W9-AWN-728

REVOLUTION

For Jessica

First published
by De Agostini Editions
Interpark House
7 Down Street
London W1Y 7DS

Distributed in the U.S.
by Stewart, Tabori & Chang
a division of US Media Holdings Inc
575 Broadway
New York NY 10012

Distributed in Canada
by General Publishing Company Ltd
30 Lesmill Road, Don Mills
Ontario M3B 2T6

UK ISBN 1 899883 73 8
US ISBN 1 899883 74 6

Printed in Spain

A CIP catalogue record for this book is available
from the British Library.

Library of Congress Cataloging-in-Publication Data

Almond, Mark.
        Revolution : 500 years of struggle for change
/ Mark Almond.
        p. cm.
        Includes bibliographical references and index.
        ISBN 1-899883-74-6
        1. Revolutions—History. 2. Military history,
Modern. I. Title.
        D214.A46 1996
        909—dc20   96-18647
                                                CIP

Publishing Director: Frances Gertler
Art Director: Tim Foster
Senior Editor: Rachel Aris
Art Editor: Manisha Patel
Editorial Assistants: Philippa Cooper, Becky Lister
Cartographic Editor: Zoë Goodwin
Picture Researcher: Diana Morris
Cartographer: Colin Earl

REVOLUTION

500 years of struggle for change

MARK ALMOND

De Agostini *Editions*

Contents

WHAT IS REVOLUTION?

What is Revolution?

ABOVE **A lone individual blocks the tanks sent by the Chinese government to crush student revolutionaries: a potent image of defiance even in defeat.**

"A revolution is a force against which no power, divine or human, can prevail.... A revolution cannot be crushed, cannot be deceived, cannot be perverted, all the more cannot be conquered..." PIERRE JOSEPH PROUDHON

Revolution is a powerful word. It evokes vivid images, strong emotions. It contains a potent mixture of hopes, romance, excitement and terror. Small wonder then that so many great works of literature, art and cinema have been inspired by revolution.

Everyone has their own image of revolution, whether it is a tumultuous scene of crowds swirling through the streets to storm a Bastille or a Winter Palace; the lonely figure of a dedicated revolutionary pursuing a vision of change regardless of the danger to himself or anyone else; or perhaps a grimmer picture of the human cost of revolution. Like grand natural phenomena, revolutions demand our attention because they stand out from the usual run of events. They change the course of life just as earthquakes divert the course of rivers and shift the features of the landscape. Suddenly every aspect of life is put into sharper focus. Politicians, ideologues, artists and ordinary people are swept up in the drama of rapid and fundamental change. Even when the turmoil subsides, life never quite returns to its old routines.

Everyone knows a revolution when they see it but no universally accepted definition of revolution exists. There is good reason for this. Revolutions are too controversial, the issues they raise cut too close to the bone to allow a consensus. Because they divide people "pro" and "contra," contradictory value judgments cloud any definition. One person's popular revolution is another's conspiratorial coup.

Over the last century, the very word "revolution" has been used in so many contexts that its meaning has become confused. It is one of the most over-used words in circulation today, and it is easy to get lost in the maze of different meanings. Even thinking of a few

BELOW **The Ayatollah Khomeini is welcomed in Tehran, Iran in January 1979. Iran's upheaval marked the resurgence of Islam as a radical force.**

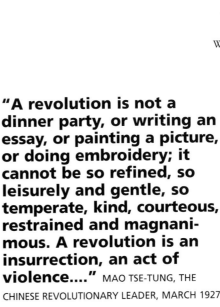

"**A revolution is not a dinner party, or writing an essay, or painting a picture, or doing embroidery; it cannot be so refined, so leisurely and gentle, so temperate, kind, courteous, restrained and magnanimous. A revolution is an insurrection, an act of violence....**" MAO TSE-TUNG, THE CHINESE REVOLUTIONARY LEADER, MARCH 1927

ABOVE **Revolutions create cult heroes. Men such as the Latin American guerrilla leader Che Guevara were turned into icons after their death as inspiration to future generations of rebels.**

common uses – "social revolution," "sexual revolution," "elite revolution," "cultural revolution," "military revolution," "abortive revolution," "world revolution," and even "conservative revolution" – helps to make at least one thing clear: any simple definition of revolution is not going to satisfy everyone or cover every possibility.

Whatever its nuances, revolution is an essentially political idea. A revolution is about a dramatic shift in power. It is a profound upheaval in which a society rejects and overthrows its government and institutions, along with the ideas that have been used to justify them. Protesting crowds, violence and often the execution of rulers are common features of revolution. Property and employment are redistributed and their legal basis rewritten. A vision of a new future replaces the old discredited way of governing and living. In other words, revolutions are radical ruptures affecting everyone in a society in different ways. They send out shock waves of imitation or revulsion across the world and across time. All the great revolutions – from America and France in the eighteenth century to Russia in 1917 and the collapse of Communism in 1989 – have been international events with long-lasting legacies.

Defining revolution

Ironically, the word "revolution" did not always have a radical meaning. Because of its suggestion of a circular movement, when the word was first applied to politics it had a conservative tinge. A revolution was when the natural order returned after a period of temporary upheaval. For instance, after the restoration of the monarchy in Britain in 1660, Thomas Hobbes wrote about the previous two decades of civil war and republic, "I have seen in this revolution a circular motion.... [Power] moved from King Charles I to the Long Parliament; from there to the Rump then to Oliver Cromwell; and back again...to the Long Parliament, and thence to King Charles II." After the expulsion from Britain of the Catholic King James II in 1688,

BELOW **Ordinary Berliners take a hand in demolishing the Wall dividing their city, November 1989. Destroying symbols of the old regime is a feature of revolutionary upheaval.**

the Protestant British celebrated a "glorious revolution" that thwarted the King's efforts to establish a Catholic despotism and restored what Protestants at least regarded as the natural way of life (*see pages 52–55*).

A century later, however, the word had acquired its modern meaning. Profound upheaval was its key characteristic. It was a clean break with the past, with society starting afresh on the basis of new ideas. Rulers and their way of governing along with much of the social order were swept away, never to return according to this new idea of revolution. In his radical pamphlet, *The Rights of Man* (1792), Thomas Paine applauded the American and French revolutions, noting that: "What we formerly called Revolutions were little more than a change of persons.... But what we now see in the world, from the Revolutions in America and France, are a renovation of the natural order of things, a system of principles as universal as truth and the existence of man, and combining moral with political happiness and national prosperity." Revolutions now became ways of transforming humanity and its way of life and government. Novelty was their key feature. Out with the old – which had become corrupt, incompetent and oppressive – and in with the new, which would herald liberty but also moral improvement. How, in fact, people were to become (or be made to be) virtuous and good citizens was to turn out again and again to be easier said than done, but the idea of the possibility of progress towards those goals became a spur to revolution ever afterwards.

ABOVE **Thomas Paine (1737–1809), an English-born radical whose essays in support of American independence from English rule were used to justify the American Revolution. He was involved in the French Revolution, but almost lost his head during the Terror (*see pages 31–33*).**

The human cost of revolution

Revolutions may be made with many honourable intentions – such as the destruction of despots, the shake-up of a corrupt regime and the birth of a new, better society – but there is also a much more sinister side to revolution, for violence is one of the most common corollaries of revolution. The relationship between violence and revolution has preoccupied many revolutionary thinkers. While the nineteenth-century Italian radical Giuseppe Mazzini believed that: "Great revolutions are the work rather of principles than of bayonets," Mao Tse-Tung (who was a most successful revolutionary, unlike Mazzini) disagreed: "power grows out of the barrel of a gun." Trotsky also took the view that violence was probably necessary to the purifying process of change. Musing on the Russian revolution of 1917 he remarked that revolutions cannot be made in white gloves on a parquet floor.

Whether or not change can only truly be achieved through bloodshed, very few revolutions have not involved violence. Indeed, the scale of human

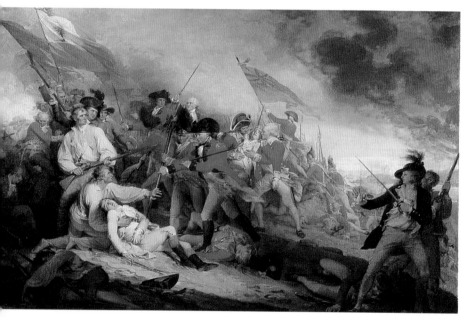

ABOVE **The death of the American General, Joseph Warren, who was killed by British troops on 17 June 1775 during the Battle of Bunker Hill, one of the first engagements of the American Revolution.**

> **"Revolutions are never waged singing 'We Shall Overcome.' Revolutions are based upon bloodshed."**
> MALCOLM X, 1964

sacrifice to the goddess of fundamental change has grown over the centuries. In some countries, revolution has been short-lived and its costs relatively minor. But the great revolutions stretched over years, even decades, and their length is reflected in the number of lives they have claimed (*see box below*). Successful revolutions have tended to demand more sacrifices than failures because the fall of the old regime is just the starting point in the process of change and purge. The old ruling elite and their supporters are by no means the only victims of revolution, for the overthrow of the government is usually followed not merely by civil war and costly social and economic upheaval, but also by in-fighting among revolutionaries over exactly which direction their cause should take.

The dawn of revolution

Revolutions are the most fascinating moments in history – and recent history in particular has been punctuated by revolutions. This makes modern times different from our more remote past. Most human societies have been remarkably static: for thousands of years they were basically agricultural societies with the vast majority of the population eking out a living on the margins of survival, devoid of the energy or education to imagine a different order. Revolutionary political change is probably impossible where social and economic change seems inconceivable. From the dawn of agricultural civilization, hopelessness was the great ally of stability. Revolutions need faith in the possibility of change.

BELOW **The dead are carried away during the 1848 revolution in Paris. An onlooker, Daniel Stern was shocked by the violence of the struggle: "Only Dante's Inferno has scenes of such mute horror."**

THE VICTIMS OF REVOLUTION

English Civil Wars, 1642–60
*c.*100,000 dead out of a population of 5 million (1 in 50)

American Revolution, 1775–83
*c.*25,000 dead out of a population of 2.5 million (1 in 100)

French Revolution, 1789–1815
*c.*1,300,000 dead out of a population of 26 million (1 in 20)

Mexican Revolution, 1910–34
*c.*2,000,000 dead out of a population of 17 million (1 in 10)

Russian Revolutions 1905–39
*c.*16,000,000 dead out of a population of 160 million (1 in 10)

Chinese Revolution 1949–76
*c.*60,000,000 dead out of a population of 600 million (1 in 10)

Cambodia (Khmer Rouge) 1975–79
*c.*2,000,000 dead out of a population of 7 million (1 in 3.5)

RIGHT **A firing squad executes a Republican in 1936 during the Spanish Civil War. The struggle cost 600,000 lives.**

Of course huge changes have shattered societies since the dawn of history, but these were usually the result of natural forces beyond human control, such as famine, plague or changes in climate. Foreign conquests, too, swept away the old social order, but were hardly popular revolutions. The historian of the greatest collapse of a society under foreign pressure, Edward Gibbon, called the fall of the Roman Empire to barbarian conquest fifteen hundred years ago, the "greatest revolution" in human history – but he was writing on the eve of the French Revolution, which he did not anticipate.

The city-states of ancient Greece and late republican Rome (1st century BC) saw frequent changes of regime, from democracy to oligarchy, or tyranny back to democracy. The urban nature of these societies was essential to their instability, for – as well as being clear centres of authority – cities can produce crowds to applaud, jeer or riot and are inhabited by educated people who can discuss new ideas and challenge the existing system. Trade in the ancient world was also important, for it brought contact with different societies and their ways of doing things. (Indeed, trade and urbanization – facilitated by the agricultural and industrial revolutions beginning around 1700 – were a crucial part of the background to the modern revolutions.) Philosophers such as Plato and Aristotle devoted much of their writings to discussing why these "revolutions" came about, but their arguments were silenced during a long gap of many centuries when most societies returned to a pre-urban state. Classical ideas about politics and revolution began to get a hearing again only after the Renaissance five hundred years ago.

> **"Inferiors revolt in order that they may be equal and equals that they may be superior. Such is the state of mind which creates revolutions."** ARISTOTLE, 4TH CENTURY BC

Despite the frequent changes of regime in these ancient states, however, the fundamentals of society were left unchanged. Ancient democracy enfranchised only a very narrow body of the population, excluding all slaves and women and the great majority of nominally freed men. The first revolutions included in Part II of this book are thus the Dutch Revolts (1568–1648) and the English Civil Wars (1642–60). Although these set out from *conservative* premises – to return to an idealized traditional order after a tyrannical monarchy – they were radicalized by the conflict, producing revolutionary consequences. Even the American Revolution began as a movement to defend the colonists' rights as British subjects to the same traditional liberties as Englishmen on the other side of the Atlantic.

SLAVE REVOLTS

Slavery was a feature of many human societies before its gradual abolition in the nineteenth century. Slave revolts were commonplace, but until the Haitians slaughtered their owners and expelled the French colonists two hundred years ago (*see pages 84–85*), no slave revolt succeeded in overturning the system. Part of the problem was that slaves rarely identified with the society that enslaved them. They were usually outsiders brought in to serve. The purpose of the most famous slave revolt in the ancient world – that of Spartacus against the Romans in 73 BC – was to rally runaway slaves into an army that would fight its way back to their homes outside Italy (in his case Thrace). The ultimate failure of Spartacus's revolt and its brutal suppression by the Romans – involving a mass crucifixion of slaves along the Appian Way to Rome – made Spartacus into a tragic hero. Subsequent myth gave life to the idea that Spartacus was an early Communist bent on overthrowing ancient Rome's unjust slave-based economy. German revolutionaries adopted the name of the Spartacus League in 1918. The writer Donald Trumbo was the most powerful proponent of the interpretation of Spartacus as a universal revolutionary, as is evident from his screenplay for Stanley Kubrick's film epic. A victim of Macarthyism in the 1950s, Trumbo was blacklisted and had to write the film under a pseudonym.

RIGHT **Kirk Douglas as Spartacus in the 1960 film of the same name.**

ВСТУПАЙТЕ ДО ЧЕРВОНОЇ КІННОТИ!

Червона кінчнота знищила, Мамонтова, Шкуро, Денікіна.
Вона била панів і Петлюру.
зараз потрібно знищити недобитка Врангеля.
Робітники й селянє—вступайте до лав Червоної Кінноти.

ABOVE **"Volunteer for the Red Cavalry!" A Bolshevik poster published in Ukrainian in 1920. Revolutions often engender civil war. The role of soldiers in ensuring the success or failure of revolutions should not be forgotten.**

The domino effect

Revolutionary disorders often come in waves. In the mid-seventeenth century, for example, Europe from the Atlantic across to the Urals was convulsed by peasant revolts and various challenges to traditional authority. At the same time, the Ottoman Empire and distant China saw peasant revolts, though the imperial regimes in these countries survived, albeit under new masters.

The late eighteenth century saw what some historians call "the age of Atlantic Revolution," when first the American colonies in 1775 and then France in 1789 witnessed violent upheaval against the old order. The French example spread across much of Europe. Yet another wave of revolution swept across Europe in 1848.

It was the early twentieth century that saw the global high-tide of revolution. The ancient Chinese monarchy finally collapsed in 1911, opening the way to decades of disorder. Mexico also descended into revolutionary chaos after 1916. But above all, the Russian empire saw the greatest revolution to date after 1917. The consequences of the Communist revolution here reverberated across Europe and around the world.

A great wave of anti-Communist revolution from Central Europe to China took place in 1989. The collapse of Communism in its heartland, Russia, after 1991 was an epochal event – just as its establishment had been about seventy years earlier. The full consequences of change in the former Soviet bloc will take decades to work their way out.

Why do revolutions occur in such waves? They seem to arise from a general crisis caused by an explosive mixture of agricultural or economic problems, coupled with cross-boundary ideological or religious issues. Naturally, when one state bursts into revolution it is likely that surrounding states facing similar instabilities will follow suit. Example and imitation have been major factors in inspiring revolutionaries in the past, and may yet do so again. Even when the high tide of revolt recedes without bringing about permanent and fundamental change, the period of excitement leaves its memory.

What triggers revolution?

Historians, sociologists and revolutionaries themselves have never stopped debating whether social and political conditions or ideas are more important for creating a climate for revolution. Throughout history most people have had just cause for complaint about their living conditions, or envy of the relatively few whose

BELOW **The Berlin Wall was a concrete expression of the East German regime's inability to satisfy its people's needs and its refusal to let them travel. The destruction of the Wall in November 1989 encouraged other East European nations to revolt against Communist rule.**

lives did not involve toil – but popular discontent about material circumstances cannot alone account for revolutions or there would have been many more of them much earlier in history. On the other hand, without the fertile soil of widespread grievance, revolutionary ideas would have little chance of seizing the popular imagination. Obviously material causes and explosive ideals are both vital to the ignition of a revolution.

"Revolutions are achieved first in the moral, and afterwards in the material sphere." GIUSEPPE MAZZINI, 1831

Every revolution is born out of a unique combination of circumstances, although one or many of the following factors may contribute to its eruption:

Material conditions such as economic downturns, sudden changes in the standard of living, heavy and regressive taxation or natural phenomena such

NUIT DU 4 AU 3 AOÛT 1789
OU LE DÉLIRE PATRIOTIQUE.

ABOVE **On 4 August 1789, not long after the French Revolution had begun, the clergy and nobles formally relinquished their privileges. This symbolic portrait of the events of 4 August shows representatives of the clergy, nobles and the common man destroying the symbols of feudalism.**

as drought, famine or epidemics often help to foster unrest. Revolutions grow out of a moral and intellectual rejection of the causes of such conditions and the belief that they can be overcome by radical change.

Oppression or **dire poverty** can contribute to a widespread sense that society is profoundly unjust. The idea of injustice is very important because it can be shared by those who do not actually suffer the consequences. From radical aristocrats in France under Louis XVI to liberal whites in South Africa there have always been members of the elite who have rejected pure self-interest and struggled for reform, even revolution.

Defeat in war discredits governments and can crystallize deeper social discontents that may have seemed hopeless while the regime's military and police forces were unbeaten. For example, Napoleon III's regime collapsed after France was defeated in the Franco-Prussian War in 1870, and this debacle set in motion the attempted revolution of the Paris Commune (*see pages 112–15*). Similarly, the inability of Tsarist Russia to fight Germany successfully after 1914 and the growing hardships imposed by the war led to the collapse of the Tsarist system in 1917 (*pages 118–33*).

Foreign rule can spark a revolutionary uprising when it becomes oppressive or incapable of improvement. Wars of independence take on revolutionary features because the struggle against the old order involves questions of how society is to be organized after the expulsion of the

BELOW **Protesters in South Africa demand democracy and an end to apartheid.**

colonial power. Colonies may also take the opportunity to break away if their motherland is defeated in war.

Foreign influence: the identification of rulers with unpopular foreign allies can destabilize them. James II was ousted from his British throne in 1688 in part because he was thought likely to imitate the intolerance towards Protestants of his French ally, Louis XIV. Foreign travel can also promote revolutionary thinking, particularly in people who have spent their lives under regimes of strict control and censorship. The

ABOVE **Protesters against the Iranian government in 1979, carry posters of the Ayatollah Khomeini. The Iranian Revolution was a reaction against the Shah's tyrannical personal rule and modernizing, pro-Western policies. The Ayatollah was the focus of anti-government unrest.**

French soldiers who had fought on the American side in the War of Independence (1775–83) often returned to France imbued with the new ideas of political liberty. Some of them, such as the Marquis de Lafayette, went on to play a key role in the French Revolution after 1789. And in 1989, many of the Chinese students protesting against the Communist regime in the capital Beijing had studied in the West and adopted Western ideas of democracy.

People can experience **tyranny** even in prosperity. When a regime tries to stifle alternative religious views, for example, believers will feel oppressed. Very often their strong religious convictions will motivate them to rebellion and the denial of the legitimacy of their ruler. Religious revolutionaries in sixteenth-century Netherlands used the argument that divine sanction had been withdrawn from an ungodly ruler (Philip II of Spain) who no longer had the right to his subjects' obedience. Denying the absolute right of Philip II to rule was a profound revolutionary step. More modern revolutionaries have used the will of the people rather than of God as the basis of legitimate authority.

New ideas can encourage revolution (see overleaf), but they can also threaten a post-revolutionary regime. Once a radical ideology loses its active appeal and becomes mere ritual, its authority vanishes. Something of the sort had happened to Soviet Communism by the 1980s: the dream of Communism had evaporated in the dreary everyday reality of Soviet life.

THE INDUSTRIAL REVOLUTION

Apart from a few marvellous mechanical and steam-powered gadgets invented in ancient Egypt, until the eighteenth century all energy was naturally produced. Man- and animal-power hauled and carried most goods. Wind-power propelled sailing ships and ground corn at mills. The application of steam technology to machinery in the second half of the eighteenth century came first in Great Britain. The political system established by the Glorious Revolution of 1688 and the so-called "financial revolution" that followed it (with the establishment of the Bank of England in 1694 and the National Debt) made rapid commercial development easier. Exactly why steam-powered machinery came into existence remains much debated. An increase in demand for laboriously manufactured goods like cloth no doubt contributed, but new thinking about technical possibilities were vital as well. Britain's lack of restrictions on trade and production also promoted the use of the new technologies (unlike other European countries that had guilds and other trade limitations). The development of the railway in the 1820s opened up the possibility of moving goods and passengers in unprecedented numbers and at unprecedented speeds.

Social and political consequences flowed rapidly from the industrial revolution. New towns grew up with astonishing speed around factories, and the demographic balance shifted so Britain became predominantly urban by 1850. Urbanization was a fundamental shift from humanity's age-old rural lifestyle. Political upheaval often followed the disruptive effects of industrialization and urbanization, and only a few European countries escaped revolution in the nineteenth century. One of these was Britain, which had already established the rule of law and elements of political participation (quickly extended after 1832) to reduce pressure for revolutionary change. However, the uprisings between 1811 and 1816 of the anti-industrial Luddites, who destroyed the new machines they blamed for unemployment and low wages, show that a potential anti-modern revolutionary class of dispossessed craftspeople existed even in Britain.

ABOVE **Inside a nineteenth-century iron foundry in France.**

"Poor people want change, want to do things, want revolution. A clean sheet of paper has no blotches... so the newest and most beautiful words can be written on it." MAO TSE-TUNG, 1958

Revolutionary ideologies

However harsh life may be, mere wishful thinking rarely stirs people to risk their lives defying authority. The dream of change has to be accompanied by a reasonable programme to get from here to there. Considering the experience of Russia in 1905 and after 1917, Leon Trotsky acknowledged that without basic general discontent revolutions could not occur successfully, but he also recognized that unorganized grievance could easily evaporate without achieving anything. Popular discontent needs to be channelled and given a clear direction. Self-conscious revolutionaries provide steerage and a destination to aim for. He wrote, "Without a guiding organization, the energy of the masses would dissipate like steam not enclosed in a piston box. But nevertheless what moves things is not the piston or the box, but the steam."

An intellectual demolition job on tradition usually sets the scene for the emergence of a new ideology justifying, even demanding change. For example, in eighteenth-century France an intellectual movement developed known as the Enlightenment. Its key thinkers – Voltaire, Diderot and Rousseau – all challenged the authority of tradition in different ways (*see page 72*). The brilliance of their writings and witticisms carried their message to the literate elite and helped undermine the legitimacy of France's system of government.

The particular character of a revolution is shaped not so much by the circumstances of its origin but by the schemes put forward to resolve the causes of dissatisfaction. The ideologies used to justify revolution obviously change from one situation to another, but offering a new vision of society – breaking with the past and denouncing its injustice – is essential to a revolutionary ideology. Reform or benevolent rule is not a substitute.

Like great religions, successful ideologies such as Communism offer practical but intellectually convincing solutions to apparently insoluble problems. They appeal to the deep, sometimes unconscious, parts of the human personality that motivate action (the hope for a better life, patriotism, ambition, the need for certainty and so on). Nationalism has also been a powerful stimulus to revolt. Even the apparently rational and enlightened aspects of the French revolutionary creed of equality and fraternity were bound up, in practice, with a dynamic French nationalism. Communism too was cross-fertilized by nationalism in Russia, China and Vietnam, which undoubtedly gave it greater appeal.

RIGHT **Revolutions need an ideological programme. Some leaders draw up their own ideologies while others rely on an existing bluprint. Thomas Jefferson (top left), Karl Marx (top right), Friedrich Engels (below left) and Mao Tse-tung (below right) were all important revolutionary thinkers.**

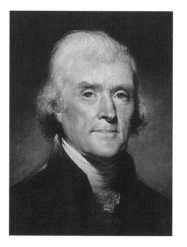
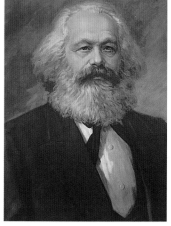

revolution
A complete upheaval in a society in which an attempt is made to change the way society is governed along with the economy and culture of everyday life.

rebellion/revolt
Organized resistance to a government. Unlike a revolution, a rebellion aims not to break with the past but very often to return to it. Unsuccessful attempts at revolutionary upheaval are often called rebellions, even if they have far-reaching revolutionary aims.

putsch/coup d'état
The seizure of political power by a small group of armed men (often regular soldiers).

counter-revolution
A radical response to revolution in which opponents of the revolutionary upheaval seek to reverse the process.

ideology
The ideas that inspire a revolution and set out its goals by explaining what is wrong with the world and how to change it. Counter-revolutionaries develop their own ideologies to explain (away) the causes of revolution and provide a plausible scheme for reversing it.

civil war
War between factions of the same nation. Many revolutions have so deeply split societies that conflict has broken out between supporters and opponents of revolution, leading to civil war. On the other hand, some societies break down into civil conflict for unrevolutionary reasons (e.g. dynastic wars).

Terror/purge
Purges of society and the revolutionary elite as a step towards achieving the revolution's ideological goals.

The best ideologists are skilled simplifiers and can adapt an ideology to suit the particular circumstances of their time and place. It is impossible to say how far the thoughts of revolutionary thinkers were implemented as they would have liked. But, for good or ill, ideologists of revolutionary change must take some responsibility for what happens when attempts are made to realize their theories. A Marx may not be able to control how a Mao operates almost a century after his death, but without the *Communist Manifesto* it is impossible to imagine a Chinese Communist leader. What made Mao successful was his adaptation of Marxist ideas and Soviet experience after 1917 to the conditions of China.

Intellectual fashion can help to create a climate of opinion favouring change, even when the people holding such opinions stand to lose as those ideas are put into practice. Lenin once described the aristocratic sponsors of fashionable radicalism in eighteenth-century France as the people who provided the rope with which they were to be hanged.

Where as indecision is a recipe for political failure, certainty is a great promoter of revolutions. Puritans in England in the 1640s and twentieth-century Marxists were certain of their views and their conviction converted many others who lacked clear ideas of their own. When success is guaranteed by divine grace or by what Marx and Lenin grandly called "the dialectical progress of history" (whereby even setbacks are just another step towards the ultimate goal of revolution and a classless society), risk-taking seems worthwhile.

RIGHT **Delegates at the Ninth Congress of the Chinese Communist Party, 1969, march past portraits of four of the great Marxist thinkers: Marx, Engels, Lenin and Stalin. The delegates all hold their Little Red Books of the "Thoughts of Chairman Mao."**

The role of propaganda

Leon Trotsky, who organized the victorious Red Army in the Russian civil war, argued that ideas need as much organization as people. A successful revolution needs a propaganda machine to disseminate its arguments, to counter those of its opponents and to stimulate popular support for the cause. Propaganda is the marriage of new ideas and people to promote them. When successful it crystallizes into memorable words or pictures the ideas and emotions that move people into pursuing a new goal. So, before a revolution has taken place it can help to persuade people of the validity of a movement, and afterwards it can be used to justify the change and discredit rivals.

All great propagandists have been masters of simplification. After 1917, the Soviet Communists needed to communicate their often complex Marxist ideas to a largely illiterate population. To do this Lenin and Trotsky made use of a striking variety of visual forms of propaganda. Cartoons, posters and public performances were widely used to get the Communist message across. At least 3,000 political posters were produced by the Soviet regime by 1921. Brilliant modern artists such as El Lissitzky (*see box page 36*) and Rodchenko put their talents at the service of the regime.

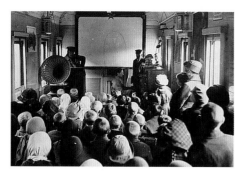

The potential of cinema to make propaganda for – and then against – revolution was recognized around the time of the Russian Revolution. Abel Gance produced his epic portrait of the young and still revolutionary Napoleon in 1927, and at around the same time in Soviet Russia Sergei Eisenstein made several films evoking the revolutionary spirit in the early Soviet period. Two of Eisenstein's quasi-documentaries stand out in particular: *Battleship Potemkin* (1926) and *October, 1917* (1927).

BELOW "**To defend Madrid is to defend Catalonia,**" a poster from the Spanish Civil War, 1936–39. Effective propaganda has to persuade people not only that the cause is right and necessary, but also that it will succeed.

ABOVE **The interior of a Russian cinema train. Trotsky and Lenin made use of the powerful popular appeal of early cinema to propagate their ideas among the Russians after 1917. According to Lenin: "Of all the arts, for us the cinema is the most important."**

RIGHT **This scene from Eisenstein's film *Battleship Potemkin*, in which an elderly woman is shot, encapsulates the portrayal of the Tsarist government as a brutal regime.**

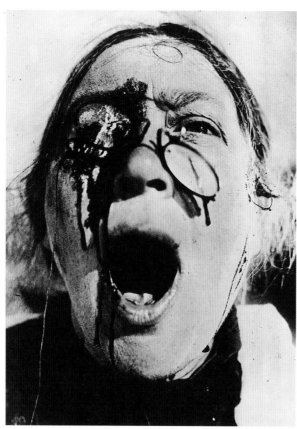

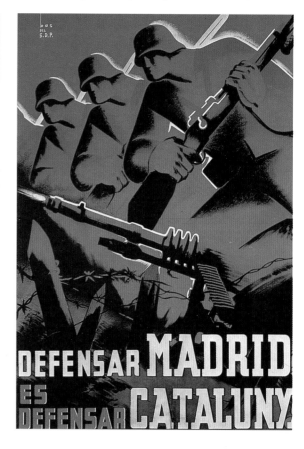

DEFENSAR MADRID ES DEFENSAR CATALUNY

Neither film was historically accurate – for instance, more extras were killed during the filming of the storming of the Winter Palace than actually died in October 1917 – but the power of Eisenstein's imagery of the energy of popular revolt or the squalid conditions aboard one of the Tsar's warships in 1905 captured the imagination of early cinema audiences. Even enemies of the Soviet Union were deeply impressed: Dr Goebbels insisted his own propagandists see Eisenstein's films. Nazi Germany never found such a talent, although Leni Riefenstahl's heroizing of the 1936 Nazi Party Rally (*Triumph of the Will*) was widely admired by cinematographers. But Eisenstein's revolutionary classics were of limited propaganda value among the Soviet masses, who preferred entertainment to ideological invocations, however well-made.

Ein Volk, ein Reich, ein Führer!

ABOVE **"One people, one empire, one leader," a Nazi poster of 1938–39. Hitler understood the need for "constant repetition" to imprint his message on people's minds and to drown out alternative views.**

ABOVE **Dr Joseph Goebbels, who masterminded the Nazi propaganda machine.**

Counter-revolutionaries recognized the importance of effective propaganda. Hitler and Goebbels, for instance, understood the power of simple and beguiling ideas and knew how to manipulate the popular psychology to promote their radically anti-Communist message and disorientate opposition. Hitler famously declared: "The broad mass of a nation will more easily fall victim to a big lie than to a small one." With its emotive use of parades and torchlight rituals as well as modern media, Nazi Germany was more successful than any other regime at transforming its ideology into propaganda.

Technological advances have made the twentieth century the true age of propaganda. Propagandists in the past were much more limited. Printed literature depended on the ability to read or the availability of an audience to hear it read aloud, and although it was possible to print cartoons and posters, distribution was often a problem. The age of cinema, radio and television has made it easy to disseminate a message simultaneously to millions of people.

BELOW **"The dead of the Paris Commune rose again under the Red flag of the Soviets." This Soviet poster of 1921 idealizes the revolutionary struggles of the Paris Commune.**

The revolutionary as romantic hero

Revolutions have captured the public imagination in a way few other historical events ever have. We have already touched on one possible explanation for this: the conflicting emotions of hope and fear embodied in the notion of profound change. But there are other reasons for the fascination of revolution. The sheer pace and apparent inexorability of events accounts for much of the excitement of revolution. Once in motion, it is hard to stop a revolution, to rein in the passions it inspires. It must either work itself out or be brutally suppressed; and the one outcome is quite as gripping as the other. There is also the fact that a people should choose to turn against its own ruling elite, which would be dramatic enough even without all

МЕРТВЕЦЫ ПАРИЖ= СКОЙ КОММУНЫ ВОСКРЕСЛИ ПОД КРАСНЫМ ЗНАМЕНЕМ СОВЕТОВ!

the – sometimes horrifying – actions carried out in the name of revolution. Like war, revolution intensifies the emotions. It is not something to believe in half-heartedly: it arouses strong passions in both the revolutionary and the onlooker. Indeed, compassion for the underprivileged must be one of the most powerful incentives for revolution – and it probably does much to explain the twentieth-century fashion for supporting revolution as a cause.

ABOVE *The Brothers Horatii Swearing the Oath*, by David. The memories of past revolutionary heroes such as the Roman assassins of the dictator Julius Caesar (44 BC) or the defiant slave, Spartacus, live on to encourage future generations of revolutionaries.

Stories of individual courage tend to be more inspiring than abstract ideals, which perhaps explains why so many revolutionaries have won cult status this century. People who believe fervently in something are often very appealing – even if their beliefs do not tally with our own – and, like all great leaders, great revolutionaries have irresistible powers of persuasion and can inspire true loyalty among their followers. But what has made revolutionaries such popular figures in history and art alike is their frequently tragic fate. The cause may triumph but often the idealist pays the ultimate price. Self-sacrifice sanctifies politics.

The revolutionary leader

The ideologues who come to the fore in the revolutionary situation are key figures for what happens next. Their characters as well as their ideas contribute to the shaping of the next stage of revolution.

Successful revolutions require organization, which implies leaders. Crowds do not topple regimes unless somebody directs them strategically. The "people" or the "proletariat" rarely achieves much by itself. Although

WORKS OF LITERATURE AND FILM INSPIRED BY REVOLUTION

It may be true that history is written by the victors, but the literature of revolution seems to be the preserve of the losers. In the aftermath of the failure of the Puritan revolution in England, John Milton laboured on *Paradise Lost*, as much a political allegory as a religious text. The success of the French Revolution spawned counter-revolutionary literature, from Balzac's *The Chouans* to English writers who celebrated England's avoidance of Terror and pitied the French for it. Although Charles Dickens described in *A Tale of Two Cities* (1859) a France ground down under a selfish aristocracy that provoked the uprising of a brutalized people, the moral of the story was that London was ruled by wiser and more virtuous heads.

The Restoration in France after 1815 and the unsatisfactory outcome of the 1830 and 1848 revolutions encouraged Victor Hugo to write his massive portrait of the oppressed as the ever-striving but losing side of history in *Les Misérables* (1862). But his portrait of revolution on the streets of Paris helped to inspire the Communards and later generations.

Official literature celebrating the Russian Revolution and idolizing Lenin in the Soviet Union never managed to create great fiction. Pasternak's long-suppressed *Doctor Zhivago* (1957), which was published in the Soviet Union only in its last years, tried not only to explain why the Communist revolution happened but also why its impact was disastrous on the lives of real people. Literature became a major means of dissent under Communism, usually in the form of home-made editions.

The cinema has often been used as a propaganda machine, and was particularly effective in the Soviet Union (*see pages 18–19*). Hollywood's attempts at revolutionary films – such as Warren Beatty's film *Reds* about the Russian Revolution or Al Pacino's *Revolution* about the American Revolution – have never carried such conviction. It is difficult for a profit-oriented industry to encourage people on to the streets rather than into the stalls. Even Hollywood's adaptation of *Doctor Zhivago*, though true to Pasternak's hardly veiled criticism of the cost of revolution, presented post-1917 Russia in too glamorous a guise to be plausible.

In 1982, the Polish director Andrjez Waijda turned aside from his *Man of Iron/Man of Marble* films (with their critical portrait of Polish Communism in the run-up to the Solidarity crisis) to produce *Danton*, his dramatic version of the perversion of French revolutionary virtue during the Terror. A few years later, the Khmer Rouge's brutal all-embracing revolution in Cambodia was dissected in *The Killing Fields*.

revolutions prosper in conditions of economic distress and are often made in the name of the poor, revolutionary leaders are rarely poor themselves, probably because it is usually only the better-off that have the education, leisure and resources to develop a revolutionary ideology. The leader of the Dutch Revolt was the Prince of Orange, as aristocratic as imaginable. The initial leaders of the French Revolution came from the privileged orders of society, though they rejected their special status. Even Jacobins such as Danton and Robespierre (*see pages 77–82*) had aspired to be accepted by the old regime before turning completely against it. Lenin was the son of a high official of the Tsars. Mao's Prime Minister, Zhou En Lai was the son of a landowner. (When Nikita Khrushchev, the son of a peasant, told Zhou En Lai that it was their different social origins that accounted for their hostility, Zhou replied: "But we have at least one thing in common – we have each betrayed our own class"!)

"The most radical revolutionary will become a conservative on the day after the revolution." GERMAN PHILOSOPHER HANNAH ARENDT, 1970

LEFT **Revolutionary leaders. Mikhail Bakunin (top left) was a prophet of anarchism in the nineteenth century. Rosa Luxemburg (top right) tried to reconcile libertarianism with Marxism. Fidel Castro (below left) allied Cuban nationalism with Marxism. Nelson Mandela (below right) hopes to reconcile parliamentary democracy with racial equality in South Africa.**

Yet such people really did break with the regime. Their dissidence was not just a way of causing a nuisance until they received patronage. Revolutionaries may come from a privileged background but they wish to abolish existing privileges even if they do not succeed in avoiding establishing new forms. The fundamental commitment to the New is a key characteristic of revolutionaries. What happens after a revolution has established itself is another story.

Why should members of the privileged orders of society wish to betray their origins? It is impossible to know exactly what motivates anyone, but we can assume a deeply held political belief coupled with some mixture of ambition, desire for a better world and who-knows-what resentments against their own class must be responsible.

Advocates of revolution are usually strong characters willing to take risks for their ideals – but rarely able to compromise. Revolutionaries are often their own worst enemies. Quarrels among revolutionaries about strategy, tactics and personalities mean that they frequently spend as much energy denouncing each other as the reactionary and unjust order that they hope to overthrow. Karl Marx, for instance, fell out with the Russian anarchist Mikhail Bakunin. Each reviled the other and their supporters. Marx ridiculed Bakunin's rag-bag of followers in Italy in the 1870s as a rabble run by "a gang of *déclassés*...by lawyers without clients, doctors without patients, or medical knowledge, by students expert at billiards, by commercial travellers and clerks, and especially by journalists of the minor press, of more or less dubious reputation." No reactionary could have better put the case for seeing the anarchists as ill-adjusted individuals! Well-publicized quarrels between revolutionaries come as grist to the reactionaries' mills.

Popular participation

Revolutionary movements may be led (even misled) by individuals or parties, but it is crucial that they are able to inspire and mobilize large sections of the population into taking direct action, for example to participate in demonstrations or strikes. In contrast, palace coups and military putsches take place without any popular participation – and frequently in defiance of public opinion.

How are the popular masses won over to a revolutionary cause? As we have seen, a leader is essential: someone with the indefinable qualities of intelligence, courage and the ability to communicate – in other words, charisma. The leader needs to appeal to the oppressed not only to foment disillusionment with the existing system but, crucially, to excite the popular imagination with the prospect of improvement. Propaganda is important here. Often it is sufficient initially to inspire only a significant dynamic minority into active support of the cause, for the popular psychology is such that many people will passively accept a movement and render opposition to it ineffective. After 1917, Lenin saw that "those who are not against us are for us." What he meant was that, in effect, those people who stand aside from political participation during a revolution are in alliance with the revolutionaries because they refuse to assist counter-revolutionary forces.

Propaganda is often used to "talk up" a cause. Nothing breeds success like success, and the more popular a movement is *seen* to be, the more supporters it will gain. Furthermore, the bigger a crowd, the more fearless it becomes, because the risk of reprisal seems to recede ("the government cannot possibly punish this many people"). It is also difficult to underestimate the excitement of having a strong belief, a purpose, and the sense of being involved in making history. People are easily swept up in a movement, particularly when it claims to improve their lot.

Is it hope or fear that makes people more revolutionary? Once a revolution gets under way it tends to release among its supporters a great tide of optimism that at last everything will

ABOVE **Chinese students demonstrate for democracy in Tiananmen Square, 1989. Taking to the streets with banners of protest is one of the oldest and most effective ways of challenging authority – but it can also be dangerous, especially if the authorities rely on force rather than dialogue to resolve the situation.**

BELOW **Crowds and police clash in Paris, May 1968, during demonstrations for improved working conditions and educational reforms. As symbols of authority, the police are the frontline in any attempt to deny the crowd control of the streets.**

ABOVE **The fall of the Bastille on 14 July 1789. Fear of famine rather than actual starvation turned Parisians on to the streets to overthrow the royal authority they blamed for the spectre of food shortages. Setbacks to rising expectations can radicalize people far more dramatically than lifelong poverty.**

be better – but a revolution is usually caused by worry rather than hope. Anxiety about a future that looks bleaker than the present is a greater cause of revolutionary disorder than despair. The destitute and hopeless never make revolutions. It is those who are losing out or who fear that life might get worse still who turn to radical solutions. It is not rising but declining expectations that lie at the root of whole social classes becoming revolutionary. Aristotle recognized this phenomenon two and a half thousand years ago when he noted that: "If the number of children exceeds what the amount of property will support" then social problems were bound to arise. "It is a sorry thing that a large number of persons should be reduced from comfort to poverty. It is difficult for men who have suffered that fate not to be revolutionaries."

For all their talk of the "will of the people" or the "working class," revolutionary leaders have often fallen into the trap of believing they know best what the people want and refusing to accept that there can be a legitimate disagreement about it. This – together with the fact that the reality of a new order often turns out to be disappointing to the people – can lead to disillusionment with the revolutionary regime, which in turn can create counter-revolution.

Counter-revolutionaries

Even dedicated opponents of revolution are affected by it. Counter-revolutionaries – who seek to reverse the effects of revolution by beginning a new one – have recognized, if unconsciously, that they can fight revolution only by using some of its own methods. Beating the radical left at its own game means mobilizing the masses, using demagogy and unscrupulous violence. A few opponents of the French Revolution who wanted to defend their traditional rural way of life against interference from revolutionaries in Paris began to do just this by mobilizing the peasantry who had lost faith in the revolution, but it was only

> **"Revolutions have never lightened the burden of tyranny; they have only shifted it to another shoulder."** GEORGE BERNARD SHAW, 1903

PEASANT REVOLTS

History is littered with examples of – usually unsuccessful – peasant revolts, such as the great Jacquerie revolt that took place in fourteenth-century France. What makes such revolts tragic is their lack of clear or realizable goals. Very often – as in England in 1381 or in Russia as late as the dawn of the twentieth century – peasants misunderstood the source of their discontents. They blamed local officials or nobles for their grievances rather than the monarchy or the system of government, and thus looked to the king for redress. The idea of appealing for justice or reform to a paternalist monarch misled by his greedy or corrupt nobles and ministers is a common one in many countries' histories. Unfortunately, kings were rarely willing or able to satisfy their peasant subjects and usually organized their suppression.

Sometimes this belief in the myth of the benevolent monarch resulted in people supporting a pretender to the throne who claimed to be the "real" ruler. In Russia in the 1770s, for instance, a rebel serf named Emilian Ivanovich Pugachev gathered a large following by claiming to be Peter III, the Tsar who had been deposed and murdered in 1762 by his wife, Catherine the Great. Although Pugachev's revolt was a severe threat to the personal rule of Tsarina Catherine, his ideology did not challenge the inherent right of Tsars to rule. Pugachev's aim was simply to be a just ruler, if he really believed he could succeed in toppling Catherine. In the event, the rebellion was defeated and Pugachev was betrayed. He ended up being tortured to death in an iron cage to discourage other rebels.

ABOVE **Wat Tyler and John Ball lead rebels in the English peasant revolt of 1381 against the heavy burden of taxation. Tyler's naive trust in King Richard II led to his murder.**

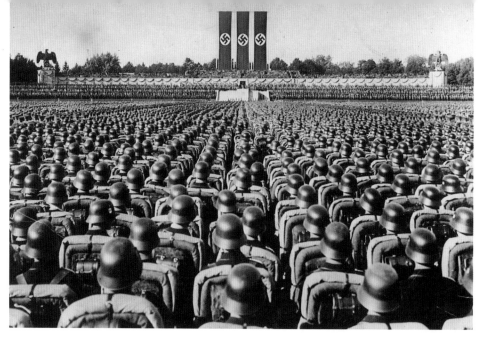

"Power is not a means, it is an end. One does not establish a dictatorship in order to safeguard a revolution; one makes the revolution in order to establish the dictatorship."
GEORGE ORWELL, *NINETEEN EIGHTY-FOUR*, 1949

ABOVE **A Nazi rally at Nuremburg. With the emotive use of parades and torchlight rituals, Nazi Germany was the regime most successful at translating its ideology into propaganda.**

after the First World War, in reaction to the Bolshevik Revolution in Russia, that a radical counter-revolutionary movement truly emerged. It is usually called Fascism. The term was first used in Italy in 1919 by the ex-Socialist turned militarist, Benito Mussolini, to describe his ideology of totalitarian government, but it has also been applied to other similar philosophies of government, the most extreme – and most successful – of which, National Socialism, was developed in Germany soon afterwards by Adolf Hitler.

The conservatives and old-fashioned reactionaries who opposed Marxism were not sure what to make of this new counter-revolutionary force. On the one hand they shared many fears with the counter-revolutionaries, but the Fascists imitated many of the Communists' worst features (secret polices and contempt for the rule of law). Whether to be saved from the Red Guard by the rabble was a question that divided the traditional conservative right. Having failed to seize power in a putsch in 1923, Adolf Hitler insisted at his trial for treason that: "If today I stand here as a revolutionary it is as a revolutionary against the revolution." The radicalism of the Fascists and Nazis may have been narrowly focused in extremely violent forms, but its uncontrollable dynamics led to the catastrophic Second World War after 1939 and almost caused the ruination of European civilization.

RIGHT ABOVE **Dramatic changes in the role of women can arise in revolutionary situations. This female Mexican guerrilla is one of many women fighting for land redistribution in rural Chiapas.**

It is too simplistic to see counter-revolutionaries simply as representatives of the old elite that lost out when the revolution abolished their privileges. Naturally, such people often have little enthusiasm for change, but nostalgia is not the main cause of counter-revolution. Disappointment with the consequences of revolution brings new players into politics, with a new ideological programme developed directly as a response to change.

RIGHT BELOW **A revolution against sexual equality: women in Iran were mobilized by the Ayatollah Khomeini in 1979 during his campaign to enforce strict Islamic codes of dress and behaviour, including the return for women to traditional veiled dress.**

Women and revolution

Whereas many absolute monarchs have been women, few women have held real power in parliamentary democracies, which suggests that individual women were more likely to exercise power in pre-revolutionary rather than post-revolutionary political systems. Nonetheless, women *have* played significant roles in revolution.

Women have acted decisively by suddenly rejecting their traditionally passive role in a moment of crisis and

ABOVE **Women on the barricades in Paris during the July Revolution of 1830, when women broke out of their traditional roles as nurses and took an active part in the insurrection.**

mobilizing to act on their grievances. In October 1789, for instance, it was poor Parisian women who led the massive march on the royal palace at Versailles to demand food. They may have been driven to revolt partly by the poverty and hunger threatening their children, that is, by the desire to defend their traditional role of the succour of children, but regardless of their motivations, the removal of the French royal family from its palace was a decisive moment in the collapse of the monarchy.

Questioning the traditional order naturally leads to a discussion of the role of women. As soon as patriarchal authority is challenged as the basis of the state, it becomes possible to imagine its abolition in the family. Women writers and male sympathizers, from the time of the French Revolution onwards, theorized about fundamental changes in the social order that would emancipate women from their traditional domestic role. Marxist thinkers, such as Rosa Luxemburg and Alexandra Kollontai, built on Engels' argument that only by transforming the economic condition of humanity could women take up new roles in society. In practice, however, women have generally found that – for all the revolutionary promises of equality – their entry into the workplace has been at the lower and less-skilled end of the scale.

Revolutionary upheaval presents unprecedented choices that sometimes lead women to the opposite, counter-revolutionary camp. The phenomenon of the counter-revolutionary widow, for example, became commonplace in France from the 1790s onwards, as men fell victim to the revolutionary Terror (*see pages 31-32*). Ironically, even decrying revolutionary change politicized women and pushed them into adopting new roles or acting as the breadwinner in exile or widowhood.

Revolution from above

For every successful revolutionary movement there have been many more that have been frustrated by well-timed reforms, or failed to ignite a popular cause, or have been stifled by repression. The history of Britain in the nineteenth century is a classic example of how reform can help to prevent revolutionary upheaval. Britain's rulers defended their constitutional political order with repressive measures, in the period immediately after the French Revolution. However,

BELOW **The female Zapatista guerrillas in modern-day Mexico have many predecessors, including these women, who were photographed with the Mexican revolutionary leader Pancho Villa in about 1914.**

as soon as the direct threat of a foreign revolutionary invasion had disappeared with Napoleon's defeat in 1815, internal political reform came on to the agenda. Mindful of the "worrying" events of the July Revolution in France in 1830, the British government passed the Great Reform Act in 1832 that broadened the franchise to include many of the urban middle classes, giving more people a stake in the existing constitutional system. This defused social tensions and helped to forestall any potential revolutionary discontent.

Otto von Bismarck, the Prussian Prime Minister from 1862 until 1890, also championed the idea of a "revolution from above:" the attempt by a traditional ruler to head off revolutionary change, which could sweep away his system altogether, by granting limited concessions and reforms within an authoritarian framework. Bismarck was characterized as a White Revolutionary. He understood that society could not stand still without provoking an explosion of discontent. What he was determined to do, therefore, was to steer developments in such a way as to avoid the most offensive aspects of change. Bismarck recognized that this meant making some concessions: to preserve the core of what he wanted to save, he had to jettison other features of Prussian society and, despite being a loyal monarchist, compromise even with elements of democracy and social reforms such as old-age pensions and state health insurance.

ABOVE **Kemal Atatürk believed that the Ottoman way of doing things was leading Turkey to ruin, so he jettisoned many of the symbols and practices of the old order to rescue the Turkish core of the defeated empire after 1918.**

Other countries have seen attempts at modernizing revolutions launched by governments anxious to guide change. The most successful was Japan's opening to the outside world and what it had to teach under the Meiji Restoration in 1868 (*see box below*). Atatürk's effort to westernize Turkey after the collapse of the Ottoman Empire at the end of the First World War also marked a real break with the past as everything from the religious basis of the law, the dress codes and the alphabet were changed. The Ottoman Sultans had felt ambiguous about modernization: they wanted the power that Western technology provided but their authority rested on their religious status as Caliphs and their upholding of a traditional society. Defeat in war by "infidels" led Atatürk to the conclusion that Turkey must be modernized.

THE MEIJI RESTORATION: A CONSERVATIVE REVOLUTION

Japan escaped the fate of the many other Asian states that fell victim to the imperialism of the more economically advanced and industrially powerful Western states during the nineteenth century. After two centuries of self-imposed isolation, Japan was forced to open its ports to foreign trade in 1853. The impact of the West divided Japanese society and resulted in the re-emergence of the Emperor as an active political figure after centuries as little more than a revered puppet in the hands of powerful clans. The fall in 1868 of the military dynasty that had ruled Japan saw the restoration to effective power of the Emperor Meiji (1852–1912, *right*), and was accompanied by a dramatic shift in policy. Instead of ignoring foreign models, the Japanese were encouraged to learn from them. The *samurai* warrior class ceased to be the only armed men and, in a revolutionary break with the past, soldiers were drawn from all classes of

the population and armed and uniformed along European lines. British advisers trained the new navy while Prussians drilled the new army and French civil servants helped to shape the bureaucracy. Japan shook off certain features of its history in order to retain its independence and develop as a force equal to the great European empires. To make the central government effective, feudal lords were persuaded to renounce their local authority and become in effect regional representatives of the central government. The Japanese Emperor and his advisers achieved remarkable results, for they managed to devise reforms that set Japan en route towards becoming a great imperial power (and, a century later, an economic superpower) without seeing the political order shattered – despite Japan's disastrous defeat in the Second World War.

ABOVE **Although French Revolution had many sympathizers abroad, it was military conquest that implanted revolutionary ideas and institutions outside France. Here members of the National Guard ("armed missionaries") leave Paris in September 1792 to join the army.**

Exporting revolution

Revolutions always have a tendency to try to export their values. Even in ancient Greece, with its astonishing variety of states (they were usually small city-states with very different constitutions), wars were fought to impose a specific system of government on another state. Some were broadly-based democracies such as Athens in the 4th century BC, others were narrower oligarchies such as Sparta, or downright tyrannies ruled by one man. Both Thucydides and Aristotle wrote about how the great Pelopponesian War between states led to political change according to the success of Sparta or Athens at its various stages: as Aristotle wrote, "The Athenians everywhere brought low the oligarchies, and the Spartans the popular governments."

The imposition of social and political change from outside rarely achieves a lasting revolution, however. Resentment against change as the work of foreigners is too natural a response. The so-called "armed missionaries" of the French Revolution carried revolutionary ideas and methods into the neighbouring countries after 1792 but succeeded in planting little loyalty to France or revolution (*see pages 76–83*) – although nineteenth-century German revolutionaries did draw extensively on French ideas and experience.

The new Soviet state after 1917 tried many ways of persuading its neighbours to accept Communism. At first, the most direct method – invasion – failed: Poland defeated an invasion by the Red Army in 1920. Communism only came to the Warsaw Pact states because of the Soviet Union's victory over Nazi Germany in World War II. As Stalin said, "Each man advances his social system as far as his army reaches." Countries to the east of the Iron Curtain were revolutionized not by internal dynamics but by Soviet power. They had been devastated by war and, as many of their traditional politicians had fallen victim to the Nazi occupier, it became easy for the Communists to pose as the only alternative – but there were some problems for them too. In 1945 there were very few Communists in most parts of Eastern Europe (apart from in Czechoslovakia, Yugoslavia, and Albania). There were less than 1,000 Communists in Romania, for example, when the Red Army arrived in

BELOW **The fall of Berlin, May 1945. A Russian soldier raises the Red flag over the Reichstag.**

August 1944. This meant that it was likely that opportunists rather than idealists would jump on the band-wagon of Soviet military success. Communism in Eastern Europe was a revolution brought in from abroad.

Even when foreign ideas have been introduced to a country with no conscious intentions of revolution, the result may be revolutionary. As the globalization of the economy and culture has speeded up in modern times, radical reactions to foreign influence have appeared in unusual revolutionary guises. Fear of losing traditional Islamic values underpinned the Iranian Revolution in 1979. The Shah's regime was accused by its opponents of being un-Islamic and "Americanized." Efforts to modernize Iran were seen as the work of the Devil intent on corrupting the Iranians with secular values.

ABOVE **An anti-American demonstration in Iran in early 1980. The popular rejection of Amer-ican influence in Iran compounded the Shah's domestic problems and helped to delegitimize his rule. The Shah himself was derided as a puppet of the US.**

THE STAGES OF REVOLUTION

Is it possible to learn from history the shape of things to come? Can any previous revolutions provide answers about what to do or avoid to achieve success? Trying to predict the exact course of a revolution is clearly impossible, but many revolutions have followed an established path of events. The

STYLE AND REVOLUTION

Revolutions have always had powerful effects on styles of dress and hair. In England in the 1640s, roundheads and cavaliers were instantly recognizable by the cut of their clothes and how they wore their hair. The repudiation of the social conventions and etiquette of the old order is well-illustrated by the wearing of ill-cut clothes and the introduction of new terms of address. The quasi-proletarian clothes of Russian Communists and the Mao suits devoid of badges of rank were visible signs of revolutionary zeal. New terms of address among people also replaced traditional and hierarchical ways of speaking to one another. In France after 1789, for example, everyone was spoken to as "citizen," especially in the most radical years of 1792–94. After the Russian Revolution – and in every Communist state – "comrade" supplanted "mister" or other titles. Conversely, the fall of a revolution is frequently succeeded by a return to old styles of dress. The reaction against the radical revolutionaries in France in 1794 was followed by a sudden popularity of lavish clothing and daring styles, particularly low-cut dresses for women. This new *jeunesse dorée* ("gilded youth") delighted in flouting yesterday's rigid puritanical Jacobin conventions of dress and behaviour. They also took pleasure in desecrating yesterday's revolutionary shrines, pulling down busts of radical heroes and agitating for the bodies of men such as Marat to be removed from their places of honour in the Pantheon. Ex-Communists in Russia after 1991 rushed to prove their new-found bourgeois credentials by dressing up in

dinner jackets or Versace. Similarly, Chinese reform Communists in the 1980s broke with Maoist convention very visibly by wearing well-cut business suits instead of anonymous military-style uniforms – although when Mao's successors want to look suitably intimidating they still pull on the olive-green fatigues of the People's Liberation Army.

With regard to styles of address, it was significant indeed when the French secret police began to note in January 1795 that citizens were once more addressed in public as "monsieur" and "madame." When Communism fell, the resumption of the self-conscious use of *gospodin* ("mister") in Russia signalled a rejection of Soviet ways – though many Russians, including "reformers" still refer to each other as "comrade." Changing one's ways is not always easy to do.

BELOW **Young Chinese wearing the distinctive "Mao suit" with white flowers of mourning for Zhou En Lai.**

French Revolution had such a profound impact on global ideology and politics that it set a pattern for the development of many subsequent revolutions. The basic sequence of events in France from 1789 was follows: after the collapse of the old order in the summer of 1789, French politics became increasingly radical. The experiment with a constitutional monarchy gave way to a republic in 1792, followed by a fearful Terror that decimated the leading figures in the republic until, in the summer of

ABOVE **"The 1789 of China." The French Revolution still has a potent international influence, 200 years after it began. Here Chinese students demonstrate in spring 1989 for the rights of man.**

1794, the radical phase was suddenly halted by a coup against the "Terrorists" by their former comrades. This new regime was eventually ousted in turn by Napoleon Bonaparte's military coup d'état in 1799. Not every revolution fits the French model, but it has certainly helped to shape expectations and fears once a revolutionary process has begun.

The collapse of the old order

BELOW **Well-intentioned reformers often open the floodgates to revolution. Louis XVI and Mikhail Gorbachev both hoped to improve the lot of their subjects through reform, but in practice their efforts to begin reform undermined their authority.**

Before it can be plausible to think of instituting a new order of society, the old one has to weaken. Powerful systems of government and society may well involve injustice and exploitation, but so long as they retain confidence in themselves and the ability to organize state power they can usually deter or suppress opposition, even when the majority are discontented. Aristotle noted that: "It is in the interests of a tyrant to make his subjects poor, so that...the people are so occupied with their daily tasks that they have no time for plotting. As an example of such measures...of keeping subjects perpetually at work and in poverty we may mention the pyramids of Egypt."

Not every ruler who came to power in a despotic system was wise or cynical enough to follow Aristotle's advice, however. From Louis XVI in

France in the 1780s to Mikhail Gorbachev in the Soviet Union in the 1980s, would-be reformers trying to improve despotic systems have helped to promote a crisis of confidence in their regime and, as a result, lead to revolution. Commenting on the French Revolution, Alexis de Tocqueville stated, "It is not always when things are going from bad to worse that revolutions break out. On the contrary it oftener happens that when a people which has put up with an oppressive regime over a long period without protest suddenly finds the government relaxing its pressure, it takes up arms against it.... The social order overthrown by a revolution is almost always better than the one immediately preceding it, and experience teaches us that, generally speaking, the most perilous moment for a bad government is one when it seeks to mend its ways." Many inveterate despots have died in their beds, but few reformers have enjoyed a happy retirement.

Liberalization often fails to satisfy grievances. Rather than promoting a favourable public opinion about the benevolent ruler, the effect of permitting freedom of speech is usually to unleash an avalanche of criticism and demands for more change. By allowing criticism of the regime, and even joining in with the criticism himself, the would-be reformer shakes the loyalty and self-confidence of the officials, troops and policemen who are the pillars of the old system. At the same time he emboldens his opponents. What had once seemed unrealistic ideas of change suddenly become plausible politics. While the radicals gain strength and push forward with renewed enthusiasm, supporters of the old order begin to drift apart. Some look for shelter and even flee the country (like the aristocratic French émigrés in 1789) while others may try to reach a compromise with the opposition and change sides, explaining that they had always really tried to promote reform. The would-be reformer soon finds himself isolated and vilified both by hard-

ABOVE **Successive generations of Russian leaders have fallen from grace. A statue of Tsar Alexander III felled in Moscow, January 1918 (left); the head of Stalin is removed from a statue in Prague in 1989 (centre); a Lenin statue being dismantled in Romania (right).**

"Is it not a simple fact that revolution in any form of government always starts from the outbreak of internal dissension in the ruling class? The constitution cannot be upset so long as that class is of one mind, however small it may be."
PLATO, 5TH-4TH CENTURY BC

liners, disappointed by his failure to crackdown, and by reformers, who decry his inability to cut every last link with the old order whose representative he remains. It is not difficult to topple the Louis XVI figure from this exposed and precarious position.

The overthrow and execution of despots is part of the classic imagery and a key feature of revolution – but revolutions are more than just coups d'état or changes of dynasty. After all, the history of human government has always been one of instability and violent change. As far back as written records or folk memories take us, rulers have been insecure – but their systems of government were usually stable. Rulers might have claimed to be "Sons of Heaven" (as the Chinese emperors have done since time immemorial) or to rule by divine right (as did so many West European kings), but that did not stop rivals from deposing and murdering them. These changes in ruler were not revolutionary, however: the new rulers took the place of the defunct ones but went on governing in the same old way.

The Romanian saying "A change of rulers is the joy of fools" recognizes that more is needed than a change in personnel at the top to alter the nature of a regime. The changing of places between government and opposition after a general election, for example, may produce change, but it is not a revolution.

The weakness of moderates

Radicalization is almost an essential feature of revolutions. Sudden change is rarely a calm or considered affair. Yet, initially at least, revolutions frequently pass through an apparent period of calming down. After the fall of the old order and the flight or arrest of its most obnoxious representatives, people seem to relax – but their expectations remain high. If the new order does not resolve the underlying social and economic issues that led to the political upheaval, then the days of moderation prove short-lived. Of course, well-intentioned moderate reformers frequently turn out to be the last people to push through radical change. Like the moderates of the unsuccessful Provisional Government in Russia in 1917, most reformers tend to want to proceed in a law-abiding and constitutional manner. However, popular pressure usually demands immediate root-and-branch reform.

The sense of an irresistible motion towards complete change set in train by the collapse of the old order is vital to promoting further change. The chain reaction taking place in the political vacuum created by the fall of the previous regime in turn opens up new possibilities undreamed of only yesterday. Dynamism is all-important force in revolutions. Moderation is anathema in these circumstances and those preaching it stand little chance of halting the tidal wave of change.

"The Revolution must be a deed beyond all measure, burning all things before it…. If mankind is ever to escape from its misery, there is only one method: the destruction of everything in fire and blood…. There is no other way, no other hope." CHE GUEVARA (ABOVE)

One effect of censorship and the denial of political participation in despotic systems is that, instead of learning the practical limitations on a government to achieve reform, the public devise all kinds of fantastic alternatives to their unsatisfactory reality. Utopian models of an ideal society that will abolish all the current causes of resentment tend to flourish – albeit underground – under authoritarian regimes. So, when the regimes topple, the dynamic of change is not behind carefully crafted alternatives that take economic or social realities into account, but behind those voices calling for a clean break with the past and the building of a New Jerusalem cleansed of all the old order's faults – and often its personnel.

BELOW **The dogmatic Ayatollah Khomeini called for a clean break with the past. He swept aside moderate opponents of the deposed Shah in the first months of the Iranian Revolution in 1979.**

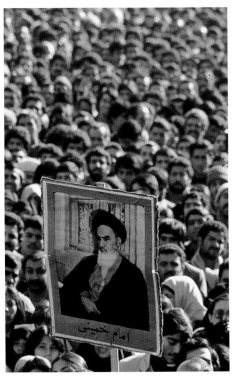

Religious revolutionaries couch their demands for a clean sweep with the past in moral terms, but even self-conscious rationalists, like many French revolutionaries after 1789, usually demand a complete break with the old order. In 1790, Paul Rabaut de St Etienne, the President of the newly-established French National Assembly, insisted that "All the established institutions of France only crown the misery of the people; to make people happy it is necessary to renovate, to change the ideas, the laws, the morals…to change the men, the things, the words…to destroy everything, yes everything; for everything must be started anew."

The Terror

The belief that everything has to be cleansed or renewed by revolution leads to the stage of Terror. Once it is

accepted that the old order and its sympathizers are not merely mistaken, but are the embodiment of evil and corruption, then physically eliminating them becomes a logical step – that is, if they have survived the initial violence of the outbreak of revolution. But soon enough, anyone tainted with the suspicion of sharing old views or harbouring nostalgia for the days before the revolution can become the target for social cleansing. In France, between the years 1793 and 1794, the guillotine claimed many more ordinary heads than aristocratic ones.

Advocates of revolutionary Terror saw it as a purifying process. After 1789, the French writer Chamfort asked (tongue-in-cheek), "You do not desire a liberty which will cost much gold and blood. Do you demand then that revolutions be made with rosewater?" The Jacobin, Danton assured the French revolutionary Convention in March 1793, "A nation in revolution is like boiling bronze regenerating itself in the crucible. The statue of liberty is not yet moulded. The metal is bubbling over. Watch the furnace or you will all be burned." George Bernard Shaw, who sympathized with no-nonsense revolutionaries who wanted to change society once and for all said, "Hot water is the revolutionist's element. You clean men as you clean milk-pails, by scalding them." Louis Aragon wrote in the 1930s, "The blue eyes of the Revolution shine with a necessary cruelty."

By the 1970s, Pol Pot's Khmer Rouge in Cambodia was so extreme in its desire to cut the links with the past that it killed people who wore spec-

ABOVE **Théodore Géricault's portrait of the victims of the guillotine during the French Revolution. Most of the executed had initially supported the revolution. Pierre Vergniaud (1753–93) noted before his own execution: "There is reason to fear that, like Saturn, the Revolution might devour each of its own children."**

REVOLUTION AND MORALITY

Revolutionary ideologies have often been fervently hostile to traditional religion, seeing it as an opium to keep the poor in their place. The rejection of religious hypocrisy led to attempts to abolish the established churches and replace religious codes of behaviour. A moral component adds weight to the revolutionary agenda.

The puritanical lifestyle of many revolutionaries earned them respect from the conventionally respectable even when their ideology required the abolition of traditional religion. Sexual frustration and self-denial were frequently parts of the revolutionary's discipline. From the eighteenth century onwards there was a strand of secular puritanism that ran through most revolutionary movements. This was in competition with the impulse of others, who saw the fall of the old order as the occasion for a carnival of liberation from all bonds, moral as well as political and economic.

Despite their puritanical fervour, revolutionaries quite often flirted at first with reforming or even abolishing the traditional family and its

legal carapace, before the fear of social breakdown or unrevolutionary indiscipline led to second thoughts. The French revolutionaries legalized divorce in 1792 but Napoleon trimmed back the justifications for divorce to the narrowest imaginable – for example, if a husband moved his mistress into the marital home, his wife might have grounds for separation.

Even though Engels doubted the necessity of the nuclear family in a socialist society, the belief in full sexual liberation advocated by Alexandra Kollontai or Rosa Luxemburg was soon quashed by Lenin and Stalin. Abortion, legalized after 1917, was outlawed by Stalin as his policies reduced the birth rate and inflated the death rate to unviable proportions.

The hedonistic neo-pagan cult of sexuality preached in 1968 was easily adopted by many of the children of the affluent societies of Western Europe and North America. These young people could afford to adopt the lifestyle revolution of the 1960s without overturning the market economy that paid for it.

ABOVE **The Sixties Revolution: the Hollywood painter Jerry Kay with two of his "works of art" under the gaze of George Washington.**

ABOVE **Evidence of the human cost of Pol Pot's drive to transform Cambodia into a Communist society survived his defeat by the Vietnamese in 1979 in the form of pyramids of the skulls of those the Communist Khmer Rouge guerrillas had executed.**

tacles on the grounds that this showed they had benefited from the old regime and had to be removed in case they corrupted the new society.

"Thermidor"

When Maximilien Robespierre, the extreme French revolutionary, fell from power in July 1794 – the revolutionary month of "Thermidor" – the event gave its name to a key stage in the revolutionary process. Until 9 Themidor, the French Revolution had seemed bent on an ever more radical trajectory. Then suddenly, this impetus stalled. The intensification of the Terror relaxed. Yesterday's radicals became opponents of extremism almost overnight. Thermidor became a concept: the moment when a revolution tries to turn back from the path of radicalism.

Whereas the ex-Jacobins who turned on the so-called "Terrorists" like Robespierre in 1794 had had enough of radical revolution, other retreats from full-fledged revolutionary enthusiasm have had the character of temporary pauses to recover strength rather than decisions to abandon the utopian impetus of revolution altogether. The most famous example of this temporary "Thermidor" was Lenin's decision in 1921 to stop the attempt to achieve Communism at one leap. Instead, Soviet Russia would pursue the so-called "New Economic Policy" (*see pages 130–31*). Within a few years, Stalin relaunched the drive to Communize Soviet Russia.

Bonapartism

The French Revolutionary model not only gave birth to the idea of the stage of setback marked by the Thermidorean reaction to radical measures, but also to the belief that the betrayal of the revolution's ideals by a dictator in the Napoleonic mould was inevitable. In 1799, the successful thirty-year-old general from Corsica, Napoleon Bonaparte, seized power and used his military prestige to establish an authoritarian regime that his ambition transformed into an empire with himself as monarch.

Latin American revolutions in the early years of the nineteenth century were also wars of liberation so it was hardly surprising that military figures dominated their politics. Nonetheless, the legacy of Bonapartism in Latin America bedevilled the continent's political development for almost two centuries. (Fidel Castro may be the only *guerrilla* leader now in power, but he may not be the last in a long line of generals turned revolutionary or counter-revolutionary.)

After 1917, many Russian Communists feared that Trotsky as organizer of the Red Army would prove to be the Bonaparte of their revolution. Ironically, they supported the growth of Stalin's power and arguably installed a different dictator over the Soviet Union, thereby achieving

BELOW **When revolutionaries fall out, history often gets rewritten. After Trotsky (standing on the right of the platform in the top photograph) lost the struggle with Stalin to succeed Lenin, who is speaking from the platform, he was "airbrushed" out of the Soviet history books (bottom).**

in effect a quasi-Bonapartist regime that devoted vast energies to militarizing the Soviet economy regardless of the high costs this forced on the civilian population.

Restoration

King Charles I of England was executed in 1649 after conflict with Parliament over his style of government led to civil war and his eventual defeat by Oliver Cromwell's New Model Army (*see pages 46–51*). In 1660, his son Charles II returned from exile to regain the throne, but only at the invitation of key members of Cromwell's army, who saw a restored monarchy as the best way to maintain order and guarantee their position. The Restoration was a compromise between monarchism and disappointed republicanism. England did not return to its pre-revolutionary ways and Charles II was wise enough not to emulate his father's style of ruling. He needed the support of some of his father's old enemies and settled for the token punishment of a handful of inveterate and irrelevant republicans.

Much the same happened in France in 1815 after Napoleon's costly wars had ended in disastrous defeat. Louis XVI's brother was restored to the French throne – by foreign bayonets rather than French ones – and it was only when his brother, like James II in Britain, seemed to threaten the compromise between restored monarchy and the legacy of the revolution that more upheaval broke out in 1830 (*see pages 92–95*).

The collapse of the Communist regimes in Eastern Europe generations after their establishment, and after a much more thorough-going purge of the old elite at their start, does not seem to have left any room for restoration. After seventy years, who could be restored?

When revolutions go wrong

If there is a tendency for revolutions to follow a pattern of great hopes, radicalization, Terror, Thermidor, then Bonapartism and even restoration, it is difficult to avoid the sense that revolutions, for all their thrills and promise, often disappoint.

> **"When the people contend for their liberty, they seldom get anything by their victory but new masters."**
> GEORGE SAVILE, MARQUIS OF HALIFAX, 1750

BELOW **Street fighting in Paris during the July Revolution in 1830. The upheaval followed the breakdown in relations between the restored Bourbon dynasty and its subjects.**

The history of revolutions is all too often a recurrent tale of hopes raised high only to be dashed. The more radical and utopian the ideology of revolution, the greater the disappointment when grim reality or human frailty thwarts the fulfilment of the dream. Despite his own enthusiasm for a Communist revolution, Friedrich Engels pointed out that revolutions have unintended consequences: "People who boast that they have made a revolution always realize the next day that they did not know what they were doing, that the revolution they had made was quite different from the one they had intended to make." Writing shortly after the Russian Revolution and the fall of the monarchies in central Europe in 1918, the Czechoslovakian writer Franz Kafka declared, "Every revolution evaporates, leaving behind only the slime of bureaucracy."

ABOVE **Victims of the Paris Commune in May 1871. The struggle failed to overthrow the existing regime.**

After 1917, many Russians came to interpret what happened in the Soviet Union according to the French pattern. The early radical phase under Lenin halted in 1921 and then – in the eyes of Trotsky at any rate – reversed under Stalin's dictatorship from the mid-1920s. The search for recurrent patterns in the past can obscure the big differences between societies and their own experience of revolution, but certainly it frequently seems true that revolutions run out of steam. No society, nor even any group of revolutionaries, can remain extremist for ever. Considerations of ambition and self-preservation undercut commitment to ideals. Sometimes the practice of those ideals repels the people who had previously preached them in theory.

Deciding when a revolution has gone wrong is a matter of personal taste or interest. To those who lose from the fall of the old order, everything is a mistake. To those who hoped for moderate change or a different direction to the revolution, its descent into Terror may mark the stage when events become unacceptable. On the other hand, the committed revolutionary determined to make a clean sweep with the past may well regard the abandonment of Terror, the so-called Thermidorean reaction, as the point of disillusionment. Others will see the appearance of dictatorship under some sort of Bonaparte as the doleful moment of loss of faith in revolution. Yet others will manage to make a career mouthing every slogan and denouncing yesterday's beliefs and tomorrow's ideals with equal abandon. Few revolutions are without opportunists.

"Every successful revolt is termed a revolution, every unsuccessful one a rebellion." ENGLISH SCIENTIST JOSEPH PRIESTLEY, IN A LETTER TO EDMUND BURKE, 1791

RIGHT **Paris has twice been the scene of "unsuccessful" revolutions: the Paris Commune of 1871 and the student riots of 1968. In both cases, however, the ruling regimes came within a whisker of collapsing.**

ABOVE *"All modern revolutions have ended in a reinforcement of the State."* So long as a regime can rely on its security forces, as the Communists in China could in 1989, mass crowds in the streets have little chance of toppling it.

Many of the revolutions that failed permanently to overturn the old order – such as those that swept across Europe in 1848 or the Paris Commune of 1871 – nonetheless had a resonance. For the emerging working-class movement, the brutal suppression of the June Days in 1848 or the Commune became part of a tragic epic that inspired future activists. Even the temporary overturning of the old regime left the ruling elite uneasy after restoration.

In 1911, Joseph Conrad summed up the tragedy of revolutionary success in *Under Western Eyes*, when the triumph of the modern wave of revolution was hardly expected. He wrote: "In a real revolution the best characters do not come to the front. A violent revolution falls into the hands of narrow-minded fanatics and of tyrannical hypocrites.... The scrupulous and the just, the noble, humane and devoted natures, the unselfish and the intelligent may begin a movement – but it passes away from them. They are not the leaders of a revolution. They are its victims: the victims of disgust, disenchantment – often of remorse. Hopes grotesquely betrayed, ideals caricatured – that is the definition of revolutionary success. There have been in every revolution hearts broken by such success." For all the libertarian hopes aroused by revolutions as diverse as the French, Russian or anti-colonial struggles of the Third World, Albert Camus concluded that: "All modern

REVOLUTIONARY ART

The link between the avant-garde in art and politics is striking. From David in the 1780s to the Russian Futurists after 1917 (and the anti-social realists in the last days of Soviet Communism) new movements in the arts have been linked to the general crisis in society. David's paintings idealized the French revolutionaries as regicide Roman republicans. His neo-classicism was subversive despite its ancient style. Bolshevik artists like El Lissitzky symbolized the 1917 Communist revolution's complete break with the past with their use of Futurism, which rejected everything old, including formal aesthetics. The very boldness of El Lissitzky's colours and forms meant that even though ordinary Russians could not analyze the content of his designs, few could miss their revolutionary meaning. The success of a revolution and the establishment of a new order posed a problem for revolutionary artists: should they conform to the aesthetic demands of successful revolution that were often remarkably conservative like Stalin's Socialist Realism, or should they risk their official status by pursuing their own muse?

ABOVE *Beat the Whites with the Red Wedge* by El Lissitzky, 1919. The red triangle symbolizes the power of the Bolsheviks' Red Army in scattered units of White Russians.

revolutions have ended in a reinforcement of the State." Camus saw this as an expression of the tragic psychology of the rebel struggling against tyranny: "The slave begins by demanding justice and ends by wanting to wear a crown. He must dominate in his turn." Sadly, being a victim of oppression and even a successful rebel with a cause does not necessarily make for the sort of moral transformation that revolutions demand.

ABOVE **History does not end with revolution. Celebrations on the day of German unification, 3 October 1990, could not mask the problems of the new Germany.**

Is the age of revolution over?

After the collapse of Soviet-style Communism, some commentators were tempted to believe that Revolution had had its day. They argued that the failure of Communism to live up to its promises of human fulfilment and social justice left only pragmatic capitalist democracy as a viable way of life. An end to history was confidently proclaimed on that basis.

Ironically, many revolutionaries had struggled for just that outcome – a society so transformed as to transcend all the pain and unsatisfactory reality of the human past. The early French Communist, Gracchus Babeuf, predicted in 1796 that: "The French Revolution is only the forerunner of a much bigger, much more solemn revolution, which will be the final one." Fifty years later, Marx and Engels predicted there would be a Communist revolution that would sweep away all existing society around the world, abolish all social distinctions and bring history as it had been known since the dawn of time to a happy if tumultuous conclusion.

Even the foundering of the twentieth century's most powerful ideological inspiration – Marxism – may not mark the end of revolutionary utopias. Most Marxist regimes have not managed to achieve Communism, and it is ironic that the few surviving, apparently Communist, rulers in China or Vietnam have made attempts to bolster their power by adopting some capitalist economic practices. But, it would be extremely simplistic to imagine that decades of Marxist education have made no lasting impact.

BELOW **Nelson Mandela's long journey from underground revolutionary via decades in prison to constitutional President of a transformed South Africa was made possible, ironically, by the waning of world revolution.**

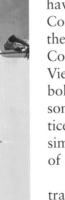

ABOVE **The collapse of the Soviet regime in 1991 brought new problems for some parts of the former Union. Here Russian troops are shown invading the breakaway Russian Republic of Chechnya in December 1994.**

It is highly unlikely that the utopian urge to transform society by eliminating injustice, inequality and a whole host of other grievances will ever entirely disappear from the human psyche. For although revolutionary hopes and dreams may not yet have been fulfilled, it is probable that hope will continue to triumph over experience and insist that another ideology offers mankind salvation from its plight, or at least a part of humanity the chance to break the shackles of the past. After all the tumults of the last few hundred years, who would like to predict a prolonged period of calm? Complacency has rarely been a good prophet.

A CHRONOLOGY
OF REVOLUTIONS

The Birth of Revolutions

Apart from the upheavals in the city-states of ancient Greece and Rome, revolution has been a modern phenomenon. Monarchs have been overthrown throughout history – merely to be replaced by other kings. It was only at the dawn of the modern age in Europe in the sixteenth century that the rejection of the idea of monarchy began to gain ground. Perhaps inspired by the remote mountain Swiss republics (which had not only repelled the encroachments of the Habsburg emperors but also rejected Catholicism in favour of the new Protestant teachings of Calvin), first the Dutch and then the English and the Scots challenged the divine right of monarchy. While religious dogma was important in motivating these early modern revolutions, they paved the way for the more radical and secular revolutions of the eighteenth century.

OPPOSITE **The public trial and execution of Charles I by his English subjects in 1649, which was followed by the establishment of a Republic, was a dramatic break with the practice of simply replacing an unpopular monarch with another.**

In the mid-sixteenth century, the Habsburgs ruled over a vast and powerful empire that included Spain, much of Italy, Austria and, to the north, the seventeen provinces of the Netherlands. But the absolutist policies of the new Habsburg King, Philip II, set in motion an epic struggle for Dutch independence from Spanish rule. This started, in 1568, as a fight to protect traditional rights but became a republican revolution against monarchy that set a powerful example for the future.

The Dutch Revolts

The seventeen provinces of the Netherlands had never been a unified state: they were bound together only by their subjection to the Spanish Crown. Each province had its own constitution and was governed by a provincial estate, which framed local laws and passed taxes. When Charles V inherited the Netherlands in 1506 he agreed to guarantee their traditional rights, and he had the wisdom to recognize that it would be imprudent to introduce schemes for greater integration by force. His son Philip, however, to whom he passed the Netherlands in 1555, appeared to lack his father's sensitivity. Whereas Charles had been born and brought up in Flanders, Philip was educated in Spain. Philip's Castilian outlook was absolutist and he had little sympathy for the patchwork of seventeen separate provinces of the Netherlands away to the north. The new King was anxious to coordinate his empire and make better use of its resources to defend it against such foreign rivals as France and the Ottomans.

The religious issue

In addition to threats from abroad, the devoutly Catholic Philip II regarded religious disunity as the main challenge to the cohesion of his domains. The teachings of John Calvin – who rejected papal authority and promoted the doctrine of predestination – were making a significant impact in parts of the Netherlands, particularly among the increasingly literate mercantile,

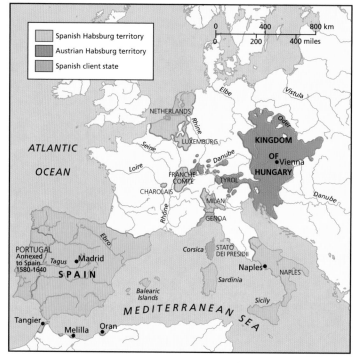

LEFT **Habsburg possessions across Europe in the mid-sixteenth century. Although the Netherlands were remote from Spain, they were a wealthy component of Philip II's inheritance and strategically valuable as a way of keeping his French rival in check.**

weaving and fishing folk of the northern coastal regions. The spread of Protestantism alarmed Philip: in his view, Calvinism and subversion were identical. As there was no Spanish Inquisition in the Netherlands to stifle the spread of Protestantism, Philip sought to stamp it out by imposing a number of religious edicts. Many of Philip's Catholic subjects in the Low Countries were more tolerant than he was, however, and they also feared that under the guise of fighting heresy Philip II was planning to introduce a centralized regime that would take away the customary self-government of the different provinces.

Bitterness about the garrisoning of Spanish soldiers and royal interference in local government and religious matters grew. By the mid-1560s, the spread of Protestantism and resentment of persecution had provoked civil disorder, especially in Flanders and the Dutch-speaking territories of the north. Protestant extremists attacked Catholic churches after August 1566 and destroyed religious works of art in protest against the heresy laws. Although the local nobility suppressed this "Iconoclastic Fury," they made it clear that they wanted the government in Spain to show tolerance in the Netherlands.

RIGHT **Philip II (1555–98). Unlike his father, Charles V, Philip II was thoroughly Castilian in outlook and unsympathetic to his subjects in northern Europe. He ruled his vast empire from Madrid.**

Philip chooses repression

Instead of compromising, in 1567 Philip II sent an army with one of his most able and brutal generals, the Duke of Alva, to suppress the Netherlands. Alva quickly arrested the leading Dutch noble spokesmen for compromise, Counts Egmont and Hoorn (both Catholics) and executed them a year later hoping to intimidate other rebels. Egmont's patriotism became a symbol to succeeding generations (he was immortalized in Goethe's play *Egmont*, for which Beethoven wrote an overture). Alva established the so-called Council of Blood to root out treason and heresy that executed or burned more than a thousand people.

Alva's heavy-handed methods proved counterproductive, however, especially as he began to levy new taxes to pay for his army of occupation. He was as efficient a tax-collector as he was a soldier, but his new taxes were bitterly unpopular and united the population against Spanish rule. He antagonized many nobles as well as

RIGHT *A village festival in honour of St Hubert and St Anthony*, 1632, by Pieter Brueghel the Younger. Despite religious war and political upheaval, the Netherlands witnessed an extraordinary flowering of the arts.

townspeople in the Netherlands, including the richest of them all: William, Prince of Orange. Born of Protestant parents, William had been a favourite of Charles V and was brought up a Catholic on Charles's insistence, but he fell foul of Philip II. Whatever personal motives the Prince of Orange may have had for defying his monarch, he also developed powerful religious and political reasons. He argued in 1564 that no monarch should impose religious beliefs on his subjects. He also began to support what was called the *politique* view that enforcing intolerance was more damaging to society than permitting pluralism. This was anathema to Philip II, who famously declared he would "rather die a thousand deaths than rule over heretics." William was willing to take no chances with Alva: he slipped into exile in Germany in 1567, where he began to raise an army to fight the Spanish.

Open rebellion

Many other Netherlanders also fled abroad. Some took up anti-Spanish piracy. These so-called "Sea Beggars" returned to raid the Spanish in the Low Countries in the spring of 1572. Finding that Alva had concentrated his troops against a possible French attack in the south, the Sea Beggars seized Brill and other ports. Soon much of Holland and Zeeland as well as Flanders was in revolt against Spanish rule. Then,

during the summer of 1572, William of Orange returned from German exile to lead the fight against the Spanish.

Orange wisely refrained from making the rebellion into an anti-Catholic crusade, even though he had now converted to Protestantism. Recognizing the unpopularity of Alva's unconstitutional taxes and brutal methods, he set about rallying disgruntled Catholics to his side as well as Protestants. He also insisted at first that he was only defending the traditional rights

ABOVE **During the "Iconoclastic Fury" of summer 1566, Protestants in Flanders and Holland attacked symbols of Catholic faith, such as statues of the saints.**

of the seventeen provinces, that he was rebelling *not* against Philip's right to rule but against Alva's cruel and illegal government. In February 1573 he affirmed that: "I have only aspired for the freedom of the country both in matters of conscience and government.... Therefore the only articles that I have to propose are that the exercise of the Reformed religion in accordance with God's word should be permitted, and that the Republic's ancient privileges and liberty should be restored, which means that foreign, and especially Spanish, officials and soldiers should be withdrawn."

Slowly Orange began to drive the Spanish out of the northern provinces. Alva's troops massacred the population of Haarlem in the hope of frightening the rebels into obedience, but cities such as Leiden, which was besieged between March and October 1574, resisted all the more desperately. The Dutch showed their will to resist by opening the dykes and flooding the fields around the city. Compromise became impossible. While the Protestants would not renounce for peace the religious freedom they enjoyed in the liberated areas, Philip wrote in 1573, "I would rather lose the Low Countries than reign over them if they ceased to be Catholic."

The breakthrough in Dutch fortunes came in 1576, when Spanish endeavours to fight war on two fronts (against the Dutch in the north and the Ottomans in the Mediterranean) bankrupted the Crown. Many unpaid Spanish soldiers in the Netherlands mutinied or deserted, sacking Antwerp and killing thousands of civilians in the process. This so-called "Spanish Fury" united the whole Netherlands: only four days later the provinces signed the Pacification of Ghent that pledged alliance against tyrannical foreign rule.

The Ghent alliance was short-lived. The more Catholic southern provinces became

> **"These troubles must be ended by force of arms without any use of pardons, mildness, negotiations or talks until everything has been flattened. That will be the time for negotiation."** THE SPANISH DUKE OF ALVA, WRITING TO HIS SUCCESSOR IN 1573

increasingly wary of Calvinism and sought to distance themselves from the unrest, while the seven Protestant states to the north – Holland, Zeeland, Gelderland (which absorbed Zutphen), Utrecht, Friesland, Groningen (which absorbed Drenthe) and Overijssel – formed the Union of Utrecht in 1579 to continue the rebellion.

Steps to independence
The rebel States-General, which united the representatives of the different provinces, were beginning to question the sense of continuing to treat Philip II as their legal sovereign while fighting his soldiers: "What reason is there why the provinces should suffer themselves to be continually

ABOVE **A sign of social tension: members of Philip II's premier order of chivalry, the Knights of the Golden Fleece, are arrested in September 1576 for siding with the Spanish.**

oppressed by their sovereign.... Why being thus oppressed should they still give their sovereign – exactly as if he were well conducting himself – the honour and title of lord of the land?"

In 1581 the states in the Union of Utrecht formally abjured their loyalty to Philip II. They denied his divine right to rule. He had betrayed his trust: "It is well known to all that if a prince is appointed by God over the land, it is to protect them from harm, even as a shepherd to the guardianship of his flock. The subjects are not created by God for the sake of the prince but rather the prince is established for his subjects' sake for without them he would not be a prince. Should he violate the laws, he is to be forsaken by his meanest subject, and to be no longer recognized as prince."

These were revolutionary sentiments in the sixteenth century, and for some time to come. Even their authors preferred to avoid becoming a republic and looked around for an alternative monarch who would satisfy their demands. There was no one suitable, however, and William of Orange made clear that he would not give Philip II the satisfaction of proving that he had rebelled to usurp the Crown.

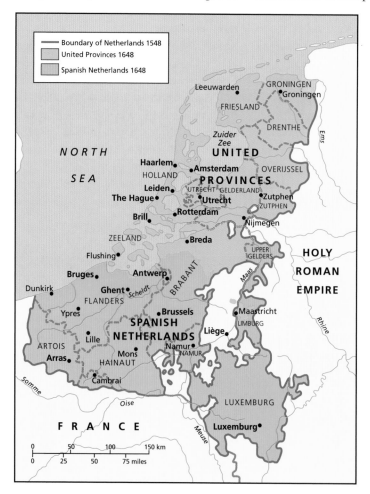

LEFT **The Netherlands during the war for independence, showing the northern provinces that eventually broke away from Spanish rule.**

Boundary of Netherlands 1548
United Provinces 1648
Spanish Netherlands 1648

The United Provinces

Philip II had no intention of accepting the declaration of independence and his new commander in the Netherlands, the Prince of Parma, proved a skilful politician as well as an able general. By a mixture of diplomacy, bribery and pressure, Parma persuaded the largely Catholic and French-speaking southern provinces to break with the Dutch and Protestant north. He made major gains in Flanders before capturing Antwerp in 1585.

The rebellious United Provinces, mean while, formed a robust unit that recognized the rights of individual provinces but organized a common war effort. The Dutch would probably have been defeated by Spain, however, were it not for profits from overseas trade and foreign aid from the French Protestants and sympathetic countries such as England. Philip II's planned invasion of England in 1588 proved disastrous: not only did his fleet, the Armada, suffer a humiliating defeat, but Parma was distracted from disposing of the rebels in the Low Countries by the need to prepare to join the Armada. A truce between the United Provinces and Spain was concluded in 1609, but war was resumed in 1621. Spain did not formally recognize the independence of the United Provinces until the Thirty Years War ended in 1648 with the Peace of Westphalia.

The importance of trade to the new state reinforced its republicanism. Although William of Orange had refused the Crown, he and his family held important positions in the government of provinces such as

Holland and Zeeland, where he was *stadholder* or chief official. Even after he was assassinated by an agent of Philip II's in 1584, the House of Orange continued to play a major role, supplying generals and political leadership. But it did not supplant the republic (not at least until after the Napoleonic wars in 1815).

During the long years of war to defend Dutch independence first against Spain and then, after 1672, against France, the burghers of the ever-richer port cities and the House of Orange cooperated in a tense but fruitful relationship. Despite almost continuous wars, the seven provinces that succeeded in breaking away from Spain developed a viable republicanism, booming trade and a flourishing culture. They became the model for how small countries with free institutions could successfully challenge powerful absolutisms.

LEFT **The Spanish laid siege to the city of Breda in 1624 during the war against the United Provinces. The Dutch garrison heroically held out until 1625. Their surrender to the Spanish commander, Ambrogio Spinola, was immortalized in this painting by Velázquez. The length and cost of such sieges made Spanish reconquest of the Netherlands prohibitively expensive.**

RIGHT **The swearing of the Oath of the Ratification of Treaty of Münster. The Dutch announced the peace with Spain on 5 April 1648, exactly eighty years after the execution of Counts Egmont and Hoorn, in order to symbolize the completion of their struggle for freedom.**

KEY EVENTS

1533	**24 April** Birth of William of Nassau
1544	William inherits Orange
1561	William marries Lutheran Princess Anna of Saxony
1565	**October** Philip II rejects pleas for leniency for heretics
1566	**10 August** Beginning of "Iconoclastic Fury" in Flanders
1567	**22 August** The Duke of Alva arrives in Brussels **9 September** Alva arrests Egmont and Hoorn
1568	**5 June** Execution of Egmont and Hoorn
1572	**1 April** Sea Beggars seize Brill
1572	**July** Holland recognizes Orange as governor even though he had been dismissed by Philip II
1573	**April** William of Orange converts to Calvinism
1576	**4 November** "Spanish Fury:" Spanish mutineers sack Antwerp **8 November** Pacification of Ghent
1579	**7 January** Union of Arras
1579	**23 January** Union of Utrecht
1581	**26 July** Act of Abjuration: declaration of independence
1584	**10 July** Assassination of William of Orange
1585	Fall of Antwerp
1609	Beginning of Twelve Years' Truce
1621	War against Spain starts again
1648	**January** Spanish finally acknowledge independence of Dutch in Peace of Westphalia

Charles I acceded to the English throne in 1625. A dignified and learned man, he was also inaccessible and obstinate, and the policies he pursued so energetically put him on a collision course with many of his subjects. The result was civil war, which broke out in 1642. His defeat was followed by his trial and execution in 1649, and England became a republic. This was truly revolutionary: monarchs had been deposed and killed before, but never legally executed by their own people.

The English Civil Wars

The fall of the monarchy in England in 1649 had many causes, but the issue of religion helped to bind them together. Religion was an important motor of politics in seventeenth-century England. Kings regarded the Church as one of their chief means of control over their subjects: from its pulpits, royal proclamations were read out. If the pulpit fell into the wrong hands, then subversive ideas could be spread.

Soon after he inherited the throne from Elizabeth I, the first Stuart King James I felt it necessary to rebuke the clergymen who wanted to shift the Church in a more Protestant direction. These Puritans – who believed that many of the Church's rituals hindered true worship – wished to get rid of what they regarded as Catholic vestiges like bishops. James I was alarmed: "no bishops, no king, no nobility," he told them prophetically in 1604. Without the church hierarchy, the social and political order would also collapse. An attack on one part of the system would topple the rest, as the Puritans would discover four decades later.

Charles I

Although there were rumblings of discontent under James I, relations between Crown and Parliament deteriorated rapidly under his son, Charles I. One of the basic causes of conflict was that Charles fervently believed that he ruled by Divine Right, whereas Parliament felt it had some rights and sovereignty independent of the King. Parliament's suspicions of royal authority were exacerbated by the fact that most continental countries were seeing a trend towards royal absolutism, and the English were sensitive to any sign that a similar situation was developing at home.

Catholicism and tyranny went together in the minds of most English Protestants, and Charles made the mistake of granting concessions to the Catholics in a secret clause in his marriage treaty with the French Catholic princess Henrietta Maria (daughter of the French King, Henri IV). Charles and the Archbishop of Canterbury William Laud also harassed the Puritans and implemented a much resented programme of religious reform that increased the power of the bishops and church courts and seemed to herald a swing towards Catholicism.

If the new King's anti-Puritan religious policies were unpopular, so was his unsuccessful foreign policy (simultaneous war against France and Spain), which was

> **"A king is a thing men have made for their own sakes, for quietness' sake. Just as in a family one man is appointed to buy the meat."** JOHN SELDEN , ARGUING THE RADICAL CASE AGAINST DIVINE RIGHT, 1654

LEFT **The King of England, Charles I (1600–49), as he liked to see himself portrayed. His lavish patronage of the arts offended his Puritanical subjects.**

expensive and led him into trying to raise taxes. Parliament was critical of the ineffcient war effort, and in 1626 impeached the royal favourite, the Duke of Buckingham, George Villiers, for his role in the disastrous campaigns in France. Charles was furious, and dissolved Parliament. He believed it was his right to choose his own ministers, run the army and raise taxes as he wished. But financial expedience forced Charles to call a second Parliament in 1628, which drew up a Petition of Right that asserted Parliament's right to vote taxes and forced loans, and declared that the forced billeting of troops, imprisonment without a fair trial and the use of martial law on citizens were illegal. Charles consented to the Petition only because he needed to raise money. It was not long, however, before he was once again collecting taxes without Parliamentary consent.

The third Parliament, of 1629, continued to oppose the King's religious and fiscal policies. Charles decided to adjourn the House of Commons yet again. But MPs defied the King's command to dissolve Parliament by holding down the Speaker of the House of Commons in his chair and passed resolutions against taxation without consent and anti-Protestant religious innovations.

The "Eleven Years Tyranny"

From 1629 to 1640, Charles I attempted to govern without Parliament (the "Eleven Years Tyranny" or "Personal Rule"). He used a variety of dubious methods to raise revenue, but their unpopularity meant that if ever he need to call another Parliament he would face much opposition.

On the religious front, Charles I pressed on with his anti-Puritan drive, which alienated many of his subjects. His tolerance of  his wife's religion and the trend of conversions at court promoted the view that he was a closet Catholic. Furthermore, his use of bishops to ram through his policies from the pulpit was resented – and in fact backfired. In 1646, a Puritan clergyman, Thomas Edwards, reflected on the counterproductive effect of this policy: "What was it that ruined the bishops and that [royalist] party, but their grasping and meddling with all at once, Church and commonwealth both, provoking all sorts of persons against them, nobility, gentry, City, ministers, common people?"

In 1637, Charles I decided to apply his religious policies to his other kingdom, Scotland, where Presbyterian Protestantism was very strong. Alienated by years of neglect and outraged by "popish" innovations, the Scots rose in revolt. Suddenly Charles I needed extra revenue to fund a war to reconquer Scotland. He did not have sufficient funds to pay his troops. So in spring 1640 the King found himself having to summon a new Parliament.

Parliament recalled

While the King hoped for money from Parliament, the newly elected MPs were intent on redress after eleven years of discontent. They would fund his war if he answered their grievances. Instead of meeting such demands, Charles I dissolved Parliament after only three weeks (the Short Parliament), but further Scottish successes compelled him to call another in November 1640. The MPs forced the King to agree not to dissolve Parliament without its consent and to accept a Triennial bill requiring him to summon Parliament at least once every three years. In fact, it sat (with interruptions) until 1660, earning it the nickname of the Long Parliament.

Having secured Parliament's position, the MPs set about dismantling the institutions that had allowed the King to maintain his quasi absolute "Personal Rule." They also indicted his chief ministers, including the Earl of Strafford (see above).

ABOVE The execution of the King's adviser, Thomas Wentworth, the Earl of Strafford, in 1641. He was suspected by many English of raising an army in Ireland to use against anti-royalists in England. A mixture of Parliamentary and mob pressure was brought on Charles I to force him to sign the Act of Parliament condemning Strafford to death in May 1641.

LEFT In the civil war, Parliament had the advantage of controlling London and the other major ports, Bristol and Hull, and much of the most valuable land in East Anglia and the south of England. Charles I's strongest support came from the poorer parts of his kingdom. The intervention of the Scots on the side of Parliament in 1644 was the key to the King's loss of northern England.

Attitudes to the monarchy began to change. Whereas most Parliamentarians had previously wished only to restrain the King's more unpopular powers, some now judged him so unfit to govern, his actions so undesirable, that they sought to transfer power to themselves, to rule on the people's behalf. But the willingness of more radical Parliamentarians like John Pym to appeal to the lower orders for support against the King began to alarm the more moderate MPs, and as 1641 went on the consensus against Charles I started to break down. With his ability to rule absolutely now gone, quite a body of MPs – led by Edward Hyde – began to fear that the *radicals* were the real threat to the traditional order rather than the King.

Both sides appealed to tradition to support their policies. Pym and his supporters were convinced that the King was insincere in his concessions, and when rebellion against English rule broke out in Ireland in October 1641 (leaving about 3,000 Protestants in Ireland dead), they worried that Charles would use his army not only to suppress the rebels across the water but also against his opponents in England. Pym responded by persuading Parliament to adopt the Grand Remonstrance, which listed all Charles's misdemeanours and demanded the abolition of the episcopacy and parliamentary control over the army and the appointment of ministers.

Suspicions of Charles's trustworthiness were confirmed in January 1642 when he stormed into the House of Commons and attempted to seize five of the most radical MPs, including Pym. Forewarned, the five had escaped by the back door. Realizing that London was broadly in sympathy with the radicals, the King left the capital to tour the provinces in the hope of rallying rural support. Civil war became a real threat as Parliament passed ordinances without royal consent putting the military under its authority.

The First Civil War

During the first months of 1642, Charles attempted to secure fortresses in the north of the country. Parliament asked him again

"That Parliaments should not make themselves perpetual is a Fundamental. Of what assurance is a Law to prevent so great an evil, if it lie in the same Legislature to unlaw it again? Is such a law likely to be lasting? It...will give no security; for the same men may unbuild what they have built." OLIVER CROMWELL ADDRESSING THE FIRST PROTECTORATE PARLIAMENT, 12 SEPTEMBER 1654

OLIVER CROMWELL (1599–1658)

Born of a strongly Protestant family of the minor English gentry, without the civil war Cromwell would never have risen to prominence. A Member of Parliament at the outbreak of the war, his military abilities, first as a cavalry commander and then organizer of the New Model Army, gave him an enormous influence. Impatient with his fellow MPs for trying to negotiate with Charles I even after two civil wars, Cromwell was the key figure in forcing through the King's trial and execution in 1649. Cromwell then conquered Scotland and Ireland for the new Commonwealth, but he fell out with the Rump Parliament (*see page 51*) over its corruption and attempts to reduce the army, his power-base. Convinced of his divine mandate to create a godly commonwealth, Cromwell struggled unsuccessfully during his regime (1653–58) to reconcile this vision with his residual belief in parliamentary government.

in June to agree to the demands set out in the Grand Remonstrance, but he refused to surrender his sovereignty. On 20 August he raised his standard at Nottingham in a formal declaration of war.

Charles I's one chance of victory was to capture London in 1642 before Parliament could mobilize its strengths, and his army of Cavaliers (from French, *chevalier*, meaning gallant) set out towards the city in October, under the command of the King's nephew, Prince Rupert. The army was met at Edgehill on October 23 by Parliamentarian troops (known as Roundheads because of their short haircuts), led by Robert Devereux, the Earl of Essex. The first major battle of the civil war took place here. The royal cavalry launched a vicious attack on their enemy, but failed to push their advantage through to victory, and the battle was drawn. Charles tried to press on to London, but his entry into the city was barred by Parliamentarian forces and he was forced to retire to Oxford. Having lost his capital, which was by far England's largest and richest city, Charles I was at a strategic disadvantage. Although country gentlemen could be found on both sides, commercial wealth overwhelmingly sided with Parliament. Thomas Hobbes wrote in 1668: "What means had he [the King] to pay, what provision had he to arm, nay, means to levy, an army to resist the army of Parliament, maintained by the great purse of the City of London, and contributions of almost all the towns corporate in England?... Those that helped the King in that kind were only lords and gentlemen."

There were no conclusive engagements in 1643 although the Parliamentarians did succeed in the autumn in securing the allegiance of the Scots. As the months went by the Roundhead army grew stronger – but also more radically Puritan. To defeat the Cavaliers, Parliament established the New Model Army in 1644, under Oliver Cromwell. Cromwell was a staunch Puritan who favoured fellow religious radicals as soldiers of high morale. He was prepared to promote officers who showed sincere faith in the Puritan cause, even if they were born outside the gentry. In 1643, he wrote to a conservative Parliamentarian worried by promotion on merit, "I had rather have a plain russet-coated captain that knows what he fights for and loves what he knows, than that which you call a 'gentleman' and is nothing else."

The royalist Cavaliers were less well disciplined and organized, and the Roundhead forces began to wear them down. In January 1644, a Scottish army (under Alexander Leslie, Earl of Leven) crossed into England and laid siege to Newcastle, while the Roundheads threatened York. Prince Rupert managed to save York, but had to face Cromwell and Leslie in a great pitched battle at Marston Moor (2 July 1644). The royalist troops were greatly outnumbered and suffered a terrible trouncing. Prince Rupert himself escaped with his life only because he hid in a bean field. Charles's forces recovered sufficiently to fight on, but they were roundly defeated the following June at Naseby. By March 1646 the King's troops were forced to surrender. The King left Oxford in disguise and tried to split his enemies by surrendering to the Scottish army, which was allied to his English opponents. His headquarters at Oxford surrendered a month later.

The Second Civil War

Many MPs had been unhappy about the war and hoped even after four years of

ABOVE **A piece of Parliamentary propaganda produced, in 1645–46. Parliament is in "England's Arke Secured" while the Royalists flounder among the "boystrous waves." Lord Strafford fires a blunderbuss at the vessel while Newcastle waves his sword at it.**

bloodshed to make a compromise with the King. The New Model Army, however, had been radicalized by the fighting and the infusion into its ranks of new men, sometimes from low down the social scale. Religious enthusiasm led many of the soldiers to look to very radical change, to bring about a godly society in England. The army became impatient with Parliament's long-drawn-out negotiations with their enemy, the King. In June 1647,

soldiers seized Charles I and defied Parliament too. The King continued to string negotiators along in the vain hope of reversing his defeats. He also inveigled the Scots into siding with him in return for England adopting their model of Presbyterianism.

A second civil war began in spring 1648. A series of royalist uprisings took place around the country that were quickly suppressed by Cromwell's troops, while the Scots were worsted at Preston on 17 August. Cromwell split the Scottish army and cut off its escape route back to Scotland. The bloody fighting lasted for days. As news of Cromwell's victory spread, most royalists surrendered. The Second Civil War was over and the King's fate was decided.

Pride's Purge

The English revolutionaries were backward-looking in many ways. They claimed that they had fought the Royalists to restore the ancient constitution and pure Protestantism. It took them a long time – two civil wars between 1642 and 1648 – to accept that Charles I would never renounce his powers with any sincerity.

LEFT **A Royalist picture of the execution of Charles I in Whitehall. Above left: the King. Below left: Charles is led to his execution. Above right: the executioner (bearing the features of the Parliamentarian Thomas Fairfax, who in fact refused to sign the death warrant) holds the King's head. Below right: people dip their handkerchiefs in the blood of the King. The execution was a most revolutionary act, but it caused widespread revulsion and produced more sympathy for the King than he had when he was alive.**

While Parliament attempted to arrange a settlement with the King, the army came to the conclusion that peace could only be achieved by calling "Charles Stuart, that man of blood, to an account for the blood that he had shed." But Cromwell knew many MPs would refuse to support this decision. It was symptomatic of the radicalization of the army that when Cromwell decided to force Parliament to accept the trial of the King, he sent a former drayman, Colonel Pride, to purge it of MPs who would not vote for the measure. On 6 December 1648, Pride and his men barred entry to or arrested all MPs considered sympathetic to the King. Of the 500 MPs elected in November 1640, only 60 remained in the so-called Rump Parliament to vote to put the King on trial. This was an index of how narrow the basis of support for the radicals was among the electors, who were drawn largely from the landed gentry and well-off.

The trial and execution of the King

Charles I's trial was a remarkable development. English kings had been killed by their subjects before (rather too often for the taste of more conservative Continentals) but none had been put on trial. It was a dramatic break with precedent. The people would sit in judgment on their King. Cromwell said, "we will cut off his head with the crown on it." This was too radical even for the majority of the judges nominated by the Rump who stayed away from the trial, but no one could defy the army.

Just before the trial, Charles was brought to St James's Palace in London, where he was stripped of his royal privileges and treated like any other prisoner. He knew nothing in advance of the charges that would be brought against him. The trial, held at Westminster Hall, began on

TOP **In this cartoon of 1649, the royal oak, a symbol of authority and stability, is pulled down under the supervision of Oliver Cromwell (left), beneath whom Hell gapes. The Church, the Crown and the Law rest in the tree's branches, and will go down with the tree.**

ABOVE **In this embroidery, entitled "The Royal Martyr," Charles grasps a crown of thorns but his vision is of eternal glory.**

20 January and went on for seven days. Charles I showed more intelligence at his trial than ever before. The verdict was foregone but he was able to get his message across: if the King, the apex of the social hierarchy, could be done away with, whose rights and privileges were safe? "If a power without law may make laws...I do not know what subject can be sure of his life, or of anything that he calls his own." He skilfully sowed doubts about whether a republic could guarantee property and hereditary rights, doubts that gnawed away at the new regime for another decade.

On 27 January, Charles I was found guilty of high treason and tyranny, and sentenced to death. He tried to speak but was silenced by the court president, who maintained prisoners were never heard after sentence had been passed. The King was executed three days later outside the Banqueting Hall in Westminster. His head was taken off with one blow of the axe.

The Republic

A week after Charles I's death, the office of King was abolished and England was proclaimed a Republic. The House of Lords – which had opposed the trial – was also abolished, while the bishops and deans had already gone about three years earlier.

The new state was led by men who had never intended to go so far and they were anxious to preserve the rest of the social order. They were challenged, however, by those who wanted the changes to go much further. Already in autumn 1647, radical lower ranks in the New Model Army had debated the future of the country at Putney and proposed the Agreement of the People that would have extended the franchise and based Parliamentary constituencies on a standard number of inhabitants. This Agreement was influenced by the Levellers, who desired to "level" society by making every citizen equal under the law. By pressing the anti-royal cause in 1647 and acting swiftly to disperse the "agitators," Cromwell had headed off trouble then. After the King's execution, however, Leveller radicalism reappeared and Cromwell showed himself stern towards challenges from the lower orders. He executed a number of soldiers who mutinied in May 1649 in sympathy with Leveller demands for a broader franchise and other reforms.

Meanwhile, Charles I's son, Charles II, in exile in Holland, was proclaimed King in Scotland and Ireland. He made plans for an expedition to England, but Cromwell held the army together and defeated challenges to the Republic by royalists. He conquered Ireland after battles at Drogheda and Wexford in 1649 and then set about incorporating Scotland into the English state. The Scottish army was crushed at Dunbar in 1650. Charles II attempted to invade England from Scotland the following year, but suffered a humiliating defeat at Worcester in September 1651.

Internal divisions among the Rump Parliamentarians, as well as their willingness to whittle down his power-base, the army, led Cromwell to seize power in 1653. The Rump was unpopular: its mixture of kill-joy Puritanism and personal corruption went down badly with the people. After the dissolution of the Rump, Cromwell noted the passivity of the people: "Not a dog barked." In its stead he summoned the Barebones Parliament of 140 members, but they surrendered power back to Cromwell in December 1653 and offered him the title of King. He refused it, but agreed to the title Lord Protector.

The Protectorate

Establishing a godly state was no easier for a dictator than it had been for Parliament. In any case, Cromwell recognized that without some kind of representation for the gentry no system would last long in England. Winning the support of the landed elites was difficult. After years of upheaval they wanted a return to normality,

> **"The meanest of men, the basest and vilest of the nation, the lowest of the people have got power into their hands; trampled upon the crown; baffled and misused the Parliament; violated the laws; destroyed or suppressed the nobility and gentry of the kingdom."**
>
> DENZILL HOLLES, ONCE A LEADING OPPONENT OF THE KING, WRITING IN 1649

even if they had supported Parliament against the King. Cromwell's reliance on upstart officers, the Major-Generals, to administer the countryside after 1655 was resented because it threatened the local rural hierarchy. Heavy taxation to maintain a large standing army was resented too, not least because the rebellion against the King had started as a result of efforts to curb his powers to establish a permanent military force that could down his subjects.

So long as Cromwell lived, no one seriously challenged his rule, but after his death in 1658 the unity of the army began to unravel, and with it the Republic. The exiled Charles II was shrewd enough to offer concessions to his father's old opponents in return for letting him return. Much of what had happened would be forgotten and the blame put on the conveniently dead, such as Oliver Cromwell. In May 1660, Charles II was restored to the throne, guarded by soldiers of the army that had overthrown his father.

BELOW **The Coronation procession of Charles II leaving the Tower of London for Westminster in 1661.**

KEY EVENTS

1629–40
Personal Rule (Eleven Years Tyranny)
1640 April–May
Short Parliament
3 November
Long Parliament meets
1641 12 May
Execution of Earl of Strafford
11 November
Grand Remonstrance passed
1642 4 January
Charles tries to arrest five MPs
20 August
Charles I raises his standard at Nottingham; civil war begins
1644 2 July
Royalists defeated at Marston Moor
25 December
Christmas abolished by Parliament
1645 14 June
Royalists defeated at Naseby
1646 5 May
Charles I surrenders to the Scots
20 June
Surrender of Oxford ends First Civil War
October
Bishops abolished
1647 2 June
Charles I seized by New Model Army
1648 March–September
Second Civil War
30 November
Army seizes Charles I
6 December
Pride's Purge of Parliament, leaving Rump Parliament
1649 20–27 January
Trial of Charles I
30 January
Execution of Charles I
19 May
England declared a Commonwealth
May
Cromwell suppresses Levellers
August 1649–May 1650
Cromwell conquers Ireland
1650 3 September
Cromwell defeats Scots at Dunbar
1651 3 September
Cromwell defeats Charles II at Worcester
1653–60
Scotland united with England, like Ireland
1653 20 April
Dissolution of Rump
July–December
Barebones Parliament
16 December
Cromwell becomes Lord Protector of Commonwealth
1658 3 September
Death of Cromwell
1659 5 May
Richard Cromwell, who succeeded his father, is deposed; Rump restored
1660 3 February
General Monck occupies London
25 May
Restoration of Charles II

Returning from exile in 1660 to claim the English throne, Charles II was content to put the years of bloody civil war behind him. But his Catholic brother, James II, who became King in 1685, managed to unite the Protestant English elite against him by seeming to imitate his absolutist and anti-Protestant French cousin, Louis XIV. The ensuing revolution resulted in the expulsion of James II, and forever changed the balance of power between the English Crown and the people.

The Glorious Revolution

Years of civil war and upheaval in England came to an end in 1660 when Charles II – son of the executed King, Charles I (*see page 51*) – returned from exile in Holland to claim the throne. He began his rule with tact and moderation, not only resisting attempts by Parliament to punish old enemies of the monarchy but also trying to promote religious toleration. Although Charles II publicly declared his allegiance to the Church of England, he was privately attracted to Catholicism (to which he converted on his deathbed), and was in favour of religious toleration. Parliament, however, was not particularly sympathetic to religious nonconformism. It recognized the extent to which charges of pro-Catholicism had undermined Charles I's popularity, and sought increasingly to introduce anti-Catholic policies.

Disagreements between the Crown and Parliament over religious issues intensified in the 1670s when it emerged that the King's brother and heir to the throne, James, had converted to Catholicism. The truth was revealed after another tough anti-Catholic law was implemented in 1673 that required all public officials to pass a test of Anglican conformity by taking communion at Easter. James failed to go to the royal chapel and soon afterwards resigned all his offices – but he remained heir to the throne.

By the late 1670s, Parliamentary politics had polarized along party lines. There were two parties: the Tories were

FAR LEFT **Charles II (1630–85) pursued conciliatory policies that assured him a relatively peaceful reign.**

LEFT **The Catholic King, James II (1633–1701), whose troubled reign ended only after his flight to France in December 1688.**

supporters of the monarchy and the Anglican domination of church and state while the Whigs were suspicious of royal power and more sympathetic to the rights of religious dissenters (provided they were not Catholics). Whatever their rivalry, however, both parties agreed that Catholicism and tyranny went hand in hand.

Charles II saves his brother's right to the throne

The idea of a Catholic king revived old fears of despotism and inquisition among the English. The Whigs made efforts to capitalize on the mood of suspicion that swept England in the late 1670s by proposing to exclude James from the succession. Charles handled the situation very skilfully, playing on the strong fears of a return to republicanism. In any case, the Exclusionists lacked a plausible candidate to replace James: his Protestant daughters,

Mary and Anne, would not desert their father, and an acceptance of Charles II's illegitimate son, the Duke of Monmouth, as heir would undermine the hereditary succession to landed estates.

With the help of the Tories, who seemed firmly behind the divine right of kings, Charles II faced down the Whigs and James inherited a peaceable kingdom on 6 February 1685, after the death of his brother. The beginning of James's reign was smooth enough. His accession was unopposed, and he immediately allayed the fears of many Anglicans by recognizing the Church of England as the country's established religion. The honeymoon period was soon interrupted, however, when the Duke of Monmouth landed on the west coast of England in June 1685, intent on claiming the throne for himself. The Duke had only a small army, and he failed to generate significant support for his cause.

In this instance, James II was swift to react: his army was easily able to crush the rebels. Under the supervision of the notorious lord chief justice, George Jeffreys, Monmouth was executed along with over 300 of his supporters, while other rebels were sentenced to transportation and slavery. The severity of the King's revenge caused some alarm among the Whigs. But it was the King's willingness to challenge the hegemony of his brother's Tory supporters that caused most trouble.

James II squanders a strong position

Unlike his brother Charles II, James not only admired his French cousin, Louis XIV, and took subsidies from him, but he also seemed likely to follow his example as a ruler. In October 1685, King Louis XIV revoked the rights of his Protestant subjects to worship freely in France, causing thousands of French Protestant refugees to flood to England. This had a damaging effect on English public opinion. Although James II himself seems to have genuinely wanted to promote religious toleration, the French example could not have happened at a worse time.

James was married to his second wife by the time he came to the throne. His first

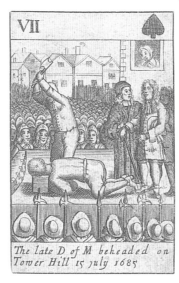

The late D of M beheaded on Tower Hill 15 July 1685

Severall of ỹ Rebells hang'd upon a Tree

LEFT **Playing cards dating from the seventeenth century that portray the events of the attempted coup by the Duke of Monmouth. The seven of clubs shows the Duke being executed on 15 July 1685, and the five of diamonds the fate of his supporters. The "Bloody Assizes" conducted by Judge Jeffreys against Monmouth's supporters helped to turn opinion against James II.**

wife, a Protestant, had given birth – before she died in 1671 – to two daughters, the older of whom, Mary (who was married to William III of Orange), was first in line to inherit the throne. Mary of Modena, James's second wife, a Catholic, had been unable to produce a surviving male heir, so the King was anxious to force through his pet schemes before his death – after which Mary might reverse them. But the King's way of promoting religious toleration was high-handed. When the Anglican-dominated Parliament declined to give him what he wanted, he would simply set the religious laws aside.

As well as flouting the law by appointing Catholics to important positions in the army, the King also revived bad memories of the social revolution during the Republic (*see pages 50–51*) when he interfered in local government – by sacking members of the gentry who did not agree with toleration – and began to appoint men from outside the squirearchy. James II threatened to turn society upside down without having any large body of support behind him: there were very few Catholics to counterbalance the Protestants whom he antagonized. When he brought in Irish Catholic soldiers to help garrison England, he simply made matters worse.

The seeds of revolution are sown

Within just three years of his accession, James II had managed to turn both Tories and Whigs against him. He may have succeeded in controlling the situation, however, were it not for two important events in 1688. The first was the birth to his second wife of a male heir, on 10 June. Far from securing the dynasty, this spurred on his discontented subjects to look for ways of replacing him. For, so long as his Protestant daughter, Mary, stood next in line to succeed, James II's Catholicizing and absolutist plans could be regarded as temporary, but a Catholic male heir threatened to make these plans permanent. Even the Tories could not accept that.

The second event was a full-scale clash between the King and the Church of England. Earlier in the year, James had issued a Declaration of Indulgence that gave full religious freedom to non-Protestants, and ordered that it should be read out in every church. Most of the clergy refused to do this in their churches, while the bishops openly denounced the Declaration. Seven of them, including the Archbishop of Canterbury, protested to the King that it was unconstitutional, whereupon they were arrested for seditious libel and imprisoned in the Tower of London. This outraged the Anglican population. Two months later, in June 1688, the bishops were brought to trial but were acquitted, enhancing the general pro-Church, anti-royal sentiment.

THE POPISH PLOT

Evidence of how powerful the fear of Catholicism was in England was revealed during the hysteria of the so-called Popish plot. In autumn 1678, Titus Oates, an ex-Jesuit, invented a tale of Catholic treason and plans to murder Charles II in order to install a Catholic tyranny that would force Protestant England to submit to the Pope's authority. Oates exploited the unexplained murder of the investigating magistrate to give credence to his fabrications. This made him enormously popular and triggered a wave of anti-Catholic fervour, culminating in the Exclusion crisis of 1678–81. Several Catholics were executed on the basis of his charges before the hysteria died down. He was later convicted of perjury and savagely whipped once a year until 1689.

Within 24 hours of the bishops' acquittal, seven leading Englishmen – a mixture of Whigs and Tories, including the Bishop of London – wrote to Mary's husband (and James II's son-in-law), William of Orange, in the Dutch Republic, seeking his intervention to restrain the King from flouting the constitution.

William of Orange had been engaged in a duel with France's monarch, Louis XIV, ever since 1672. William's key interest was in protecting his native Holland from French domination, and he saw that if he could replace James II as King of England then he could rally England's resources to the anti-French cause. Defending his wife's claims to the English succession gave William a way of interfering in England to Holland's advantage.

William began to make preparations to invade England straight away, and it was not long before rumours of an impending offensive began to reach the shores of England. James panicked, and hurriedly began to reverse many of his most unpopular policies. He abolished the Ecclesiastical Commission, reinstated many of the men he had removed from public office and dismissed numerous Catholics from the army and other prominent positions. But these concessions did nothing to earn him the respect or support of his subjects. The King's main hope, therefore, was that Louis XIV would come to his aid in the event of an invasion. But even this hope was dashed in September 1688 when the French King committed 70,000 troops elsewhere.

An invasion is launched

William made his first attempt to sail from Holland on 20 October, but was obliged to turn back almost immediately because of bad weather. His second attempt was more successful. A providential change of wind allowed the Dutch fleet to speed down the English Channel unopposed. James had been wrong-footed: he had somehow expected the Dutch forces to land on the northeast coast, but in fact they sailed to the southwest and landed at Brixham near Torbay (*see map page 47*) on 5 November.

In spite of months of preparations for an invasion, James II played into William's hands. While the English soldiers became increasingly demoralized on the long march from London, in terrible weather conditions, to meet the invading army, William and his troops had time to rest and regroup. James joined his army at Salisbury on 19 November, but he had developed a nasal infection that not only incapacitated him physically but also affected his confidence. He bungled military resistance to the Dutch invasion and was shocked by the desertion of key officers to his enemies. Even his second daughter, Anne, changed sides, along with

> **"If the King may suspend the laws of our land which concern our religion, I am sure there is no other law but he may suspend; and if the King may suspend all the laws of the kingdom, what a condition are all the subjects in for their lives, liberties and properties."** COUNSEL FOR THE SEVEN BISHOPS, 1688

ABOVE **The "Warming-Pan" baby. Opponents of James II attempted to spread the absurd rumour that James's son was an impostor, who had been smuggled into the Queen's bed in a warming pan. In this engraving the baby holds a toy windmill (it was alleged that his true father was a miller) while the King pokes his head through the curtains above the Queen's head.**

her husband, causing James to moan, "God help me, my own children have forsaken me." In fact, only a very small minority of Englishmen took up arms against their King. (The Tory, Lord Willoughby, expressed the dilemma of old royalists in 1688: "It was the first time any [member of the family] was ever engaged against the Crown and it was his trouble – but there was a necessity either to part with our religion and properties or do it.") More importantly, however, even fewer English subjects were willing to come to the aid of their King. Within a few days of his arrival at Salisbury – and with scarcely a shot being exchanged – James II had ordered a retreat.

Most of the grandees of English political life who had invited William of Orange to invade hoped that he would find a way of making James II behave himself, perhaps as a regent, but William recognized that so long as James II remained in England, the situation would never be stable and France could always intervene to restore him to full power. Thus it was almost certainly with his connivance that James II – who was afraid of meeting his father's fate: *see page 50* – escaped to France, following his wife and son. (The King's first attempt at flight had been foiled when he was captured and returned to London.) James's departure left William in a strong position to propose a most peculiar arrangement: with the King and Prince of Wales abroad, William not only arranged that his wife, Mary, should become Queen, but also that he should share sovereignty with her as King William III.

The Whigs accepted this arrangement because it weakened the idea of divinely sanctioned hereditary right. But the Tories were in a quandary: try as they might to avoid the idea that James II had been deposed by his subjects, the Tories could not really explain his "abdication by reason of flight" in any other way. The Scots were clearer: they said that James II had forfeited the Crown because of his misgovernment. Future kings

BELOW **William and Mary were the only joint-sovereigns in English history – an elegant solution to William of Orange's insistence on having a share of power in return for deposing James II.**

should beware of trying their subjects' patience. Daniel Defoe remarked of Charles I that: "If the King could do no wrong, then someone had done the late King a great deal of wrong." James II chose exile over murder or execution. Even his conservative subjects preferred the novelty of joint-monarchs to anarchy.

The consequences of revolution

Despite the bloodless nature of the fall of James II, the Glorious (or "Bloodless") Revolution marked a decisive turn in British history. The divine right of kings was effectively buried in Britain after 1688. There was some resistance to the revolution in Scotland and Ireland, not least because it was an English Protestant event – to the disadvantage of both (Catholic) societies. The revolution was also to have repercussions elsewhere in the world, for the weakening of royal authority helped to lay the foundations for the revolution in America eighty years later, when mem-

bers of the colonies rebelled against British sovereignty (*see pages 58–69*).

At home, however, Britain saw the change to a parliamentary monarchy and bucked the continental trend towards absolutism. Parliamentary government was responsible to the taxpayers, encouraged trade and above all maintained the rule of law. The Bill of Rights and Toleration Bills of 1689 both made fundamental changes in the balance between government and subject: the Crown could no longer use arbitrary arrest, torture and other heavy-handed methods to get its way. Habeas corpus was at last guaranteed. Religious toleration of non-Anglicans (provided that they were not Catholics) discouraged radicalism among the dissenters and helped to encourage political stability. Religious liberty also encouraged philosophical and scientific inquiry. The myth grew up that 1688 had not been a revolution but a return to the natural state of British political life. According to this view, James II had been trying to upset the traditional order. It was a comforting conservative argument for those who had benefited from the Glorious Revolution and did not want any further change.

KEY EVENTS

1685 6 February
James II succeeds to throne on Charles II's death
June
Duke of Monmouth attempts, unsuccessfully, to seize throne

1688 April
Declaration of Indulgence issued
10 June
Birth of heir to the throne, James Edward Stuart
30 June
Bishops acquitted of libel; William of Orange invited to invade Britain
5 November
William of Orange lands at Brixham
19 November
James II joins his army at Salisbury
11 December
James II tries to escape to France but is captured and returned to London
23 December
James finally takes ship for France

1689 13 February
William and Mary proclaimed joint sovereigns
May
Toleration Act given royal assent
December
Bill of Rights receives royal assent

1694 28 December
Mary dies; William III reigns until 1702

1701 16 September
James II dies in France. Act of Settlement: Parliament limits Crown's powers and decides succession to throne

1745–46
Bonnie Prince Charlie's invasion of Britain marks last effort by Jacobites to recover throne

Revolutions of the Enlightenment

In the late eighteenth century, a new tide of revolution swept both sides of the Atlantic. Influenced by the ideas of the Enlightenment – which challenged the notion of hereditary monarchy and the domination of the Church – insurgents overthrew the traditional order in both America and France. The war that broke out in 1775 between the thirteen North American colonies and Britain was the first revolutionary war for independence and a new society. It also helped to spread revolutionary principles to France, where revolution erupted in turn in 1789. The upheaval in France was the most dramatic and influential yet, and its reverberations disturbed the world for decades to come.

OPPOSITE **Washington crossing the Delaware during the American Revolution; detail of a painting by Emanuel Gottlieb Leutze.**

The revolt of the thirteen American colonies against British rule that erupted in 1775 marked the start of the age of transatlantic revolution. Appealing to many of the principles that the English had invoked against Charles I and James II the previous century, the Americans developed an ideology of rights that had profound consequences across the globe. The American struggle was also the prototype revolutionary war of liberation from colonial rule.

The American Revolution

It is difficult to imagine today how Britain could have expected to keep the North American colonies under her control forever, given the great distance of the colonies from their mother country and their growing prosperity and sense of identity. But even in the thirteen colonies that were to break away from British rule in the 1770s, there was considerable reluctance to cut the links with Britain. After all, the majority of the colonists' families were recent arrivals from Britain and they had brought with them much of the British style of life and traditions.

The conflict that developed between the Americans and the British in the eighteenth century in many ways grew out of their common traditions. Oscar Wilde once joked that they were "two peoples divided by one language," but it would be truer to say that it was Britain's refusal to apply the principles of its own government and constitution to the thirteen colonies that led to the revolt after 1775.

The revolt was also an indirect consequence of the Seven Years War (1756–63), a world-wide conflict between Britain, Prussia and Hanover on one side and France, Austria, Russia, Sweden and Spain on the other, that involved a protracted struggle for colonial supremacy between France and Britain. Although Britain was on the winning side, she had accumulated a huge debt from fighting France around the globe, not least in North America. King George III's government decided it was

time to make the colonies, and particularly the North Americans, pay what it regarded as their share of the burden of empire, specifically the cost of new garrison.

To American understanding, these troops and the taxes that went with them were now even less necessary than ever. Before the conclusion of the Seven Years War in 1763, Britain's American colonies had been repeatedly threatened by France – which controlled Quebec and claimed much of the land to the west of the Appalachians – as well as by conflicts with the native Indians. But afterwards, with Britain taking Quebec, her colonies were secure from the old enemy and they saw no reason to pay for an unnecessary defence. They also resented the so-called Proclam-

ation Line of 1763, which was imposed on the colonies by the British government at Westminster in order to protect the Indians and the colonists from each other. The colonists considered this another example of British interference in their way of life.

Like the Stuarts' subjects in seventeenth-century England, who considered a standing army a threat to their liberties, so Americans in the 1760s began to fear that Westminster's intention was to subordinate them and tax them for its own purposes. After generations of a lax and often corrupt local tax regime, they were in no mood to surrender its advantages to a more rigorous scheme invented across the Atlantic to pay for imperial rule.

The Stamp Act

After 1763, the British Parliament passed a series of laws that tightened imperial control over America. A long list of American products could be exported only via Britain. New duties were also introduced. Especially hated was the Stamp Act of 1765 that required Americans to pay a fee on legal transactions. At the same time, redcoated British soldiers began to be billeted on American homes. Reviving the English slogan used against Charles I more than a century earlier, the Americans took

LEFT **An American cartoon of 1774, showing anti-Stamp Act protesters forcing British tea down the throat of a tax collector, who has been tarred and feathered. Behind them the Stamp Act has been nailed upside down on the Tree of Liberty.**

up the demand for "No taxation without representation." Without MPs representing colonial interests in Parliament, Americans had no say in framing the laws and setting the taxes that directly affected them.

Already after the fall of James II in 1688, the American colonies had asserted themselves by reversing his attempts to institute new forms of royal government among them. It was an early sign of how attached to self-government the colonists were. Parliament's claims to absolute sovereignty over the American colonies created a similar tension between government and people that existed in Britain in the seventeenth century. British sympathiz-

ers with the American cause were aware of the comparison between the Glorious Revolution and the situation emerging in North America. Edmund Burke, for example, "considered the Americans as standing at that time and in that controversy, as England did to King James II in 1688," while William Pitt the Elder told the House of Lords in January 1775 that: "The spirit which now resists your taxation in America is the same which formerly opposed loans, benevolences and ship-money in England; the same spirit which called all England on its legs, and by the Bill of Rights vindicated the English constitution; the same spirit which estab-

lished the great, fundamental maxim of your liberties – that no subject of England shall be taxed but by his own consent."

The road to rebellion

Resistance to the Stamp Act and other attempts to tax or subordinate the colonies was organized on several different levels. Stamp distributors and royal officials were intimidated and threatened, sometimes also tarred and feathered, while, more formally, nine colonies sent representatives to a Stamp Act Congress in New York in October 1765, which issued a Declaration of Rights and Grievances. The British response to these American protests was inept. Sometimes the government tried to uphold the new rules by using troops, at others it backed off and withdrew the offending duties, only to pass a Declaratory Act in 1766 insisting on its right to tax the Americans as it chose.

The arguments used to uphold British sovereignty also backfired. In January 1773, the Governor of Massachusetts, Thomas Hutchinson, tried to bring the local House of Representatives to see that it had no choice but to obey Parliament otherwise it would embark on a course unthinkable to him: "I know of no line that can be drawn between the supreme authority of Parliament and the total independence of the colonies." To which the Boston lawyer John Adams replied, "If

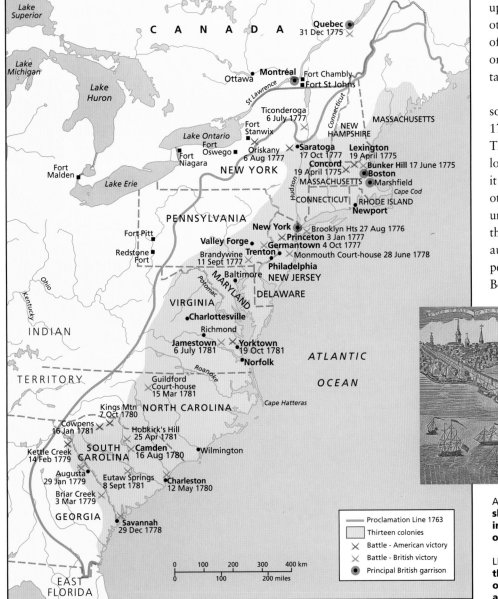

ABOVE A view of the city of Boston, showing British ships landing their troops in 1768. Boston was an early centre of opposition to British colonial rule.

LEFT The thirteen American colonies during the revolution for independence. At the outbreak of revolution, America was only a strip of land on the east of the continent.

there be no such line, the consequence is, either the colonies are the vassals of the Parliament, or that they are totally independent." Even moderate American opinion was being pushed into concluding that whether or not the colonies kept the same king as Britain, they should no longer obey any of Britain's laws, not just stop paying taxes. Others were moving to a republican position from principle, but in any case it was clear that George III would never side with his American subjects against the Parliament in Westminster.

Violence begins

By 1770, the temperature was rising as the colonists insisted on their rights and clashed with the representatives of royal authority. The port of Boston was particularly radicalized by new customs duties, including a tax on tea, and a downturn in trade. Escalating tensions here between demonstrators and soldiers culminated in the Boston Massacre of 5 March 1770, when British redcoats opened fire on a crowd that had been taunting them. Five citizens died. Whether the British intended to fire or not, the bloodshed left a bitter legacy.

Boston was to remain a centre of opposition to the British government and took the lead in resisting British attempts to off-load cheap tea on the colonies to benefit the financially struggling East India Company, which had close links with the government in London. The famous Boston Tea Party of December 1773 – in which a group of Bostonians, disguised as Indians, boarded tea ships and dumped their cargo into the harbour – provoked Parliament into closing the port of Boston.

Other acts of Parliament gave wide powers to colonial governors, interfered with the local legal system, extended the billeting of redcoats on civilians and established a new government in Quebec that did not allow for a colonial assembly of the sort usual in the thirteen English colonies to the south. These measures convinced many Americans that Britain was intent not only on imposing unjust taxes on them but, worse still, on taking away all their rights to self-government.

ABOVE **Paul Revere's famous engraving of the Boston Massacre, published in the** *Boston Gazette* **on 12 March 1770. The illustration, which not entirely accurately shows British redcoats firing at point-blank range on the defenceless civilians of Boston, helped to win Americans round to the patriot cause.**

RIGHT **The Boston Tea Party, 16 December 1773, when rebels disguised as Indians threw chests of tea into the harbour.**

Massachusetts may have been the focus of discontent with British rule, but along the American seaboard similar resentments existed against British high-handedness. The disparate colonies began to find ways of acting together. In September 1774, representatives from twelve colonies gathered in Philadelphia to form the First Continental Congress to coordinate their response to British policy. Georgia soon joined in. Delegates at the Congress condemned the coercive attitude of the Parliament at Westminster, voted to adopt a policy of non-importation of British goods and called on all Americans to raise troops. This provoked outrage in Parliament, which resolved to reimpose order in the colonies – where necessary by force.

The battles of Lexington, Concord and Bunker Hill

The first true fighting of the revolutionary war began at Lexington in April 1775 with an unintended skirmish. Determined to disarm the mutinous state of Massachusetts the British commander General Thomas Gage sent his troops to seize an arsenal of rebel ammunition at Concord and arrest the rebel leaders Samuel Adams and John Hancock. To maintain an element of surprise, the British soldiers were to march silently through Boston on the night of 18 April, row across the bay in boats with muffled oars, wade ashore at Phipps Farm and quietly make their way to Concord (*see map opposite*). Despite their precautions, however, their movements were discovered and two messengers were dispatched immediately to warn Adams and Hancock. One of these messengers was Paul Revere, who rode through the night to raise the alarm.

I set off upon a very good horse; it was then about eleven o'clock and very pleasant. After I had passed Charlestown Neck.... I saw two men on horseback, under a tree. When I got near them, I discovered they were British officers. One tried to get ahead of me, and the other to take me. I turned my horse very quick, and galloped towards Charlestown Neck, and then pushed for the Medford road. The one who chased me, endeavouring to cut me off, got into a clay pond.... I got clear of him, and went through Medford, over the bridge, and up to Menotomy. In Medford, I awakened the captain of the minute men [the local militia, so-called because they were willing to take up arms at a minute's notice]; and after that I alarmed almost every house, till I got to Lexington [where] I found Mssrs. Hancock and Adams.... We refreshed ourselves, and set off for Concord to secure the stores, &c....

We had got nearly halfway, Mr. Dawes and the Doctor stopped to alarm the people of a house. I was about one hundred rods ahead when I saw two men, in nearly the same situation as those officers were near Charlestown. I called for the Doctor and Mr. Dawes to come up; in an instant I was surrounded by four.... The Doctor, being foremost, he came up and we tried to get passed them; but they being armed with pistols and swords, they forced us into the pasture. The Doctor jumped his horse over a low stone wall and got to Concord.

Thus forewarned, the minute men of Lexington drew up on the village green to await the arrival of the British, who appeared at first light. Although the rebels refused to hand over their weapons, they had begun to disperse when the redcoats

opened fire on them, killing eight and wounding another ten. A more serious clash took place later that day after the British were forced to withdraw from Concord by the arrival of groups of local militia-men. As they retreated to Boston, the British troops found themselves being fired upon by rebels hidden within buildings and behind farm walls. Despite the arrival at Lexington of a relief column commanded by Lord Hugh Percy, the British suffered heavy losses. The following day Lord Percy gave an account to General Gage of the retreat: "As soon as [the rebels] saw us begin to retire, they pressed very much upon our rear guard, which for that reason, I relieved every now and then. In this manner we retired for 15 miles under an incessant fire all round us, till we arrived at Charlestown, between 7 and 8 in the evening and having expended almost all our ammunition. We had the misfortune of losing a good many men in the retreat, though nothing like the number which from many circumstances I have reason to believe were killed of the rebels."

Far from calming the situation, Lexington set the whole of Massachusetts in

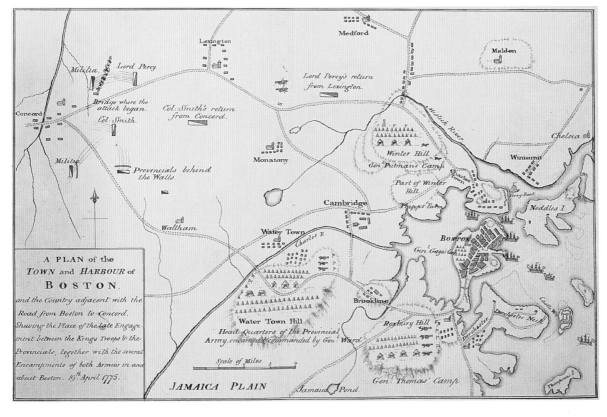

A PLAN of the
TOWN and HARBOUR of
BOSTON.
and the Country adjacent with the
Road from Boston to Concord.
Shewing the Place of the late Engagement between the Kings Troops & the
Provincials, together with the several
Encampments of both Armies in and
about Boston. 19th April 1775.

LEFT **The earliest known map of the opening clashes of the American Revolution at Lexington and Concord and the encampments of both armies. British troops were sent to seize military equipment at Concord but they were observed leaving Boston, and Paul Revere crossed the bay at the north of the town and rode through the night to alert the militia. A clash took place at Lexington** (ABOVE RIGHT) **before the redcoats came under heavy fire as they retreated from Concord at the "Bridge where the attack began"** (ABOVE LEFT) **and were forced retreat to Boston.**

arms. Within a few weeks, thousands of rebels (drawn from the surrounding area, and soon from across America) had set up camp in the hills overlooking Boston where British troops were based. The British soon found themselves under siege. Reinforcements – including three major-generals, William Howe, John Burgoyne and Henry Clinton – began to arrive from Britain in May, and General Gage made plans to occupy the heights of Charlestown and Dorchester on the promontories to the north and south of Boston. But before he had a chance to launch an offensive, word of his plans reached the rebels, who fortified their positions. A bloody battle ensued at Bunker Hill on 17 June 1775 that saw the British victorious but at a heavy cost. Some 228 redcoats fell at Bunker Hill, and a further 826 were wounded; the rebels lost 100 men and 271 were wounded.

In March 1776 the British decided to evacuate Boston. Even after Bunker Hill the British had illusions that a few thousand regular troops would soon disperse the American rebels and restore the colonies to obedience. In part this wishful thinking was fostered by the fact that

RIGHT **A British artist's impression of the attack on Bunker's Hill in June 1775, that misleadingly shows the Americans at Charlestown with much stronger fortifications than they actually had.**

BELOW **The Death of General Montgomery at Quebec, painted by John Trumbull.**

Britain could not afford to deploy a large army 3,000 miles (5000 km) from its shores. After all, it was the need for money that had led Westminster into collision with the colonies in the first place.

Meanwhile, the American Congress authorized rebel troops in summer 1775 to invade British-ruled Canada. The American Commander-in-Chief, George Washington, commissioned a two-pronged attack: one, led by Richard Montgomery, was to take Montreal and the other, led by Benedict Arnold, was to take Quebec. On 12 November, Montreal was surrendered to Montgomery, who then went on to join Arnold in Quebec. The Americans attempted to storm the city of Quebec on New Year's Eve 1775, but heavy snow, the death of Montgomery and the wounding of Arnold resulted in defeat for the rebels.

The Declaration of Independence

By 1775, the British government had sufficiently alienated public opinion in

AMERICAN SOCIETY

The early colonists who settled the North American seaboard from the 1620s onwards were often refugees from religious persecution in England. At different times, Puritans went to Massachusetts, Catholics to Maryland and Quakers to Pennsylvania. Freedom of conscience was important to such people and its defence reinforced their attachment to traditional English liberties. They took advantage of the Glorious Revolution in England in 1688 to reassert the limitations on the Crown's governors in the colonies.

Big differences developed between the society they left behind and the one that developed across the Atlantic. Although there were wide variations in wealth among the colonists – and slavery existed in the southern colonies – class differences were much less marked than in Britain. There were no aristocrats in America.

American self-confidence grew after 1763. The British conquest of Canada removed the threat of French invasion, and the colonies' wealth and population exceeded many European states. There were more than 2.5 million colonists in 1715, and the population had doubled by 1800. Philadelphia was the British Empire's second city. Americans felt increasingly hemmed in by British trade controls to the east and attempts to prevent expansion across the vast continent to the west. Tom Paine gave expression in his pamphlet, *Common Sense*, to the growing sentiment that "There is something absurd in supposing a continent to be perpetually governed by an island." His views chimed in well with American feeling; and the pamphlet was reprinted 25 times and sold about 150,000 copies.

When the revolution began, pride in the equality of Americans was a common theme. In June 1776, one broadsheet urged Pennsylvanians then thinking about electing delegates to the Constitutional Convention to remember: "It is the Happiness of America that there is no Rank above that of Freeman existing in it; and much of our future Welfare and Tranquillity will depend on it remaining so forever; for this reason, great and over-rich men will be improper to be trusted.... Let no Men represent you...who would be disposed to form any Rank above that of Freemen." Even though the vote was generally limited to property-holders in colonial America, the majority of settlers did own some property and so most could vote, making American legislatures much more democratic than the British House of Commons.

America that radicals there began to find growing support for the notion of severing the ties with Britain. The Americans soon turned to framing a new constitution for themselves. The ideas of Enlightened Europe (*see page 72*) were already well-known and developed in North America. First principles were now invoked instead of relying on tradition alone. Natural rights in fact had roots in English thought. John Locke had justified resistance to the Stuart kings and the Glorious Revolution by invoking the idea of an original state of human equality, famously looking across the Atlantic to the primitive societies there and proclaiming, "in the beginning all the world was America."

Delegates at the Second Continental Congress agreed that the time had come to proclaim formally America's independence from the British Crown. Drafted by Thomas Jefferson (an eloquent planter from Virginia and a member of the Congress), the momentous Declaration of Independence contained a long list of grievances against the government at Westminster – including taxation without consent, the billeting of troops and so on – but it was the opening words that gave the document its historical standing as a revolutionary document. Instead of using arguments based on precedents in English law and history, the Declaration proclaimed first principles of its own: "We hold these truths to be self-evident, that all men are created equal, that they are endowed by their Creator with certain unalienable Rights, that among these are Life, Liberty and the pursuit of Happiness. That to secure these rights, Governments are instituted among Men, deriving their just Powers from the consent of the governed. That whenever any Form of Government becomes destructive of these ends, it is the Right of the People to alter or to abolish it."

A fresh start seemed possible to political thinkers in the New World. In 1777,

> **"We hold these truths to be self-evident, that all men are created equal, that they are endowed by their Creator with certain unalienable Rights, that among these are Life, Liberty and the pursuit of Happiness. That to secure these rights, Governments are instituted among Men, deriving their just Powers from the consent of the governed."**
> DECLARATION OF INDEPENDENCE, 4 JULY 1776

ABOVE **Thomas Jefferson presents the Declaration of Independence to Congress. John Adams is on Jefferson's right (in a brown suit), and Benjamin Franklin on his left; John Hancock, President of Congress, is seated behind the table.**

the New York lawyer, John Jay, saw America's ability to start anew as a blessing from Heaven: "The Americans are the first people whom Heaven has favoured with an opportunity of deliberating upon, and choosing, the forms of government under which they shall live. All other constitutions have derived their existence from violence or accidental circumstances."

The Declaration, approved by Congress on 4 July 1776 and signed by its members on 2 August, was greeted with incredulity by the British. The British *Gentleman's Magazine* ridiculed the idea of equality: "We hold, they say, these truths to be self-evident: That all men are created equal. In

what are they created equal? Is it in size, strength, understanding, figure, civil or moral accomplishments, or situation of life?" The American statesman and scientist Benjamin Franklin, who was a delegate to the Continental Congress, understood how momentous were the implications of the Declaration, not least for the signatories, who now were committed to pure treason in the eyes of Britain. He remarked after the signing ceremony, "We must all hang together, or most assuredly we shall all hang separately." John Adams, another signatory, recognized that the revolutionary war against King George also had consequences for the hierarchy of American society. In April 1776 he admitted "that our struggle has loosened the bonds of government everywhere; that children and apprentices were disobedient; that schools and colleges were grown turbulent; that Indians slighted their guardians, and negroes grew more insolent to their masters."

The war intensifies

Although the Declaration helped to rally Americans to the rebel cause, it had little immediate effect on the American military campaign. The Continental army was disorganized and under-trained as well as being ill-equipped, and although the regular British troops – supported by German mercenaries – were harried by the Americans during the first few years of the revolutionary war, the redcoats could usually beat the rebels in open battle.

At the end of August 1776, the British forces – under General William Howe and his brother Admiral Richard Howe – launched an attack on New York. Ever since word of the Declaration had reached New York in July, the city had been a centre of rebellious resistance, which the British were now determined to crush. On 22 August, British troops were landed on Long Island where, over the next few days, they succeeded in outmanoeuvring

Washington's troops. The Americans lost thousands of men: some were killed in action, others drowned on the retreat, considerable numbers deserted the army and a further 2,000 were taken prisoner. Smaller-scale skirmishes took place on the outskirts of New York until the British were able to march triumphantly into the city on 15 September 1776.

By the winter of 1776–77, American morale was flagging. George Washington's brilliant surprise attack on Trenton at Christmas 1776 and on Princeton on 3 January 1777 helped to raise rebel spirits, however. The publication in December of Paine's pamphlet *The Crisis*, with its frank admission of the strains on the revolutionaries, had also done much to encourage the rebels: "These are the times that try men's souls. The summer soldier and the sunshine patriot [rebel] will, in this crisis, shrink from the service of their country; but he that stands it now, deserves the love and thanks of man and woman."

Loyalism

Support for the anti-British cause was not wholehearted. A mixture of loyalty to old ties, suspicion of the motives of the revolutionaries (particularly those from other colonies) and self-interest encouraged thousands of Americans to support the British Crown, while many others tried to avoid nailing their colours to either mast.

Almost everywhere, however, revolutionary activists were more numerous and aggressive than their loyalist counterparts. Active loyalism, or Toryism, usually depended on the presence of the British army. When the army appeared in autumn 1776 in New Jersey, 2,500 local loyalists volunteered to join it, but when the redcoats went away loyalism waned. The British general, Henry Clinton, wrote in 1776, "Tis clear to me that there does not not exist... in America a number of friends of the Government

ABOVE **The Battle of Princeton, 3 January 1777. An American detachment sent to destroy a bridge south of Princeton was initially dispersed by the redcoats, but when Washington (shown in the foreground on a charger) arrived with reinforcements, the Americans succeeded in routing the British.**

sufficient to defend themselves when the troops are withdrawn." He noted that whenever British troops left a colony, resistance to the American side collapsed.

Loyalism lent the bitter elements of a civil war to the War of Independence. Reprisals were not unknown. Even whole towns risked punishment for siding with the British. New York was considered a hotbed of loyalism. In summer 1776, Washington's colleague, General Nathaniel Greene, seriously proposed burning New York rather than surrendering it intact to the British. This would be little loss to the American cause, he argued, because "Two-thirds belong to the Tories so we have no great reason to run any risk for its defence and burning it will deprive the enemy of an opportunity of barracking the whole army together."

LEFT **When word of the Declaration of Independence reached New York on 9 July 1776, a statue in the city of King George III was pulled down by local militiamen and civilians. While the head of the statue was taken for display in a local tavern, the body – made of lead – was carried off to be melted down into bullets.**

Frustration at their inability to mobilize adequate local support led some British officers to advocate and even carry out savage reprisals directed at intimidating the entire civilian population. However, these generally had the effect of driving more Americans to the patriot camp. Loyalists such as Banastre Tarleton committed brutal atrocities against alleged rebels and those accused of harbouring them, but succeeded only in alienating local opinion. It was hardly surprising given the animosity bred by civil war that, faced by defeat, scores of thousands of American Tories preferred to flee to Canada or back to the home country rather than stay in America.

From the start, the rebels delighted in humiliating other Americans who were loyal to King George. As one patriot reported: "August 8 1775. Riflemen took a man in New Milford, Connecticut, a most incorrigible Tory, who called them d__d rebels, etc., and made him walk before them to Litchfield, which is twenty miles and carry one of his own geese all the way in his hand. When they arrived there, they tarred him, and made him pluck his goose, and then bestowed the feathers on him, drummed him out of the company, and obliged him to kneel down and thank god for their lenity."

Changing fortunes for the British

British expectations that the harsh realities of war would soon persuade the Americans of the virtues of obedience were frustrated. Although the American troops were frequently worsted in battle, the British seemed unable to hold down the vast country; and although American morale waned, it did not collapse.

Lacking the manpower to subdue the colonies with permanent garrisons, the British adopted in 1777 a bold strategy to split the northern rebels from the southern colonies by a two-pronged invasion. General Howe's army was supposed to march up to the Hudson River to meet another, under General Burgoyne, coming south from Canada. The two campaigns were badly coordinated, however, and what should have been a good year for the British ended in defeat.

One of the British objectives of 1777 was to seize the key city of Philadelphia – home of the Continental Congress. After considering an overland march, Howe decided in the spring to approach by sea. It was not until July that his troops set sail, however, and in the meantime the first half of 1777 was spent trying to engage Washington in battle. The rebel army was beset with difficulties (smallpox, dwindling volunteers, shortages of food and other supplies), and the British felt that a decisive military victory would have brought about a permanent end to the American rebellion; but Washington, too, was aware of the odds against an American success, and did everything he could to avoid being drawn into battle.

Howe's troops landed at the tip of Chesapeake Bay in Maryland in late August and, after a brief rest, began their advance towards Philadelphia. On 11 September

ABOVE **American troops under fire at the Battle of Germantown, 4 October 1777.**

they were met by Washington's army at Brandywine Creek, roughly halfway to Philadelphia. While one British column engaged the rebels in battle, another, larger column (under Lord Cornwallis) crossed the Creek unobserved in order to threaten the Americans' rearguard. The rebels were forced to retreat, and on 26 September the redcoats entered the city of Philadelphia. Howe immediately set about opening the Delaware River to British ships, but while he was thus distracted, Washington was able to launch an offensive on the British camp at Germantown. Although the Americans were narrowly defeated, the attack proved to both sides that the rebels were capable of taking the initiative.

Meanwhile, General Burgoyne had made good progress on the march down from Canada. He managed quite easily to take Ticonderoga on 6 July 1777, and proceeded on towards Albany, where he was to join forces with General Howe and Lieutenant-Colonel Barry St Leger. They never reached Albany, however: Howe was held up at Philadelphia while St Leger – who had successfully ambushed the Americans at Oriskany Creek and then continued on to besiege Fort Stanwix – was forced to retreat to Canada after rumours of the approach of a large rebel army caused the Indians fighting for the British to desert.

Burgoyne pressed on towards Albany, but his troops were halted at Saratoga by the patriot army. Isolated in difficult terrain and harried by the Americans, Burgoyne's army was surrounded and forced to surrender on 17 October 1777.

Saratoga marked the turning point in the war. It proved that the Americans could beat the British and encouraged Britain's old enemies, France and Spain, to enter the war on the rebels' side in 1778 and 1779 respectively. The involvement of the powerful French navy and the landing of French

LEFT **The surrender of Burgoyne at Saratoga on 17 October 1777 was a major morale boost for the Americans and encouraged France to enter the war on the rebels' side.**

troops and supplies as well as cash subsidies altered the military balance in favour of the Americans.

Even in the grim winter of 1777–78, Washington's army held together in bitterly cold conditions at Valley Forge, where they lacked supplies. The French volunteer, the Marquis de Lafayette (who was later to play a prominent role in the French Revolution), wrote in February 1778: "The unfortunate soldiers are in want of everything; they have neither coats, hats, shirts or shoes. Their feet and legs have frozen until they become black, and it is often necessary to amputate them." About 3,000 troops died of disease and hunger before the weather improved.

War-weariness in Britain

As the war went on some politicians in London recognized that it had been Parliament's dogmatic insistence on its absolute sovereign rights that had led to rebellion. In 1778, schemes were proposed to offer the Americans representation in Parliament, to renounce taxes on anything except trade and to withdraw British troops. But the new situation after Saratoga and French intervention made these concessions meaningless.

One Member of Parliament, Charles Mellish, still hoped that traditional anti-French feeling would rally the Americans to King George III, overlooking the bitterness built up during the last years of fighting with the British: "No more than one-fifth of the [American] people were ever in any revolution, and consequently, though the quiet men were silenced by the [American] army, it was no proof that this country had not friends in America...and we should have still more when the Americans found their governors were giving them up to France." But Americans were more concerned with fighting their present enemy than they were with past foe.

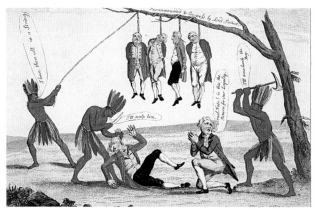

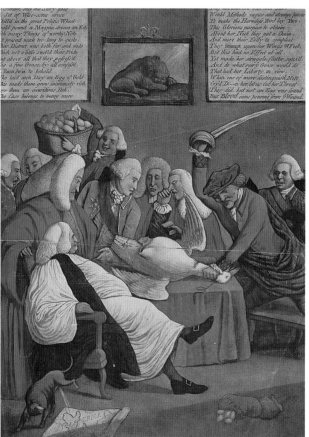

TOP **This British satire entitled "The Savages let loose or the Cruel Fate of the Loyalists" expressed the widespread feeling that American loyalists were not afforded the protection they deserved.**

ABOVE **"The Wise Men of Gotham and their Goose," a Whig cartoon lampooning the rapacious British Tory Government for trying to make the goose – America – lay two golden eggs a day instead of one.**

The war shifts south

For a while after Saratoga, the British army still seemed to dominate the battlefields. The end of 1778 saw victory for British troops at Savannah, but there were no decisive victories for either side in 1779. On Boxing Day 1779, Clinton set sail from New York with over 7,500 men, bound for South Carolina. Winter winds and strong currents carried several ships off course, and it took over a month for the troops finally to arrive. Once disembarked, the soldiers set out for Charleston, where the Americans were entrenched. By March, the British had taken the fort across the harbour from Charleston and in April, after laying siege to the town, they opened fire. The shelling was so relentless that Clinton reproached the artillery commander, saying that it was "absurd, impolitic, inhuman to burn a town you mean to occupy." The American Major-General in Charleston, Benjamin Lincoln, refused on several occasions to surrender, but finally capitulated on 12 May 1780. Clinton then returned to New York, leaving Cornwallis in charge in the south.

The British proceeded to gain control of most of South Carolina, taking Camden three months after Charleston. The Americans were to suffer a further setback in September 1780 when Benedict Arnold defected to the British. Arnold felt he had been ill-rewarded for his services to the rebel cause, and resented French involvement in the war. Now in command of the fortress of West Point on the Hudson River, he offered to betray the fortress to the British in return for a large sum. Clinton was keen on the plan as it would have hindered any American attack on New York. The conspiracy was discovered, however, when the go-between was captured by American militia-men on 23 September. Unlike the unfortunate go-between, who was hanged, Arnold managed to escape to a British ship, in which he sailed to New York.

Despite Arnold's treachery and British defeats in South Carolina, the year was to end inconclusively. For although Cornwallis was able to ravage the southern colonies, he lacked the ability permanently to pacify the area.

Yorktown: the world turned upside down

In 1781, joint operations by the French and Washington put Cornwallis on the defensive. He abandoned the south and marched north intending to join up with Clinton's forces based in New York. Clinton constantly changed his mind, however, about the threat posed to New York, and eventually commanded Cornwallis instead to establish a base in the Chesapeake Bay area. Cornwallis set about fortifying Yorktown in August.

Meanwhile, the American and French generals had been considering their next move. After rejecting an offensive against New York (which was heavily defended by the British), they agreed to march against Cornwallis. In several letters to Clinton, Cornwallis had expressed his doubts about the worth and security of a base in the

"Although I never dared promise myself that any exertions of mine, with my very reduced force...could bring the war to a happy conclusion; yet I confess that the campaign of 1781 terminated very differently from what I once flattered myself it would."
SIR HENRY CLINTON, WRITING IN 1783

Chesapeake, but when Clinton finally recognized the vulnerability of Cornwallis's position and sent naval support, the help came too late. The French navy had gained control of the sea off Virginia and French and American troops hemmed in Cornwallis on land at Yorktown.

Leaving Williamsburg on the morning of 28 September, the allied French and American army reached Yorktown that evening and took up positions surrounding the British camp. Believing reinforcements were finally on their way, Cornwallis

abandoned the outposts and proceeded to bombard the besiegers with heavy artillery fire. Washington's troops were forced at first to keep their distance, but once their artillery arrived on 6 October they set to work digging a trench – the first parallel – around the town. After three days this was completed and they were able to begin their own artillery bombardment. Shot after shot showered into British lines, inflicting heavy casualties among Cornwallis's men. The allies then dug a second, closer parallel on 11 October, and three days later captured two British redoubts blocking the path of the parallel to the river.

Trapped and short of supplies, Cornwallis knew he could hold out little longer. He made a desperate attempt on the night of 16 October to move his troops across the river to Gloucester Point, but a storm prevented more than one detachment from reaching safety. The next day, Cornwallis could see no alternative but to capitulate to the Americans, so he sent an emissary to Washington's headquarters to negotiate terms for surrender. While Washington refused to guarantee there would be no recriminations against American loyalists or army deserters, he did allow the British to retreat with dignity. Thus, as the British troops marched out to surrender their arms on 19 October, the bands played the old song, "The World Turned Upside Down."

The battle of Yorktown was a momentous event, for Britain's most serious defeat on land in America spelled the end of her rule there. In London, Lord North reacted with despair to the news from Yorktown, "Oh God! It is all over." Even before Cornwallis surrendered to Washington at Yorktown, his commander Clinton foresaw the disastrous consequences of any defeat in a letter to the Duke of Newcastle in Britain: "If Lord Cornwallis's army falls I shall have little hope of seeing British dominion re-established in America, as our country cannot replace that army."

RIGHT **Hemmed in at Yorktown by a Franco-American force on land and the French fleet out to sea in Chesapeake Bay, the mobile British land army in North America was forced to surrender on 19 October 1781. It marked the end of British hopes.**

INSET **The British General, Charles Cornwallis, whose fateful Yorktown campaign resulted in defeat for the British.**

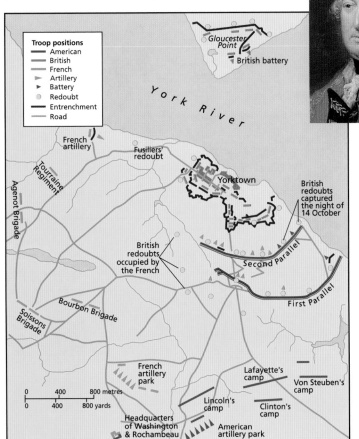

The end of the revolution

The British lost the will to conduct serious military operations in North America after Yorktown, even though they still had 28,000 regular troops there. On 27 February 1782, the House of Commons passed a resolution opposing "the further prosecution of offensive warfare on the continent of North America," preferring instead to concentrate Britain's resources against her European enemies. Garrisons were withdrawn even from strongly defended ports such as Savannah in Georgia, leaving local American loyalists an ugly choice between emigration with the retreating British or subjection to the advancing revolutionary army.

In 1783, Britain recognized the independence of the United States, but the end of the war did not mean that the revolution was yet over. The question of how the thirteen colonies were to be governed had still to be resolved. Having defeated an attempt by the British to exert central control, the Americans were not about to submit to a national government that would take away their rights and identity. The Articles of Confederation, ratified in 1781, provided a legal basis for the United States and granted limited powers to Congress. Yet experience quickly showed that the confederated status of the new states was a shaky foundation for the future: no one was certain how far Congressional decisions had the force of law in the individual states, and a host of economic and practical problems arose from the jealous protection of their sovereignty. Above all, there was the question of taxation to fund central needs – the very issue that had sparked the revolution.

While some of the ex-colonists were anxious to preserve the sovereignty of the individual states and have only the loosest ties with the others, others had visions of a common constitution for the thirteen states. Given the deep common bonds of language, culture and the experience of the revolutionary war, it was natural that federalism should prove the strongest ideological force in America. After all, federalism had been a central element in the American Revolution.

In May 1787 delegates assembled at a Convention in Philadelphia to draft a constitution. The Constitution was ratified in 1788, and George Washington became the first President of the United States in 1789. Compared with other constitutions, the US Constitution has been astonishing in its continuing vitality. France, for example, had seen ten constitutions come and go by the time the American reached its centenary, and another four by its bicentenary.

Revolutionary legacy

Federalism and limitations on government authority were at the heart of the US Constitution. The delegates drafting the document were haunted by the fear that future generations could become corrupt and let the republic slide under the rule of a despotic government. Not only were the individual states guaranteed rights but throughout the United States the principle of the *separation of powers* was enshrined: the executive authority of the President was checked by the separate powers of the legislature (the two houses of Congress), and both were held accountable by independent courts, like all the citizens. Checks and balances that had evolved in Britain were consciously and logically

BELOW **The siege of Yorktown. In front of American headquarters, the French general, the Comte de Rochambeau, is giving a direction to Washington, to his left.**

BOTTOM **The official ceremony of surrender at Yorktown, 18 October 1781. Behind the troops marching in the foreground, British redcoats are laying down their arms.**

enshrined in the US Constitution. But a very un-English right lurked there too: fearful of too much government power, the Founding Fathers enshrined the right of Americans to bear arms in defence of their other rights. Jefferson wrote in 1787 to the future US President, James Madison: "I hold it, a little rebellion now and then, is a good thing, and as necessary in the political world as storms in the physical.... It is a medicine for the sound health of government." At his inauguration as President in 1861, Abraham Lincoln assured his audience, "This country, with its institutions, belongs to the people who inhabit it. Whenever they shall grow weary of the existing government, they can exercise their constitutional right of amending it, or their *revolutionary right* to dismember or overthrow it." To this day, the right to bear arms to protect the citizen against potential tyranny is invoked to resist the introduction of gun-controls.

Dislike of rank and titles also remained a feature of American society. When the

GEORGE WASHINGTON (1732–99)

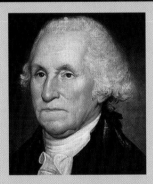

Born on 22 February 1732, Washington was a gentleman farmer from Virginia. He gained his military experience fighting the French during the Seven Years War before returning to his tobacco plantation. Unhappy with British policy, he joined the American army in 1775. His qualities as a commander were less spectacular than those of some of his contemporaries but his rugged determination and organizing ability, along with skilful management, helped to carry the American forces through to victory. His status as America's most famous soldier-citizen made him a natural candidate for the new position of President. He took office in 1789 and was re-elected in 1793. He died on 14 December 1799.

"Freedom hath been hunted round the Globe. Asia and Africa have long expelled her. Europe regards her like a stranger, and England hath given her warning to depart. O! receive the fugitive, and prepare in time an asylum for mankind." THOMAS PAINE, 1776

Presidency was created, the idea of addressing even George Washington as "Your Excellency" was rejected in favour of plain "Mr President." Social hierarchy was associated by many revolutionaries with loyalty to George III. According to one British observer in Boston after Independence, even the Governor had to wait in line with his fellow citizens: "When they are desirous to praise a man 'that he was a good sort of man – that he had nothing of a *gentleman* about him'.... Their own [mock] Governor durst not keep a *valet de chambre*, but went regularly to the barber's shop to be shaved; and that, the rule there being that the first comer should be first served, the Governor, if he found a cobbler before him, was obliged to wait till that worthy cobbler had been shaved first."

Consequences of the revolution

French assistance to the rebel Americans helped to bankrupt the royal regime in France and create the conditions for revolution in 1789 (*see pages 70–83*). French volunteers who had fought for the Americans helped to spread the subversive ideals of republican self-government when they returned to Europe. Tom Paine, who did so much to radicalize America in the 1770s, noted in 1787: "The French...were once the freest people in Europe and as nations appear to have their periodical revolutions, it is very probable they will be so again. The change is already begun." Spain had only reluctantly joined in the war against her old enemy, England, and though she recovered Florida for her pains, the independence of North America set a dangerous precedent for Spain's colonies to the south (*see pages 88–91*).

KEY EVENTS

1765	**22 March** British Parliament passes Stamp Act
1770	**5 March** Boston Massacre
1773	**10 February** France cedes Canada to Great Britain
	16 December Boston Tea-Party; port closed
1774	**5 September** Ist Continental Congress meets in Philadelphia
1775	**19 April** Battles of Lexington and Concord
	17 June Battle of Bunker Hill
	10 May 2nd Continental Congress meets
	August Americans invade Canada
	12 November Montreal surrendered to rebels
1776	**9 January** Tom Paine publishes *Common Sense*
	17 March British evacuate Boston
	4 July Declaration of Independence
	15 September British take New York
	26 December Washington defeats Hessians at Trenton
1777	**3 January** American forces win Princeton
	25 September Philadelphia captured by British
	17 October Burgoyne surrenders at Saratoga
1777–1778	Washington's army winters at Valley Forge
1778	**6 February** France signs alliance with Americans
	29 December Savannah captured by British
1780	**12 May** Charleston captured by British
	23 September Benedict Arnold defects to the British
1781	**19 October** Cornwallis surrenders at Yorktown
1782	**11 July** British evacuate Savannah
	18 December British evacuate Charleston
1783	**September** Treaty of Versailles ends war
	25 November British leave New York
1787	**14 May** Constitutional Convention opens
	17 September Constitution of United States adopted
1789	**30 April** Washington inaugurated as first United States President
1790	**May** Rhode Island is the last state to ratify the Constitution

The French Revolution was really the coming together of several revolutions at one explosive moment. Louis XVI's regime faced simultaneous challenges from disgruntled members of the elite, the population of Paris and the rural poor. But the monarch lacked both the intelligence and the character to control the situation, and violence erupted in 1789. The storming of the Bastille in Paris, on 14 July of that year, was the symbolic moment of the collapse of royal power.

The French Revolution

As day broke on 14 July 1789, rumours were flying round Paris that royal troops were marching on the city with orders to occupy the capital and crush dissent. Responding to this threat, a huge crowd of about 60,000 Parisians converged on the parade ground in front of the Invalides – which housed a store of muskets – demanding to be armed. The demonstrators forced their way into the cellars of the building and seized all the weapons they could find. But they still lacked ammunition – and for this they looked to the prison-fortress of the Bastille.

To the people of Paris, the Bastille represented a despotic regime that sanctioned the King to arrest and imprison his people without trial. As the protesters drew near, their worst fears about the fortress appeared to be borne out, for they noticed cannons on the battlements, menacingly aimed at the streets below. The crowd dispatched a delegation to the Governor of the prison, requesting the withdrawal of the cannons and the peaceful surrender of the gun-powder. But negotiations were interrupted when the crowd outside became anxious and impatient, and lowered the drawbridge. Fearing an assault, the Governor ordered shots to be fired, igniting the angry mob outside to surge into the fortress. The first man to reach the

tower of the Bastille, a watchmaker named Jean-Baptiste Humbert, gives his account of the events that followed:

We found the gate behind the drawbridge closed: after a couple of minutes an invalide [veteran] came to open it, and asked what we wanted: Give up the Bastille, I replied, as did everyone else: then he let us in. My first concern was to call for the bridge to be lowered; this was done.

Then I entered the main courtyard.... I rapidly climbed up to the keep...[where] I found a Swiss soldier squatting down with his back to me; I aimed my rifle at him, shouting: lay down your arms; he turned round in surprise, and laid down

his weapons, saying "Comrade, don't kill me, I'm for the Third Estate and I will defend you to the last drop of my blood; you know I'm obliged to do my job, but I haven't fired."

Immediately afterwards I went to the cannon that stood just above the drawbridge of the Bastille, in order to push it off its gun-carriage and render it unusable. But as I stood for this purpose with my shoulder under the mouth of the cannon, someone in the vicinity fired at me, and the bullet pierced my coat and waistcoat and wounded me in the neck; I fell down senseless.

INSET Angry Parisians pillage the Invalides for weapons on the morning of 14 July 1789.

RIGHT Crowds storm the prison fortress of the Bastille later the same day.

Humbert survived, but when the Governor eventually capitulated to the crowd and mutinous soldiers outside the Bastille, the bodies of nearly one hundred besiegers lay scattered on the ground.

The image of an enraged crowd storming the citadel of tyranny is a powerful one, but in fact the Bastille was more sinister in appearance than it was in reality. The Governor had only seven captives in his custody – not the scores of wretched political prisoners of popular belief. This revelation did nothing to save the Governor, however, who was slaughtered by the mob along with several other hated government officials.

While the Bastille was being demolished by its captors, King Louis XVI was at his palace of Versailles, a few miles away to the west. The date 14 July 1789 must be one of the most memorable in history, but the King's diary for that day records "nothing!" It had been a bad day's hunting. The entry had no political significance, but it speaks volumes about the last absolute monarch of France. The whole political system revolved around him and it was a time of most acute crisis. Yet the King spent much of his day like a country gentleman at leisure.

The King's underestimate of the significance of the fall of the Bastille was not shared by most contemporary observers. For instance, the American ambassador to France, Thomas Jefferson, was impressed by the storming of the Bastille and the lynching of key royal officials: "What country before ever existed a century and a half without a rebellion? And what country can preserve its liberties if their rulers are not warned from time to time that their people preserve the spirit of resistance? Let them take arms.... What signify a few lives lost in a century or two? The tree of liberty must be refreshed from time to time with the blood of patriots and tyrants. It is its natural manure." While the regime had been visibly decaying for some time, this first great day or *journée* was rightly seen ever afterwards as the key moment in the revolution. For the date was more than symbolic. The mob violence that had accompanied the storming of the Bastille was to set a precedent for much of what was to happen over the next five years.

The monarchy in crisis

The dramatic events of the summer of 1789 did not come out of the blue: the French King had faced a mounting crisis for years. First of all, the Crown was heavily in debt. Although France had avenged herself on her old enemy, England, by helping the American rebels to victory during the American Revolution (*see pages 65–69*), the cost was near bankruptcy. The only way the French monarch could finance these expensive wars was through new taxes. But the two richest social groups, the Catholic clergy and the nobility, were exempt from paying direct taxes, meaning that the full weight of taxation fell on the common people.

By the 1780s, France was facing a deep economic crisis caused by her rapidly rising population. Louis XVI ruled over 26 million subjects, the largest number outside Russia, and agricultural techniques had not kept pace with the birth rate. Food shortages were made worse by poor weather in 1788, and by mid-summer 1789 many people – particularly those in the cities – faced near starvation as the previous year's harvest was depleted before the new one had been brought in. High food prices combined with high taxes made for an explosive mix.

At the same time, the frivolous – and extremely costly – lifestyle of the royal court at Versailles, just outside Paris, threw into even sharper relief the harsh realities of life for the majority of the population. The group most resentful of the royal extravagance consisted of the skilled craftspeople, who found their standard of living collapsing as food prices rocketed. These so-called *sans-culottes* (men who wore trousers rather than aristocratic breeches) formed the backbone of the revolutionary crowds.

Added to this political discontent there was also tremendous social discontent. Honour, and to a great extent wealth, in France were based on birth. Hereditary privilege was a vital feature of French

society: the King ruled by hereditary right, and noble birth meant immunity to much taxation. The most privileged group in France was not the nobility, however, but the clergy. The Catholic Church was the only legal faith, as well as being the greatest landowner and employer in France. By the later eighteenth century, new philosophical ideas – known collectively as the Enlightenment (*see overleaf*) – were undermining the Church's claims to divinely sanctioned authority, but it was the Church's privileged status, its courts and its right to levy a tithe on the population that made it resented more than any widespread decline in religious faith. In fact, the peasantry were to show a remarkable capacity to rebel against the Church's privileges one year and to rise in defence of its religious beliefs the next.

French society was divided by a web of inherited special rights. By 1789, many voices had begun to denounce these arbitrary inequalities. The will to reform was perhaps the most striking feature of Louis XVI's regime, but the King tragically mismanaged the situation and ended by alienating every significant section of society – including the urban poor and the peasants, of whom no one had taken much notice until then.

The King attempts reform

By the late 1770s, the financial position of the Crown was in a parlous state. Although the King and his ministers recognized the problem, attempts to reform the royal finances were blocked each time by the privileged orders, who were outraged by every effort to abolish traditional tax immunities. In 1787, Louis XVI called an Assembly of the Notables, who again refused to countenance any fundamental changes. Faced with imminent bankruptcy, and lacking either the resolve or the power to establish an open dictatorship, Louis XVI tried to appeal to his subjects as a whole by summoning an Estates-General: an assembly of the three orders or Estates of France (the clergy, the nobles and the common people) that had last been called in 1614. Such an assembly spelled the end of the absolute monarchy: it was politically as well as

ABOVE **The inauguration of the Estates General (the assembly of representatives of the three orders or Estates of society: the nobles, the clergy and the common people) in the presence of Louis XVI and the imperial court on 5 May 1789.**

financially bankrupt. Any hopes Louis might have had that this body would do as he wished soon proved illusory. But for all his frustrations at the earlier refusal of the two privileged orders to accept reform, Louis XVI refused the chance to ally himself with the Third Estate, whose representatives resented the fact that they had only as many votes as the two privileged orders, despite representing the vast majority of the King's subjects. It was not until the end of December 1788 that the King finally conceded to the demands of the Third Estate and agreed to the election of 600 deputies – as opposed to the 300 allowed to both of the other two orders.

When the traditional three Estates assembled on 4 May 1789, it soon became clear that many of the members had no intention of playing their part in a loyal medieval pageant. A number of radical nobles, such as the Comte de Mirabeau, had had themselves elected to

LEFT **The National Guard: a grenadier, a fusilier, a rifleman and a sapper.**

THE ENLIGHTENMENT

The Enlightenment was an intellectual movement in the eighteenth century that challenged traditional ways of thinking about the world. Enlightenment thinkers rejected religious dogma, superstition and custom in favour of a rational and scientific approach to society and its institutions. They believed that nature, society, politics, morality and the economy were all governed by rational laws that, once discovered, would indicate how society should be organized. The major proponents of this theory were known as the *philosophes* – such as Diderot, Voltaire (*below*) and Rousseau (*bottom*) – who popularized Enlightenment ideas for the general public.

The Enlightenment emphasis on reason and scientific and historical methodology led the *philosophes* to attack the Catholic Church, the hereditary monarchy and the aristocracy, for these were incompatible with rational society. They argued that the role of religion should be to serve useful social purposes, rather than be interpreted as absolute truth. While some Enlightenment thinkers such as Voltaire and Diderot hoped to influence well-educated contemporary monarchs into making reforms, others, such as Rousseau, saw pagan ancient Rome as the model for a just society based on republican virtue. Most *philosophes* wrote before the Revolution, but their influence on the Declaration of the Rights of Man and the revolutionary constitution are clear.

LEFT **Jacques Louis David's painting of the taking of the Tennis Court Oath on 20 June 1789.**

represent the common people in the Third Estate. It was not long before the question arose over whether the deputies of the Three Estates should meet separately and vote by order, or meet together and vote by head, which would have ensured a majority for the Third Estate.

On several occasions the Third Estate invited the nobles and clergy to meet in joint session but, receiving no positive reply, the representatives of the Third Estate decided to proclaim themselves members of a National Assembly on 17 June. They were joined by a few deputies from the clergy and notables. Rebellious members of the Estates gathered on the tennis court at Versailles on 20 June, having been denied entry to their usual meeting place. Here they swore – in what became known as the Tennis Court Oath – to defy any attempt to disperse the National Assembly until the country had a new constitution. Instead of being summoned at the King's pleasure the deputies now insisted that they be assembled by the will of the people.

Efforts to save the special interests of the clergy and nobility were doomed after the King conceded the point to the National Assembly by not dispersing the takers of the Tennis Court Oath. Only the King failed to recognize that he now had to deal with a new political system – and one that was still in the making. Mirabeau suggested that, in this fluid situation, the monarchy could seize the initiative by promoting popular reforms. Without the privileged orders and their special rights hemming in the Crown, it could get on with governing. Unfortunately this was too subtle for the King. Louis XVI could never accept the abolition of the old regime: reform it by all means, but do not tamper with its traditional orders and ranks. This proved to be impossible. But the King's will was no longer law, and even his veto would soon be challenged – and then ignored.

The Great Fear sweeps France

While the National Assembly challenged the King at Versailles, royal authority across the whole kingdom began to collapse in the face of disorder. Rumours that Louis XVI was intending to sack his new reforming ministers – and also that he had ordered troops to Versailles and Paris – helped to spark a series of violent outbursts that culminated in the storming of the Bastille on 14 July (*see pages 70–71*).

Meanwhile, a tremendous peasant revolt broke out across much of north-central France. Goaded by rumours that aristocrats or brigands were about to slaughter them or steal their meagre crops, the peasants became gripped by panic – the so-called Great Fear – and reacted violently. Dearth had caused trouble for the last few years, but the rural poor now went beyond attempts to seize food: they

"The National Assembly, considering that it has been summoned to establish the constitution of the kingdom…decrees that all members of this assembly shall immediately take a solemn oath not to separate…until the constitution of the kingdom is established on firm foundations…" THE TENNIS COURT OATH, 20 JUNE 1789

attacked manor houses and destroyed feudal records of their rents and obligations. High summer was a natural period of tension because the last year's harvest had been eaten and this year's was not yet in. In town and country alike fears for the size and safety of the harvest made people easily roused. Summer was to prove a radical time for years to come.

Yet, in spite of the tension, many people in France felt optimistic about the future. Madame de la Tour du Pin remembered the naive expectations of reform shared by many aristocrats in the summer of 1789: *Amid all the pleasures, we were drawing near to the month of August, laughing and dancing our way to the precipice. Thinking people were content to talk of abolishing all abuses. France, they said, was about to be reborn. The word "revolution"* was never uttered. Had anyone dared to use it, he would have been thought mad. In the upper classes, this illusion of security misled the wise who wanted to see an end to the abuses and to the waste of public money. This is why so many upright and honourable men, including the King himself who fully shared the illusion, hoped that they were about to enter a Golden Age.... People were particularly insistent on the need to base the new French constitution on that of England, which very few people knew anything about.

Popular involvement was a key feature of the French Revolution – and from July

"Men are born free and equal in their rights.... These rights are liberty, property, security and resistance to oppression.

The fundamental source of all sovereignty resides in the nation.

Liberty consists in being able to do anything which does not harm another.

The law is the expression of the general will. All citizens have the right to take part personally, or through representatives, in the making of law."
THE DECLARATION OF THE RIGHTS OF MAN

1789 it became clear that the people of Paris could play a decisive role. Aware of their grievances, the new National Assembly voted on 4 August to abolish feudal rights, and three weeks later, on 26 August, adopted the Declaration of the Rights of Man and Citizen. This guaranteed the "inalienable rights" of the individual to liberty, equality, property, security, resistance to oppression and freedom of speech. But despite these liberal reforms, suspicion of the King's sincerity combined with the newfound confidence of the Paris crowds, led to more radical action.

LEFT **The National Assembly's Declaration of the Rights of Man marked the high-tide of the liberal phase of the French Revolution and is its most important legacy. It has remained the basis for all subsequent declarations of human rights.**

The royal family is brought to Paris
In October 1789, a great crowd led by hungry women set out from Paris to bring the King back to his capital from the unpopular palace at Versailles. There was still a residual respect for monarchy: the King's presence was almost magical and perhaps people thought if he lived among them then life would get easier. But after his two brothers had fled abroad in the summer of 1789 along with the first wave of so-called émigrés, many people feared that the royal family too might flee and set up a counter-revolutionary government. Suspicions of Louis XVI's sincerity were not misplaced: he could not reconcile himself to his role as a figurehead. In October 1789 Louis XVI wrote to his cousin, the King of Spain, admitting that he had no intention of abiding by the concessions forced from him: "I owe it to myself, to my children, to my family, and to my entire dynasty, not to...let the royal dignity, *confirmed in my dynasty by the passage of centuries*, become debased in my hands.... I have chosen your Majesty, the head of the second branch of our

family, as the person to whom I entrust my solemn protest against all the decrees contrary to royal authority to which I have been compelled by force to assent since 15th July of this year. I beg your Majesty to keep my protest secret until its publication becomes necessary."

The Assembly also moved to Paris, where it began work on a new constitution to limit the power of the Crown and create a one-chamber elected legislature. The Catholic Church was another institution to come under attack, and in November 1789 it was deprived of its privileged status and property, which became the so-called *biens-nationaux* (the national wealth). Briefly it seemed that liberty, equality and fraternity would flourish, but the trend towards radicalism continued.

The King's behaviour certainly accelerated the radical current. Half-hearted attempts to veto legislation under the new constitution and a half-baked attempt to flee the country, which ended with his capture at Varennes in June 1791, only served to convince the Parisians that their King was at heart an enemy of the changes.

When Louis XVI next visited the National Assembly on 14 September 1791, the Republic was already symbolically becoming a reality as the deputies *sat with their hats on* in the presence of the King.

The origins of the Terror

Worse still, Louis XVI had potential allies abroad: his royal cousins. At first they had welcomed the revolution in France – either because, like the English, they

ABOVE **Women dragging cannons depart Paris for Versailles on 5 October 1789.**

thought it would lead to a desirable reform of French society or, more cynically, because confusion in France would weaken her power to intimidate her neighbours. By 1792, however, many European kings were becoming alarmed at the developments in France and feared that subversive ideas might spread to their peoples. At the same time, evidence that Louis and his Queen hoped to be rescued from their humiliating position by her brother, Emperor Francis II of Austria, or the King of Prussia encouraged the revolutionaries to see treachery everywhere and to look for ways of stamping it out.

Demanding a revolutionary war of national defence made the careers of previously unknown but ambitious politicians such as Jacques Pierre Brissot – only to prove disastrous for them a few months later as the war went badly. Alarm about

reactionary revenge fuelled the savagery of what became known as the Terror. Fearful for their own future and convinced of the righteousness of their cause, many revolutionaries abandoned their previous humanitarian scruples about violence and the death penalty to demand a rooting out of anyone entertaining nostalgia for the old regime or sympathy for the King.

The fall of the monarchy

The outbreak of war with Francis II of Austria and the King of Prussia in the spring of 1792 was followed by a string of defeats for France. In the fevered atmosphere of the times, hysterical fear of potential traitors from Louis XVI downwards gripped much of France, especially Paris. Moderate elements lost control of the streets, and soon of the government. On 20 June 1792, the Tuileries (the royal residence in Paris) was occupied by an angry crowd who forced the King to prove his allegiance to the revolution by donning a symbolic red cap of the Girondins and drinking a toast to the people of Paris.

With the advance in late July of the allied Austrian and Prussian army led by the Duke of Brunswick, the fate of the monarchy was sealed. The Duke issued a manifesto on 25 July 1792, saying: "Since

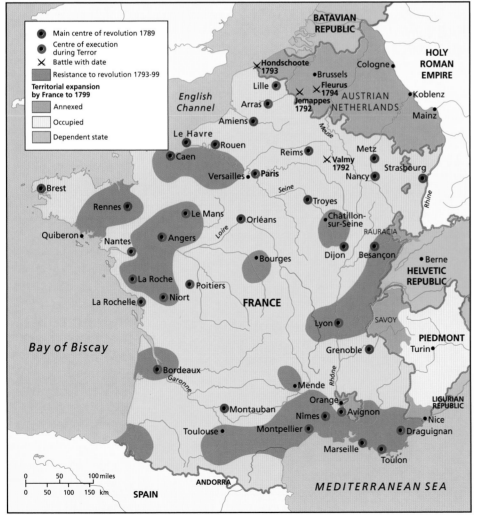

ABOVE **The thwarting of Louis XVI and his family's farcical attempted escape from France at Varennes in June 1791 contributed to the final collapse of the monarchy.**

LEFT **The French Revolution was not just a Parisian event: it erupted in many areas across France from the summer of 1789, although resistance was widespread. Revolutionary ideas soon spread abroad to neighbouring countries.**

their Majesties, the [Holy Roman] Emperor and the King of Prussia have entrusted me with the command of their combined armies on the frontiers of France, I have resolved to announce to the inhabitants of that Kingdom...[that those] who dare defend themselves against our troops, and fire on them...shall be punished immediately, according to the rigour of the law, and their houses demolished or burned.... If the Palace of Tuileries is entered by force or attacked, or if the least outrage is done to Their Majesties...an exemplary vengeance [will be carried out on] delivering the city of Paris to military punishment and total destruction."

Far from calming the situation, the Duke's threats enraged the crowds, and on 10 August they stormed the Tuileries once again, slaughtering over five hundred members of the King's Swiss Guards and servants. The reaction of the politicians was to suspend the monarchy and call elections for a National Convention that would draft a new constitution.

The French Revolution as an international crusade

"Come, children of the Motherland, the day of glory has arrived! Against us, the tyrant has raised his bloody banner, has raised his bloody banner! Don't you hear across our countryside the roar of his merciless soldiers? They are coming right into your arms to butcher your friends and family! Citizens, to arms! Form up your battalions! Let's march! March! So that our very fields shall wash with their evil blood! Wash with their evil blood!" (Words of the French marching song, "La Marseillaise")

Although the revolution encouraged the first great wave of French nationalism, it saw itself as international. After all, it had declared the "rights of man," not just of French men. Nationalism among the French fuelled their armies' defiance of foreign reactionaries, but for all the blood-curdling nationalism of "La Marseillaise," the French Revolution had an enormous international following.

While in the past new religions had offered a divine sanction for sweeping all before them, converting the peoples of new lands by persuasion or force, after 1792 the "armed missionaries" (as the revolutionary leader Maximilien Robespierre called them) of the French Revolution spread a secular faith – but a most intense one. For a long time, people had no word for this new political religion, but by the twentieth century the notion of ideology had become central to interpreting

revolutionary ideals. Under the banner of "liberty, equality and fraternity," the French armies presented a political and ideological as well as a military threat.

When France declared war it emphasized that it was the French "nation" versus foreign kings. The Declaration of War insisted that the French nation "adopts in advance all foreigners who, abjuring the cause of its enemies, range themselves under its banners and devote

"Until the enemies of France have been expelled from the territory of the Republic all Frenchmen are in a state of permanent requisition for the army. The young men will go to fight; married men will forge arms and transport food and supplies; women will make tents and uniforms and work in hospitals ...old men will appear in public places to excite the courage of warriors, the hatred of kings, and the unity of the Republic."

DECREE ON THE *LEVEE EN MASSE*, 23 AUGUST 1793

LEFT **Members of the National Guard and other citizens. The caption reads "Liberty or Death."**

their efforts to the defence of her liberty." This made the French Republic subversive of the loyalty of neighbouring monarchs' subjects. Quite a few flocked to the revolution's banners, although some of them came to regret their enthusiasm as the Terror made even friendly foreigners suspect.

At first the monarchs seemed to present a greater threat to the revolution in France than the revolution did to the monarchs, but on 20 September 1792 the invading Prussian Army was defeated at Valmy, to everyone's surprise. As with so much else connected with the revolution, myth soon enshrouded this battle. It became a decisive clash between the courageous people in arms and cowardly mercenary troops serving a tyrant. (In fact the decisive role was played by the professional artillery men, upon whom the deposed King had lavished vast funds.) Nonetheless myth counts more than reality in history and the German writer Johann Goethe caught the mood when he told his defeated comrades in the Duke of Brunswick's camp: "From this place and from this day commences a new era in world history, and you can all say that you were present at its birth."

The trial of Louis XVI

Meeting for the first time in September 1792, the National Convention lost no time in abolishing the monarchy and declaring a Republic. Louis XVI was now no longer King even in name. A new generation of politicians such as Georges Danton and Maximilien Robespierre were convinced that what the crowds called for was right: the revolution would be saved by shedding royal blood in defiance of Europe's crowned heads.

Like so many enlightened young men, Robespierre had originally opposed the death penalty (as he had war as a means of spreading the revolution), but by the autumn of 1792 he had been radicalized and now encouraged others to follow suit. Louis must be punished. Robespierre even

wanted to deny Louis the formality of a trial like that of Charles I of England 150 years earlier (*see pages 46–51*). In Robespierre's view, Louis was guilty of tyranny simply by virtue of his title of King. It was possible that the deposed monarch might be acquitted by a trial and the revolution found guilty of injustice in his place. This was an intolerable idea for Robespierre, but the residue of enlightened respect for the rule of law was still just strong enough for other members of the Convention to decide to try Louis for his life.

The atmosphere was hardly conducive to a fair trial. Unlike Charles I, the ex-King did not refuse to recognize the court, but instead denied the charges. Revolutionary passions and pressure from the Parisian radicals made his plea hopeless. A vote to

LEFT **The Battle of Valmy on 20 September 1792. A combination of regular French soldiers and revolutionary volunteers defeated the invading Prussian Army at Valmy, saving the new republic. Johann Goethe told the retreating Prussians that they had witnessed the beginning of a "new era in history."**

acquit him would have been unpatriotic. Robespierre insisted that "Louis must die because the motherland must live." On 23 January 1793, Louis Capet (as the revolutionaries called him) went to the guillotine in the Place de la Concorde in Paris, where a magnificent statue of his predecessor, Louis XV, had once stood.

The Terror

"Today the machine invented for the purpose of decapitating criminals sentenced to death will be put to work for the first time. Relative to the methods of execution practised heretofore, this machine has several advantages. It is less repugnant: no man's hands will be tainted with the blood of his fellow being, and the worst of the ordeal for the condemned man will be his own fear of death, a fear more painful to him than the stroke which deprives him of life." (The official executioner, Charles-Louis Sanson, 25 April 1792)

FAR LEFT **Maximilien Robespierre, who dominated the revolutionary government until his arrest and execution in the counter-coup of July 1794.**

LEFT **The more moderate revolutionary leader, Georges Danton.**

The King was not the first to die. Occasional lynchings had accompanied the revolution from the start. In September 1792, for example, hundreds of suspected royalists had been massacred in the Paris prisons. The introduction of the guillotine was supposed to end the savagery of old-regime executions. Public executions had been popular under the old regime. It was early ordained that to assist the republican education of women, they might sit and knit during trials. Soon they could count heads rolling as well as stitches as the revolution came to provide grisly public entertainments with a vengeance. After Louis' execution, the dynamics of Terror began to accelerate.

Following the extension of the war to include England, Holland and Spain in the early months of 1793, two important institutions were established in Paris in March: the Revolutionary Tribunal and the Committee of Public Safety. According to Danton the Tribunal was set up to bring order to the random and chaotic nature of the people's terror. By July 1794, the Tribunal had ordered the execution of 2,400 people in Paris. But that was only a small proportion of the 30,000 people

LEFT **Louis XVI addresses the crowd from the scaffold shortly before his execution: "I forgive those who are guilty of my death."**

BELOW **The public execution of Louis XVI in the Place de la Concorde, 23 January 1793.**

executed across France. During the suppression of the revolt in the Vendée (*see below*) scores of thousands died.

Counter-revolution

The Terror was about waging war at home and abroad, and the machinery of government it developed to conscript soldiers, collect taxes and commandeer foodstuffs and supplies antagonized much of the population. It provoked the very thing the Terror was supposed to stop: counter-revolution.

Although the revolutionaries tended to caricature their opponents as resentful beneficiaries of the old order, their worst opponents were usually losers under the new regime. The Revolution coincided with renewed food shortages and inflation, and it soon became the target of criticism from the poor. Worse still, the revolutionaries interfered with the lives of peasants much more than the royal regime ever had. Conscription, taxation and de-Christianization all went down badly in the countryside. They had to be imposed by force. Soon enough they were resisted by violence too. Some revolts, such as that in

ABOVE **The Festival of the Supreme Being, Paris, June 1794. The cult of the Supreme Being was introduced as an acceptable alternative to Christianity by the revolutionary leadership, which recognized that religion was necessary for social stability.**

the far western region of the Vendée, took on massive proportions and took huge efforts to quell, leading to as many as a quarter of a million deaths. The rebels were by no means all nobles.

De-Christianization turned out to be a great mistake, but for radicals brought up on the cult pagan republics of antiquity and the sceptical writings of the Enlightenment, the Catholic Church was an obvious target for criticism. The revolutionaries not only invented a new calendar abandon-

ing Christ's birth as the start of the modern era and replacing it with one dating from the deposition of Louis XVI, but they also tried to replace the old feast-days of the Catholic Church with new republican festivals of their own. These ceremonies often parodied Catholic practices but were held in honour of the nation or the Supreme Being. For true republicans, the "nation" replaced God as the object of worship. One of the charges against Louis XVI had been that he "permitted...the nation [to be] blasphemed."

Although there was much local support for counter-revolution, it was never coordinated. The revolutionaries based in Paris could isolate and pick off provincial rebellions. Later on, after the Terror, the government could also rig elections and disqualify candidates when the wrong result was returned. Whoever controlled the machinery of government in Paris controlled the revolution.

Everyday Terror

Although the "terrorists" as they became called regularly denounced their victims as "aristocrats," most of the people rounded

---

HARMONIZATION AND RATIONALIZATION

The revolutionary calendar. To mark the break with the past, the Republic introduced a new calendar in October 1793. Out went the old months and days of the week and in came a new age: Year I was backdated to the proclamation of the Republic on 22 September 1792. The revolutionary calendar was rational, like the revolutionary metric system of weights and measures (*below*). Ten-day weeks replaced the old order's seven days, and twelve regular months of thirty days each were established. Individual days were named after flowers and plants. But the earth's journey around the sun was not quite so rational: to make up the extra five days required, five holidays were added to the end of the republican year in the middle of what had been September. For many people, however, these holidays and the single day off once every ten days did not make up for the many lost Sundays that had been abolished. The calendar survived until 1806.

Weights and measures. One of the most frequent demands in 1789 was for a national system of weights and measures. Weights and measures varied widely under the old regime, which made fraud and extortion by crooks and unscrupulous seigneurs easy. One of the revolutionary slogans was: "One king, one law, one weight and one measure." In Year III of the Republic (1795), the metric system was imposed and later spread by Napoleon's armies across much of Europe. Jacques Prieur, a member of the Convention, hailed the metric system: "It is worthy of the great nation to whom it belongs and of other civilized peoples, who are also probably destined to adopt it sooner or later."

ABOVE **The revolutionary calendar.**

LEFT **An engraving showing tradespeople using the new weights and measures that were introduced in 1795.**

up in the growing hysteria were ordinary folk, often of the poorer sort who had let slip some foolish remark that bread had been cheaper under Louis XVI! Inflation (produced by the new regime's paper money to pay for the war against the reactionaries) and the "maximum" imposed on wages made life hard. And the worse life became, the more the new dominant group of Jacobins began to turn on its head the revolution's denunciation of the vices of the old order.

Before 1789 informers had been despised, but the revolutionaries now made denouncing suspected traitors a republican virtue: "Denunciations, which were hateful under the old regime because they served tyranny, have now become legitimate because today they are intended for the good of all." The rabid journalistic "terrorist," Jean-Paul Marat, urged that informers should be well-regarded whether their charges were true or false: "It is essential that every justified denunciation should entitle the informer to public respect. Each unfounded denunciation, if made from patriotic motives, should not expose the informer to any penalties." He even thought "at least 70,000 more heads are necessary to re-establish the Republic."

Normal rules of evidence were suspended in favour of classifications such as "aristocrat." At the height of the Terror, the Convention decreed: "If material or moral proof exists, independently of the evidence of witnesses, the latter will not be heard, unless this formality should appear necessary, either to discover accomplices or for other important reasons concerning the public interest." Witnesses for the defence were not needed.

Robespierre insisted in February 1794 that "Pity is treason." At the same time the twenty-four-year-old Louis de Saint-Just told the Convention, "You have no right to be merciful or compassionate where traitors are concerned. You are working not on your own account, but on behalf of the people."

With this sort of thinking, it was not surprising that the Terror began to consume earlier advocates of radicalism who

> **"What surprised me was, as each head fell into the basket, the cry of the people was no other than a repetition of *'A bas le Maximum!'* which was caused by the privations imposed on the populace by the rigorous exaction of that law which set certain prices upon all sorts of provisions and which was attributed to Robespierre."**
> AN EYEWITNESS, ARCHIBALD HAMILTON ROWAN, DESCRIBING ROBESPIERRE'S FATE

had either failed to keep pace with their colleagues or fallen foul of them as rivals. Successive groups of erstwhile revolutionaries made their way to the guillotine as the due process of law was increasingly put aside in the mounting panic. Paris was the centre of a new wave of executions that took up to 30,000 lives. Amongst the victims of this purge were Danton and other so-called "Indulgents" who were arguing for greater clemency.

The end of the Terror

So long as the enemies of the revolution at home and abroad seemed about to overwhelm it, the Jacobin leaders could justify their harsh measures and even their settling of scores as a necessary response to the terrible threats to their cause. But once the revolutionary armies began to rout their foreign enemies and suppress counter-revolution at home, the spectacle of the revolution devouring its children began to alarm and revolt even the most sincere revolutionaries.

Victories over the revolution's foreign enemies, combined with a dread of who might be next to depart in a tumbril to the guillotine and worries that Robespierre was becoming too powerful, led some of Robespierre's colleagues to mount a sudden coup against him and the leading "terrorists" on 9 Thermidor (27 July 1794). He was beheaded the next day. An eyewitness wrote the following account of his execution:

On 10 Thermidor, at four o'clock in the afternoon, the sinister procession issued from the courtyard of the Palais de Justice. No crowd of such dimensions had ever been seen in Paris.... Most of the watchers fixed their eyes on the cart in which the two Robespierres [Maximilien and his

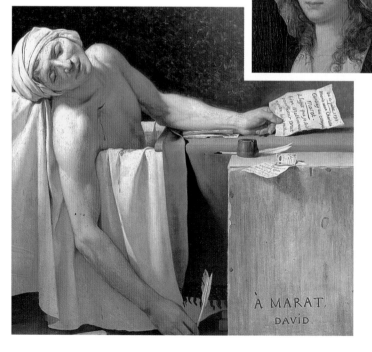

LEFT **David's famous painting of Marat dying in his bath after being stabbed by Charlotte Corday** (INSET) **on 13 July 1793. Far from stopping the Terror as she hoped, Corday's act gave it fresh impetus. Marat had been a police informer under Louis XVI but his newspaper,** *L'Ami du Peuple* **(The Friend of the People), was one of the most radical promoters of the Terror.**

LEFT *Saturn*, by Francisco Goya. The French revolutionary Pierre Vergniaud (1753–93), who was guillotined for opposing Robespierre, once remarked: "There is reason to fear that, like Saturn, the Revolution might devour each of its children in turn."

BELOW The wounded Robespierre lies on a table after his arrest on 9 Thermidor (26 July 1794). He had tried to shoot himself in the head but was taken to the guillotine with a bandaged jaw on 28 July.

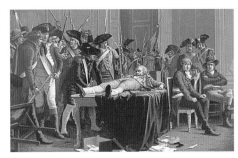

brother Augustin], Couthon and Hanriot were riding. These miserable creatures were all mutilated and covered with blood, and looked like a group of brigands whom the gendarmes had surprised in a wood.... Robespierre kept his eyes shut and did not reopen them until he felt himself being carried up to the scaffold.... The wretched man's head was now no more than an object of horror and repulsion. When at last it was severed from his body and the executioner took it by the hair to show to the people, it presented an indescribably horrible spectacle.

Using the same sort of methods as Robespierre's group had made notorious, the new ex-radical leaders exterminated their rivals but began to calm the extremism of the last two years. The Paris mob had lost its potency. Hyper-inflation, the unpopular "maximum" on wages and prices that did more to hold down the former than the latter, and bewilderment at the twists and turns of the Terror had all served to weary the so-called *sans-culottes* of their willingness to go on the streets. Throughout the country, the poor were very badly hit by the revolution. However much the radical Jacobins despised the top few thousand idle aristocrats, their wrath was also directed at millions of the poor who depended in part on charity. For the revolutionaries, idleness was a sign of suspect civil virtue. They closed down many

of the charities provided by the Church under the old regime.

The cult of pseudo-antique republican virtue was followed by a release of pent-up dissolute desires. The *jeunesse dorée* deliberately outraged *sans-culotte* virtue. As early as January 1795, the police reported that "citizens" were once more calling each other "monsieur" and "madame." On 8 February, the Convention ordered the remains of the murdered radical, Jean-Paul Marat, to be removed from the Pantheon to signify its rejection of the Terror.

On 20–21 May, angry *sans-culottes*, whose poverty was now exacerbated by the about-turn in the revolution's direction, rioted in the streets of Paris. The new regime showed no compunction about using force to disperse them. The politicians had grown tired of letting the mob force decisions on them. The new constitution of August 1795 forbade mere citizens to organize themselves: "All citizens are free to address petitions to public authorities, but they must be submitted by *individuals; no association may present a collective Petition.*"

Just as war had accelerated the Terror, with unexpected defeats on the frontier multiplying fears of treachery at home, decisive military success from summer 1794 onwards helped to relax domestic tension. The first fruit of victory was the fall of the "terrorists" around Robespierre.

KEY EVENTS

1789 **4 May**
Estates-General meet at Versailles
20 June
Tennis Court Oath
14 July
Fall of Bastille
5–11 August
Decrees abolishing feudalism
27 August
Declaration of the Rights of Man
6 October
Royal family is brought to Paris
1790 **December–January**
France divided into 83 *départements*
17 April
First *assignats* (paper-money) issued
1791 **21 June**
The King's flight to Varennes
27 September
Civil Constitution of the Clergy
1792 **20 April**
France declares war on Austria
20 June
Mob jostle royal family in Tuileries
10 August
Storming of the Tuileries
20 September
French defeat Prussians at Valmy
21 September
France declared a Republic
22 September
First day of Year I of the Republic
2 October
Committee of General Security set up
1793 **23 January**
Execution of Louis XVI
10 March
Revolutionary Tribunal established
6 April
Decree establishing Committee of Public Safety
4 May
Maximum decreed on food prices
31 May–2 June
Jacobin coup in Paris
23 August
Proclamation of the *levée en masse*
16 October
Execution of Marie Antoinette
31 October
Execution of 31 Girondins
1794 **5 April**
Execution of Danton
10 June
Powers of Revolutionary Tribunal extended
26 June
French defeat Austrians at Fleurus
27 July (9 Thermidor)
The fall of Robespierre
14 November
Jacobin Club closed down
24 December
The "maximum" abolished
1795 **October**
Directory of Five established
1799 **9 November (18 Brumaire)**
Napoleon's coup d'état
1804 **2 December**
Napoleon proclaims himself Emperor

But if his civilian rivals expected to enjoy their new power easily, their reliance on generals of the revolutionary armies – the new heroes of the age – made them vulnerable in their turn to coups.

The Directory

From 1795, an oligarchy of ex-radical revolutionaries turned conservative statesmen tried to rule France. Five Directors were appointed to run the executive. Elections to the assembly were fixed, but even that could not disguise growing discontent with a regime that retained republican symbols but lacked any real commitment to them.

Ultimately, it was the youngest and most successful of the French generals, Napoleon Bonaparte, who emerged as the beneficiary of the fall of Louis XVI and Robespierre. Despite military victories against foreign enemies, the Directory in Paris still faced enemies at home as a result of high taxes, conscription and residual anti-Catholicism. Counter-revolutionaries continued to resist the Republic across large areas of western France. It was only after Napoleon's coup on 18 Brumaire (9 November) 1799, that a ruler emerged ready to sacrifice certain revolutionary principles in order to calm the situation and reinforce his own power.

Full circle under Napoleon?

For the five years following his coup, Napoleon ruled France as a dictatorial First Consul. He restored relations with the Vatican – largely on his own terms – and even let émigrés return if they took an oath of good behaviour. To encourage the old nobility's loyalty and to satisfy his vanity, he proclaimed himself monarch as "Emperor of the French" in 1804. As a gesture to the revolutionary roots of his new power, Napoleon even staged a (rigged) referendum to let the people endorse this restoration of monarchy. But things had not come quite full circle.

Victories by generals such as Bonaparte helped to spread not only the ideals but also the practice of the new revolutionary state into conquered territories. The abolition of feudalism and the establishment of legal conformity as well as metric weights and measures were lasting consequences of the Revolution. Another result was the stimulation of nationalism, which became an anti-French and anti-revolutionary force, among the peoples conquered and exploited as cannon fodder by the French.

After Napoleon established himself in power, the downgrading of the role of the population went on. Under the Republic they had been dignified as "*citoyens*" even when they were ignored. Now they were dismissed as "*administrés*." To strengthen his hold on France, Napoleon added to the rational plan of more less equal *départements* (regions) across the country a layer of officials – the prefects – who held absolute sway in the *départements*. It was a revival of the old regime's intendants except in paramilitary uniform and without any of their aristocratic independence of mind.

Napoleon's declaration in 1799 that the revolution had come to an end proved premature. The legacy of the French Revolution continues to agitate French people, and many others too. For decades after 1789, the ideas of the French revolution were fiercely debated and fought over

ABOVE **Napoleon Bonaparte's propaganda machine portrayed him as a romantic hero. David painted for every regime from Louis XVI's to Napoleon's empire.**

RIGHT **The Napoleonic empire at its height in 1812. Napoleon built an empire on revolutionary France's early armed missionary conquests. His nominees – frequently relatives – occupied new thrones as he redrew boundaries for his own convenience.**

in France. The basic principles of the Declaration of the Rights of Man are still more honoured in the breach around the globe than enshrined in law, but the impact of the French Revolution in all its varied aspects remains an emotive subject.

INTERNATIONAL REPERCUSSIONS OF THE FRENCH REVOLUTION

French revolutionary ideas and ways of doing things were spread across large parts of Europe as much through Napoleonic conquest after 1799 as by example. Long years of French occupation in places such as Belgium or the Rhineland encouraged the retention of French legal norms even after Napoleon had been defeated in 1815. Wherever the French army arrived, it brought with it the *Code Napoléon* (which reformed the legal system), metric weights and even the prospect of a career based on talent as the occupiers tried to recruit local collaborators.

In Italy, Napoleon's conquests brought the peninsula closer to unity than it had been at any other time since the fall of the Roman Empire. After 1815, anti-restoration secret societies such as the Carbonari owed much of their revolutionary democratic and nationalist ideology to the Jacobins and Napoleon. (In exile, Napoleon's nephew, Louis-Napoleon Bonaparte, joined the Carbonari.)

Napoleon's invasion of Spain sparked popular resistance. The term "liberal" came into existence in 1812 when the Spanish opponents of French occupation gathered in Cádiz to pass a constitution that better reflected the principles of 1789 than the regime of Napoleon's brother, Joseph, who had been installed by Bonaparte as puppet-king of Spain. Throughout the coming decades in the nineteenth century, "liberalism" came to be seen as the ideology of the representatives of the French Revolution's ideals.

Even in distant Latin America, the news of the fall of the Bastille and the developments in France travelled fast. In 1790, the Archbishop of la Plata wrote

"The French Revolution and the doings of Napoleon opened the eyes of the world. The nations knew nothing before and the people thought kings were gods upon earth..."
THEODORE KOLOKOTRONIS, DURING THE GREEK WAR OF INDEPENDENCE IN THE 1820s

ABOVE **Tory populists in Britain emphasized the brutality of the French Revolution in brilliant caricatures. This satire is entitled "A Family of Sans-Culotts [sic] refreshing after the fatigues of the day."**

that the region was "quite full of eyewitness letters and accounts of the monstrous occurrences in France," while a merchant in Potosí in Bolivia wrote to a friend in Buenos Aires, "I thank you with all my heart for the news of the revolution in France, which this post has brought me, and I hope more will come, as in these parts we greatly appreciate such news." Copies of Rousseau and revolutionary decrees such as the Rights of Man were widely smuggled into the Americas.

Britain avoids revolution

At first the British establishment was complacent about the French Revolution. A common view was that France was about to pursue the path of constitutional monarchy blazed by Britain since 1688. The House of Lords even considered making 14 July a public holiday in Britain. But the radicalization of the revolution in France, the outbreak of war in 1792 and growing evidence of sympathy for Jacobin ideals among urban craftsmen and even

the armed forces led to a hardening of official attitudes as the 1790s went on. In 1797–98, the stability of Britain was threatened first by naval mutinies, then by rebellion in Ireland. In both cases the threat existed that France would actively intervene to promote a revolution, though French involvement even during the Irish rebellion in May 1798 was marginal.

An important legacy of the French Revolution was the development of a conscious counter-revolutionary movement. While Britain avoided real revolution, it produced the leading theorist of counter-revolution. As early as 1790, Edmund Burke (1729–97), who had defended the Americans' right to rebel, denounced the French attempt to recast society on the basis of abstract principles. Burke's insistence that social change should be evolutionary and tempered by respect for the legacy of the past was taken up by Continental critics of the revolution. Authoritarian critics such as Joseph de Maistre also appeared and championed complete opposition to change. The Austrian statesman Clemens von Metternich tried to put into effect opposition to any influence of French or other liberal ideas across Central Europe in the years between 1815 and 1848.

The Decembrists in Russia

It was in one of the countries that had defeated Napoleon that the ideas of a thorough-going revolution to sweep away the old order nonetheless took root. Napoleon's invasion of Russia in 1812 left an important legacy there. The Tsar's armies not only defeated the Grand Army of France but also captured Paris in 1814. Prolonged contact with France encouraged the spread of neo-Jacobin ideas among the officer class. These culminated in the attempted revolution against the new Tsar, Nicholas I, in December 1825. The failure of this coup left the tragic myth of principled revolutionaries suppressed by a cruel autocrat, which lived on to inspire fresh generations of disaffected children of the elite in the coming century.

The French colony of Saint-Domingue (Haiti) in the Caribbean was one of the most valuable possessions of the French crown. The revolution in France after 1789 encouraged radical new ideas among Haiti's huge slave majority, resulting in the outbreak of a rebellion against the colonial elite. The savage revolutionary war led to the creation of an independent state whose forms caricatured those of Napoleonic France.

The Slave Revolt in Haiti

The island of Hispaniola had been a Spanish colony for about 200 years when, in 1697, the western portion was ceded to France and renamed Saint-Domingue. By 1789, Saint-Domingue was France's most prosperous colony. It relied for its wealth on the cultivation of plantation crops – and particularly sugar – which in turn depended on slave labour. By 1791, slaves accounted for nearly 90 per cent of the total population.

The white elite in France's Caribbean colonies had no intention of letting events in Paris in 1789 influence their way of life. The Rights of Man – which promoted liberty and equality – may have been declared in France, but slavery remained in force on the other side of the Atlantic.

Imported from West Africa, the slaves tended to be subjected to appalling living and working conditions, and small-scale slave rebellions were not uncommon in the Caribbean colonies during the eighteenth century. The slaves maintained many of their traditions, however, including their voodoo religion, which they used as a means of defying French efforts to catholicize and subjugate them. (Ironically, the great leader of the slave revolution, François Dominique Toussaint, was a practising Catholic.)

Apart from tensions with their black slaves, the white elite was also involved in rivalries with the mixed-race free mulattos,

LEFT **The colonial possessions of the European powers in the Caribbean at the end of the eighteenth century. Before its independence in 1804, Haiti was the French-owned western half of an island; the eastern half was ruled by Spain.**

BELOW LEFT **Slaves attack French troops in Haiti in 1791.**

who were excluded from positions of authority. A system of racial segregation existed in Saint-Domingue: intermarriage between whites and mulattos was prohibited, and mulattos were forced to sit apart from whites in churches, theatres and other public places. In 1790, a mulatto named Vincent Ogé was tortured and executed by the white planters for trying to bring the new rights of man from France to Saint-Domingue. Jean-Marie d'Augy, the white President of the colonial assembly declared, "We have not brought half a million slaves from the coasts of Africa to make them into French citizens."

The revolution begins

On 22 August 1791, the black slaves of Saint-Domingue rose in revolt in many plantations. They slaughtered their masters and set about destroying white properties and sugar-factories. The revolt spread from one end of the colony to the other. The fighting was confused by shifting loyalties: at first the whites and mulattos united

FRANÇOIS DOMINIQUE TOUSSAINT

François Dominique Toussaint was born into slavery in 1743 near Cape François on Haiti. Recognizing his gifts, Toussaint's master liberated him in 1777. During the first great slave revolt in 1791, Toussaint repaid his master by rescuing him from the rebels. Unlike many of the ex-slaves, Toussaint was not utterly hostile to the whites and their culture. He wanted the liberated population to learn from the French. He was also a Catholic and hostile to voodooism. Once the French Republic abolished slavery in 1794 Toussaint was prepared to cooperate with it, but this was unpopular with many of the ex-slaves and the returning French distrusted him. The remaining whites and creoles hoped to recover their property under French protection. The arrival of a large French force sent by Napoleon sealed Toussaint's fate: the French were determined to eliminate the most capable rebel leader and deported Toussaint to prison in France in 1802 where he died a year later.

against the slaves, but this alliance soon broke down and the mulattos tended to side thereafter with the slave majority. Although a number of ex-slave leaders appeared, it was the freedman, Toussaint, who became the most widely accepted. He was able to unite blacks and mulattos most effectively and showed rare skills as a military leader.

The French Commander attempted to crush the revolt and restore order. His army briefly won the upper hand, but when news reached the island of the execution of King Louis XVI, many of his troops deserted. Spain entered the fray after declaring war against France in 1793 by invading from Santo Domingo (the other half of the island). At first Toussaint sided with the Spanish, but when the French Republic declared freedom for all slaves in 1794 he switched sides and helped France to gain control of Santo Domingo as well as to recover their own colony.

To add to the chaos, Britain invaded Saint-Domingue with the encouragement of the white elite, who preferred the idea of British sovereignty to that of having to free their slaves. The French Commissioner, Léger-Félicité Sonthonax, who came from France to represent the revolutionary regime, denounced the white planters as "aristocrats of the skin" and looked to the blacks as allies in France's struggle to protect her colonies from Britain. In June 1793 he declared: "It is with the natives of the country, that is, the Africans, that we will save Saint-Domingue for France." By the end of the decade, both Spain and Britain had been forced out.

Although nominally loyal to France, Toussaint was effectively in charge of Saint-Domingue until 1802. His system in the 1790s was very authoritarian. Slavery was abolished, but to preserve order Toussaint decreed that labourers were confined to the plantations and a strict passport system was introduced to register the population. He ruled in effect in the fashion of an enlightened despot.

The war of independence

In May 1802, Napoleon's forces tried to re-establish slavery. To make matters worse, the French Commander kidnapped Toussaint and deported him to France. The effect was to enrage the black majority and provoke an even greater rebellion. By now black soldiers had gained experience in organizing an army. The French were at a disadvantage: they were more susceptible to disease (particularly yellow fever) than their opponents, and reinforcements were difficult to obtain from France. The French troops were also demoralized by fighting against enemies who sang the Marseillaise and invoked revolutionary ideals. One officer, Lacroix, asked, "Have our barbarous enemies justice on their side? Are we no longer the soldiers of Republican France? And have we become crude instruments of policy?"

The slave army was victorious, thanks in large part to the military leadership of the African-born Jean-Jacques Dessalines.

At the beginning of 1804 Dessalines declared the independence of Saint-Domingue, which he renamed Haiti, and then proclaimed himself Emperor. Europeans mocked the grand titles that Haitian officials adopted, but they were hardly more ridiculous than the magnificent ranks Napoleon invented for his marshals.

A sad legacy

Although Dessalines's savage anti-white policies were widely supported by the former slaves, when he turned on the mulattos (who saw themselves as Haiti's natural elite), he provoked civil war and was killed in action in 1806. The war impoverished Haiti. Rivalries between commanders and between mulattos and blacks became entrenched after independence. But even if its subsequent history was hardly a tribute to the principles of the revolution, Haiti was the only genuinely independent state created as a result of the French Revolution. One of Dessalines's successors – Alexandre Pétion – supported Simón Bolívar in his struggle against Spanish rule, so Haiti also had a direct influence on decolonization elsewhere in Latin America.

KEY EVENTS

1789	**July** National Assembly in France admits delegates from Saint-Domingue
1790	**October** Revolt against white rule; Ogé broken on wheel
1791	**15 May** Civil Rights for free blacks in French dominions
	22 August Slave revolt breaks out
1792	**April** Full equality to all free blacks
1793	**29 August** The abolition of slavery is declared in Saint-Domingue
1794	**4 February** Convention abolishes slavery in French territory
1802	**May** Napoleon restores slavery
1803	**7 April** Toussaint dies in prison in France
	18 May Rebellion starts again
	31 December Declaration of Independence
1804	**October** Dessalines proclaimed Emperor

Liberalism, Nationalism, Communism: The Spread of Revolution

The French Revolution unleashed two great subversive forces: liberalism (embodying the still radical ideas of liberty, equality and fraternity) and nationalism. Together these two ideologies threatened the old order, which had been precariously restored after Napoleon's defeat in 1815, resulting in repeated waves of revolution in the nineteenth century. In Latin America, the potent mixture of revolutionary zeal and nationalist enthusiasm swept across a whole continent, while a similar wave of nationalist revolutions erupted in central Europe in 1848. It was not long, however, before another revolutionary idea – Marxism – made its appearance, and by the end of the century nationalism and Communism were emerging as rivals for intellectual hegemony in the twentieth century.

OPPOSITE *Liberty leading the people* in the July Revolution of 1830, by Eugene Delacroix.

Between 1808 and 1820, the peoples of Latin America rebelled against Spanish domination and fought for independence. The French Revolution had a profound effect on the events in South America (despite the three thousand miles that separated the two continents), not only indirectly through the spread of ideas and symbols, but also through the French invasion of Spain in 1808, which helped to cut the links between Spain and her colonies.

Revolution in Latin America

The success of the North American colonies in breaking away from their European motherland in 1783 at first seemed to encourage little imitation in the Spanish empire to the south. Relations between English-speaking colonists in America and their Hispanic counterparts had long been marked by political, religious and commercial rivalries as well as warfare and piracy, but there were some common causes of discontent, particularly the imperial monopoly of trade between the Old World and the New. Spanish officials recognized that if manufacturing developed in South America the colonies would no longer need Spain, so they encouraged the colonies to continue in their role as providers of raw materials.

While the snobbery of British colonial officials often irked American self-esteem, there was nothing in the British Empire to compare with the second-class status imposed on Latin American descendants of Spanish settlers, so-called creoles. In the Spanish Empire almost all high posts in the Catholic Church and the colonial administration were reserved to Spaniards, meaning they enjoyed exclusive access to high status and incomes (through bribes).

Radical ideas began to penetrate the vast region of South America in the 1790s. The outbreak of the French Revolution also had profound effects, partly because Spain was drawn into war on the losing side. Jacobin literature and translations of Tom Paine's writings found their way to Venezuela from nearby Trinidad and French Haiti. Even a few concessions, such as the ending in 1796 of the monopoly enjoyed by Spaniards on trade between Spain and her American colonies, did little to stifle growing discontents. But it was Napoleon's conquest of Spain in 1808, rather than events in the Americas, that truly precipitated the sudden break of transatlantic relations.

Napoleon's conquest of Spain casts the colonies adrift

"America was not prepared for secession from the mother country; secession was suddenly brought about." (Simón Bolívar) Years of growing resentment and revolutionary sentiment in South America came to a head suddenly in 1808 when Napoleon deposed King Ferdinand VII of Spain and installed his (Napoleon's) brother, Joseph, in his stead, shattering the legal links between the colonies in South America and the Spanish monarchy. Prior to 1808, Spain had increasingly left Latin America to look after itself. Local militias were formed for defence against British or French attack (such as the assault launched in 1806–7 by the British on the Río de la Plata province in modern-day Argentina), and these local defence forces soon turned into quasi-independent juntas when the monarchy collapsed in Spain.

Initially the juntas still professed a loyalty to the Spanish government precariously resisting Napoleon in southern Spain, but soon many parts of the Empire – including Venezuela, Paraguay, Chile and

LEFT *Execution of the defenders of Madrid, 3 May 1808* by Francisco Goya. The brutality of the French reprisals sparked Spanish resistance against Napoleon's conquest and the first guerrilla war.

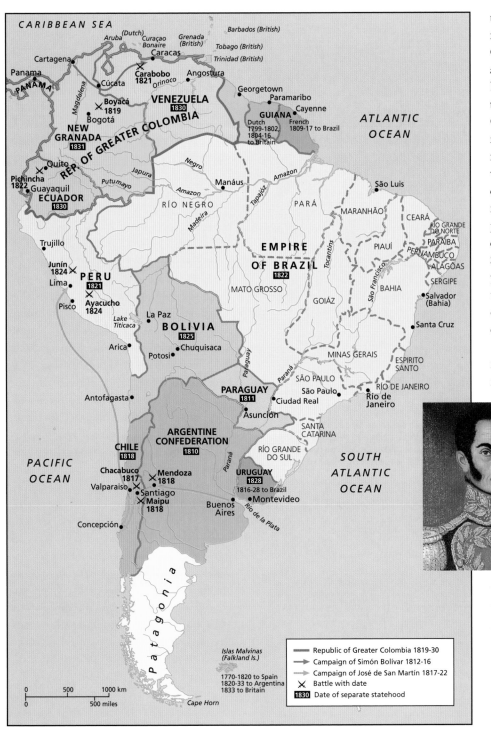

ularly cruel. In 1812 the Spanish garrison from Puerto Rico was sent to recapture Caracas, which it did, destroying the rebel army. Bolívar was determined not to be beaten, however, and in 1813 he returned to Venezuela with a small army and took Caracas. He showed no mercy towards royalist traitors, as his decree of Trujillo makes clear: "Any Spaniard who does not work against tyranny in favour of the just cause, by the most active and effective means, shall be considered an enemy and punished as a traitor to the country and in consequence shall inevitably be shot. Spaniards and Canarios, depend upon it, you will die, even if you are simply neutral, unless you actively espouse the liberation of America." Up to 1,200 Spanish prisoners were executed on Bolívar's orders.

Once again, however, the Spanish forces overcame the patriots, and Bolívar fled to Jamaica and then to Haiti.

Tensions among the Latin Americans

One of the biggest problems for the rebels was that cultural antagonisms between the Spaniards and the settlers were compounded by other racial tensions. Officials from Spain (*peninsulares*) and the creoles ruled over much larger populations of mixed Indian, Spanish and black African origin. The gradations of interracial heritage were treated as degrees of social stigma. If the creoles resented Spanish superiority, they in turn looked down on other social groups.

The new liberal ideas and tricolour flags that appeared in Latin America after the French occupation of Spain rarely meant that the creole rebel elites intended to advocate an end to slavery or to establish legal and political equality for Indians and blacks. For example, the Congress of the new Venezuelan Republic was elected in March 1811 on a whites-only franchise, and when its Supreme Junta ordered the citizenry to defend the Republic in July of that year, segregation between racial

ABOVE **Following Simón Bolívar's lead Spanish and Portuguese colonies in South America broke away from their motherlands during two decades of struggle.**

INSET **Simón Bolívar (1783–1830), the key figure in the struggle against Spanish rule.**

New Granada (now Colombia) – broke away more formally. The revolutionary leader Simón Bolívar believed it was time for Latin America to throw off the yoke of colonial rule. In 1811 he managed to persuade the Venezuelan Congress to declare independence.

Spain moved rapidly to crush the rebellions. In each province there was a party of royalists loyal to the Spanish Crown, as well as a Spanish garrison, who resisted and harried the revolutionaries. The result was a series of civil wars, often of great savagery. The war in Venezuela was partic-

groups was part of the call-up: "The Whites would enlist before the Church; the blacks to the east; and the mulattos to the south....The slaves should remain at home at their masters' commands."

To promote dissent among the revolutionaries, the royalists abolished slavery and could frequently rely on support from ex-slaves against the republicans. In 1813, Bolívar admitted that the Spanish had been able to start "a revolution of blacks, free and slave" against the newly proclaimed Republic. In areas overrun by these forces, whites were killed indiscriminately; the republicans then took horrible revenge.

Bolívar showed political as well as military acumen in 1816 when he broke with many of his fellow landowners in Venezuela and advocated an end to slavery. He offered slaves freedom if they would fight the Spanish, but few were enthusiastic for this risky bargain. In 1819, he tried to overcome the racial divide and announced that: "We are neither Europeans nor Indians, but a mixed species midway between aborigines and Spaniards. Americans by birth and Europeans by law, we find ourselves engaged in a dual conflict, disputing with the natives titles of ownership, and at the same time struggling to maintain ourselves in the country of our birth against the opposition of [Spanish] invaders. Thus our position is most extraordinary and complicated."

Even after the defeat of the Spanish forces, Bolívar was still pessimistic about the prospects of overcoming racial antagonisms. In August 1826, for example, he wrote about their deep roots in South and Central America: "A great volcano lies at our feet. Who shall restrain the oppressed classes? Slavery will break its yoke, each shade of complexion will seek mastery."

Even in largely European Argentina, conflicts between the domineering city of Buenos Aires and the countryside were frequent. The great estate owners were anxious to shake off the control of the capital, but imposed a rigid discipline on their *gauchos* [Argentinian cowboys] and the poor *peons* [peasants who tilled the soil] under their economic thumb.

TOP AND ABOVE **The battle of Carabobo in Venezuela on 24 June 1821 was the decisive defeat of the pro-Spanish forces in the Caribbean basin and secured Venezuela's independence from Spain.**

THE BRAZILIAN EXCEPTION

Although Portugal was not occupied by Napoleon, the Portuguese royal family took refuge in Brazil while the war against the French continued. Río de Janeiro became the capital of the Portuguese empire. This helped to cement Portugal's relations with the Brazilian elite – even if, ironically, it weakened the dynasty's hold on Portugal itself. The Portuguese King, John VI, eventually returned to Portugal in 1820, leaving his son, Pedro, as regent in Brazil. But Lisbon's politicians wanted to resubordinate Brazil and ignored its years as centre of the Portuguese empire. In October 1821 the Brazilian elite reinforced Don Pedro's desire not to return to Portugal himself by insisting he uphold Brazil's status as an equal partner with Portugal. On 9 January 1822, Pedro announced he would not return and on 7 September he proclaimed an independent Brazilian empire. by 1824, he had suppressed the last pro-Portuguese resistance by troops loyal to Lisbon. Some Brazilian landowners resented Pedro's willingness to end the slave trade in return for British recognition in 1826, but Pedro I provided a constitution that lasted from 1823 until 1889 – a rare period of stability in the region.

Restoration in Spain, rebellion in the Americas

Following the defeat of Napoleon in 1814, the Spanish King, Ferdinand VII, was restored to the throne. Ironically, this did much to ensure that rebellion in the colonies would grow in popularity, for the King promptly revoked the liberal constitution of 1812 (around which Spaniards had rallied to resist French invasion) and restored the inquisitorial power of the Church. These reactionary changes were enforced in Spanish America as well, where many locals had become used to running their own affairs.

With France no longer posing a threat, Spain was able to mount a more serious campaign against the rebels in South America. Ferdinand VII sent an experienced general, Pablo Morillo, to deal with the revolutionaries. Venezuela and New Granada were quickly retaken by the Spanish, who carried out vicious reprisals and confiscated the land of the rebels. About two-thirds of the more wealthy creole families were punished in this way, which reinforced animosity towards Spain. Far to the south in Chile, heavy-handed repression between 1814 and 1817 triggered a serious revolutionary struggle against royal authority. Latin America was ready to fight back. Returning to Venezuela in 1816, Bolívar set about building a revolutionary army, which was supplemented by foreign mercenaries. In 1819, his troops undertook their legendary crossing of the Andes, which surpassed even Hannibal's feat of bringing his army across the Alps two thousand years earlier. Despite the effects of altitude sickness and the cold at 13,000 feet (3,950 metres), Bolívar's army was still able to rout the royalists and on 10 August it took Bogotá, the Colombian capital.

Meanwhile, in the south, the fight for freedom was being led by the Argentinian José de San Martín and his so-called Army of the Andes, ably supported by the Chilean revolutionary Bernardo O'Higgins. On 5 January 1917, San Martín set out towards the southern Andes, with about 5,000 men, 1,600 horses and over 9,000 mules. By the time they arrived in Chile only 500 horses and 4,300 mules remained – the rest victims, like many of the soldiers, of the cold and altitude. Nevertheless, the rebel army managed to defeat the Spanish army at Chacabuco and Maipú, which led to the liberation of Chile. San Martín then marched on to Santiago, where he prepared a naval force which would attack the viceroyalty of Peru, the base of Spanish power in South America. The rebels

RIGHT **José de San Martín (1778–1850) spent twenty years in the Spanish army before returning to Argentina. He led the army to liberate Peru in 1820. A disagreement with Bolívar, however, was followed by his exile to Europe in 1824.**

landed in Pisco, south of Lima, where San Martín tried to rally Peruvians to the revolutionary cause. In July 1821, the Spanish forces fled into the mountains, but San Martín failed to consolidate his victories, and it was not until Bolívar invaded Peru from the north in 1824 that the Spaniards were truly driven out.

Rivalries mar independence

Liberation from Spanish rule did not resolve the internal social and racial tensions of the new states. Even when slavery was abolished, race relations remained a source of recurrent trouble and the non-whites generally made up the poorest part – and great majority – of the population.

Although several prominent figures played a key role in the liberation struggle across South America, regionalism outweighed common Latin American feeling even at the moment of liberation from Spain. Wars between the new states were as common as in Europe in the nineteenth century. In theory, as in post-colonial Africa 150 years later, the Spanish colonies became the new states. But it was not quite so simple. In South America, for instance, the old Viceroyalty of Río de la Plata included Bolivia, Paraguay and Uruguay as

well as Argentina. The first three broke away from the rule of Buenos Aires early on and even large parts of Argentina were reluctant to accept the authority of the big city in the north for decades to come.

Under Spanish rule individual regional identities and loyalties had emerged, and even as popular a figure as Bolívar could not wish them away. A British observer noted after Bolívar's triumphant entry into Lima in 1825, "Although Bolívar himself is extremely popular, as popular as it is possible a Colombian should be in Peru, still there is such jealousy, if not hate, between the Peruvians and the Colombians that there can be no real cordiality between the two peoples until time and intercourse may lessen the prejudice." Peruvians had little love for their other neighbours who, like the Chileans, tended to reciprocate the antagonism. Just as racial and class divisions bedevilled Latin America after liberation, so national rivalries led to much bloodshed in the coming century.

Disillusionment

Political instability cursed almost all the new states after independence. The irresponsible ambition of individual leaders compounded the deeper causes of the coups and revolutions. Apart from Chile, none of the Spanish ex-colonies could avoid the cycle of revolution and coup d'état for long.

Bolívar disliked political competition and called elections "the greatest scourge of republics [which] produce only anarchy," but his preference for life-presidents with strong executive powers were worse than the scourge of which he spoke, since this type of quasi-dictatorship naturally stimulated the ambition of would-be dictators. In Mexico, for instance, the creole general, Agustín de Iturbide, who turned against the Spanish and established independence, imitated Napoleon and proclaimed himself Emperor in 1822, only to be deposed the next year.

Like many successful revolutionaries, Simón Bolívar lived to see success turn

sour. In January 1830, he told the new Colombian congress: "I am ashamed to admit it, but independence is the only benefit we have gained at the cost of everything else." Later he became even more bitter and on his way to self-imposed exile in Europe commented on the seeming futility of his life: "America is ungovernable. Those who have served the revolution have ploughed the sea. The only thing to do in America is to emigrate."

KEY EVENTS

1808 March
Napoleon deposes Spanish Bourbons
1810 25 May
Coup in Buenos Aires sets up junta
16 July
Chileans establish their own government (still nominally loyal to King of Spain)
1811 March
Congress elected in Caracas, Venezuela
4 July
Chilean Congress meets
5 July
Venezuela declares independence
1812 March
Spanish royal troops suppress Venezuelan revolt
1813 August
Bolívar recaptures Caracas and declares Venezuelan Republic again
1814 October
Royalist troops try to restore King's full authority in Chile
1816 January
Royal army recovers control of Venezuela
9 July
Republic of United Provinces of Río de la Plata declared
1818 12 February
Declaration of Independence in Chile
5 April
Royal army defeated by Chileans (led by San Martín) at Maipu, resulting in Chilean liberation
1819 February
Bolívar refounds Venezuelan Republic
August
Bolívar establishes Republic of Colombia
1820 January
Spanish army mutinies before sailing for America
1821 San Martín captures Lima; Peruvian Independence proclaimed
1824 24 December
Final collapse of Spanish authority in Peru
1826 Failure of Bolívar's Congress in Panama to discuss Pan-American union
1830 17 December
Bolívar dies

At the end of the French Revolution, the Bourbon dynasty was restored to the throne. But the Bourbons came back to France in 1815 having apparently "learned nothing and forgotten nothing" since 1789. The reign of Charles X was a futile attempt to return to the past that only provoked a revival of revolutionary feeling. By July 1830, Charles X had alienated many of the supporters of the Restoration and also enraged sympathizers with the ideals of the Revolution.

The July Revolution in France

Napoleon's supremacy finally came to an end in 1815, following the cataclysmic defeat of the French army by allied Prussian and British troops at Waterloo. But the victorious Allies did not want to pay the cost of remaining in charge of France. The only solution seemed to be to restore the Bourbon dynasty in the person of Louis XVIII, brother of the executed King, Louis XVI (whose son "Louis XVII" had died in prison during the revolution). Although Louis XVIII insisted on some traditional rights of the Bourbon dynasty (he came to the throne as hereditary "King of France" not just of the French – which might imply his subjects had some choice in the matter – and he restored the white fleur-de-lis flag of the Bourbons instead of the tricolour), he also had to grant a constitutional Charter. He claimed to issue this on the basis of his divine right, but in fact it was a major concession. The Charter admitted certain important revolutionary concepts: legal equality and religious tolerance, for instance. Moreover, although the Chamber of Deputies still had only limited rights, parliamentary consent was now needed to implement new laws on taxation, which was a key improvement on the pre-1789 situation.

The Charter was a reassuring compromise for members of the liberal elite, who could argue that the ideal world of 1790 had been restored. It offered the rule of law instead of an untrammelled monarchy, and yet it also avoided the dangers of

LEFT **The Battle of Waterloo in 1815, which saw the Allies victorious over the French army. Napoleon's defeat resulted in the restoration of the Bourbon ruling dynasty to France, but the country had greatly changed since the reign of the last Bourbon King, Louis XVI.**

popular sovereignty: the gains of the early revolution need not now be dissipated by a descent into the violent chaos that had wrecked the noble aspirations of 1789 by 1793. Louis XVIII's conciliatory stance towards both the elite and former revolutionaries ensured that his regime could count on at least qualified support from most of the population. But the fragile status quo was upset when the Duc de

"I consider the revolution of 1789 to be over and done with. All its interests and legitimate wishes are guaranteed by the Charter. I am not afraid of counter-revolution; we have both the force of law and fact against it…. What France needs now is to do away with the revolutionary spirit which still torments her…" THE LIBERAL PROTESTANT HISTORIAN, FRANÇOIS GUIZOT, 1820

Berry, heir to the throne, was assassinated in 1820. The crisis precipitated a clampdown on censorship, the introduction of repressive social controls and changes to electoral law. Ironically, it was not the radicals who undermined François Guizot's vision of an enlightened constitutional monarchy (*see quotation below left*): the radicals might have remained a negligible force on the sidelines of French politics had the ultra-royalists supporting Louis XVIII's younger brother, Charles – who acceded to the French throne in 1824 – not tried to turn back the clock.

Charles X provokes his own downfall

Unlike Louis XVIII, Charles X seemed to go out of his way to antagonize the bulk of the French population. His appointments restricted favour to the old nobility, stirring up the new elites that had emerged under Napoleon. He also granted compensation to émigrés whose property had been confiscated after 1789 – which offended everyone who stayed in France during the long years of revolution and empire – and introduced a law against sacrilege.

Charles X's rigid religious views were out of fashion. The clericalism of the restored monarchy was probably caricatured, but exaggerated feelings were all the rage among the romantic youth of post-Napoleonic France. While their childhoods had resonated with news of glorious victories, they came to adulthood in an age of soporific calm. Alfred de Musset spoke for a generation "conceived between two battles, brought up in colleges to the roll of drums...[who] had dreamed for fifteen years of the snows of Moscow and the sun of the Pyramids.... When the children spoke of glory, they were told 'Become priests;' when they spoke of ambition, 'Become priests;' of hope, love, force, and life, 'Become priests'!"

Charles X moved steadily away from the lazy compromise that had meant that his brother had lived out his days in relative calm. Along with his sympathy for hardline émigré demands, the King's open contempt for the limitations on his authority established by the Charter and his censorship of criticism dangerously narrowed the base of support for his regime. At the same time, his successful invasion of Algeria established a new

RIGHT **An unflattering caricature of the restored King Louis XVIII (1755–1824), who owed his shaky Crown to the Allied victory over Napoleon**

French colonial empire but denuded France of regular troops during a period of growing unrest at home.

Discontented would-be ministers, diplomats and officers felt they had a convenient alternative to Charles X, and they looked to the Glorious Revolution in England (*see pages 52–55*) for inspiration. The Duc d'Orléans could play the role of William of Orange to Charles X's James II. Guizot wrote: "We did not choose a king but negotiated with a prince [Orléans] we found next to the throne and who alone could by mounting it guarantee our public law and save us from revolutions.... Our minds were guided by the English Revolution of 1688, by the fine and free government it founded, and the wonderful prosperity it brought to the British nation."

The crisis

Opposition to Charles X's regime began to grow as increasing numbers of the middle class found themselves excluded from positions of power. In August 1829 the King asked the ultra-royalist Prince de Polignac to form a cabinet. This alienated both moderates and liberals. The liberal association "Aide-toi le ciel t'aidera" (Heaven helps those who help themselves) responded by organizing a protest against the government, calling for a nationwide refusal to pay taxes.

All this was happening at a time of economic depression. Fear of unemployment among the urban population, as well as under-employment among the educated shut out of the bureaucracy by an ageing noble elite, made for instability. Opposition on the Left and the Right united against the King, although almost all of his opponents were looking for a change of policy, not a revolution.

All that was required was for Charles X to ignite the flames of revolution. He did this in 1830. Although elections to the Chamber of Deputies were held under a very narrow franchise that restricted the vote to the rich, an overwhelming majority of oppositionists was elected in July of that year. And yet instead of recognizing the

THE CORONATION OF CHARLES X

Charles X's coronation at Reims in 1825 (pictured *right*) was intended to symbolize the monarchy's reassertion of its ancient rights. The ceremony was a pastiche of medievalism. Pins were stuck into Charles's hands, feet and side to simulate the wounds of Christ, and he revived the practice of touching the sick for the King's Evil, scrofula – a ritual that had gone out of fashion in Britain more than a century earlier. This rigmarole was scoffed at by sceptics. The writer and peer, the Viscomte de Chateaubriand, dismissed the pomp as absurd: "The monarchy perished, and the cathedral was for some years converted into stables. Seeing it again today, does Charles X remember that he watched Louis XVI receive the unction just where he will receive it in his turn? Can he believe that a coronation ceremony will keep him safe from all misfortune? There is no longer any hand virtuous enough to cure scrofula, or any holy phial beneficial enough to render kings inviolable."

gravity of the situation, Charles X decided on 25 July to flout the will of the electors, dissolve the newly elected Chamber and censor the press.

News of the King's action slowly spread through Paris the next day. On the morning of 27 July, four newspapers appeared in defiance of the King. The police prefect sent policemen to close down the presses of the rebellious newspapers. This only enraged the people of Paris further, who now began to hold more organized protests. A radical mixture of students, young lawyers and clerks, along with the perennially discontented journeymen and apprentices who had traditionally made up the unruly Paris mob, went on to the streets to defy royal authority. The revolutionary tricolour flag reappeared. That afternoon, police fired on a crowd that had gathered in the Place du Palais

Royal, killing several protesters. This did nothing to calm the populace, which responded by arming itself during nocturnal raids on weapon shops.

As if in conscious imitation of his brother forty-one years earlier, Charles X spent the first day of the rioting in Paris out hunting! The next morning the military commander Maréchal de Marmont dispatched a note to the King at Saint-Cloud outside Paris warning that "it is no longer a riot, it is a revolution." Meanwhile, the situation in the capital was deteriorating: trees were uprooted and paving stones wrenched out to erect barricades. By the time the King began to react to events, his troops had lost control of the capital and desertion was rife.

Marmont decided to send his troops in three columns through Paris to clear the barricades. But more were erected in their place and by the morning of 29 June almost every street on the right bank of the Seine was blocked.

To many opponents of the regime, the obvious solution seemed to be to ask another member of the Bourbon dynasty – the Duc d'Orléans, Louis-Philippe – to assume command. An envoy was sent to the Duke at Neuilly, just outside Paris, to persuade him to come to the capital,

but he proved unwilling. Meanwhile, Marmont – despairing at the hopelessness of the task he faced – sent another message to the King urging him to negotiate with his subjects, and ordered a cease-fire. This did nothing to appease the insurgents, however, who continued on towards the Louvre where the troops were lodged. The soldiers fled, leaving the mob to storm through the Louvre. Finally recognizing the seriousness of the revolt, the King sacked the unpopular Polignac, replacing him with a liberal. But his concession came too late to save the situation.

Pamphlets distributed the next day by the rebels declared that the King was no longer fit to rule. They promoted Louis-Philippe as a "prince devoted to the cause of revolution." One of the chief supporters of this scheme was the journalist Adolphe Thiers, who now set off for Neuilly to persuade the Duke once more to return to Paris. As Louis-Philippe was not at home, Thiers spoke instead to his sister, who agreed that her family should aid the revolutionary cause. That night, Orléans slipped quietly into the city.

Although many moderates hoped that Louis-Philippe would act as a regent for the young heir to the throne, the nine-year-old Henri, Duc de Bordeaux (the son of the assassinated Duc de Berry), the Duc d'Orléans agreed on 31 July to become Lieutenant-General of France. Two days later Charles X abdicated and – unwilling to imitate Louis XVI any further – he and his family set sail after a fortnight for England. Louis-Philippe became King.

The new monarchy: more a change of flags than system

The wealthy elites who were generally glad to see Charles X go did not want the

LEFT **Fighting at the Porte St Denis in July 1830. Clashes between troops and civilians in Paris led to the rapid flight of the King, Charles X, but the street-fighting also alarmed the more conservative bourgeoisie who joined in the pressure for a rapid transfer of power to a new regime to calm the situation.**

INSET **Conflict at the Hôtel de Ville (the town hall) in July 1830.**

populace of Paris to get above itself – as it had done in the past – and so there was a closing of ranks around the new King. Louis-Philippe agreed to some symbolic changes: he abandoned the white flag of the Bourbons for the revolutionary tricolour and called himself "King of the French." Nevertheless, while the hereditary upper chamber of peers was replaced by a nominated body, the franchise was extended only to include men who paid the considerable sum of 200 francs in taxation – just three per cent of the adult male population.

This was much less representative than the British model of constitutional monarchy praised by Louis-Philippe's promoters. Although agitation for constitutional as well as electoral reform was widespread in Britain in 1830, more than 400,000 British men (out of a much smaller population than that in France) had the vote, whereas the July Monarchy enfranchised only 270,000 or so. In fact, fear of a July-style revolution was one factor in encouraging further parliamentary reform in Britain. The British Whig reformer Thomas Babington Macaulay urged the Tories to accept a broader

"[Louis-Philippe] had on his side that great designation for the throne – exile. He had been proscribed, a wanderer, poor. He had lived by his own toil...he had been in the Jacobin club; Mirabeau had clapped him on the shoulder...he had been present at the trial of Louis XVI.... The Revolution had left a tremendous mark on him."
VICTOR HUGO, *LES MISERABLES*, 1862

franchise by consent rather than have it forced on them from below, so another 400,000 British males were added to the electoral register by the Great Reform Act of 1832. Thus, while Louis-Philippe's

ABOVE **The Duc d'Orléans, Louis-Philippe leaves the Palais Royal for the Hôtel de Ville on 31 July 1830.**

regime steadfastly resisted all calls for further electoral reform and the widening of the franchise, the British system proved adept over the coming century at including new waves of voters inside the system before public discontent broke out against it.

Louis-Philippe's assumption of the throne alienated many of the old monarchy's natural supporters without gaining him many true adherents on the left. Chateaubriand wrote in 1831, "For myself, a republican by nature, a monarchist by reason, and a Bourbonist by honour, if I could not have kept the legitimate monarchy, I would have been happier with a democracy than with a bastard monarchy granted by God knows whom." The split between the two wings of the French royal house bedevilled the chances of monarchy for the next half century, finally scuppering its best chance of restoration after 1871 (*see pages 112–15*). The unwillingness of so many aristocrats to compromise on their allegiance to the Lord's Anointed (the King) and accept the Orleanist compromise with revolution helped to thwart efforts to head off further republican challenges later on. As so often, without the pig-headedness of the reactionaries revolution would have stood little chance.

Guizot, who became Prime Minister in the 1840s, wanted the July revolution in 1830 to mark the end of violent upheavals in France. He thought freedom could best be protected by cautious reform. In December 1830 he told Parisians: "The spirit of revolution, the spirit of insurrec-

tion, is a spirit radically opposed to liberty." But to many of his fellow countrymen, Guizot's arguments sounded like the hypocritical defence of an oligarchy that had achieved what it wanted with the fall of Charles X and had no desire to share its gains with a broader public. Eighteen years later it was to be challenged on the streets of Paris in its turn (*see pages 97–101*).

The impact of the July Revolution

The July Revolution had repercussions abroad. In particular, it stimulated a revolt among the Catholic Belgians against their incorporation in 1815 into a Protestant and Dutch-dominated Netherlands. The French-speaking liberals in Belgium had been agitating for change since 1828, but the decision of the Dutch King, William I, to send troops against demonstrators in Brussels in September 1830 resulted in crisis. The European powers recognized Belgian independence in 1831 but did not want to give France an excuse to support Belgium's revolutionaries and so imposed a German prince, Leopold of Saxe-Gotha, as a constitutional monarch in Belgium. Under the 1831 constitution only 2 per cent of Belgian men were entitled to vote.

KEY EVENTS

1815 8 July
Louis XVIII is restored after Waterloo
1824 16 September
Charles X succeeds to the throne
1825 19 June
Charles X is crowned at Reims
1829 2 August
The King invites the Prince de Polignac to form a ministry
1830 25 July
Charles issues Four Ordinances, dissolving the newly elected Chamber
28 July
Revolution begins in Paris
29 July
The King sacks Polignac
30 July
Louis-Philippe of Orléans enters Paris; Charles X flees from Versailles
31 July
Louis-Philippe becomes Lieutenant-General of France
2 August
Charles X abdicates

The year 1848 saw a revolutionary explosion across Europe. From France, south to Sicily and eastwards to Poland, the post-Napoleonic order established in 1815 was challenged from below. Inspired by a potent mixture of social discontent and nationalism, a loose coalition of radicals and liberals, bourgeoisie, intelligentsia and under-privileged united against the common evils of autocratic monarchy, nobility and the Church.

The Springtime of the Peoples

On the eve of 1848, Karl Marx wrote in his *Communist Manifesto* that "a spectre is haunting Europe – the spectre of Communism." Marx was right that a revolutionary ghost haunted ageing reactionaries, but the name of their nightmare was not Communism but nationalism.

The wave of revolutions across Europe in 1848 offered the chance for subject peoples of the great empires to assert their national identity. Hopes for German or Italian unity were high, and the Poles believed that at long last their country would be restored. This "springtime of the peoples" proved brief, however, and one by one the revolutions were suppressed by force. The revolutions failed for a variety of reasons, most notably because the insurgents were fighting for too many irreconcilable causes (social and economic reform, nationalism, liberalism). The diversity of their demands helped to divide and ultimately to defeat the uprisings. Moreover, many of the moderates who assumed control of the insurrections became alarmed at the radical agenda of some of their colleagues and failed to coopt the crucial support of the lower classes.

Literacy and industry: new forces of revolution

Literacy was essential for the promotion of a new consciousness. Everywhere the old regime had maintained censorship to stifle new ideas, but educational improvements were widespread across northern and central Europe in the decades before 1848. The rise in levels of literacy were related to the demands and possibilities of the new industrial age.

From the mid-1830s railways spread across Europe improving communications and facilitating the growth of industry,

TOP **A nineteenth-century iron foundry. The spread of the rail network and industrialization helped destabilize traditional societies.**

ABOVE **A Chartist meeting in London on 10 April 1848. The generally peaceful manner of Chartist protest reflected as much the moderation of the authorities in Britain as the demonstrators' own law-abiding nature.**

which helped to cause unrest in two ways. First, a whole new class of people rose to wealth on the back of the new technologies, but were denied the political rights or influence appropriate to their new standing. At the same time, a novel and sinister urban working class emerged that grew by leaps and bounds as old cities entered the industrial age and new towns sprang up.

Second, while industry was creating fresh opportunities, its means of production were wiping out older forms of occupation. Thousands of handicraft workers found their livelihoods disappearing overnight. Tragically, much of the rural population had depended on handicrafts to supplement their agricultural labours: selling or bartering home-made cloth or leather often made the difference between living above or below the subsistence level. So, when in the 1840s economic change combined with poor harvests across large parts of Europe, the ingredients for rural discontent were mixed explosively.

Ironically, the country that had first experienced the industrial revolution and gone furthest down the track of urbanization – Britain – was the least threatened by revolution in 1848. This was because the Great Reform Act of 1832 had effectively satisfied the middle classes. A wider franchise, which offered modest property-owners the chance to vote, produced a great body of middle-class support for the government. One British group, known as the Chartists, offered a radical challenge to this consensus, demanding voting by secret ballot, universal adult male suffrage, annual elections and paid Members of Parliament. But behind the apparent radicalism of their demands lay the core request: that ordinary people should share in the British constitution. On the whole the Chartists showed respect for law and order. The huge demonstration in April 1848 to demand the extension of the franchise fizzled out in the rain without violence.

The British authorities were prepared for trouble and had recruited thousands of special constables (including Charles Dickens and Louis Napoleon Bonaparte, nephew of the great Emperor, then in exile in London) to support the police in the event of rioting. The use of unarmed police for crowd control was an important innovation. Elsewhere in Europe in 1848, the accidental or unauthorized discharge of muskets led to bloodshed and a radicalization of public opinion, but this was avoided in London.

The situation was different in Ireland. In the aftermath of the Great Potato Famine (1845–49), the population was preoccupied with survival, and attempts to raise a rebellion quickly faltered. Emigration rather than insurrection had become the main way to escape British rule.

FRANCE IN 1848

France was the classic centre of revolution in the romantic age, and any new outbreak of revolution here was bound to be an international event. Just such a revolution occurred in 1848 when traditional adherents of the July Monarchy withdrew their support, resulting in vicious fighting on the streets of Paris. The fall of the King, Louis-Philippe, resulted in tragic internal divisions amongst French society and led eventually to the triumph of a new dictator: Louis Napoleon Bonaparte.

BELOW **During the so-called "Springtime of the Peoples" in 1848, almost every regime in Europe faced popular revolution, or at least the threat of it.**

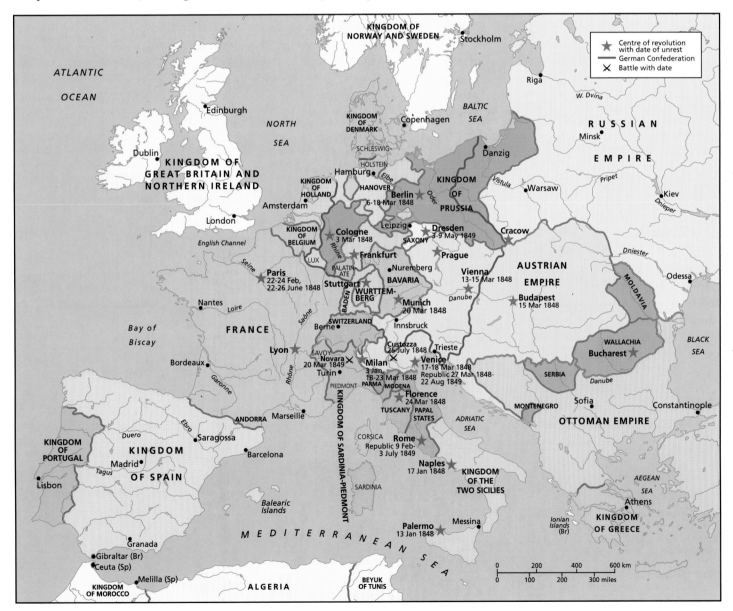

The undoing of the July Monarchy

As the years passed since 1789, the cult of revolution grew rather than diminished. New generations of Frenchmen felt inferior to those aged souls that had seen the great upheaval, and as the last witnesses of the fall of Louis XVI passed away, books and pamphlets started to appear that promoted the idea of revolution with an almost religious faith. A cult of Napoleon Bonaparte also emerged.

Louis-Philippe tried to attach himself to Napoleon's reflected glory in 1840 by arranging a state reburial for the Emperor in Paris. The King's ambiguity towards France's revolutionary past and his own approach to the role of Citizen-King meant that the July Monarchy never had a clear ideology. Criticisms of the government were bound to become attacks on the monarch and his dynasty.

Poor harvests in 1845 and 1846 produced rumbles of discontent that even a better harvest in 1847 could not dispel. Although famine on the Irish scale was not experienced, food shortages and high prices made for a tense situation. The rapid growth of Paris in the first half of the century also created many sources of unrest. The population doubled to more than a million by 1848, but housing was slower to develop. Over-crowding, disease and under-employment constantly replenished the well of lower-class discontent.

Disappointed by the failure of the July Monarchy to improve their lot, an unlikely alliance of artisans (whose livelihood was threatened by the new industrial revolution) and workers in the new industries who felt badly paid, frequently broke into rebellion, particularly in the early 1830s. Students and old Bonapartists also rioted against the new regime in Paris, but by the 1840s Louis-Philippe's government thought it had weathered the storm.

RIGHT **Although the King, Louis-Philippe, had fled from Paris, the seat of government in Paris, the Château d'Eau, was stormed on 24 February 1848.**

INSET **The Parisians had developed an expertise in rapidly putting up barricades, such as this one in rue St Martin.**

Complacency was the greatest undoing of the July Monarchy. It was easy for the government to manage the narrow electorate to produce a favourable majority in the Chamber of Deputies. The King was elderly and easily caricatured as smug. His Prime Minister, François Guizot, regarded the regime as the best of all possible worlds and confidently proclaimed that "universal suffrage will never see the light of day."

Others were less certain. The liberal politician, Alexis de Tocqueville, predicted on 27 January 1848 that the revolutionary tide was returning: "The old monarchy [of Louis XVI]...was stronger than you, stronger because of its [hereditary] origin; it had better support than you from ancient practices, old customs ancient beliefs; it was stronger than you, and yet it fell into the dust.... Can you not feel – how shall I put it? – the wind of revolution in the air?"

February 1848

By late 1847, a serious campaign had developed in Paris to promote the extension of the franchise. The campaign was conducted largely through a series of banquets (held in private venues to circumvent the law on public meetings) at which promi-

LEFT **Louis-Philippe (1773–1850), shown here clasping a tricolour flag, owed his Crown to the July Revolution of 1830 but lost it again during the revolution of 1848.**

nent republicans would speak. These so-called "banquets for reform" were popular as a way of letting ordinary people express their grievances.

When a mass banquet planned for 22 February 1848 was banned by the government, opposition leaders called for a demonstration against the King and the unpopular Guizot. Protesters assembled in the Place de la Concorde in Paris, and a few scattered barricades appeared, but by and large the few clashes were not violent. Crowds gathered the next day as well. At first they were peaceful, singing the Marseillaise and rude ditties about unpopular politicians. Eyewitnesses reported

banter across the newly erected barricades: "You won't shoot without letting us know?" the demonstrators asked the soldiers, who replied, "Don't worry, we have no orders yet." But then shooting began – no one was certain from where. The troops fired on the crowd in a half-hearted way. The National Guard, sent to assist the soldiers, generally refused to cooperate. The rioting got worse as demonstrators sensed the weakness and indecision of the regime. In a desperate bid to restore calm, Louis-Philippe decided to sacrifice Guizot and replace him with the more liberal Comte de Molé. But the news did little to stabilize the situation. Barricades spread across Paris as the casualty list passed fifty. Victor Hugo described the events of 23 February: *The crowds which I had seen start cheerfully singing down the boulevards, at first went on their way peacefully and without resistance.... But on the Boulevard des Capucines a body of troops, both infantry and cavalry were massed on the two pavements and across the road, guarding the Ministry of Foreign Affairs and its unpopular minister, M. Guizot. Before this impassable obstacle, the head of the popular column tried to stop and turn aside; but the irresistible pressure of the huge crowd weighed on the front ranks. At this moment a shot rang out, from which side is not known. Panic followed and then a volley. Eighty dead or wounded remained on the spot. A universal cry of horror and fury arose: Vengeance! The bodies of the victims were loaded on a cart lit with torches. The cortège moved back amidst curses at a funeral pace. And in a few hours Paris was covered with barricades.* By the end of the street-fighting about 370 people had been killed. Lacking clear instructions, the military commander ordered his troops on the morning of 24 February to cease fire. This left the insurgents to gain control of the city. At this point, Louis-Philippe lost his nerve and abdicated. Although he hoped to see his grandson succeed, the republican mood of the city was too powerful. A Provisional Government was formed and the Second Republic proclaimed. Even quite conserv-

"I saw society cut in two: those who possessed nothing, united in common greed; those who possessed something, in a common fear. No more links, no more sympathy, everywhere the idea of an inevitable and close struggle." THE LIBERAL POLITICIAN, ALEXIS DE TOCQUEVILLE, APRIL 1848

ABOVE **A naive view of the new French Republic as a harmonious society.**

ative politicians preferred to try to steer the revolution by joining it rather than stand by their panicking monarch, who fled to England, the first of so many other political refugees in 1848 (first reactionaries, then defeated revolutionaries). For the moment everyone was a republican. Baudelaire rhapsodized on 27 February 1848: "For three days now the population of Paris has been wonderful in its physical beauty.... The people and the bourgeoisie have shaken the lice of corruption and immorality from the body of France."

The Second Republic
The flight of Louis-Philippe seemed to mark the triumph of republicanism, but it also opened the divisions between those who merely wanted an end to any kind of monarchy and those who saw a republic

as the first step to further reforms. The immediate policy of the motley crew who made up the self-proclaimed Provisional Government was to calm the Parisians and to arrange elections to guarantee the democracy of the new Republic.

The inclusion in the Provisional Government of Albert Martin, a mechanic – the first of many token "representatives of the labouring people" – was a sign that the new regime meant to do something for the urban poor. It was also a harbinger of trouble to come. The urban unemployed were a big issue, especially in Paris, but outside the capital sympathy among rural taxpayers for poor "townies" was in short supply. Class antagonisms quickly emerged after the euphoria of February wore off.

Democracy and the right to work were the two key promises of the radicals who led the Provisional Government. Universal male suffrage was announced at once, increasing the electorate from 250,000 to more than 9,000,000. France's first Socialist minister, Louis Blanc, also established a system of labour schemes, National Workshops, for the urban unemployed. By June 1848, 120,000 Parisians were employed by these workshops, but they were expensive, and to cover the budget deficit the Provisional Government hiked the land tax by 45 per cent. Nothing could have been better designed to alienate the rural population, who regarded this tax as a way of making them pay for urban layabouts.

The provinces versus the city
It is important to remember that not all the property-owners in France were rich. One effect of the revolution in 1789 had been the encouragement of a property-owning peasantry in France. Huge numbers of otherwise poor people owned a plot of land and were jealous of anyone who might take it from them or tax it.

Paris was the home of radicalism. Both the intellectual radicals and the urban poor were based here. They were all too ready to assume that they represented France as a whole. The rest of France took a different view, and public opinion outside Paris began to swing to the right. As the radicals began to suspect that suffrage would not bring about the election result they hoped for, they became indignant and tried to intimidate the countryside with a grim vision of urban outrage. This backfired.

The elections to the Constituent Assembly (which was to draw up a new constitution) took place on Easter Sunday, 23 April 1848. The turnout was a huge 84 per cent and briefly democracy triumphed with liberal aristocrats waiting their turn to vote in alphabetical order. The result, however, was a stunning victory for the right. When the 900 new deputies met, only 72 supported the right to work and 110 voted for a graduated income tax. The new Constituent Assembly had a massive monarchist majority, but the monarchists were divided as to who should be the next King – the choice was between heirs of Charles X or Louis-Philippe – and they were not certain what Paris would accept.

Pierre Joseph Proudhon recognized the significance of the popular vote that Easter. It marked the death of hopes that the people could be relied on to support revolution. Three years later he proclaimed, "Universal suffrage is counter-revolution." Part of Marx's contempt for peasantry – transmitted with such terrible consequences to later generations of revolutionaries – grew out of a recognition that country folk in France and elsewhere in 1848 were not natural allies of social revolutionaries.

Tension grew in Paris and disgruntled radicals stormed the National Assembly on 15 May, but their protest was largely peaceful and it was dispersed by troops and the National Guard. The new right-wing majority took the chance to arrest the radical leaders Auguste Blanqui and Armand Barbès. This left the crowds without leadership. The Assembly's next step was to abolish the National Workshops. This was done in the most insensitive way.

The June Days

"The February revolution was the *beautiful* revolution.... The June Revolution is the *ugly* revolution, the repulsive revolution, because deeds have taken the place of phrases." (Karl Marx, 29 June 1849)

ABOVE **Ernest Meissonier's painting of the remains of this barricade was based on his experience as a National Guard officer who helped destroy the barricade.**

Anger at the betrayal of the promises of February was widespread among the Parisian poor. Victor Hugo sympathized with them but could not justify their rebellion: "It must be repressed. The honest man devotes himself to it, and, for the very love of that multitude, he battles against it." Hugo was nostalgic for the rule of the mob that threatened to seize Paris in June 1848. He argued: "June, 1848, was...a thing apart, and almost impossible to classify." It was a case of "labour demanding its rights," but threatening the very republic just established: "It must be put down, and that was duty, for it attacked the republic. But at bottom, what was June, 1848? A revolt of the people against itself." From 1848 to the imposition of martial law in Poland in 1981, revolutionaries would explain the need for troops to suppress the workers as an attempt to stop the people behaving illogically: how could they challenge their own Republic?

Determined to close down the National Workshops and to disperse the gathering of the poor, the new government acted quickly and harshly. The recipients of public funds were peremptorily offered a brutal choice: to depart Paris for public works in the remote provinces (such as draining the unhealthy marshes of Sologne), to join the army or to do without public aid altogether. This decree was published on 21 June. By 11 o'clock the next morning a crowd had gathered outside the Hôtel de Ville, and the police reported, "The men who impose it say that they will not leave for the Sologne, they would prefer to die here. They add that they will take up arms against the National Assembly." By the evening, columns of workers were marching into the centre of Paris shouting, "Work! Bread! We will not leave!"

The narrow streets of the old city of Paris were blocked yet again with makeshift barricades. Disillusioned citizens of the city turned out in their thousands to defend their Republic, but this time the forces of law and order proved superior. While the newly elected deputies were unwilling to pay for unemployment relief, they had not stinted on the police. Twenty-

> **"When the barricade in the rue de la Mortellerie was taken I realized all the horror of such warfare. I saw the defenders shot down, hurled out of windows, and the ground strewn with corpses, the earth red with the blood it had not yet drunk."**
> THE PAINTER, ERNEST MEISSONNIER

four battalions of Mobile Guards were rapidly recruited from the ranks of the unemployed and paid 1.50 francs a day – more than regular soldiers, and more than enough to persuade them of the need to shoot down less fortunate, unemployed workers in June. About 1,500 revolutionaries were killed. A further 3,000 were killed in the following reprisals.

The savagery of repression foreshadowed the events of the Commune in 1871 (*see pages 112–15*). Hugo describes a terrible scene on the barricades of a "young woman, beautiful, dishevelled, terrible. This woman, who was a whore, lifted her dress up to her waist and shouted to the National Guard: 'Fire, you cowards, if you dare, on the belly of a woman!' A volley of shots knocked the wretched woman to the ground. She fell, letting forth a great cry."

The results of the revolution: the Second Empire

Having defeated the forces of social revolt, the Constituent Assembly went on to enact an ideal liberal constitution. This constitution contained a classic separation of powers between an executive president and a parliamentary National Assembly to make the laws, and provided for the election of a president. But the age of bourgeois rule was not about to be born.

The real beneficiary of the 1848 revolution in France was not the conservative political class, but an outsider: Louis Napoleon Bonaparte, nephew of the Emperor. After the savagery of June 1848, his return to France as the heir of his uncle offered something for everyone. He did not alarm the forces of order: as a Bonaparte he inherited the right to represent them, but at the same time his earlier writings on the need to abolish poverty ensured he was popular among the poor.

In the presidential election campaign, Louis Napoleon routed his main rival, General Cavaignac, the army commander during the June Days. Cavaignac was hated by the poor but even many bourgeois voters thought his reputation too divisive to make him a viable president for the much-desired calm. The Bonapartist manifesto was clear in its appeal across the social divide: "The unfortunate die of hunger; the worker is without work; the cultivator is no longer able to dispose of his crops; the merchant sells nothing; the proprietor no longer receives his rent; the capitalist no longer dares to invest, lacking security. The nephew of the great man, with his magic name, will give us security and save us from misery."

Some 74 per cent of those who voted on 10 December 1848 voted for Louis Napoleon. The new Prince-President as he was called had little affection for the constitution. He wanted to restore his uncle's

LEFT **Napoleon III (1808–73), here photographed during the 1860s.**

imperial glory. Aware of how unpopular the politicians in the National Assembly were with the French public, he gave them time to discredit themselves further with their disagreements and inaction while at the same time blaming his own inactivity on their obstructiveness. If only the constitution would let him act he would fulfil his manifesto – but that required sweeping away the political class. On 2 December 1851, he staged his famous coup d'état. Few people went on to the barricades to stop it. As one character from Gustave Flaubert's novel, *L'Education sentimentale*, put it: "We're not fools enough to get ourselves killed for the bourgeois! Let them settle it themselves!" A year later Louis Napoleon proclaimed himself Napoleon III. Only another revolution, or defeat in war – or both – would remove him from power (*see pages 112–15*).

KEY EVENTS: FRANCE

1848 22 February
Demonstrations begin in Paris
23 February
Guizot resigns; the first protesters are killed
24 February
Louis-Philippe abdicates
23 April
Constituent Assembly is elected
4 May
Constituent Assembly meets
15 May
Crowds invade Constituent Assembly
20 June
Assembly votes to dissolve national workshops
22–26 June
"June Days"
10 December
Election of Louis Napoleon Bonaparte as President
1851 2 December
Louis Napoleon's coup d'état
1852 2 December
Proclamation of the Second Empire

ITALY IN 1848

Italy was still divided into different states in 1848. The majority of northern states were dominated by Austria while the Kingdom of the Two Sicilies (Naples and Sicily) was governed by Spanish Bourbon kings. Poor economic performance and growing social problems in the first half of the nineteenth century fuelled opposition to foreign rule. For a few months in 1848, liberal campaigners for the granting of constitutions and press freedom joined forces with supporters of Italian unification – but Habsburg military power and social and regional divisions ultimately thwarted the hopes of both liberals and nationalist radicals.

Sicily leads the way

"No state in Europe is in a worse condition than ours.... In the Kingdom of the Two Sicilies...which is said to be the garden of Europe, the people die of hunger, are in a state worse than beasts, the only law is caprice...." (Luigi Settembrini, 1847)

Inspired more by resentment against Bourbon rule and despair about the rising cost of living than by any nationalist zeal, the Sicilians of Palermo rose up in revolt on 12 January 1848. A fortnight of vicious fighting between insurgents and royalist troops culminated in the people sacking the Royal Palace and the withdrawal of government troops. King Ferdinand had no choice but to grant a constitution to Sicily and Naples.

Trouble was already stirring across the rest of Italy when the Austrian military commander in Italy, Marshal Joseph Radetzky, heard the "sad news from Paris" of the fall of Louis-Philippe. "I took it to be a stock-exchange rumour since it was too incredible.... I cannot foresee...whether the weak Italian governments will survive for 24 hours after receiving the news and whether the revolutionary party will not use this moment to realize their old dream of a united Italy." The rulers of Tuscany and Piedmont tried to pre-empt the spread of any disorder to their states by granting constitutions. The Pope, Pius IX, also enacted liberalizing reforms in the Papal States and granted his people a constitution on 14 March 1848. But he soon came to distrust the radical forces his reforms unleashed, and when his own general called for a nationalist war in the spring of 1848 against the Habsburg troops in northern Italy "to exterminate the enemies of God and of Italy," Pius IX denounced the enterprise reminding his subjects and the world that "According to the order of Our supreme Apostolate, We seek after and embrace all races, peoples, and nations, with equal devotion of paternal love." This was good Christianity but reactionary politics, and the Pope was later driven into exile from Rome, where a republic was proclaimed in 1849.

Rebellion against the Habsburgs

Italian nationalists recognized that only the expulsion of the Austrians from Italy could open the way to a unified liberal state. As news reached Italy of the fall of the Austrian Chancellor Clemens von Metternich in the middle of March 1848 (*see page 109*) this suddenly seemed a feasible goal – but it required effective military action by the best-prepared Italian

ABOVE **By mid-February 1848, in Sicily only the town of Messina remained in royal hands. This illustration shows the fighting that took place in Messina.**

ABOVE RIGHT **Civilians face Austrian troops in St Mark's Square in Venice on 18 March 1848. Austrian rule in Venice collapsed almost bloodlessly and a Venetian Republic was proclaimed.**

RIGHT **A barricade in Milan on 22 March 1848. After five days of street-fighting, Austrian troops retreated from Milan.**

state, Piedmont, whose territory bordered the Austrian province of Lombardy.

Rioting erupted in Venice on 17 March, with bands of the populace parading the streets, breaking windows and crying "Viva l'Italia!" Troops were called out but withdrawn the next day, as the people won their appeal for constitutional rights. The Austrian governors of northern Italy calculated that they could turn the peasants against the towns in the event of an uprising, but their hopes proved premature. When rioting began in Milan, country-dwellers rushed to help the insurrection. An Austrian officer reported, "The city was surrounded by armed and uproarious peasants who came running in their thousands, shooting at the soldiers standing on the bastions just as they were being shot at from inside the city."

ABOVE **Street fighting in Naples between royal troops and civilians on 15 May**

The violence in Milan took Marshal Radetzky by surprise: both sides suffered terrible losses. In spite of the uncoordinated nature of the insurrection initially, the Milanese quickly organized a military committee that directed the uprising with extraordinary skill. Members of the city's noble and bourgeois elite had led the opposition prior to the insurrection and were now quick to take charge against the risk of peasants or urban poor demanding social reform as well as political liberaliza-

tion. Radetzky wrote in a dispatch of 21 March that: "The streets have been pulled up to an extent you can hardly imagine. Barricades close them by the hundred, even by the thousand. The revolutionary party is moving with a caution and cleverness which makes it obvious that they are being directed by military officers from abroad. The character of this people has been altered as if by magic, and fanaticism has taken hold of every age group, every class, and both sexes." After five days, Radetzky was forced to withdraw. "It is the most frightful decision of my life," he wrote, "but I can no longer hold Milan. The whole country is in revolt."

Piedmont declares war on Austria
King Charles Albert of Piedmont followed the events taking place in Milan from a safe distance. Once it became obvious that the rebels were going to win, he decided the time was ripe for his army to intervene. The intervention backfired, however. Taxes and requisitions from the peasantry were unpopular and Charles Albert added conscription to the grievances of the Lombard peasants whom he wanted to turn into his new subjects. Meanwhile, Radetzky prepared to recover Lombardy by force. He soon found himself cheered by peasants as a liberator as he marched back towards Milan. He also cancelled debts owed to rebellious landlords as he went. After capturing Milan on 6 August 1848, Radetzky billeted his troops on nobles and bourgeoisie, not the poor, and demanded huge fines from the top 200 families resident in the city. Class warfare was turning out to be a powerful weapon in the imperial arsenal.

The revolutions in Italy are overturned
It soon became clear that the reactionary forces could recover ground if they kept their nerve and played up the divisions among their enemies. Although insurrection was widespread across Italy in 1848, there was very little coordination between the revolutionaries. This was fatal when outside powers such as Austria and France began to intervene with a clear strategy

and powerful forces. The Tuscan radical, Giuseppe Montanelli, admitted that for all their nationalistic rhetoric, the Italian revolutionaries failed to think in national terms when it came to strategy. "There was no unity of direction, therefore there was no national government. We fought as Piedmontese, as Tuscans, as Neapolitans, as Romans, not as Italians."

KEY EVENTS: ITALY

1848 3 January
Demonstrations begin in Milan against Austrian rule
13 January
Revolution in Sicily against King Ferdinand
17 January
Demonstrations in Naples supporting Sicilians
29 January
Ferdinand of Two Sicilies grants constitution
17 February
Constitution granted to Tuscany
5 March
Charles Albert grants Piedmont a constitution
6 March
Ferdinand grants Sicily a separate parliament
14 March
Pius IX grants Papal states a constitution
17–18 March
Anti-Habsburg rebellion in Venice
18–23 March
Anti-Habsburg rebellion in Milan
25 March
Piedmont starts war against Austria
27 March
Restoration of Venetian Republic proclaimed
25 July
Piedmont defeated by Austrian army at Custozza
9 August
Piedmont signs armistice with Austria
1849 9 February
Proclamation of Roman Republic
12 March
Piedmont reopens war against Austria
20 March
Piedmont defeated at Novara; ends war with Austria
27 April
Neapolitan troops reoccupy Palermo
3 July
French troops occupy Rome and suppress the Republic
28 July
Grand Duke Leopold returns to Tuscany
22 August
Venetian Republic surrenders to Austrian troops
1850 12 April
Pius IX returns to Rome

Many Italian liberals harboured the delusion that the French Republic would intervene to assure their national independence and protect constitutional states, but their hopes were soon dashed. Louis Napoleon Bonaparte sent French troops in 1849 to restore the Pope and crush the Roman Republic.

Further north, the Austrians reconquered Milan and Venice. Contrary to the nationalistic myth, most of the troops in the Austrian army were not foreigners but poor Italians who regarded the urban revolutionaries with suspicion. The Bourbon King of the Two Sicilies also found allies against his bourgeois rebels among the Neapolitan poor.

Venice continued its resistance after the forces of reaction had triumphed across the rest of Italy, but it too eventually fell to the Austrians on 22 August 1849. Once they had recovered Lombardy and Venetia, the Austrians forgot their divide-and-rule tactics and within a few years heavy land taxes and conscription had alienated the peasants. By the mid-1850s, instead of noble-led rebellions, sudden local revolts and stabbings of officials were the main worry for the Austrian garrison.

But it was not merely the parochial nature of the revolutions that prevented their success. As in Central Europe, fear of radicalization split the ranks of the opponents of reaction. Already in 1846, Count Cavour had argued that: "If the social order were to be genuinely menaced, if the great principles on which it rests were to be at serious risk, then many of the most determined oppositionists, the most enthusiastic republicans would be...the first to join the ranks of the conservative party." It was not by chance that in the end Cavour's conservative approach did more to unite Italy than Garibaldi's dashing but disastrous tactics of 1848–49.

The reactionaries were aware of the advantages of international cooperation: it was the alliance of France and Austria that eventually defeated the Italian revolutionaries. Ten years later, however, Napoleon III had a change of heart and sent his

LEFT **Giuseppe Garibaldi (1807–82), one of Italy's most romantic revolutionary nationalists. Apart from his role in the events in Italy of 1848–49 and his famous conquest of Sicily (with his army of a thousand men) in 1860, he played a key part in South America's turbulent politics before 1848.**

troops to assist Piedmont against Austria. Liberal Italy was created as a by-product of one great power's intervention against another – but by then unification was no longer a revolutionary cause.

GERMANY IN 1848

In 1848, "Germany" was still almost as much of a "geographical expression" as Italy. After 1815, all the German-speaking states belonged to the German Confederation, but the Austrian Emperor ruled over millions of non-Germans too, and Prussia had a sizeable Polish minority. Nationality issues, along with political and social questions, played a major part in the events of 1848–49 in Germany.

Problems beset the German regime

Trade and industry began to develop quite rapidly in northern Germany in the first half of the nineteenth century. In 1834, Prussia and all the other German states except the Austrian Empire formed a customs union, the *Zollverein*, to promote trade between them. It was a step towards political unification, which was widely supported by the growing numbers of students and educated people in the cities.

Some sort of representation of the people existed in most states, but royal governments were not responsible to Diets or elected chambers. Discontent among the subject peoples began to mount in the 1840s. By 1848, groups as diverse as artisans, peasants, manufacturers, lawyers and students all had grievances. Although none of the regimes were as rigorously reactionary in Germany as they had been after the Napoleonic wars, the strait-jacket of official censorship was still irksome. In

April 1847, as the first sign of a thaw, the King of Prussia, Frederick William IV, permitted the press to report on the proceedings in the Diet, but still insisted that "no power on earth" would make him grant a constitution. He would not let "a piece of paper" come between him and his people. Their representatives were not impressed and called for a full constitution limiting the powers of the monarchy.

Economic problems made life worse. Already in June 1844, Silesian weavers had risen in a desperate protest against their poverty (due in large part to the new machinery) and had been suppressed by the Prussian army. By the beginning of 1848, there was a widespread feeling that revolution was in the air and that the "Metternich System" – named after the Austrian Chancellor, Clemens von Metternich – would soon collapse. Metternich himself told his doctor, "I am not a prophet, and I don't know what will happen, but I am an old physician and can distinguish between temporary and fatal diseases. We now face one of the latter.

THE RISE OF GERMAN NATIONALISM

For all their liberalism, most German revolutionary activists in 1848 had little sympathy with the national aspirations of their neighbours, the Poles and the Danes. In 1848 the Frankfurt Parliament endorsed a short war against Denmark over the Schleswig-Holstein question: these two duchies were ruled by the King of Denmark but had a majority German population. The Prussian army was applauded when it led the attack on the Danes. With regard to Poland, the overwhelming majority of the Frankfurt Parliament (342 to 31) voted in favour of incorporating the Duchy of Posen, with its large Polish population, into the new Germany. Wilhelm Jordan, an East Prussian MP, ridiculed the Poles as a "few families who revel in court splendour and a few charming mazurka dancers." He believed: "It is time to wake up to a policy of healthy national egotism." Heinrich von Gagern, a prominent liberal, argued: "It is not enough to warm ourselves at our own firesides. We want a unity that can incorporate, like satellites in our planetary system, all the peoples in the Danube basin, who have neither ability nor claim to independence." It was a harbinger of attitudes to come.

ABOVE **Barricades in Berlin, 18–19 March 1848. The liberal protesters were non-violent in their demands for constitutional reform after the news of Metternich's fall reached Berlin, but chance incidents led to violent clashes with the army. To stop bloodshed, the King withdrew his troops.**

We'll hold on as long as we can, but I have doubts about the outcome." As early as 9 March 1848, the King of Württemberg told the Russian ambassador, "I cannot ride a horse against ideas." Later on his Prussian cousin, Frederick William IV, learned a different lesson: "Against democrats only soldiers are any use."

It was not only fatalism that limited the capacity of the old regimes to use force against their critics in 1848: the role of members of the respectable classes in the agitation for reform was also a problem. It was one matter to send soldiers to stop strikes in the new industries or to disperse disgruntled handicraft workers, but quite another to shoot down professors and lawyers. On 5 March 1848, middle-class intellectuals with a few noble supporters had met in Heidelberg to call for an all-German parliament to assemble in Frankfurt. This was a challenge to the states of the German Confederation, of which Austria and Prussia were the most important. Prussia was the state most likely to gain from German unification

because its Polish minority was much smaller than Austria's non-German majority. But absolutism was deeply ingrained in the minds of the Prussian royal family.

Revolution in Berlin

Traditionally, Prussia had been a highly militarized state. Mirabeau once defined Prussia as an army with a state, and Prussian militarism was a great issue in 1848. Across the German Confederation, troops were used to suppress opposition. In Berlin, there was a garrison of 15,000, but only 209 policemen. Liberals and radicals alike believed in the need to replace the army (which was an instrument of royal absolutism) with a civic guard that would uphold human rights.

The first demonstrations against the government began in January 1848 in the Rhineland provinces. News of the revolution in Paris and then the fall of Metternich in Vienna promoted the spread of open discontent. The demands were for political reform: a constitutional monarchy with a ministry responsible to an elected parliament and a civic guard on the model of the French National Guard. Demands for German unity were also loud. ·

When the crowds became noisy in their demands for reform, the King refused to leave Berlin because his Queen was too ill to travel. This made it difficult for the generals to use force without endangering the life of the King, so they dithered. Frederick William was anxious that the barricades should be cleared, but he ordered his troops not to fire. Between 16 and 18 March there were incidents involving gunfire – though no one was certain who started the shooting. The troops had not been trained for crowd control and the street-fighting that followed was confused. But civilian casualties inflamed the situation.

Workers from the Borsig engineering works turned out in the streets to make

barricades alongside bourgeois students. There was a brief period of solidarity in opposition to the brutal army. The liberal, Varnhagen von Ense, wrote about the social solidarity of the motley demonstrators shot down by troops in Berlin: "Never have I seen greater courage, a more resolute contempt for death, than in those young men who were beaten down and lost beyond all hope of rescue. Well-bred students in fine clothes, men-servants, apprentices, youths, old labourers, all went to make up a single company and vied with one another in courage and endurance."

On 18 March, the King appeared on the balcony of his palace wearing the revolutionary cockade of black, gold and red (like Louis XVI seventy years earlier) and saluted the dead citizens. He announced that "henceforth Prussia merges into Germany" and was cheered, though the crowd called for the regular soldiers to be withdrawn from Berlin. Indecisive at this stage, Frederick William IV permitted the army's withdrawal. In the short term this weakened his position, but within months

ABOVE **A Berlin newspaper of 21 August 1848. Anti-government riots continued in Berlin and other big cities throughout 1848, but fear of disorder slowly shifted support among the propertied back to the regime.**

it became clear that the army had been able to regroup away from the pressures and agitation of the radicals in the capital. In practice the King had no intention of giving up his state and began to look for ways to delay German unity. Recognizing that the Habsburgs in Vienna would never agree to give up to a new Germany either their German-speaking lands or their non-German lands, Frederick William was soon sounding more nationalist than the so-called "little Germans" who were prepared to accept a unified Germany minus Austria. He announced: "Germany without the German provinces of Austria would be worse than a face without a nose."

Social tensions began to reappear in Prussia soon enough. The young German scientist Rudolf Virchow wrote to his father from Berlin on 1 May 1848: "You are quite right, essentially it has been the workers who have decided this revolution, but I also believe that you in the provinces do not fully realize that this revolution was not simply a political one, but essentially a social one." Fear of disorder and social breakdown was never far from the surface. The liberals wanted a constitution not chaos. Although Prussia saw nothing like the June Days in Paris, the bourgeois civic guard was prepared to support the social order and property holders against the radicals.

The Frankfurt Parliament

While in the individual German states the local political struggle went on between kings and people, at the end of March, a preparatory parliament (*Vorparlament*) met in Frankfurt to prepare for a fully democratic all-German parliament and a new constitution. Under pressure from events in the states, their ambassadors to the Confederation, which also met in Frankfurt, agreed to the elections.

Later, after the ineffectiveness of the Frankfurt Parliament was revealed, it was ridiculed by disappointed radicals and

"[The Paulskirche] is still set up as the National Assembly left it, a lot of black-red-gold flags and curtains, even four lamps on the speaker's table.... The church was so quiet as a grave above the empty benches that it was hard to imagine all the Parliamentary hubbub."
OTTO VON BISMARCK, VISITING THE FORMER SEAT OF THE FRANKFURT PARLIAMENT IN 1851

ABOVE **Fighting in front of St Paul's Church in Frankfurt, 18 October 1848. Tension mounted between the moderate majority of the Frankfurt Parliament and radicals outside it. Ironically the MPs depended on the Prussian army to protect them from the more revolutionary demonstrators.**

reactionaries alike as the "Professors' Parliament." In fact there were only 50 professors and 60 teachers among its members. But it *was* overwhelmingly a parliament of the higher educated, many of whom had become lawyers or civil servants. Few landlords (38) and fewer noblemen (25) were elected, but then there were only four journeymen elected, and no ordinary labourers. Reasonableness and

willingness to debate were simultaneously its virtues and its vices.

The majority in the Frankfurt Parliament wanted change to be acceptable to the conservative princes. This was to prove its downfall. Concessions, such as electing a Habsburg Archduke to act as Reichvicar to head the executive (which in fact did not yet exist), were taken as signs of weakness.

Differences soon arose over what sort of constitution the united Germany (which almost every member supported) should have. Some were federalists, others were for a unitary state. Radicals wanted to do without a standing army while pragmatists argued Germany would be vulnerable to attack without one. Above all, there was the question of who should be head of state. If it was to be a monarch – as most people agreed – choosing the King of Prussia or the Austrian Emperor was a sensitive issue.

Nationalism also haunted the proceedings of Parliament. The deputies endorsed Prussia's taking the lead in a war against Denmark to keep two northern duchies, Schleswig and Holstein, in Germany. But when Prussia high-handedly decided to halt the war on its own terms, the lack of real power in the hands of Frankfurt was revealed. The deputies also compromised their liberal credentials by ignoring Polish demands for self-determination.

When radicals murdered two conservative deputies to the Frankfurt Parliament in August 1848, many of their colleagues began to look more favourably on the Prussian army as a guarantor of law and order. A state of siege was proclaimed in Frankfurt to protect Parliament from radical attacks. The dependence of the deputies on reactionary armies became apparent.

Counter-revolution in Prussia

Throughout the summer and autumn of 1848, Frederick William IV became bolder in his refusal to accept liberal reforms. By November, he had accepted what his military advisers had long been telling him: that the determined use of the army would not be resisted. The largely peasant soldiers with their Junker (aristocratic) officers shared a dislike of urban radicals. On 10 November, Field Marshal Wrangel and 40,000 troops entered Berlin and disarmed the citizens' guard.

Even in Prussia, the reactionaries around the King recognized that the clock could not be turned back entirely. Instead, the restored regime intended to steer change. On 5 December, the Prussian King graciously "conferred" a constitution on his "subjects." Although there were to be elections and votes on taxes – key liberal demands – the only oath of obedience was to the King, not to the constitution, and the army and civil service were to be controlled by him. The elections too were significantly watered down: every adult male retained the right to vote, but the whole electorate was divided into three classes according to their taxable incomes, weighting the results in favour of the richer two classes against the much more populous third class.

Frederick William IV's refusal to accept the German Crown offered by Frankfurt in April 1849 marked the end of hopes for liberal unification. The King rejected the democratic election as insulting, like picking up a crown "out of the gutter." Instead his forces were to become the spearhead of suppressing what remained of the radical revolutionaries, who took heart from the failure of moderation and tried to arouse more mass protest.

The Dresden revolution, May 1849

Encouraged by the growing tide of reaction in Prussia and Austria, the King of Saxony dismissed his liberal ministers in February 1849. Over the next three months tension rose until street-fighting broke out in his capital, Dresden, on 3 May. The Dresden revolution might have been just a footnote to 1848 but for the participation of two famous figures. The Russian anarchist, Mikhail Bakunin, found himself in the city on the run from Prague, and his enthusiasm for anarchic

ABOVE **Counter-revolution in Saxony provoked a radical revolt in May 1849 – here crowds are storming the Hotel Rom in Dresden – but Prussian troops arrived to suppress the uprising as they were doing across Germany.**

revolutionary destruction was shared by Richard Wagner, who abandoned his post as court conductor to join the revolutionaries. He advocated universal suffrage, the abolition of the standing army and a civic guard and fled into exile in Switzerland after Prussian troops put down the revolution. Some 250 people were killed in the street-fighting in Dresden in May 1849. Clara Schumann (wife of the famous

LEFT **The young court composer Richard Wagner (1813–83) supported the revolutionary ideals of 1848 and openly sided with the Saxon rebels. He was forced into exile in Switzerland after 1849 where he was to remain until 1864.**

composer) wrote in her diary on 10 May: "We heard of the awful atrocities committed by the troops; they shot every insurgent they could find and our landlady told us later that her brother...was made to stand and watch while the soldiers shot one after another twenty-six students they found in a room there.... When will the time come when all men have equal rights?

Wagner was not the only exile after 1849. England and America in particular received a stream of disappointed German radical and liberal refugees. Ordinary folk left the country too: about one in twenty of the people of Baden emigrated after 1849. Political reasons along with economic hardship combined now to encourage emigration instead of revolution. By the end of July 1849, all organized resistance to the Prussian-led restoration had collapsed. Only in the Habsburg Empire did the embers of revolution still glow (see below).

Reasons for the failure of revolution in Germany

After 1849, cynics argued that the events of 1848 had been a "pantomime revolution," or that it was nothing more than an academic theory. However, the failure of the attempt to create a liberal united Germany had deeper causes than the shallowness of the revolutionaries in 1848.

The old order could rely on the social composition of the Prussian army in particular to provide a reliable instrument of reaction. The opposition was divided: many liberals feared uncontrolled disorder more than the reactionaries. The radicals had few levers of power in their hands. The Frankfurt Parliament was not only split between conservatives, liberals and radicals, it also had no power base. The Frankfurt Parliament depended on the individual states to turn its votes into reality. This was something they increasingly refused to do as 1848 went by. German nationalism also began to rear an ugly head. Too many deputies put national interests above liberal principles, as indicated by the war against the Danes and the attitude to the Poles.

Failure was was by no means total, however. Certain important liberal ideas, such as some form of constitution, were conceded in almost every German state. Censorship did not return to the stifling norms of pre-March 1848. Above all, German unity came about only twenty years later. Ironically, it was the Prussian reactionary, Otto von Bismarck, who had learned from the mistakes of the Frankfurt Parliament that such a question as national

RIGHT **Nationalism was a great revolutionary force in the nineteenth century. Ruling over at least fourteen different ethnic groups during this period, the Habsburg emperor had no choice but to resist the spread of nationalism.**

LEFT **Otto von Bismarck (1815–98) learned from the downfall of Metternich to shape a new type of effective counter-revolutionary policy mixing nationalism, social reform and cynical power politics.**

unity was "not decided by speeches and resolutions, but by blood and iron."

THE HABSBURG LANDS IN 1848

After 1815, the Austrian Chancellor Clemens von Metternich made the Habsburg Empire into the bastion of reaction. By 1848, however, nationalist tensions among the many nationalities of the Empire, as well as social and economic issues and political radicalism, were threatening to topple his system.

When news of the February Revolution in France reached Vienna, the elderly Metternich declared, "The situation was just what it was in 1792." It became clear within days that the revolutionaries were

strong in Vienna as well as Paris. In fact, France was less of a threat to the old order in Europe than its own subjects.

The failure of the French Republic to march to the support of revolutionaries across Europe in the style of the Jacobins was a relief to monarchs, and surprised subject peoples everywhere from Italy to Poland. The Poles especially had enjoyed close relations with French radicals. Gallant Polish revolts in Russian-occupied Poland in 1830 and then in Austria's Polish province of Galicia in 1846 had led to outpourings of romantic sympathy from the French, not least the poet Alphonse Lamartine, who became foreign minister in 1848. But the Polish question also united the monarchs in Berlin, Vienna and St Petersburg. Nicholas I of Russia was certainly prepared to fight to keep his Polish territories, and the rest of Europe knew it. When a delegation of Polish émigrés came to see Lamartine in Paris to ask for help in liberating their country, he told them, "We love Poland, we love Italy, we love all the oppressed nations, but most

of all we love France." Even reactionary monarchs had little to fear in reality from the Second French Republic.

Austrian generals had learnt lessons in Galicia in 1846 that they would belatedly apply in Italy and other parts of the Empire after hesitations in 1848. Faced by a revolt of the Polish gentry in February 1846, the Austrian regime encouraged the peasantry of Galicia to revolt against their masters in turn. The Austrian Commissioner in Tarnów paid the peasants on a per capita basis for any rebel gentleman they brought in. Eventually, the government became alarmed by the very success of its setting of peasants against lords, as the peasants came to see their strength. One German-speaking lord wrote, "I see in the present condition of Galicia, the first victory of Communism; others must follow.... The peasants, who in their looting and brigandage have met no resistance, have come to realize, or even over-rate, their collective strength."

The eruption of revolution inside the Habsburg Empire came among peoples divided by class and nation. At first it seemed that the radicals could make the best use of this reality, but only a few months later things looked very different as nation fought nation. There were fourteen different linguistic groups inside the Empire. Once their sense of identity was aroused, cooperation between them was virtually impossible.

The revolution

By 1848, Metternich's age (he was in his mid-seventies) counted against him. His Emperor, Ferdinand, was mentally subnormal, and various Habsburg archdukes and their wives hoped to gain influence by throwing Metternich to the wolves. Appeasing widespread hostility towards the architect of the pre-March system seemed to make sense.

With astonishing rapidity, the imperial court conceded to the radical demands from the streets. A Citizens' Guard of 30,000 was formed along with a student Academic Legion of 7,000. On 15 March, a constitution was promised. Censorship

"If the revolution is victorious here [Vienna], it can regain its momentum, but if the revolution is defeated, then Germany will be as quiet as a tomb."
ROBERT BLUM, A RADICAL DEPUTY IN THE FRANKFURT PARLIAMENT, WRITING TO HIS WIFE ON 20 OCTOBER 1848

TOP **A barricade in Vienna in 1848. While events in Paris sparked the wave of revolutions in 1848, the fall in Vienna of Metternich, the architect of reaction, helped to sustain it.**

ABOVE **A parade of the Citizens' Guard in Vienna on 13 March 1848. As elsewhere in Europe the formation of a citizens' militia was a key step in the revolution in 1848.**

was abolished and the remains of feudal serfdom were quickly done away with. Within a matter of weeks, the gentry and aristocratic-dominated traditional estates of Bohemia and Hungary had voted for the abolition of obligatory labour (the so-called *robot*) so as to put themselves on the right side of the peasants.

Emancipation from the remaining religious and national restrictions was

embodied in the prominent part played in the events of 13–15 March by Adolf Fischhof, a young Jewish surgeon and liberal who addressed a crowd of mainly students and assured them that together the various peoples of the Austrian Empire would promote liberty. It was a short-lived dream.

Nationalities in conflict

The Frankfurt Parliament expected to include the German-speaking parts of the Habsburg empire in its united Germany. But the imperial court could hardly agree to a division of its empire with one part disappearing into the new Germany and the other falling into the hands of the increasingly republican Hungarians. At the same time, the Frankfurt Parliament forgot that the Czechs of Bohemia and Moravia, parts of the old German Confederation, would not want to lose their identity inside a new united Germany.

It was Hungarian nationalism that presented the Habsburgs with their greatest challenge. On 15 March, the Diet put forward the Fifteen Demands of the Hungarian People. The first twelve (the most important) were: "1. Freedom of the press and abolition of censorship. 2. A responsible ministry based in Budapest. 3. An annual parliament in Budapest. 4. Political and religious equality before the law. 5. A national guard. 6 Taxes to be paid by all without exemption. 7. The abolition of serfdom. 8. Trial by jury. 9. A national bank. 10. Soldiers to take an oath to the constitution; foreign soldiers to be removed from Hungary; Hungarian soldiers not to be sent abroad. 11. Release of political prisoners. 12. Union with Transylvania.

These demands were broadly enacted in the so-called March Laws that reduced the relationship of the Habsburg Emperor with Hungary to a purely personal union. In Budapest the public was convinced that a new liberal age was about to dawn in Hungary. However, although the Hungarians were anxious to demand many liberal rights for themselves they were unwilling to extend them to the non-Magyar half of the population. Nationalism was a much more powerful force than liberalism in Hungary. Despite the liberal March Laws, the Hungarian rebels showed no sympathy for the non-Magyar peoples who lived in the traditional kingdom of Hungary. For instance, speaking Hungarian was a qualification for election. Denying participation to Slovaks, the Romanians of Transylvania, Croats and other minorities was the Achilles heel of the Hungarian revolution.

While Hungarians effectively nullified the powers of their Habsburg King, they could not guarantee the loyalties of other subject peoples inside the half of the Habsburg dominions known as the Crown Lands of St Stephan. The Croats in particular resented the Hungarians' assertion of domination over their part of the territory. A Croat soldier, Jellaćić, put himself at the head of a loyalist movement to the Habsburgs. Denounced as a traitor to Hungary by the liberal-nationalist regime that had established itself in Budapest, Jellaćić marshalled his forces to support other imperial commanders. But, at first, it was the new, largely volunteer Hungarian forces that seemed to pose a greater threat to the vestiges of imperial authority.

Creeping restoration in Austria and Bohemia

As the spring progressed, the Habsburg court began to recover its nerve. Neither the constitution proclaimed on 25 April nor the election law announced on 9 May were satisfactory to the bulk of the Viennese liberals and radicals. A senate nominated by the Emperor could block the lower house's proposals and it was to be elected indirectly by property-owners. The democrats were outraged. Crowds demonstrated for universal suffrage and a single popularly elected chamber. The Emperor Ferdinand conceded this before fleeing to Innsbruck.

Vienna became radicalized. But when the Constituent Assembly finally met in Vienna in late July, it became apparent that the countryside had elected a more conservative set of deputies than had the

big cities. By 23 August, the more moderate reformers felt strong enough to use the bourgeois civil guard to disperse the unemployed workers whose public works had been cancelled.

By then, the imperial general Windischgrätz had already captured Prague and suppressed the Czech radicals in June 1848 and the Austrian Field Marshal Radetzky (immortalized in the march by Johann Strauss) had defeated the Piedmontese at Custozza. Vienna's turn for the restoration of imperial order looked imminent. Ferdinand even briefly returned to the capital in August, but banking on support

LEFT **Franz Joseph I (1848–1916), who became Emperor at the age of eighteen and almost lived to see the monarchy's fall at the end of the First World War. He was the only focus of loyalty of his empire.**

from the Hungarians who were by now in open rebellion, radicals seized power in Vienna in the name of the Central Committee of Democratic Clubs on 23 August. Their domination lasted only until the imperial army entered the city after a siege on 20 November.

As in Italy and Poland, so in Hungary the Habsburgs found that the slogans of liberalism and nationalism were loudest from the mouths of the nobility and the gentry. The imperial Chancellor, Schwarzenberg, admitted, "One can be of old lineage, have an old title, and call oneself an aristocrat, but still be a supporter of revolutionary subversion."

The restoration of Habsburg authority depended almost entirely on the army. Although the aristocracy were losers from revolution, most noblemen showed little initiative in resisting change. In fact even the strict hereditary principle was abandoned when Ferdinand's eighteen-year-old nephew, Franz Josef, was installed as Emperor in December 1848, in the hope of putting someone with a greater sense of

direction in place on the throne. Schwarzenberg wrote to his brother-in-law, Field Marshal Windischgrätz, "I know of not a dozen men of our class with sufficient political wisdom or the necessary experience to whom an important share of power could be entrusted.... To rely on an ally as weak as our aristocracy unfortunately is, would be to damage our cause more than to help it."

The troops proved able to turn the tide against urban revolutionaries. The soldiers were drawn from the poor of town and country alike and had little sympathy for revolutionaries whose leaders and spokesmen at any rate came from the better off.

The failure to mobilize the peasantry was the key to the revolutionaries' failure in Austria. Some had recognized this by the autumn of 1848. Hans Kudlich, for example, who was sent out into the countryside in September to explain the Viennese rebels' scheme to abolish serfdom, found little sympathy among the rural population: "In October [1848] we were punished for our sins of omission.... The Viennese party of movement had only agitated in Vienna. It had built up the revolutionary explosive force [there] to the most extreme levels but had neglected the hinterland, the provinces completely."

Hungary defeated with Russian help

Whatever their faults with regard to the insensitive handling of the non-Magyars, the Hungarians showed remarkable

ABOVE **Lajos Kossuth (1802–94) was the chief architect of Hungarian independence from the Habsburgs. With his fiery oratory he resisted compromise after fighting began, but his fate was to spend more than forty years in exile after 1849. Huge crowds gathered when he was buried in Hungary.**

RIGHT **Faced by a huge Russian army, the Hungarian forces were obliged to capitulate at Villagos in August 1849. The Austrians ignored the clemency offered by the Russians and executed thirteen Hungarian generals and the Prime Minister when they fell into their hands after the surrender.**

solidarity. Even though there were differences between the republican political leader Kossuth and the conservative monarchist general Görgey, the Hungarian armies put up such resistance to the imperial forces that it was only when a huge Russian army of 300,000 men intervened in 1849 that defeat became inevitable.

The role of the Croats and another nationalities in helping to suppress the Hungarian revolution caused a backlash against them among revolutionaries and their sympathizers across Europe. Engels summed up the resentment against "reactionary peoples" on the part of those who saw their own nations as "progressive:" "There is no country in Europe which does not have in some corner or other one or several ruined fragments of peoples.... These relics of a nation mercilessly tram-

ABOVE **Nationalist and liberal stirrings appeared among other peoples in 1848, such as the Romanians. Influenced by French ideas, young radicals, such as Ana Ipatescu pictured here, led demonstrations for independence from Hungarian and Russian domination.**

pled under foot in the course of history... always become fanatical standard-bearers of counter-revolution."

The antagonism of Marxists towards some nations helped to explain the slow progress of their Socialism after 1848. In any case, cynical supporters of the Emperor did more to promote radical reform than any of his opponents ever had. In February 1850, Windischgrätz told Franz Josef: "The most pronounced Communist has not yet dared to demand what Your Majesty's Government now enacts." It was not strictly true, but it had abolished forced labour and let peasants keep land they formerly tenanted.

The failure of revolution in the Habsburg lands

If German nationalism helped to stifle liberalism and radicalism north of Austria in 1849, then nationalist divisions paved the way for restoration inside Austria. Amid the cacophony of demands and counter-claims, the Habsburgs and their army represented a clear-cut proposition, with force to back it up. The intervention of the Russian army confirmed the defeat of the revolution.

After Habsburg defeats in war at the hands of Bismarck's Prussia in 1866, Franz Josef had to concede to the Hungarians the kind of quasi-independent stature most of them had sought in 1848. The so-called Compromise of 1867 even saw the return to high office of previous rebels such

as Gyula Andrassy. Unfortunately, this Hungary proved no more willing to concede political equality to the non-Hungarian majority than had the old one in 1848. In 1918, Hungary was dismembered to make way for national states. It was the final fruit of 1848's springtime of the peoples, though by then it tasted sour.

The revolt of the Paris Commune in 1871 was the last dramatic gasp of the French revolutionary tradition in the nineteenth century. Although the revolution was relatively short-lived, the myth of the Commune endured for decades: for radicals it became a symbol of martyrdom, while for reactionaries it represented a nightmare. Its failure marked the defeat of the radical city by the conservative countryside.

The Paris Commune

The Second Empire, established by Napoleon III in 1852 (*see page 101*), came to a rather abrupt end in 1870 following France's defeat in war against Germany. The conflict had begun on 19 July 1870, after Napoleon III – who was worried about Prussia's growing power – protested when the Spanish throne had been offered to a prince of the ruling house of Prussia. Weeks of heavy fighting resulted in a string of defeats for the French. The Prussian troops, who had begun their march on Paris in August, scored their most decisive victory on 2 September at Sedan, where Napoleon III was forced to capitulate. News of the defeat provoked the politicians in Paris to declare an end to Napoleon III's regime and to establish a provisional government, with Adolphe Thiers at its head. The Third Republic, proclaimed on 4 September, tried to rally the defence of France, looking back to the example of the First Republic eighty years

"Paris goes her own way. France, irritated, is forced to follow; later she calms down and applauds; it is one of the forms of our national life. A coach passes flying a flag; it comes from Paris. The flag is no longer a flag, it is a flame, and the whole trail of human gunpowder catches fire behind it." VICTOR HUGO, 1867

earlier: "The Republic was victorious over the invasion of 1792. The Republic is declared." But the dearth of trained soldiers and equipment made resistance to the Germans very difficult, and by 19 September the German army had surrounded and laid siege to Paris.

Paris under siege

The siege was the essential ingredient in the radicalization of the city's population. The famine and other burdens reduced many of the recently prosperous to penury, even prostitution. Edmond Goncourt recalled hearing a respectable girl's murmur: "Monsieur, would you like to come upstairs with me...for a piece of bread."

Some 350,000 men formed a National Guard to defend the city; most of them depended on their soldier's pay for their livelihood because the economy had collapsed during the siege. Attempts to break out of the city failed on 27 October 1870 and 19 January 1871, and provoked demonstrations at the Hôtel de Ville. Already the suspicion was spreading that politicians outside Paris were less devoted to resistance than the people of the capital.

Distrust of the Parisians was common to the Republic's governing class, many of whom – including the new Prime Minister, Adolphe Thiers – could still remember the June days of 1848 (*see pages 100–1*) and were haunted by the fear of another workers' revolt. In fact, Napoleon III's regime had started to rebuild Paris, partly to

ABOVE **Elections to the general council of the Seine *départément* were held on 26 March 1871. This cartoon, entitled "Le jugement de Paris," shows the choice between the wholesome young Republic or the decrepit figures of Monarchy and Empire.**

reduce its revolutionary potential. His prefect of Paris, Baron Haussmann, had designed broad new boulevards that would make the building of barricades difficult. During the reconstruction in the 1860s, scores of thousands of poorer Parisians were pushed out of their traditional homes in the centre of the city to new, ill-planned suburbs. During the siege they came back, with their resentments, inside the city walls.

Paris against the rest of France

Despite the efforts of the Parisians to hold out against the besieging army, the French government felt it was futile to continue the war and signed an armistice with Germany on 28 January 1871. This treaty brought an end to the siege but imposed humiliating terms on France, including the surrender of Alsace-Lorraine and a crippling war indemnity of 5 million francs.

France went to the polls on 8 February to vote for a new government that would (in accordance with the armistice) take responsibility for accepting or rejecting Germany's terms for peace. The results revealed how different Paris was from the rest of France. Paris elected a group of radicals to the Assembly, while monarchists dominated the elections elsewhere. The monarchist majority wanted peace with the Germans, whatever the humiliation.

To achieve this peace, the Prime Minister, Thiers, had to disarm the National Guard in Paris. He ordered the Guard to hand over its artillery to the regular army on 18 March 1871. But he had already antagonized the Guard by cutting its pay, which hit the poor much as the abolition of national workshops had done in 1848 (*see pages 100–1*). The poor had also been hit when the new National Assembly voted to end the wartime moratorium on debts and rents. Thus the people of Montmartre, especially the women,

rallied to stop their cannons being hauled away. Bloody clashes occurred between the army and the people. The mayor of Montmartre, Georges Clemenceau, was shocked by the violence of the outburst:

The mob which filled the courtyard burst into the street in the grip of some kind of frenzy. Amongst them were chasseurs, soldiers of the line, National Guards, women and children. All were shrieking like wild beasts without realizing what they were doing. I observed then that pathological phenomenon which might be called blood lust. A breath of madness seemed to have passed over this mob...

Several hours of fighting and rioting followed, at the end of which the government troops appeared to be no nearer to capturing the guns of Montmartre. Thiers decided to withdraw his forces and remove the Government from the capital city to Versailles. The rebels in Paris, meanwhile, voted to revive the Commune (on the model of 1792) in defiance of the government.

Only four members of the Commune represented the recently founded Marxist Workingman's International. Twenty-five out of the Commune's ninety members worked with their hands, but mainly as skilled artisans. They were outnumbered by professionals, such as

ABOVE **The artillery at Montmartre, back in government hands, trained on the city below.**

journalists, radical doctors and teachers. But two-thirds or more of the Commune's members would have described themselves as the heirs of the Jacobins of 1793. Karl Marx himself did not at first recognize the Communards as the proletarian revolutionaries of his future Communist society, but his sympathy for their struggle against the French bourgeoisie encouraged the romanticization of the Communard as a premature Communist revolutionary.

The ideals of the Commune

Along with renewed antagonism towards an insensitive regime led by Thiers, which seemed determined to cut the main source of livelihood for the capital's poor, nationalist resentment at the willingness of the government to accept defeat by the Germans was the key element in the revolt of the Paris Commune. But it showed no nostalgia for past Napoleonic glory. The debacle of Napoleon III had undoubtedly tarnished respect for his uncle's memory, and the Commune ordered the demolition of Napoleon's column in the Place Vendôme on 12 April 1871, describing it as: "a monument of barbarism, a symbol of brute force and false glory, an affirmation of militarism, a denial of international law, a permanent insult directed at the conquered by their conquerors, a perpetual attack upon one of the three great principles of the French republic."

LEFT **The toppled statue of Napoleon III in Place Vendôme in Paris, April 1871.**

INSET **Parisians pulling down a statue of King Louis XVI from the same spot in Place Vendôme during the French Revolution, about ninety years before the Commune.**

The Commune emerged in such confused conditions and was so short-lived that it had no opportunity to develop a clear programme, let alone enact it. Nonetheless, certain reforms *were* introduced: employers were no longer to have the right to fine their workers, and, most strikingly, "widows" of men killed in the siege were to receive pensions whether they had actually been married or not. Night work was restricted and a moratorium on debts to last three years was enacted.

Nationalism and popular local government rather than social revolution were the rallying cries of the Commune, but the flight from Paris of Thiers' government and most of the wealthy members of society created a new social situation. In the absence of many of the bourgeois elite, Paris fell into the hands of members of the lower orders, who had little experience of administration. Marx noted that the

Communards lacked effective leadership. "They should at once have marched on Versailles," he wrote, before Thiers had time to complete amassing his army. But the Communards' revolutionary hostility to rank meant that their forces lacked an effective commander-in-chief who might have seized the moment. Spontaneity without strategy was bound to fail.

Thiers' strategy

From March 1871, two rival authorities existed in France, the national government at Versailles and the Commune in Paris, each with its own armed force and each

jockeying for political power. Half-hearted negotiations between the two authorities did take place, but when these broke down Thiers decided to attempt once more to retake the capital. He brought up an army of provincial Frenchmen, suspicious and resentful of what they saw as arrogant Parisians trying to dictate politics to France as so often before. Naturally the Germans looked favourably on any bloodletting among the French that would weaken them further.

On 2 April, government troops seized Courbevoie, a suburb of Paris, and began a new siege of Paris. For several weeks

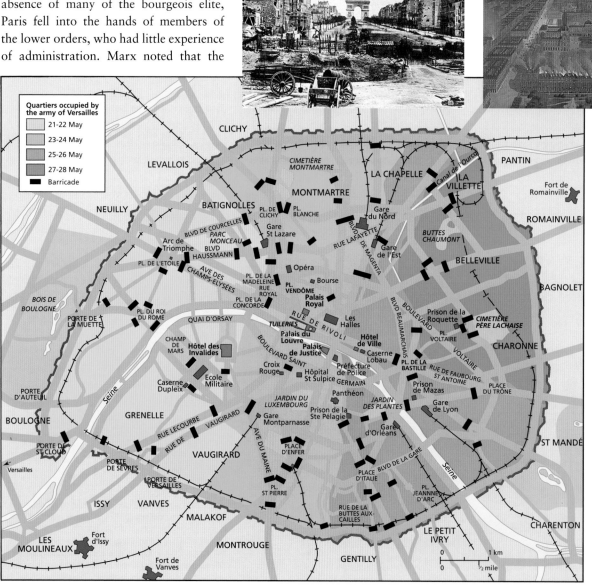

Quartiers occupied by the army of Versailles
- 21–22 May
- 23–24 May
- 25–26 May
- 27–28 May
- Barricade

ABOVE LEFT **The destruction at Porte Maillot on 29 May 1871, at the end of the "bloody week."**

ABOVE RIGHT **Paris is set ablaze on the evening of 24–25 May 1871.**

LEFT **After breaking through the fortifications that had protected Paris during the German siege of 1870–71, the army took a week to retake Paris from the Communards.**

FAR LEFT **Edouard Manet's painting of the execution of Communards. The newspaper Le Figaro demanded that: "The people of Paris must submit to the laws of war. Mercy is madness."**

LEFT **Coffins with the bodies of those killed during the fighting in Paris in May 1871.**

Government troops bombarded the fortresses protecting the capital, taking them one by one, and by 21 May the army was able to force its way into Paris through an undefended point to the south-west of the city. Over the next seven days, known as the "bloody week," the army methodically reconquered the capital from west to east. Each *quartier* defended itself, giving the army the opportunity to pick off district after district. In the course of the struggle, the Communards set fire to ancient buildings like the Tuileries and the Hôtel de Ville. They also shot their hostages, including the Archbishop of Paris, Georges Darboy. Given the anti-clerical tradition of revolution in France he might have seemed an ideal reactionary scapegoat, but Darboy himself was disliked by French conservatives: he had voted against Papal Infallibility at the Vatican Council two years earlier and was something of a liberal. The Communards ensured that Paris would not have another liberal archbishop for almost a century.

Savagery

The respectable bourgeoisie outside Paris were outraged by reports of arson and vandalism by the Communards, as well as their shooting of hostages; so the brutal reprisals carried out by Thiers' troops were widely endorsed. Even a progressive such as the writer Emile Zola was caught up in the hysterical fear inspired by the breakdown of public order in Paris. He described the savage suppression of the Communards but justified it by citing their alleged depravity:

The slaughter was atrocious. Our soldiers...meted out implacable justice in the streets. Any man caught with a weapon in his hand was shot. So corpses lay scattered everywhere, thrown into corners, decomposing with astonishing rapidity, which was doubtless due to the drunken state of these men when they were hit. For six days Paris has been nothing but a huge cemetery.

"The working men's Paris, in the act of its heroic self-holocaust, involved in its flames buildings and monuments.... The bourgeoisie ...looks complacently upon the wholesale massacre after the battle but is convulsed by horror at the desecration of brick and mortar." KARL MARX, *THE CIVIL WAR IN FRANCE*, 1871

As many as 20,000 Communards – including women and children – were killed as the army fought its way forward through the streets of Paris, while another 40,000 insurgents were taken prisoner. About half of these were released soon enough, but 10,000 were transported to the colonies, including the remote New Caledonia in the South Pacific.

Paris may not have hosted another revolutionary revolt, but fear of it and bitter memories of the Commune's failure ran through the coming decades. The Commune lasted only seventy-three days, but its example was long-lasting.

The bloody suppression of the Paris Commune had wide ramifications. For all the bitterness stored up among the surviving defeated and their sympathizers, it taught a terrible lesson for the future: urban revolutionaries often lack the numbers and power to sweep aside the conservative classes. Reform rather than revolution came increasingly to be the motto of the radicals, both in France and elsewhere in western Europe.

KEY EVENTS

1870 2 September
Napoleon III defeated at Sedan
4 September
Third Republic proclaimed
25 September
Beginning of siege of Paris by Germans
27 October
First radical disorders inside Paris
1871 5 January
Germans begin to bombard Paris
18 January
Failed sortie against Germans outside Paris
28 January
France signs armistice with Germany
6 February
General elections produce reactionary majority; Paris votes for Left
1 March
National Assembly ratifies treaty with Germany
18 March
Thiers attempts to seize guns at Montmartre
28 March
Election of Paris Commune
19 April
Paris Commune appeals for support to other cities
16 May
Napoleon I's statue in Place Vendôme is toppled
21 May
French army attacks Paris; "Bloody week" begins
29 May
Resistance ends

The High Tide of Revolution

The first half of the twentieth century witnessed a tide of revolutionary hopes that utopian change could be achieved. Even before the First World War broke out in 1914, revolutionary turmoil seemed inevitable as economic and social change accelerated across much of the northern hemisphere. Russia's Tsar barely survived one revolution in 1905 before being toppled forever in 1917, while both China and Mexico sank into decades of upheaval after 1910. The success of the Russian Communists in taking and holding power and then establishing a completely new socio-economic order produced enthusiastic imitators (and enraged opponents) around the globe. The Marxist model of revolution became the dominant one for much of the twentieth century.

OPPOSITE **A Soviet revolutionary poster of 1917.**

Urbanization, poor living and working conditions, inflation, food shortages and the hardships of the First World War all helped to create widespread disaffection across the Russian Empire with the autocratic rule of Tsar Nicholas II. The result was the outbreak in 1917 of the most profound and far-reaching revolution since the French Revolution of 1789. Its consequences have reverberated around the world throughout the twentieth century.

The Russian Revolutions

At the start of the twentieth century, many observers thought the Russian Empire was set on a period of growth. Industrialization was under way, new factories were built and the rail system was extended. The already vast empire began to expand further in the Far East, and the new emperor, Nicholas II, inaugurated the massive trans-Siberian Railway project to link European Russia with Vladivostok.

There was also a shadow side to these developments, however. Although Russia boasted some of the most modern factories in the world, the bulk of her population remained illiterate peasants. The emancipation of the peasants from serfdom in 1861 had been a concession of great political significance, but failed in practical terms to calm the uneasy social situation. Migration into the new urban industrial centres, such as the capital St Petersburg, created problems for the authorities. The very dynamism of the Russian economy was destabilizing to a political system whose authority rested on the divine right of the Tsar to rule without any restraint by his subjects. Even the rich had no right to participate in politics, unlike their counterparts across liberal Europe to the West.

Russia was a strange and unstable mixture of the old and the new by 1900. Primitive agriculture was practised next to modern factories. Ancient rituals of the Orthodox Church existed side by side with an intellectual life that discussed atheism and every new ideology from the West.

Censorship interfered with Russia's blooming literary life but permitted "works of economics by Dr Marx." The pace of chance and its lack of clear direction contributed to the general sense of foreboding.

Premonitions of doom

Disaster overshadowed the start of the reign of the young emperor, Nicholas II. Poor crowd control at his coronation in 1896 led to a stampede of people trying to grab the free souvenirs on offer and a murderous crush resulted in the deaths of hundreds of people. Unlike his stern father, the new Tsar lacked the personality of an autocrat but he was determined not to give up any of the powers he had inherited. In December 1904, Nicholas II insisted, "I shall never, under any circumstances, agree to a representative form of government because I consider it harmful to the people whom God has entrusted to my care."

But events were moving beyond his control. He was a limited man, devoted to

"The time has come, an avalanche is moving down on us, a mighty wholesome storm is brewing, which... will sweep away from our society its idleness, indifference, prejudice against work, and foul ennui."
BARON TUZENBACHIN FROM ANTON CHEKHOV'S PLAY, *THREE SISTERS*, 1901

his family, but unintellectual and incapable of learning from his mistakes or trying to win over the populace. An overconfident assumption of European superiority led Russia to challenge Japan in February 1904 for domination in the Far East. Russia was unprepared for such a war, however, and it proved deeply unpopular with the Russian people. Unexpected and costly defeats shattered imperial prestige at home as much as abroad. Domestic discontents reared their head.

Bloody Sunday: 9 January 1905

Defeat in the war against Japan combined with bad economic conditions to promote general unrest. Inflation cut into the wages of the poor, and wretched living conditions added to their grievances. Nevertheless, outright opposition to the regime was crystallized only by the events in St Petersburg of Sunday 9 January 1905.

Led by a priest, Father George Gapon, a gigantic but peaceful demonstration of workers from the industrial suburbs came to the Winter Palace, the seat of the imperial government, carrying icons and portraits of Nicholas II, requesting that the Tsar hear their petition. Among their demands were a constituent assembly, universal suffrage, improvements in living conditions and an end to the war with Japan. The Tsar was away from the city, however. Panicked by the scale of the demonstration, his guards opened fire on it and the Tsar's loyal cavalry, the Cossacks, charged into the crowd. About 200 people were killed and a further 800 injured in what became known as "Bloody Sunday." The shock of the bloodshed did more than any single event to smash the popular

image of the Tsar as the benevolent father of his people. Nicholas II may not have ordered the shooting, but as the head of the government he was held responsible.

Bloody Sunday provoked outrage: the following day workers in Moscow walked out in protest against the massacre, and strike action quickly spread to Warsaw, Vilna, Kharkov and other cities across the empire. By the end of January, over 400,000 workers were on strike, and before long unrest had spread to the rural populations. Furthermore, a number of small-scale mutinies took place among the army and navy – the most famous being the seizure of the battleship, *Potemkin*, the flagship of the Black Sea fleet.

Russia in chaos

Ironically, although Russia had a long tradition of revolutionary activists, few played an important role in the events of 1905. For almost a century, the Tsarist

regime had faced trouble from revolutionary groups, many of whom, like the Decembrists in 1825 (*see box*), were influenced by foreign models. Suppression had forced critics abroad or underground. Occasional assassinations of imperial officials created a sense of tension, but their influence on the mass of the rural population was slight. In 1905, underground

RUSSIA'S REVOLUTIONARY TRADITION

The autocratic system of the Russian Tsars had been shaken by individual acts of revolution throughout the nineteenth century, of which the most important were:

1825 14 December
A group of army officers in St Petersburg revolted against the new Tsar, Nicholas I, under the influence of French republican ideas. The conspirators intended to establish a constitution and abolish serfdom. However, loyal troops suppressed the mutiny (*see picture below*) and a prolonged period of repression started.

1848–49
Tsar Nicholas I's suppression of political opposition was such that the revolutionary movement affecting the rest of Europe (*see pages 96–111*) did not spread to Russia. Some political meetings did take place, however, and in 1849 a group of radical intellectuals known as the Petrashevsky Circle (which included the young writer, Fyodor Dostoevksy) was arrested.

1866
The first of several assassination attempts on the life of Tsar Alexander II.

1875–76
The so-called Land and Liberty movement tried to arouse peasant unrest.

1879
The formation of the terrorist revolutionary group, the People's Will.

1881
On 1 March, Alexander II was assassinated by a bomb thrown at his carriage. Instead of continuing his father's reforms, Alexander III resorted once more to repression.

ABOVE **Demonstrators fall as Cossacks charge into the crowd outside the Winter Palace on Bloody Sunday, 9 January 1905.**

INSET **Father George Gapon, who led the ill-fated demonstration. One commentator remarked of him: "For each of his words men were ready to give their lives."**

LEFT **The famous (and historically inaccurate) scene of loyal troops shooting at the crowds on the Odessa steps from Sergei Eisenstein's film *Battleship Potemkin*, which dramatized the mutiny on board one of the Tsar's naval vessels in 1905.**

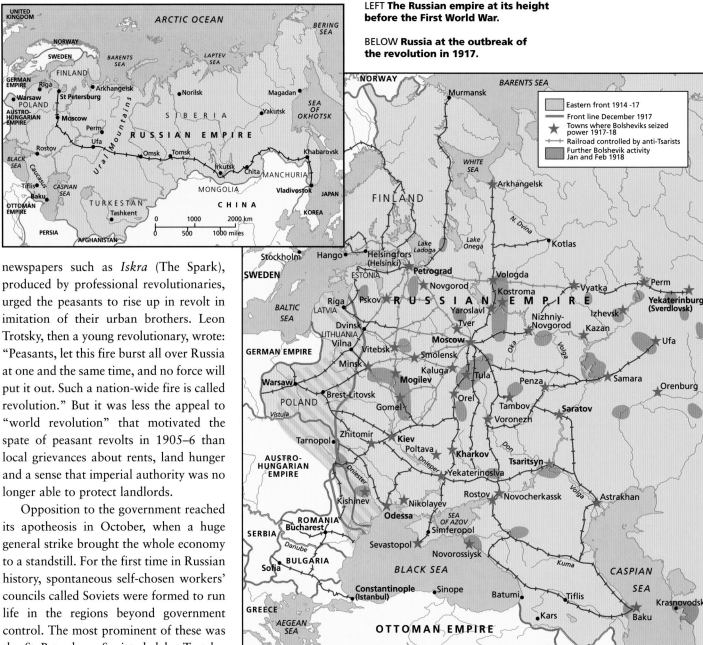

LEFT **The Russian empire at its height before the First World War.**

BELOW **Russia at the outbreak of the revolution in 1917.**

newspapers such as *Iskra* (The Spark), produced by professional revolutionaries, urged the peasants to rise up in revolt in imitation of their urban brothers. Leon Trotsky, then a young revolutionary, wrote: "Peasants, let this fire burst all over Russia at one and the same time, and no force will put it out. Such a nation-wide fire is called revolution." But it was less the appeal to "world revolution" that motivated the spate of peasant revolts in 1905–6 than local grievances about rents, land hunger and a sense that imperial authority was no longer able to protect landlords.

Opposition to the government reached its apotheosis in October, when a huge general strike brought the whole economy to a standstill. For the first time in Russian history, spontaneous self-chosen workers' councils called Soviets were formed to run life in the regions beyond government control. The most prominent of these was the St Petersburg Soviet, led by Trotsky. The government tolerated this Soviet until December, when the leaders were arrested and put behind bars (Trotsky was exiled to Siberia but he managed to escape abroad). This was followed by an armed uprising in Moscow, organized by the Moscow Soviet, that was violently suppressed after ten days by the army. Over 1,000 people died in the insurrection, and numerous others were killed in reprisals.

Had the army or police been unable or unwilling to stand firm, the Tsar would have faced disaster, for there was no social group (not even the rich) organized to support the system. Fortunately for the Tsar, though, the army remained largely loyal to the Crown. Relying on royal troops and the firm direction of imperial officials, the government was able to put down the disorders. But calm returned only after significant concessions had been made. At the end of October 1905, the Tsar reluctantly agreed in his so-called October Manifesto to permit the election of a parliament, the Duma. The Tsar insisted on keeping his right to rule by decree whenever he considered that a state of emergency existed, however, which meant that he could flout the will of the Duma as he saw fit. The Duma, like the local councils or *zemstvos*, exercised little power and soon enjoyed little respect. The new Prime Minister, Pyotr Stolypin, tried to manipulate the elections to achieve the most favourable result for the Tsar, but a few revolutionary critics continued to be elected.

RIGHT **"Death stalks the barricades."** This cartoon from 1905, inspired by the fighting that took place in Moscow prefigured the terrible cost of the revolution and civil war after 1917.

Even after Stolypin had been assassinated in 1911, economic recovery and heavy-handed police measures seemed sufficient to counter any threat to the system, although revolutionary terrorists continued to take their toll on its officials. The reliability of the army and police as pillars of the system misled Nicholas II into over-confidence. Apparent calm after 1906 encouraged him to enter World War I in 1914 on the side of the Allies with much the same optimism as he had against Japan ten years earlier. But Germany was to be an even more deadly enemy than Japan.

War against Germany

If anyone thought that war would rally people to the Tsarist system they were soon disillusioned, as much by the incompetence of the war effort as by any lack of patriotism among the millions of peasants who joined the army. As early as August 1915, the Minister of War, Aleksei Polivanov, painted a grim picture of breakdown: "The army is no longer retreating but simply fleeing.... The slightest rumour about the enemy, the appearance of an insignificant German detachment leads to panic.... Headquarters has completely lost its head. Contradictory orders, absence of a plan, feverish changes of commanding officers, and general confusion upset even the most courageous men...." Russia had been ill-prepared for war. The economy was simply unable to cope with the demands for munitions and food at the front, and the disorganization led to

massive demoralization among the troops. The civilian population was also suffering: food and fuel was in short supply, inflation rocketed and refugees from the fighting flooded to the already overcrowded cities.

But the height of folly was reached by the Tsar in 1915 when, spurred on by his wife, he took active personal command of the Russian troops fighting Germany. As his horrified ministers recognized, this made the Tsar personally liable for any defeats – for victories were not in sight – and left the unpopular Tsarina in charge of day-to-day government in Petrograd, which had a disastrous effect on public opinion. It also meant that Nicholas II left the capital to go to army headquarters at Mogilev far away in Belorussia. The immense challenge of the First World War showed that Nicholas II lacked any of the attributes of an autocratic ruler. His father, Alexander III, had not been particularly intelligent but he had been decisive and his physique was impressive. Nicholas II, on the other hand, neither radiated natural authority nor was able to find ministers who could. In fact, he was deeply suspicious of sharing his authority with any of his subjects. Instead of delegating power to those able to exercise it, Nicholas II tried to run everything himself, even doing without a private secretary.

RIGHT **A satire of 1916 showing the Tsar and Tsarina as puppets in the hands of the evil Rasputin. Rasputin's grisly murder by three ultra-conservatives in December 1916 did not stop the regime's slide to ruin – in fact it probably only discredited the Tsar further.**

By the middle of the war, things were so bad that the Minister of the Navy, Prince Shcherbatov, wrote: "the government enjoys the confidence neither of the Sovereign, nor the army, nor the towns, nor the *zemstvos*, nor the nobility, nor the merchants, nor the working men – such a government cannot perform its duties or even exist."

Alexandra and the scandal of Rasputin

The influence over Nicholas II of the German-born Tsarina, Alexandra, was disastrous. She was even less attuned than he was to the changes that had taken place in Russian society, and behaved in ways calculated to alienate it. Her fostering of the disreputable holy man, Grigory Rasputin, was a key factor in undermining the imperial family's reputation. Rasputin supposedly had powers as a faith healer, and it was in this capacity that the Tsar and Tsarina engaged him to look after their only son, Alexis, who suffered from haemophilia. But rumours of his corruption and immorality around the capital St Petersburg, out of sight of the court, led to

"The appearance in Court of Grigory Rasputin, and the influence he exercised there, mark the beginning of the decay of Russian society and the loss of prestige for the throne and for the person of the Tsar himself...." MIKHAIL RODZYANKO, CHAIRMAN OF THE DUMA, WRITING IN EXILE

scurrilous gossip. Many saw his influence as the cause of Russia's misfortunes.

Alexandra may have been innocent of any impropriety with Rasputin, but her faith in his moral authority was so at variance with public opinion that, like Marie Antoinette before her (*see page 71*), she was open to every charge. Even her protégé, the Interior Minister Aleksandr Protopopov, noted how criticism of the imperial family's private life and of government policy went hand in hand. Worse still, the imperial elite shared the disillusionment with the lower orders: "Even the very highest classes became *frondeurs* [political rebels] before the revolution; in grand salons and clubs the policy of the government received harsh and unfriendly criticism. The relations that had been formed in the Tsar's family were analyzed and talked over. Little anecdotes were passed about the head of state. Verses were composed. Many grand dukes openly attended these meetings.... A sense of danger of this sport did not awaken until the last moment."

As the war dragged on, unrest continued to mount. Huge numbers of Russian

LEFT **German soldiers stand guard over the bodies of dead Bolsheviks in May 1918.**

soldiers were killed or injured at the front, and thousands of others were taken prisoner. The growing burdens placed on frontliners provoked increasing numbers of desertions – although life in the cities was little better. The scarcity of food and other commodities had resulted in the introduction of rationing, as well as general corruption and profiteering. Disaffection caused by hunger, military humiliation, government mismanagement and economic dislocation soon led to renewed strike action that, by late 1916, had begun to creep up to pre-war levels.

The February Revolution, 1917

"Situation serious. In the capital anarchy. Government paralyzed. Transport of food and fuel completely disorganized. Public disaffection growing. On the streets chaotic shooting. Army units fire at each other. It is essential at once to entrust a person enjoying the country's confidence with the formation of new government. There should be no delay. All delay is death. I pray to God that in this hour responsibility not fall on the sovereign."

Thus read a telegram sent to the Tsar on 26 February by the President of the Duma, Mikhail Rodzyanko. The events of February 1917 caught the imperial regime by surprise, despite all the rumblings of discontent with the war situation. Even Vladimir Lenin (then an obscure middle-aged Russian exile in Switzerland) was unprepared. As late as January 1917 he

LEFT **The mutiny of the Petrograd garrison sealed the fate of the Tsarist system. Soldiers continued to play a central role in the Russian revolution after 1917.**

INSET **One of the many demonstrations held in St Petersburg during February 1917.**

told a group of Swiss radicals that he did not expect to see the fall of the Tsarist system in his lifetime: "We old-timers perhaps shall not live to see the decisive battles of the looming revolution." Six weeks later the Tsar had abdicated.

Short of food and fuel for a third winter of war, Russia's capital Petrograd (as St Petersburg had been renamed) was already discontented when a cut in the bread ration sparked demonstrations. Oblivious to the explosive atmosphere in the city, Nicholas II left the capital on 22 February for the army headquarters at Mogilev. The following day (23 February) was International Women's Day, and thousands of women processed through the city in protest against the lack of bread. Until this moment, the demonstrations had been relatively peaceful, but as local Socialist groups awoke to the gathering momentum of the situation, the protests now became better organized, acquired a more political nature – and also grew more aggressive. Looting became widespread, shops were smashed and policemen were attacked.

On the night of 25 February, a telegram arrived from the Tsar instructing the army to suppress the disorders by force. Notices were posted throughout the city, outlawing demonstrations and threatening that troops would shoot anyone who disobeyed. The posters were torn down almost immediately. Government forces imposed a curfew on 26 February, arrested known revolutionary leaders and blocked the bridges over the Neva River. But the people ignored the wishes of the Tsar. Large crowds gathered in the city centre, giving the government no choice but to bring in soldiers to disperse the mob. About forty civilians were killed in Znamenskaya Square when troops opened fire on the crowds; others were killed in incidents elsewhere.

Just when it seemed that order would be restored, members of one of the Petrograd regiments mutinied and refused to fire on an unarmed crowd. Other regiments soon followed suit, and by 28 February it was clear that the government had lost control of Petrograd.

The Tsar abdicates

Nicholas reacted very slowly to this crisis. Out of touch with what was happening, he was suddenly confronted by demands to abdicate – even from his generals. The politicians in the Duma hoped to maintain order by dropping the Tsar as an unpopular symbol. Almost forgotten in the dramatic turn of events and trapped by a train strike en route to the capital, Nicholas II had no choice but to abdicate on 2 March 1917. He had hoped to pass the throne to his brother, Michael, instead of his sickly son Alexis, but Michael recognized the unreality of the proposal and rejected the Crown. The Romanov dynasty thus passed into history after three centuries in power.

The Duma tried to assume responsibility for government, but the Tsar gave an order to dissolve the parliament. In defiance of imperial orders, prominent members of the Duma formed a Provisional Govern-ment on 27 February, consisting of a coalition of moderates, liberals and Socialists. However, workers and soldiers in the capital distrusted the Provisional Government, and its authority was challenged by

ABOVE **Members of one of the many Soviets founded in Russia at the beginning of the revolution in 1917 along the lines of the 1905 Soviet. The establishment of Soviets in the army and among civilians signified the collapse of traditional authority.**

the new Petrograd Soviet, which had been formed on the same day to coordinate and consolidate the uprising. Following the lead of Petrograd, Soviets quickly began to emerge all over Russia, and it soon became clear that these carried more weight than the Provisional Government.

RUSSIA'S POLITICAL PARTIES

Russia had many competing groups jostling for power during the revolutionary period. The main opposition parties, from Left to Right, were as follows:

Anarchists
Key figure: Prince Peter Kropotkin
Key idea: no state

Social Revolutionaries (SRs)
Key ideas: peasant ownership of land; republicanism
Method: terrorism (responsible for many assassinations)
Split in 1917 into Left and Right: the Left SRs were prepared to cooperate with the Communists at first.

Social Democrats (Marxist–Communists)
Key figures: Karl Marx, Georgi Plekhanov (the father of Russian Marxism), Julius Martov, Vladimir Lenin
Key ideas: Marxist-style Communism; the abolition of the state after a world-wide working-class revolution
In 1903 the Social-Democrats split into two rival groups, the "majority" (Bolsheviks) led by Lenin and the "minority" (Mensheviks) led by Martov. The Mensheviks believed the Revolution must follow the laws of development laid down by Marx: it would start in the most advanced industrial countries and only then spread to Russia. Lenin's Bolsheviks hoped to bypass such development through the careful organization of a revolutionary party to seize power and then establish the conditions for Communism.

Kadets
A Constitutional Democratic Party consisting of liberal reformers who hoped to establish a constitutional monarchy on the Western model after the revolution of 1905.

Octobrists
A more conservative reformist party, which derived its name from the Tsar's October Manifesto of 1905.

Black Hundreds
Extreme right-wing and anti-Semitic groups, officially called the Union of the Russian People.

The struggle for power

The Provisional Government had to agree that troops who had taken part in the revolution could not be sent from the capital without their consent. Few wanted to go to the front, but the continuing war made keeping 200,000 troops idle in Petrograd a military nonsense. Any politicians who took up the soldiers' case and played on their fears of being sent to the front to fight the Germans – as the Socialists did – were likely to find a ready hearing.

The Provisional Government completely misjudged public opinion. As educated men they looked back to the French Revolution in the attempt to understand what to do next. The patriotic revolutionary war against the Germans and Austrians in 1792 had rallied many Frenchmen to the new Republic, and to the members of the Provisional Government it was obvious that Russia should do the same. But unfortunately for them, the lessons they drew from the French Republic meant nothing to the mass of Russian peasant soldiers and hungry city-dwellers. For the war was in many ways the *cause* of the revolution in Russia. It had disillusioned people with the old order. It had cost not only millions of lives, but driven up the price of every necessity and reduced the availability of all goods. Anyone who carried on the war was likely only to gain the unpopularity of Nicholas II – and yet this was exactly the strategy pursued by the new government.

The Soviets soon showed they were unhappy with this policy. On 2 March, the Petrograd Soviet issued a resolution known as Order No. 1, which called for military units to be run by their own committees. "The orders of the military commission of the state Duma are to be obeyed only in such insistence when they do not contradict the orders and decrees of the Soviet." This was the first sign of the impending clash between the Soviets and the Provisional Government. The latter proved ineffective on non-military matters as well. Out of democratic principle it insisted that key questions such as the constitution of the new Republic or land

---

MARX AND HIS REVOLUTIONARY IDEAS

Karl Marx (1818–83) believed that all history was the history of class struggles, that is, conflict between the haves and the have-nots. The industrial revolution during his lifetime led him to believe that a final clash between the owners of industrial capital and the workers, the proletariat, would result in the abolition of private property by the victorious proletariat, who would use modern industrial technology to produce an affluent Communist society. Marx expected this development to take place first in advanced industrial societies like Britain. Only after decades of development would a largely rural society like Russia be ready for a Marxist revolution.

"The Soviet of Workers' and Soldiers' Deputies... enjoys all the elements of real power, since the troops, the railways, the post and the telegraph are in its hands. One can say flatly that the Provisional Government exists only so long as it is permitted by the Soviet." WAR MINISTER, ALEKSANDR GUCHKOV, MARCH 1917

---

rights could be decided only by a properly elected Constituent Assembly. However, it was slow in organizing the elections, which were held only after a second revolution had taken place, in October 1917.

Meanwhile, the breakdown of authority went on throughout 1917. Failures at the front against the Germans compounded the social difficulties in the rear. Factory production continued to fall and living conditions deteriorated. Radical schemes for a complete break with the past now became more plausible.

Russia's long autocracy had not encouraged moderation among its opponents. Unable to participate in day-to-day decision-making and tackle everyday problems, Russia's intellectual revolutionaries became utopian schemers. They liked to dream about abolishing the Tsarist system and introducing a completely new and just system. Some form of Socialism was widely popular as the opposite of the

---

hierarchical system that had been in place before 1917. The ideas of Karl Marx were taken seriously by many of the revolutionary intellectuals, who had visions of a world-wide working-class. But putting a radical ideology into practice required more than wishful thinking. Even the Provisional Government's ineffective steps towards reform showed that.

Political anarchy

Russia's growing anarchy after February 1917 was bound to be short-lived. It was only a matter of time before an organized force stepped into the chaos to restore order. Most Russians feared that this would be the army, but in practice the army was disintegrating and the generals did not have enough authority over the troops for a coup d'état. The real threat to Russian anarchy came from a little-known political party, the Bolshevik wing of the Social Democrats, whose leader – Lenin – was not even resident in Russia.

Events began to run out of the control of the Provisional Government. As Aleksandr Kerensky, the Socialist leader of the Provisional Government, later admitted: "Between February and October the tide of revolution became a flood, and we could not halt or direct it." It was the dedicated world revolutionary, Lenin, exiled in Zurich, who sensed that neither the Provisional Government nor any of the other revolutionary parties had a clear vision of how to proceed. He anxiously urged his supporters in Russia to oppose the new Provisional Government in every way: "Our tactics: absolute mistrust, no support of the new government. Kerensky particularly suspect: to arm the proletariat the only guarantee.... No rapprochement with other parties."

A strange alliance then appeared between Lenin and the German army. The Germans wanted to knock Russia out of the war and Lenin's anti-war message appealed to them. Lenin, for his part, wanted to get back to revolutionary Russia and was willing to accept any help to get there. The Germans thus provided the famous "sealed train" to transport

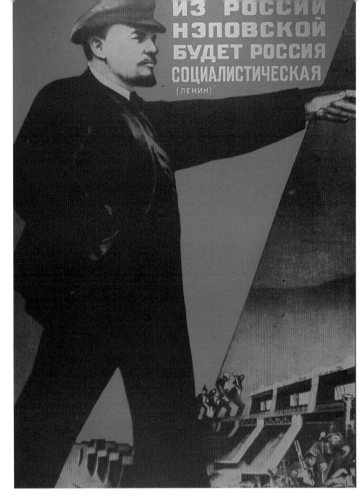

125

LEFT **After his death in January 1924, Lenin became a quasi-deified figure in the Soviet Union. His mummified body was venerated on Red Square in Moscow and countless millions of busts and posters, such as this one, were produced over the next seven decades, presenting him as the heroic guide to the future.**

WHO WAS LENIN?

Born the son of a senior civil servant in 1870, like many children of the elite the young Vladimir Ilyich Ulyanov turned revolutionary. His elder brother, Alexander, blazed the way as a conspirator against Alexander III, and paid for it with his life: he was executed in 1887 for plotting against the Tsar. Lenin rejected assassination and bomb-throwing as the way to overthrow the Tsars in favour of a careful preparation of revolution. This would require a clear vision of the future social order and a well-organized revolutionary party to bring it about. First arrested in 1895, he became a Marxist activist and adopted the revolutionary pseudonym "Lenin" to disguise his identity from the police. After 1902 he lived as a political exile in western Europe, from where he organized the Bolshevik party, only returning to Russia in April 1917.

Taking advantage of the chaotic situation in Russia that year, Lenin revealed extraordinary talents as a revolutionary organizer and propagandist. After his party seized power, he led the world's first Communist state through its birthpangs until he was incapacitated by a wasting disease in 1922. After his death in January 1924, his mummified body was put on display in Moscow's Red Square as the totem of the new society.

Lenin and another thirty or so Russian revolutionary exiles through German territory. Winston Churchill compared the quarantining of Lenin and his comrades to the transport of a "plague bacillus." The scheme worked better than the Germans could have hoped – but it was to produce nightmares for them in the long run.

Returning to Petrograd in April 1917, Lenin immediately launched an all-out attack on the Provisional Government's policies. His slogans, "Peace, land and bread!" and "All power to the Soviets!"

were a mortal threat to the Provisional Government. The latter was loyally determined to carry on the war and to leave major reforms until the population had elected a Constituent Assembly. This was laudably democratic – and very naive.

Lenin's rise to power

At first Lenin's return to Russia aroused little trepidation among the supporters of the Provisional Government. One of them wrote: "A man who talks such nonsense is not dangerous." But Lenin had been preparing for this moment for a long time. He was the galvanizing personality behind the transformation of a fringe group of about 10,000 activists to a revolutionary party in power.

It took two decades of fruitless revolutionary activity, much of it abroad, for Lenin to become a major figure in Russian politics. During that period, he adapted the ideas of Marx to a Russian context, but most importantly he established his party. With skill but dogmatic ruthlessness, he took over the existing underground Russian Social Democratic Party and remodelled it to fit his version of a disciplined and ideologically driven party.

In the process, Lenin fell out with most other Russian Social Democrats, but by skilful manoeuvring he kept the majority of its key committees. For a long time the rivalry between Lenin's so-called "Bolsheviki" (the "majority") and the more numerous "Mensheviki" (the "minority"!) was of little concern to the world. But Lenin's insistence on control and obedience set the pattern for how his Party would rule, once in power.

Some contemporary Marxists saw that. Trotsky, then still a Menshevik, criticized Lenin's dictatorial tendencies. The Polish-German revolutionary, Rosa Luxemburg, argued in 1919, not long before she was murdered by German counter-revolutionaries, that Lenin's technique of revolution would be stultifying, saying that: "Freedom is always freedom for the man who thinks differently." What would come about was a "dictatorship it is true, but not the dictatorship of the proletariat, but of a handful of politicians." In fact, it was soon to become the dictatorship of one man under Joseph Stalin (*see pages 131–33*). But in the turbulent events of revolution and civil war, few Russian Marxists had patience with such reflections.

The Bolsheviks gain popular support

Opposition to the war was the key to the growing support for the Bolsheviks in 1917. Lenin's close comrade, Nikolai Bukharin, argued, "For the bourgeoisie keeping the war going means stopping the Revolution, and for the working class stopping the war means keeping the Revolution going."

In July 1917, the Bolsheviks launched a premature attempt to topple the Provisional Government. Briefly it looked as if Lenin's career was over when he fled to Finland to avoid arrest, but by the end of the summer, the Bolsheviks had gained majority support in the Petrograd Soviet and others. The revolutionary anti-war message was spreading. The disintegration of military morale and the home front led the army commander, General Kornilov, to try to stage a coup to restore Kerensky's authority, but Kerensky lost his nerve and distributed weapons to the Petrograd workers, including Lenin's Red Guards. He was arming his own enemies.

From September 1917, life drained out of the Provisional Government. With its authority gone, and support waning, the question was who would step into the vacuum of power? Russia had many competing revolutionary groups (*see the box on page 123*). There were the Social Revolutionaries who represented the terrorist tradition of the 1870s, and who quarrelled with each other as much as with other groups. Anarchists were noisy but naturally ill-organized. There were the Mensheviks who wanted a Marxist society but thought a long period of capitalist development was needed before the final revolution. And many others. Then there were the Bolsheviks.

Lenin's party was the only one to combine a vision of the future with an organization and a leader who thought he could bring this vision about. By the autumn of 1917, there were probably only 250,000 confirmed supporters of Lenin in

LEFT **Government troops open fire on a demonstration on Nevskiy Prospekt in Petrograd in July 1917.**

Russia, but they were concentrated where it mattered: in Petrograd and the other big cities. They possessed discipline and drive in a sea of confusion and growing apathy. Their vision of a Soviet Russia leading a worldwide proletarian revolution had a powerful appeal to people humiliated and angered by Russia's backwardness and defeat. Lenin intended the Bolsheviks not only to leap-frog to power in Russia over the other parties, but also to light the spark for a Communist revolution across the globe. It was time to act.

The October revolution, 1917

From his hiding place in Finland, Lenin bombarded his supporters in Petrograd with messages urging them to seize power. However, it was not until he had returned to the city (in disguise) that he managed to

RIGHT **The centre of Petrograd as it was in 1917. The key objectives of the Bolsheviks during the October Revolution are shown in red, with the most important in bright red.**

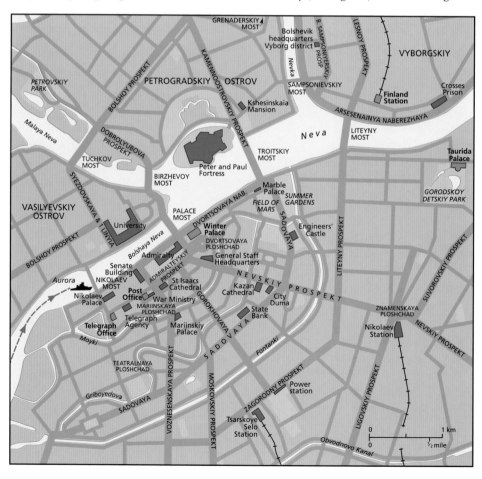

RIGHT **The Bolshevik assault on the Winter Palace.**

BELOW **The storming of the Winter Palace, as recreated for a film. The film had more to do with heroic propaganda than reality (night photography was impossible) but it was no less powerful for that.**

ABOVE **Members of the Red Guard around a tank captured from the Junkers (Cadets). The tank was renamed Lieutenant Schmidt in honour of a hero of the 1905 Revolution.**

convince the Central Committee of the Bolshevik Party to agree to an uprising. On 16 October, Trotsky created a Military Revolutionary Committee (MRC) to stage the coup. As a first step, the MRC dispatched commissars to all the military units in the region of Petrograd to win over troops and workers to the revolutionary cause – or at least persuade them to remain neutral in the event of an armed rising. Not all of the garrisons agreed immediately, however: it took a personal appeal from Trotsky himself on 23 October to persuade the soldiers of the important St Peter and Paul fortress

(which overlooked the Neva River and the Winter Palace) not to oppose the coup.

The same day, as rumours of the planned insurrection began to circulate the city, the Prime Minister Kerensky decided he had to do something. He ordered government soldiers to arrest Bolshevik and MRC leaders and to close down two Bolshevik newspapers. Little did he guess that this was just the impetus needed by the Bolsheviks to rally people to their cause. The next day, declaring that the Petrograd Soviet was under threat, the MRC sent out Red Guards and sympathetic soldiers to seize all the key bridges and communication facilities in Petrograd. While mutinous sailors on the warship *Aurora* trained their guns on strategic points in the city, the Bolsheviks quietly went into action. One by one, on the night of 24/25 October, each station, bank, bridge and post office fell to Bolshevik units without a shot being fired. It was a strangely uneventful revolution for an episode with such profound implications. Later Soviet propagandists (such as Sergei Eisenstein in his film *October, 1917*) produced a much more dramatic picture of what had happened. The American sympathizer with the Bolsheviks, John Reed, also wrote a famously dramatic account of the October Revolution (*Ten Days that Shook the World*), but the Menshevik, Nikolai Sukhanov, described events in a more matter-of-fact way:

No resistance was shown. Beginning at 2 in the morning the stations, bridges, lighting installations, telegraphs and telegraph agency were gradually occupied by small forces.... In general the military operations in the politically important centres of the city resembled a changing of the guard.... The decisive operations that had begun were quite bloodless; not one casualty was recorded. The city was absolutely calm. Both the centre and the suburbs were sunk in a deep sleep, not suspecting what was going on in the quiet of a cold autumn night.

At 10 am on October 25, Lenin released a statement, posted all over the city, declaring that the Provisional Government had fallen and power had passed to the Soviets. But the coup was not yet complete: the cabinet of the Provisional Government had refused to surrender and were holding out at the Winter Palace. At 6.30 that evening, the MRC issued an ultimatum to the ministers to surrender. Receiving no reply, the Bolsheviks ordered the *Aurora* to fire. It fired a single, blank shot, but this was sufficient to persuade the remaining government sympathizers of the seriousness of the Bolshevik challenge. As darkness fell, the troops defending the palace began gradually, peacefully to melt away. By midnight the palace was almost deserted, and at 2 am the last ministers were arrested and marched off. The Winter Palace had fallen.

The collapse of the Provisional Government was announced immediately to the Congress of Soviets, which was meeting elsewhere in the city. Protests by Mensheviks against the coup as they saw it were met by

Trotsky's brutal dismissive response: "You are – pitiful isolated individuals, you are – bankrupts; your role is played out. Go where you belong from now on – into the dustbin of history." The Soviet regime had been born.

A red star over Russia

Lenin was well aware that seizing power was one thing, keeping it quite another. As the days passed after the proclamation of the Soviet regime, he liked to compare its longevity with shorter-lived revolutions such as the Paris Commune (*see pages 112–15*). Despite his rhetoric about how a Socialist society would do without the need of any state or police, in practice he recognized that coercion was needed to bring his vision of society about: "As long as there is a state there is no freedom; when there is freedom there will be no state." Far from the state "withering away," as Marx had expected after a Communist revolution, within weeks of seizing power from the Provisional Government a new secret police, the Cheka, had been established; a new Red Army was in embryo; and a huge bureaucracy to manage society was coming into being. The Workers' State would leave little to chance or spontaneity. Lenin liked to quip, "Trust is good but control is better."

Lenin recognized that the Provisional Government's failure to stop the war and to solve the land question had destroyed it. He was determined not to go the same way, so his new government immediately issued its first decree calling for an end to the war without annexations. The second decree told the peasants to take land from landowners, the church or others for themselves. "Private ownership of land shall be abolished for ever.... [All land] shall become the property of the whole people, and pass into the use of those who cultivate it.... The employment of hired labour is not permitted." Other new legislation included the adoption of the Gregorian calendar, to bring Russia into line with Western Europe; the removal of the seat of government from Petrograd to Moscow; and the abolition of the existing judicial system.

LEON TROTSKY (1879–1940)

Born in 1879 into a Ukrainian Jewish family, Lev Bronstein became a Marxist revolutionary in his late teens. He was arrested in 1898 and sentenced to exile in Siberia, but he escaped and made his way to London using a false passport bearing the name of Trotsky. Returning to Russia in 1905 he became leader of the St Petersburg Soviet, but he was arrested once again and exiled to Siberia. This time he escaped to Vienna. A Menshevik and for a long time a fierce critic of Lenin's methods, Trotsky suddenly joined the Bolsheviks in mid-summer 1917. He was the architect of the military aspects of the overthrow of the Provisional Government in October that year. First foreign commissar of the new Soviet state, he then became organizer of the Red Army during the civil war. After Lenin's death, however, he was marginalized by rivals in the Communist leadership, which resulted eventually in his expulsion from the Soviet Union in 1929. From abroad he denounced what he saw as Stalin's betrayal of Communist ideals. He was murdered by a Soviet agent in Mexico in 1940.

Disappointed by the fact that neither peace nor the revolution had spread, Lenin made peace with the Germans in March 1918, though Russia had no choice but to accept Germany's crippling terms. The treaty of Brest-Litovsk took away roughly a quarter of Russia's territory, about a third of her population and half of her industrial strength. Lenin admitted "Our impulse tells us...to refuse to sign this robber peace. Our reason will in our calmer moments tell us the plain naked truth – that Russia can offer no physical resistance because she is materially exhausted by three years' war." Let Germany and her Western enemies fight it out while Soviet Russia recuperates: "Let the Revolution utilize this struggle for its own ends."

> **"The execution of the Tsar's family was needed not only to frighten, horrify and dishearten the enemy, but also in order to shake up our own ranks to show that there was no turning back, that ahead lay either complete victory or ruin."** LEON TROTSKY, 1935

The Whites challenge the Bolsheviks for supremacy

Peace with Germany helped to spark a terrible civil war in Russia. Many army officers regarded Lenin's regime as treacherous, in league with Germany. The Western Allies sent help to the dissenters in the hope of drawing Russia back into the war with Germany, but their plan backfired. Allied intervention was half-hearted, and it probably helped merely to rally Russians who resented foreign interference to Lenin's side.

In the war against the opponents of the Soviet regime – known as the "Whites" – Lenin's "Reds" had many advantages. They held Russia's main industrial centres and the hub of the railway network at their new capital, Moscow, while the Whites were scattered around the fringes of the Russian Empire, and often faced rebellions by local non-Russian nationalities wanting independence from Russia. The Whites were divided about what they wanted to achieve: the Tsarist system was discredited, but so too was the liberal Provisional Government. The Bolsheviks, on the other hand, offered a vision of a transformed Russia in an ideal world. By satisfying the peasants' immediate demand for land, Lenin outmanoeuvred the Whites in the struggle for popular support. On the whole, the peasants were suspicious of the Whites' intentions – but, unfortunately for them, they did not know what the Communists' long-term plans were either.

The ex-Tsar and his family were among the early victims of the civil war. Almost forgotten by the world, the ex-imperial family had been taken as prisoners to Yekaterinburg, beyond the Ural Mountains, and there they were murdered in July 1918, as potential White rescuers approached the city. Unlike the fanfare of publicity that accompanied the deaths of autocratic rulers in so many other revolutions, no effort was made to dramatize the slaughter of Nicholas II and his family as a great act of revolutionary justice. Perhaps Lenin wanted to avoid antagonizing the ex-Tsar's royal cousins abroad, or perhaps it was just indifference. Lenin believed ruthlessness was necessary for any successful revolution. Scruples about harsh treatment of opponents and their families had no place in his thinking. He told young Communists in 1920: "Our morality is entirely subordinated to the interests of the proletariat's class struggle. Morality is what serves to destroy the old exploiting society." The result of this policy was the so-called Red Terror. Anti-Bolsheviks were given no quarter: thousands were killed or imprisoned between 1918 and 1921.

In retrospect, opponents of Lenin such as Pavel Milyukov, Foreign Minister of the Provisional Government, admitted that the Communists' single-minded approach to revolution was the key to their success: "They knew where they were going, and went in the direction which they had chosen...." Everyone else had either compromised or lost their way. By the end of 1920, the superior organization of Trotsky's Red Army had managed to overcome the half-hearted resistance of the White forces.

Building Communism during the civil war

At the same time as the Communists were fighting their White enemies, they were also involved in a headlong attempt to establish a Communist system – later called "War Communism" – which led not only to terrible food shortages but also to economic breakdown. Florence Farmborough, an English nurse, observed the food shortages in Moscow in January 1918: "The Red commissioners agreed to give me a

ABOVE **An anti-Bolshevik poster of 1917 depicting Leon Trotsky as a ruthless monster of death.**

ABOVE **The Tsar and his family on the roof of the house in Yekaterinburg where they were held prisoners. Left to right: Olgar, Anastasia, the Tsar, Tsarevich, Tatiana and Marie. This is one of the last pictures taken of them before they were killed in July 1918.**

LEFT **Russia during the years of civil war and famine, 1918–21. Mobilizing all the resources of the key central region of Russia, the Communists were able to defeat the Whites, who operated from the fringes of the old Russian Empire (with limited assistance from abroad). The period of so-called War Communism led to the collapse of the economy, for food was requisitioned from the peasantry to feed the armies and the cities. The famine in 1921 was a greater challenge to the new regime than the Whites, and led to Lenin's adoption of the New Economic Policy (overleaf).**

Map labels:
BARENT SEA
NORWAY
SWEDEN
Murmansk — BRITISH FRENCH CANADIANS ITALIANS SERBS
WHITE SEA
Gulf of Bothnia
Arkhangelsk — CANADIANS AMERICANS BRITISH FRENCH
FINLAND — FINNS
Lake Onega
Helsingfors (Helsinki)
Lake Ladoga
Petrograd
BRITISH
Kronstadt
Lake Pskov
BRITISH
GERMANS
Vitebsk
POLAND
Mogilev
Brest-Litovsk
POLES
Kiev
AUSTRO-HUNGARIAN EMPIRE
Kharkov
ROMANIANS
Dniester
Odessa
ROMANIA
Sevastopol
BULGARIA
FRENCH
BRITISH
Constantinople (Istanbul)
OTTOMAN EMPIRE
Vologda
Perm
Vyatka
Yekaterinburg (Sverdlovsk)
Kazan
Chelyabinsk
Moscow
Oka
Simbirsk
Ufa
Tula
Penza
Samara
Saratov
Don
RUSSIA
Ural
Tsaritsyn
Volga
Guryev
Rostov
Dnieper
SEA OF AZOV
Novorossiysk
Kuma
BLACK SEA
CASPIAN SEA
Astrakhan
Batumi
Tiflis
Baku
Krasnovodsk
PERSIA
Tehran
BRITISH

Legend:
Treaty of Brest-Litovsk boundary 1918
Soviet Union boundary 1921
Non-Russian army
White Russian army
Red army counter-attack
Principal famine area
Widespread famine conditions

0 200 400 600 800 km
0 200 400 miles

permit for my own rations. Two potatoes or one eighth of a pound of bread was the daily ration per head. We preferred the potatoes, for, washed and cooked, every bit of them could be eaten – that is when they were not bad! Whereas the bread inevitably contained sawdust and other 'foreign bodies,' calculated to augment the weight.... No treasure could buy salt; it had ceased to exist."

To ensure that the revolutionaries were fit to lead the revolution, special rations and canteens were set aside for them. From early on in the revolution, a system of privileges for Communist activists appeared, ultimately developing into the hated *nomenklatura* – the list of names of the privileged Communist elite. At first it was justified by necessity, but as time passed joining the privileged *nomenklatura* became an end in itself because its members had access to the good things in life as well as essentials that were unavailable elsewhere in Soviet Russia.

Victory in the civil war did not mark the end of opposition. The new Soviet state now had soldiers and policemen enough to suppress resistance, but this opposition now came no longer from the beneficiaries of the old order but rather from disillusioned workers and peasants who had expected to do better under the new order. The harsh winter of 1920–21 saw the first

of many revolts by the proletariat against its self-proclaimed leaders.

Famine threatened to destroy the new revolutionary society, leading Lenin to announce in March 1921 a sudden retreat in economic policy. Under the so-called New Economic Policy (NEP), peasants would be allowed to grow crops for profit again, which horrified many Bolsheviks. Worse still, private traders would be allowed to hawk goods around and sell them. Known as "bagmen," these traders were regarded as "parasites" and "speculators" by the Communists, but Lenin insisted that unless there was food there could be no hope of Communism. A step backwards was required.

In any case, a serious direct challenge to Communist power had emerged at the same time. The sailors and dockyard workers of the Kronstadt naval base outside Petrograd had revolted against Comn unist rule. Their slogans denounced the new Red Bourgeoisie and accused Lenin of exercising a dictatorship far worse than the tyranny of the Tsar. Only four years earlier, Lenin had praised the sailors as the "reddest of the red." Now he determined to crush them using the Red Army and the Cheka (the secret police). Ironically, the troops who eventually suppressed the Kronstadt mutiny were led into action by Marshal Tukhachevsky, a

ABOVE **A Soviet propaganda poster dating from 1921 proclaiming the benefits of the New Economic Policy.**

former colonel in the Imperial Guard who had switched sides.

Although the Kronstadt rising failed, it was just the first in a series of working-class revolts against the Communists who claimed to rule on their behalf. Eventually, in the 1980s, Polish shipyard workers would succeed where the Kronstadt rebels failed (see *pages 176–77*), but in the meantime Lenin's uncompromising insistence that the Party knew best won out.

But even inside the Party by 1921 Lenin was no longer prepared to tolerate dissent. As news of the suppression of the Kronstadt rebels came through at the Party congress in March, Lenin introduced a new rule outlawing factions or even honest disagreement. Party members now had to believe that it was "better to be wrong with the party, than right against it."

The New Economic Policy was never intended by Lenin to be anything other than a tactical retreat to buy time before the Communists could work out how to run a completely socialized economy. The leader of the Communist Party in Petrograd, Grigory Zinoviev, insisted in December 1921, "The New Economic Policy is only a temporary deviation, a tactical retreat, a clearing of land for a new and decisive attack of labour against the front of international capitalism."

LEFT **Evidence of the catastrophic effects of the civil war and the attempt to abolish agriculture at the same time: victims of famine in Russia's once fertile Volga region and** (INSET) **starving children at the Samara relief camp in October 1921.**

ABOVE **"Long Live the Revolution!" an early
Bolshevik poster illustrating the Red Guards
in a commandeered vehicle.**

Lenin's legacy

Lenin fell mortally ill in May 1922, before he could decide how to return to a strictly Communist economic model, but by the end of his life he had laid the foundations of a Socialist society. This society was not, however, what most Russians had expected or hoped for in the anarchic year of 1917. Earlier dreams of workers running a workers' state had been abandoned. In 1921, Lenin asked, "Can a worker administer the state?" and answered his own question contemptuously, "Practical people know that that is fantasy...!"

Convinced of the correctness of his vision, Lenin had established a coercive state to control the people and transform them into a new type of humanity. It was left to Joseph Stalin – who took over as Party leader following Lenin's death in 1924 – to reinvigorate the utopian dream after the brief period of NEP. It was also left to Stalin to turn the secret police against the Party as well as the people. Most of Lenin's other close comrades-in-arms fell victim to Stalin's purges as the revolution devoured its children and he completed the construction of a totalitarian Communist state.

Seventy years earlier, the great Russian liberal, Aleksandr Herzen, foresaw the tragedy of a Socialist triumph in his motherland. Russians would take the idea to its logical extreme and create an egalitarian autocracy in place of the Tsar's absolutism. Then eventually another revolution would be needed: "Socialism will develop to extremes...to the point of absurdity. Then once again a cry of rejection will erupt from the bosom of a revolutionary minority, and again a decisive struggle will begin in which Socialism will take the place of conservatism and be defeated by a future revolution as yet unknown to us."

It took another seventy years – and many more revolutions – before that would happen (*see pages 174–91*).

THE INTERNATIONAL IMPACT OF THE RUSSIAN REVOLUTION

For the Bolsheviks, seizing power in Russia was the beginning of their revolutionary work: world revolution was their aim. In May 1918, Lenin insisted that "The interests of world socialism are superior to national interests." Even temporary set-backs such as the treaty of Brest-Litovsk, which conceded huge and valuable areas of the old Russian empire to Germany, was justified as a necessary short-term concession that would be reversed when the revolution spread to Germany and a Soviet regime was established there.

Lenin's hopes for the rapid spread of revolution across Europe were revived in Autumn 1918. The Central Powers – Austro-Hungary, Bulgaria and Turkey, led by Germany – were defeated by the Western Allies (Britain, France and the USA). Mutinies broke out across central Europe and monarchs fled into ignominious exile to avoid the fate of Nicholas II. Briefly, revolutionaries inspired by the Soviet model tried to imitate Lenin's success in the defeated countries. But in Germany, Austria and Hungary, the disintegration of the old order was not as complete as it had been in Russia. Nor were the local Communists well enough prepared to seize power. Superficial similarities, such as the role of mutinous sailors in starting the German revolution, disguised major differences between conditions in Russia in 1917 and Central Europe a year later.

The Spartacist uprising in Germany

Following the overthrow of Germany's Kaiser Wilhelm II in 1918, the German

Communist Party (known until January 1919 as the Spartacists, after the slave leader Spartacus: *see box on page 12*) launched a propaganda campaign against the government and initiated a series of terrorist attacks. At the beginning of 1919, insurrections against the newly established Weimar Republic broke out in both Berlin and the Bavarian capital, Munich. A general strike was organized and revolutionaries took over certain key government buildings. But although the new German Chancellor, Friedrich Ebert, was a Social Democrat, he had no sympathy with the Bolshevik model. Convinced that a Communist revolution would bring only the chaos of civil war and starvation to a

country still reeling from defeat, Ebert allied with generals of the old imperial army to suppress the Communists. The revolutionaries were not widely supported: reports about conditions in civil war-torn Russia did nothing to encourage the German people to experiment with Communism, while many committed Communists, such as Rosa Luxemburg, were critical of Lenin's ruthless methods.

The army, police and paramilitary groups were much better prepared than the Communists and, unlike their Russian counterparts, had not lost their self-confidence. They suppressed the Spartacist rising with real savagery: Luxemburg and other revolutionary leaders were brutally

murdered in 1919 and their supporters were defeated in street-fighting in Berlin. Altogether 100 revolutionaries were killed.

By calling early elections and ensuring that the newly elected Parliament met at once, Ebert avoided the constitutional

"Civil war has flared up throughout Europe. The victory of Communism in Germany is absolutely inevitable. In a year, Europe will have forgotten about the fight for Communism because all of Europe will be Communist. Then the struggle for Communism in America will begin, and possibly in Asia and other continents." GRIGORY ZINOVIEV, 1919

confusion that had bedevilled the Russian Provisional Government. Instead of facing a legal vacuum, Germany's Communists were wrong-footed by having to defy a Parliament elected by universal suffrage. It was not easy to agitate against a democratic republic. In any case, some of the pro-Soviet revolutionaries were almost comic in their attempts at revolution. In Munich, the self-appointed Foreign Minister of the Bavarian Soviet Republic sent scurrilous telegrams to the Pope, but did little to establish an effective revolutionary government. The Bavarian rising, too, was bloodily put down by the German army.

The struggle for Hungary and Poland

In Hungary, local Communists led by Béla Kun seized power in March 1919, but soon faced a successful onslaught from both ex-Hungarian soldiers and the Romanian army that advanced westwards to stifle revolution before help might come from Soviet Russia.

The threat of Soviet intervention grew more real when Poland became embroiled in war with Soviet Russia in April 1920 after the new government in Warsaw tried to take advantage of the Russian civil war to recover lands it regarded as traditionally

RIGHT **The spread of Communism. Lenin expected the Russian Revolution to be the first in a chain-reaction across the globe. Factors such as war-weariness and hardship sparked revolutions in Central Europe, much as they had in Russia a year earlier. Haunted by the Russian example, the officer corps and moderate politicians in Germany acted decisively to crush local Marxists. Only in Hungary and Slovakia did a local Soviet regime come to power – briefly. The Red Army's attempt to march westwards in 1920 after its victory in the Russian civil war united newly independent Catholic Poles in resistance against what they saw as "godless atheism" and renewed Russian imperialism.**

Polish. After defeating the Whites in the civil war, the Red Army began a rapid westward advance, but this was turned into a sudden retreat outside Warsaw in August 1920. The Polish peasants and workers did not see the Red Army as their liberators, but as another form of Russian imperialism. Supported by French military advisers, the Polish army struck back. Part of the reason for the defeat of the Red Army lay in divisions among its leaders over how best to attack Poland. Trotsky and Stalin were attached to different wings of the Red Army and each blamed the other for the defeat. A bitter feud followed that ended only years later with the murder by Stalin of Trotsky and his associates.

For a few more years, Communists in Central Europe hoped to start a Soviet-style revolution in their countries, but by the end of 1923 hopes for a Communist seizure of power had faded, even in inflation-racked Germany.

Coordinating global revolution from Moscow

Lenin had often expressed his scepticism about the revolutionary potential of the German Social Democrats (once sarcastically remarking that they would only occupy railway stations after they had first bought platform tickets!). He felt that the international Communist movement needed firm direction from Moscow. Two previous Marxist Internationals had collapsed before the First World War, and in March 1919 Lenin gathered a motley band of foreign supporters of the Soviet regime to form the Third International. This so-called Comintern was intended to coordinate the newly established Communist parties around the world. Each party would be merely a "section" of the Comintern, whose guiding committee in Moscow would direct the world revolution. Efforts were made to rally the subject peoples of Western colonial empires to the Soviet cause. Lenin was prepared to back-pedal his anti-religious views to promote rebellion among Muslims and Hindus in the British Empire, for instance. But enthusiasm for the Soviet model was still weak in the colonies in the 1920s.

The Comintern proved to be a mixed blessing to the foreign Communist parties. Often its directives showed little knowl-

LEFT **Joseph Stalin in 1935. The Comintern's control of foreign Communist parties made them follow the Soviet model in every detail, including the cult of Stalin. But blind obedience to Stalin's orders often proved disastrous to Communists outside the Soviet Union.**

edge of what was happening in their countries, but strict discipline required that they be followed. Money and other forms of support from Moscow, however, were often essential to keeping the frequently illegal Communist parties going. Another problem for these groups was that as the chance of revolutionary upheaval receded, the Soviet government preferred to use Comintern agents for espionage activities rather than political roles. In Stalin's time, the Comintern became completely subordinate to Soviet interests and was officially wound up in 1943 when Stalin wanted to persuade his Western allies in the war against Hitler that the Soviet Union was no longer a subversive threat.

Mexico was Spain's first colony on the American mainland and it remained the most important until it broke away after 1810. Even after independence, Mexico's republican tradition was repeatedly challenged before being definitively established in 1867. The long years of stability under Porfirio Díaz collapsed in 1910, and more than two decades of upheaval followed. For all the violence and revolutionary slogans, Mexicans were left wondering what had really changed.

Revolution in Mexico

Preaching at Mass in the village of Dolores on Sunday 16 September 1810, the priest Miguel Hidalgo provoked a great anti-Spanish revolt when he issued his *Grito de Dolores*, a cry (*grito*) for greater racial and material equality in Mexico. Although the revolt was suppressed, it was an important step to the formal declaration of independence from Spain on 6 November 1813. The Spanish King Ferdinand VII refused to recognize this declaration, however, and it was not until the creole general Agustín de Iturbide turned against the Spanish and defeated the royalists in 1821 that Spain formally granted independence to Mexico. Iturbide imitated Napoleon and proclaimed himself Emperor in 1822, only to be deposed the next year by another general, Santa Anna, who established a Republic.

Foreign occupation

Despite the frequent changes in government, by 1857 Mexico had acquired a liberal constitution. But in 1861 the country faced a new challenge when, taking advantage of Mexico's inability to pay her debts, France invaded Mexico. The recently elected Mexican President, Benito Juárez, had many adversaries, not only among the conservatives and Catholics offended by the constitution but also among the

wealthy landowners hostile to his partly Indian origins. These opponents sided with the French and supported Napoleon III when he installed the Habsburg prince, Maximilian, as Emperor. But Maximilian turned out to be a mistake: he wanted to benefit his subjects, not the clique that endorsed him. Neither group trusted him.

Juárez resisted the French and was almost defeated, but then the situation changed. Napoleon III needed to recall French troops to bolster his defences against Prussia, while the defeat of the Confederacy in the Civil War left the United States in a strong position to insist on the

removal of foreign troops from Mexico. Left without any military support, the empire quickly crumbled and Maximilian himself was shot.

Although the threat of recolonization had now receded, Mexico found herself

INSET **Mexico once covered much of what is now the southwest of the United States. Texas and California were lost in 1848.**

RIGHT **The revolutionary struggles were conducted mainly in the uplands of Mexico.**

more dependent on the United States after 1867, largely because Juárez refused to honour Maximilian's debts to European bankers, so Mexicans could only look to the Americans for loans. What's more, Mexico's social problems remained unresolved. Juárez had found it difficult to assert his authority over the whole of liberated Mexico and the liberal regime was soon in disrepute after his death in 1872.

The long rule of Porfirio Díaz

A military rebellion brought Porfirio Díaz to power in 1876. His regime restored central authority but often by compromise with the local elites. Rapid economic development during Díaz's thirty-year rule did much to destabilize Mexican society, however. While the population grew rapidly, and cities such as the steel town, Monterrey, boomed, conditions in the countryside worsened and life expectancy actually fell. Inflation also cut into the real value of wages. Everywhere across Mexico, state power and economic dominance tended to intertwine in a tight oligarchy. Even some of the middle classes felt excluded.

Old age took its toll on Díaz (who was eighty in 1910) and his ministers (who were generally over seventy). The elderly ruling elite lacked the mental agility to keep in touch with a youthful population. Widespread strikes and the use of force to suppress them heralded a crisis in Díaz's regime. A sudden drop in prices for mining products turned the boom towns into centres of discontent. As early as August 1907, the commander of US troops on the border looked south and concluded, "There exists...a great unrest due to the current situation. If there were a revolutionary explosion, a capable leader would have numerous followers."

Díaz is forced to step down

One such leader was Francisco Madero, who came from a wealthy landowning family in the north. He was a key opponent of the Porfirian regime and was the

LEFT **Revolutionaries take over a locomotive at Cuernavaca, Morelos, 1910–20. Between 1884 and 1910, 13,000 miles of rail tracks were laid; mining output quadrupled; and foreign investment increased thirtyfold. But the rapidity of the changes unsettled Mexico and helped spark the revolution.**

first Mexican politician to make a campaign tour of the country on the American whistle-stop model. He proclaimed such populist slogans as "The people do not want bread but liberty," and announced that "the Mexican people are willing to die in order to defend their rights...it is not that they want to incinerate the national territory with a revolution, it is that they are no longer afraid of the sacrifice." His arrest in 1910 only increased his popularity.

Meanwhile, in agriculturally depressed Morelos to the south, a much more radical leader was soon to appear. On 12 September

ABOVE LEFT **Porfirio Díaz (1830–1915) was twice President of Mexico, but he lost his political grip in old age.**

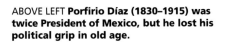

ABOVE RIGHT **Emiliano Zapata (1879–1919) led a guerrilla army in the fight for land rights.**

1909, Emiliano Zapata was elected leader of Anenecuilco in Morelos. Zapata represented all those resentful of the loss of land to railway, mining and large farming interests – especially those owned by foreigners. New laws had allowed land customarily farmed by poor peasants and Indians to be bought by those with cash.

The combination of discontent among the rich and poor forced Díaz to admit the bogus nature of his reelection for the seventh time in 1910 and to retire. Madero was elected President in 1911, but he did not enjoy the fruits of victory for long.

Coup and counter-coup

The fall of Díaz left a vacuum in Mexican politics that Madero could not fill. Supporters of the old regime tried to forestall change but were suppressed. Then, in February 1913, the general who did the suppressing, Victoriano Huerta, decided to seize power himself. Madero was promptly murdered. The bloodletting got steadily worse as faction fought faction and peasants and workers revolted.

Huerta, too, was unable to restore Díaz's stability. Within weeks, the governor of the state of Coahuila, Venustiano Carranza, had challenged Huerta's right to rule. Carranza was supported by real radicals such as Francisco "Pancho" Villa, whose origins in banditry had earned him a Robin Hood-like reputation. Villa and Zapata promoted social reform and called for the return of land to the Indians, making them very popular among the rural poor.

Huerta admitted defeat in July 1914 and went into exile – but the victors fell out with each other. Carranza and his military chief, General Obregón, turned on Zapata and Pancho Villa, who raised substantial armies to fight Carranza. The rebels fought tenaciously to win Mexico City and control of the rail network, but the years of rural war ended in defeat for the radicals – and led to hundreds of thousands of deaths and the destruction of property, railways and other assets. Villa and Zapata were both assassinated.

Carranza enacted a new constitution in 1917 whose key principle was that the powerful president could not be reelected. Importantly, the constitution also pronounced the end of debt-peonage, which had kept many Mexicans effectively in life-long service to their landlords; declared the mineral wealth of Mexico a national asset; and tried to abolish the Catholic Church's influence in Mexican affairs. Carranza in fact defied many provisions of the constitution (as did so many of his successors) and hoped to install a stooge in 1920, but Obregón defied him and had himself elected President on 5 September 1920.

LEFT **Ragtag troops in Mexico City in 1912.**

The Cristero war

The radical anticlericalism of the government in Mexico City provoked a violent backlash in the mid-1920s. For, across much of the countryside, the revolutionaries in the capital were more unpopular than the rural clergy. During the early summer of 1926, the Catholic Church faced more and more restrictions while the government press waged a propaganda campaign against it. Recalcitrant Catholics responded by proclaiming Mexico the "Kingdom of Christ," which was followed by a government ban on the practice of Catholicism. Some 50,000 peasants took up arms against the government. Their slogan was "Viva Cristo Rey!"

(long live Christ the King), hence their name: the Cristeros.

The new President, Plutarco Calles, completely underestimated the attachment of ordinary people to the Church. Like the Jacobins during the French Revolution (*see page* 79) he saw the Church as a mixture of superstition and exploitation, while the rebels for their part saw Calles as the representative of a hypocritical revolution that had not benefited them and now was trying to destroy their souls.

After three bloody years a compromise between the Church and State was agreed in June 1929. It paved the way for the "institutionalization" of the revolution.

Bloodletting among the revolutionaries

Even while the Cristero rebellion was going on, Obregón and Calles fell out with Arnulfo Gomez and Francisco Serrano, their former allies, over Obregón's controversial decision to seek reelection as President. A conspiracy to stop Obregón was stifled in October 1927 and

ABOVE **Pancho Villa's (1878–1923) "invasion" of the United States provoked US offers of rewards for this "bandit" in 1916. He was eventually murdered by General Obregón's agents on 20 June 1923.**

LEFT **A firing squad executes a guerrilla in 1914. The revolution was to lead to recurrent civil wars, and savage reprisals became the norm.**

LEFT **A by-product of the revolution was the flowering of a new art style that married radical rhetoric and peasant Indian aspirations, minus the sordid reality of the revolution. This mural, *History of Mexico*, is by Diego Rivera.**

both Serrano and Gomez were brutally murdered. Photographs of their bullet-riddled corpses were widely displayed to discourage other plotters. But on the eve of taking office again in July 1928, Obregón was shot by a lone Cristero. The six years after Obregón's assassination saw three presidents, but real power was held by Calles, who helped to institutionalize the revolution by establishing the National Revolutionary Party in 1929.

The victorious revolutionaries tended to be wealthy men from northern Mexico (unlike the Zapatas and Villas) and were much less radical in practice than rhetoric. By the mid-1920s, foreign businesses were usually safe from expropriation and even the great estates were left in private hands provided they were profitable. Thus, by the time Lázaro Cárdenas became President in 1934, decades of revolution had produced very little change: 70 per cent of Mexicans still worked in agriculture, while only 14 per cent worked in industry and about 15 per cent had jobs in trade or the professions. About 800,000 peasants had received land, but 3,000,000 others had not.

Cárdenas was not content with the status quo. While denying genuine popular participation, he wanted to produce a dramatic revolutionary act to confirm his credentials. On 18 March 1938, "like a bolt of lightning in a blue sky" according to the US ambassador, Cárdenas announced the nationalization of the foreign oil companies. It was a bold move. Apart from the Soviet Union, no state had ever dared such a revolutionary act – though in the coming decades some Middle Eastern rulers would imitate such a profitable move. It certainly made Cárdenas immensely popular, as anti-foreign feeling surged in a fit of national pride. Unfortunately, the foreign-

ers were able to do without Mexican oil, so the negative long-term economic effect outweighed the brief psychological boost.

Institutionalized revolution

After World War II, Mexico relapsed into political immobility, but economic growth was combined with the firm grip on power of the Party of Institutional Revolution (PRI), set up in 1946. It was the natural product of efforts by Calles and his successors to find a way of avoiding a return to all the strife that had disfigured the early years of the revolution. An effective if undemocratic way of transferring power was developed whereby every six years the President nominated a successor who was duly "elected" by the Mexican people, whether they liked him or not.

By the mid-1990s, the PRI's unity and hold on power were beginning to show signs of strain. In the poor Indian province of Chiapas, self-proclaimed Zapatistas rose

ABOVE **Masked Zapatista guerrillas in the state of Chiapas, southwest Mexico, 1994.**

in revolt demanding land redistribution, while in 1994 members of the PRI apparently arranged the assassinations of its presidential candidate and party secretary general for fear that they were too liberal. Mexico was trapped between the pressures from her past and the harsh consequences of trying to join the world economy.

The combined impact of the First World War and the Russian Revolution provoked a powerful backlash in Europe. Fear of Communism, political and economic disorder and disillusionment with the postwar settlement and liberal democracy encouraged the emergence of radical right-wing movements in Europe that rejected the respectability of traditional conservatives in favour of highly authoritarian schemes for transforming both government and society.

Fascism as Counter-revolution

Whereas in Russia the far-reaching disruption caused by the First World War helped to spark the Bolshevik revolution in 1917, in other parts of Europe it promoted the most radical form of *counter*-revolution: Fascism. Although Fascism differed in detail from one country to another, all Fascists believed in an authoritarian, nationalist and militaristic single-party state ruled by a strong leader.

Both the main Fascist leaders, Benito Mussolini and Adolf Hitler, were veterans of the war, like tens of thousands of their early supporters. The scale of destruction and terrible conditions in the trenches helped to desocialize a whole generation of soldiers and accustom them to violence. Returning home, they were often contemptuous of the civilian population and the political elite that had led them into such a horrific war. Defeat for Germany and disappointment with a costly victory for Italy, together with inflation and unemployment, helped to radicalize the population.

Although the Left gained some support in these conditions, neither the newly founded Communist Parties nor the more traditional Socialists were able to dominate politics, partly because of their own rivalry. Instead, it was the new Fascist parties that truly managed to capitalize on post-war anxiety and build mass support.

The Italian model

Initially a Socialist, Mussolini broke with the party in 1914 by advocating Italy's entrance into the Great War. Despite abandoning pacifism (which was a key Socialist principle), Mussolini kept a lot of radical rhetoric from his left-wing past when he established a new party in 1919. Named the *Fasci di combattimento* (hence Fascists), it was an openly authoritarian party. Its name derived from the *fasces*, the bundle of rods and axes that symbolized harsh Roman justice. Nostalgia for a past age of Roman greatness and the determination to restore it was part of Fascism's appeal.

Mussolini recognized that war veterans disillusioned with peace made excellent material for his paramilitary party. Strikes and other left-wing disorders offered the

LEFT **Mussolini and Hitler in Berlin, 1936. Relations between the two leaders were uneasy despite agreement in public. Mussolini was sceptical about the German imitation of Fascism: "I should be pleased, I suppose, that Hitler has carried out a revolution on our lines. But they are Germans. So they will end up by ruining our idea."**

Fascists the opportunity to show that they could maintain order even if the police could not. This attracted the financial backing of industrialists and landowners initially suspicious of the new movement.

Within three years, Mussolini had built a power base large enough to attempt to seize power. On 28 October, Fascist "black

LEFT **Mussolini taking the salute at a Fascist rally ("The March of Triumph") by Fascist Youth in the Piazza Venezia in Rome in 1935.**

BENITO MUSSOLINI (1883–1945)

Named Benito by his radical father after the Mexican president, Benito Juárez, who shot Emperor Maximilian (*see pages 134–37*), the young Mussolini joined the Marxist Italian Socialist party, and became editor of its newspaper, *Avanti!* But in 1914, he rejected the party's pacifist approach and demanded Italy's entry into the First World War on the Allied side. Although Mussolini still uttered radical sentiments, his thought became dominated by militaristic and disciplinarian language. Pro-interventionists became the core of the early Fascist Party in 1919. A master-journalist and orator, Mussolini's post-war propaganda was very effective. He also understood that the Italian establishment would accept his violence in order to defeat the Left.

shirts" (so-called because of their attire) stormed public buildings across north and central Italy before converging on the capital in the "March on Rome." The Left proved a paper tiger, doing almost nothing to stop the march. The next day the King, Victor Emmanuel III, sent for Mussolini, who took the train to Rome from Milan, the birthplace of his movement. Mussolini emerged from the interview as Prime Minister. He had come to power in alliance with members of the old order who feared Communism and disliked democracy or considered democracy helpless to deal with severe economic and social problems.

Consolidation of the regime

It took Mussolini several years to make himself dictator, although legally speaking he always owed his power to nomination by the King and endorsement by a majority in the Parliament he claimed to despise. From the start, Mussolini encouraged arbitrary action by his supporters, but it was only after the murder (by Fascist hitmen) of the Socialist MP Giacomo Matteotti in 1924 that Mussolini decisively rejected the rule of law and openly showed that he would not tolerate opposition even in Parliament. Once he had established himself as dictator, he set about fashioning a Fascist state and society.

Fascists rejected Marxist ideas of class struggle and insisted on national solidarity against foreign rivals, but Mussolini claimed that there was a social component to his movement. "Corporatism" was the principle on which Fascism operated: workers and employers should cooperate, but strikes and independent trade unions were forbidden. The term "totalitarian" was coined by one of Mussolini's ministers to describe the Fascist dictatorship that claimed to supervise every aspect of life. In practice, the regime was riddled with corruption and cronyism: behind the facade of obedience all sorts of individuals and groups struggled for their own interests.

Nazism in Germany

While Mussolini had enjoyed a distinguished career as a journalist before he entered Fascist politics, Hitler was an Austrian-born drifter who found himself in the German army, resentful at the end of the war of its defeat and willing to accept and propagate the myth that it had been "stabbed in the back" rather than beaten by the Allies. Almost by chance, Hitler discovered his gifts as a speaker, voicing the resentments of millions like himself. After the war he entered a fringe party, the National Socialist German Workers' (Nazi) party, which had as its programme a mixture of socialism and racist nationalism.

Although the Nazis had come into existence before Mussolini seized power in Italy, much of the style of the Nazis – uniformed, saluting stormtroopers – and their methods – violent attacks on opponents and the cult of the "Leader" – were modelled on the Italian Fascists. But from the start Hitler's rhetoric contained one radical element that Mussolini came to copy only years later: a brutal anti-Semitism. The Fascists were Italian nationalists and shared a widespread European disdain for non-Europeans, but

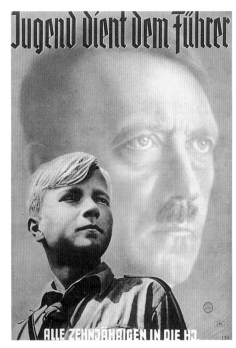

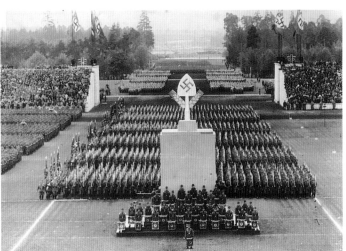

ABOVE **This Nazi poster of *c.* 1935 urges all ten-year-olds to serve their Leader (Führer) by joining the Hitler Youth. Youth and dynamism were key elements in Nazi propaganda.**

LEFT **Massive well-drilled rallies of Party members and Hitler Youth, such as this one in Nuremberg in September 1938, replaced genuine popular participation in politics.**

Hitler's followers were distinguished by their belief that Jews were at the root of all evil, ranging from Germany's defeat in the First World War to the ruthlessness of the Russian Revolution.

Hitler's coming to power

The Great Depression after 1929 enabled Hitler to come to power. He had tried to seize power in 1923 in a farcical putsch in a Munich beer hall. Defending in court his resort to radicalism, he declared: "If today I stand here as a revolutionary it is as a revolutionary against the revolution." Later he recognized that his party would do better to *use* democracy than to confront it head-on. The propaganda chief, Joseph Goebbels, was quite brazen about their approach: "We enter parliament in order to supply ourselves in the arsenal of democracy with its own weapons. We become members of the Reichstag in order to paralyze the Weimar sentiment with its own assistance. If democracy is so stupid as to give us free tickets and salaries for this work, that is its affair!"

By January 1933, with almost seven million people unemployed in Germany, the Nazi party was the largest in the country. Hitler's popularity was based on his criticisms of democracy for having failed Germany and his claim that he could restore full employment and national pride. Reactionary politicians around the aged President Hindenburg persuaded him that installing Hitler as Chancellor would at least foil the Communists, then Hitler could be pensioned off. But this was a naive belief, especially given Mussolini's consolidation of power in Italy after a similar deal ten years earlier.

With Hindenburg's compliance, Hitler forced through the banning of the Communist Party, his own electoral victory (with only 44 per cent of the vote) and then an Enabling Act that gave him dictatorial powers for four years. Within weeks, all other parties and trade unions had been abolished or merged with Nazi organizations.

The Nazi counter-revolution

When Hitler was appointed Chancellor in 1933, Goebbels proclaimed that this event marked the reversal of 1789. The French Revolution had promoted the principles of the rights of man, but the Nazis sought to deny them. Hitler had already declared that instead of revolutions to promote the rights of man or human equality, "There are no revolutions except racial revolutions: there cannot be a political, economic or social revolution – always and only it is a struggle of the lower stratum of inferior race against the dominant higher race...." Whereas Marx saw history as the story of class struggles, Hitler insisted that it was one of race conflicts.

Social Darwinism was the essential element in Hitler's thinking. What this meant

ABOVE **Poster for an anti-semitic exhibition in 1937. Depicting Jews as Germany's enemies was a central theme of Nazi propaganda.**

was that every aspect of life was part of a crude struggle for survival. Darwin's ideas about the survival of the fittest had been vulgarized by many people by 1900 and their writings had been read by Hitler and countless others in Central Europe. Thus, when Hitler set his biological vision of history against a Marxist one, his ideas fell on fertile soil. So-called "racial hygiene" had been widely disseminated by scientists long before Hitler's regime began to enforce the segregation, sterilization and finally extermination of "undesirables."

The elitism of Nazism was exemplified not only in its racism but also in its emphasis on the "Leadership Principle." All Fascist movements insisted on blind obedience to a single dominant leader who embodied the people's will and directed it. Thus, while Mussolini came to be known as "Il Duce," Hitler became the "Führer" (both titles meaning "Leader").

Fascists and their sympathizers liked to argue that conformity to a Leader's will would make societies more efficient. In fact, for all its efficiency at mass murder, Nazi Germany proved remarkably ill-organized as a war economy when it came to fighting the Allies in the Second World War. Hitler's interference in areas in which he had no specialist knowledge hindered the German war effort after its initial successes, while his subordinates quarrelled among themselves and frequently wasted research resources duplicating projects.

Racist revolution

By scapegoating a small proportion of Germany's population, the Jews, as the architects of all the country's misfortunes, Hitler used a skilful propaganda technique. This was not merely a cynical trick to get votes, but a gigantic and cruel experiment in "racial hygiene." As primary victims, the Jews were steadily subjected to worse treatment. At the height of his

success in 1938, Hitler unleashed a pogrom against Jews, the "Crystal Night," when Jews remaining in Germany were attacked and their property vandalized. After the war broke out, the Nazis moved from brutalization to extermination.

So-called Aryans were also subject to Hitler's racial hygiene. Even before the mass murder of Jews began, a programme of euthanasia was initiated to weed out the mentally and physically handicapped. The Nazi obsession with heredity led to efforts to control breeding among the Germans as if the Reich (the state) was a stud farm, boosting births among the desirable types and preventing unwanted conceptions.

Although the Nazi regime lasted just twelve years and implemented its full programme only during the war years, its terrible consequences were profound. Millions of Jews, hundreds of thousands of gypsies and vast numbers of Soviet prisoners of war were deliberately murdered or starved to death. The seriousness of Hitler's racism can be judged by his willingness to squander scarce sources and manpower on killing defenceless people rather than on fighting his armed enemies.

The defeat of counter-revolution

The aggressiveness of the Fascist regimes brought them into conflict with a vast coalition of states ranging from western democracies to Stalin's Russia. The Fascist cult of war as a virtue for its own sake proved self-destructive.

Mussolini fell under Hitler's spell as the Nazis achieved dramatic successes against defenceless or ill-prepared enemies. The Duce began to imitate his German counterpart and to adopt Nazi policies, including anti-Semitism. Fascist Italy tied its fate to Germany by joining the war against the Allies in 1940, and in so doing doomed itself. Not only would it be defeated if Germany lost, but an alliance with Hitler went against the nationalist grain (Germany was traditionally Italy's enemy) and undermined the popularity of the regime.

Whereas even Italian Fascists turned against Mussolini in 1943 as the Allies invaded the country, Hitler preserved a charismatic hold over most Germans until his suicide in the ruins of Berlin in April 1945. Ironically, neo-Fascism achieved a much stronger position in Italian political life after the war than neo-Nazism ever did in West Germany. The massive destruction of Germany and the revelation of Nazi crimes against humanity shocked Germans out of any residual loyalty to Hitler.

The Fascist movements turned out to have been a meteoric and devastating revolt against liberal as well as Socialist values, but the sheer scale of their defeat rendered them redundant after 1945. Even sympathizers felt obliged to distance themselves from the actions of the Nazis and Fascists, or to deny their worst crimes.

KEY EVENTS

1918 **9 November**
Germany declared a Republic
11 November
Germany signs armistice to end First World War
1919 **23 March**
Mussolini founds the Fascist Party
1922 **28 October**
Mussolini's "March on Rome"
29 October
Mussolini appointed Prime Minister
1923 **9 November**
Hitler's "Beer Hall putsch" in Munich
1924 **10 June**
Murder of Italian Socialist, Matteotti
1933 **30 January**
Hitler appointed Reich Chancellor
27 February
The Reichstag fire
23 March
Enabling Act grants Hitler dictatorial powers
2 May
Abolition of free trade unions
1938 **9 November**
"Crystal Night" – anti-Jewish pogrom
1939 **1 September**
Germany invades Poland
1940 **10 June**
Italy enters Second World War
1941 **22 June**
Germany invades the Soviet Union
1943 **25 July**
Mussolini deposed as Duce
3 September
Italy surrenders to Allies
1945 **28 April**
Mussolini executed by Communist partisans
30 April
Hitler commits suicide
8 May
Unconditional surrender of Nazi Germany

Unemployment, disillusionment with Republican government and other domestic problems in the early 1930s led Spain down the road to civil war, with fierce attachment to revolutionary goals on one side and equally determined reaction on the other. The conflict was not just a bitter ideologcal struggle between the Spanish Left and Right: support from different European regimes for one side or the other marked the great dividing line of European politics in the 1930s.

The Spanish Civil War

After the disastrous war against the USA in 1898, Spain lost the last vestiges of her transatlantic empire. The days of glory after Columbus had blazed the way for a vast overseas empire were over. Spain was beset by economic, social and political unrest. Not only was the constitutional monarchy far from truly representative: it was also incompetent. Defeat by Moors in Spain's last colony (Morocco) precipitated a military coup in Madrid in 1923. The new dictator tried to modernize Spain in an authoritarian way, but his regime collapsed in 1929. King Alfonso XIII gained no credit for dismissing the dictator, and in February 1931 local elections produced a republican majority. The King abdicated.

The Republic

The new Republic was born in somewhat inauspicious circumstances. Unemployment in the cities combined with rural under-employment to create a volatile situation. Both the Communists and anarchists had made considerable progress in gaining the support of the under-privileged, and a widespread feeling of revolutionary optimism existed on the Left that change could succeed. On the Right, however, a fear of rapid change was equally pronounced.

Reforms proposed by the Republic were often more impressive in word than they were in deed. Although an eight-hour day and protection against summary eviction of rural labourers were introduced, other laws aroused unrealistic hopes on the part

ABOVE **Socialist demonstrators march through Madrid in February 1936 demanding the release of political prisoners.**

LEFT **General Franco's hopes of quickly seizing the Catalonian city of Barcelona were thwarted by workers' militias that barricaded the city's streets.**

of many peasants and deep fear among many of the landowners. The traditional elites also felt threatened by the anticlericalism that flourished after the King had fled. The Prime Minister Manuel Azaña did nothing to stop the burning of church property, claiming: "All the convents in Madrid are not worth the life of a single republican." The head of the Catholic Church, Cardinal Segura, was exiled.

The failure to satisfy either the Left or Right provoked the downfall of the

government and a general election in November 1933. The united right-wing coalition won the election (despite getting fewer votes than the divided Left) but, as its leader José María Gil Robles later admitted, it wasted its victory with two years of "suicidal egoism." Resentments built up as employers and landlords felt free to reverse some of the Republic's early reforms. At the same time, events abroad influenced Spanish politics: the Right looked with admiration at Hitler's success in Germany at destroying the Left, while Spain's left-wingers saw this as an ominous portent of what might happen to them. Radicals on both sides came to see violence as the best way to achieve their goals. A general strike in 1934 was followed later that year by an armed revolt in Asturias, which was brutally suppressed by the army. A fresh bout of elections were held in February 1936, and this time the Left – united in the Popular Front of Socialists, Communists, radicals and anarchists – won most votes and a majority of seats. While supporters of the new government celebrated the dawn of what they hoped

ABOVE **Rifles are distributed to members of the left-wing trade union, CNT, in Barcelona.**

BELOW **Spain during the Civil War, showing the gradual advance of the Nationalists.**

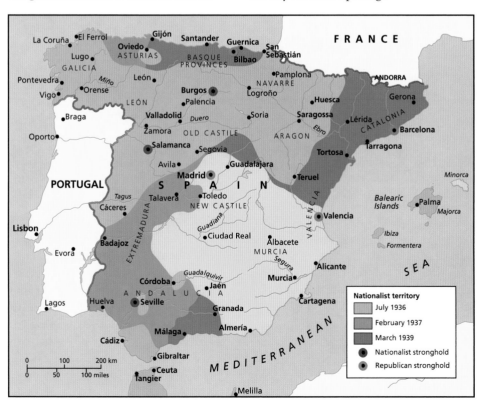

would be profound social change, on the Right the advocates of violent counter-revolution conspired, arguing that democracy could not produce the right result for Spain.

The coup

The Spanish army, which had *not* profited under the Republic, saw itself as the guarantor of traditional Spain – or at least its generals did. They feared that genuinely radical social policies would follow the February elections, and were worried by the growing disorder as peasants in the country and anticlericals in the cities took matters into their own hands and began local revolutions. The core group of military conspirators had no intention, however, of relying on legal means to express their grievances: they began to plot a coup.

The spring and early summer of 1936 saw growing political polarization and an increase in violence. The murder by Republican assault guards of the leading conservative politician, José Calvo Sotelo, on 13 July 1936 was a useful propaganda gift to the generals, who had set 18 July as the day for their uprising.

LEFT **Francisco Franco. Born in 1892, he had a brilliant career in the army, fighting the Moors and then suppressing strikes in the Basque country in 1934, before leading a military coup in 1936 that sparked the Spanish Civil War. His regime lasted until his death in 1975.**

The rising actually began with a military revolt in Spanish Morocco. Most army officers on the mainland were sympathetic to the rebel (Nationalist) cause, and the following day similar risings began in Seville and spread to many towns across Spain. When the leading insurgent died in a plane crash on 20 July, the youngest Spanish general, Francisco Franco, took over as rebel leader. The rebels made contact with sympathetic regimes abroad. With the aid of Italian and German aeroplanes, Franco was able to fly troops from Morocco to Spain at the start of August 1936 to spearhead the coup.

The start of the civil war

Although key elements of the security forces, particularly the police, refused to support the generals, the authorities in Madrid lacked the strength to crush the uprising. They attempted at first to negotiate with the rebels, but finally submitted to left-wing demands that the people be armed to resist. In cities such as Madrid and Barcelona weapons were distributed to hastily formed workers' militias that helped thwart the seizure of power by Franco's Nationalists. In other places the rebels found themselves besieged by local forces loyal to the Republic. Only the arrival of troops from Morocco relieved mutinous garrisons on the mainland.

The military coup promoted a revolutionary reaction in the areas beyond the generals' control. In some places a spontaneous and often brutal purge of real and imaginary Fascists started. At the same time local government collapsed, as did central control, and local revolutionary juntas established themselves, occupied, factories and redistributed land. Even the wearing of hats and ties – bourgeois styles – went rapidly out of fashion: workers' dungarees became the style for intellectuals as well as workers. In all this confusion, the new agricultural collectives often proved inefficient and were unhelpful when it came to supplying the big cities.

Divisions open on the Left

Rivalries among the Republicans were often as bitter as the antagonism towards Franco's forces. Right from the start, the Republic had been divided between the pragmatists, who wanted to maximize support for the government against Franco by minimizing social change, and those who believed that only a revolutionary upheaval behind Republican lines would arouse enough popular support to rout the Nationalists. The Communists were on the side of the moderates. Stalin felt that a radical republic would promote an alliance between the Fascist states helping Franco and Britain and France – something to be avoided at all costs. Thus the Communists not only opposed radical social changes but also tried to stop peasants from taking land for themselves. They wanted as many allies as possible, even the bourgeoisie and the military. Other radicals regarded all officers as Fascists and all landowners as reactionaries.

Franco's forces refused to recognize any minorities in Spain so the Basques and Catalans were naturally hostile to the Nationalists, but they also resisted coordination from Madrid. Castilian officers, loyal to the Republic, found they had little authority among the Catalans.

Splits within the Republican camp deepened as time went on. The civil war on the Republican side between Communists and their rivals was as savage as it was against Franco. In May 1937, fighting erupted in Barcelona between Communist-led forces and a motley array of local anarchists and Catalan separatists. Eventually, the non-Communists agreed to lay down their arms to avoid further bloodshed that could only serve Franco's cause. The Communists then used their influence in the police

LEFT **Joan Miró's famous poster calling for international help for the Republican cause.**

BELOW **An anti-Fascist Popular Front was difficult to establish. Despite popular support for the Republican struggle neither Britain nor France – two of the great democracies in Europe – would send official aid. They adopted instead a policy of non-intervention, trying to prevent arms from reaching either side. In practice, however, this meant blockading the Republic while arms could flow freely to Franco via Portugal.**

"It was the first time I had ever been in a town where the working class was in the saddle. Practically every building of any size had been seized by the workers and draped with [flags] ....The revolutionary posters were everywhere... loudspeakers were bellowing revolutionary songs all day and far into the night."
GEORGE ORWELL, ON BARCELONA IN 1936

and security services to hunt down anarchists and Trotskyites just as Stalin was purging his enemies inside the Soviet Union. Jesus Hernandez described the fruitless efforts of Communist interrogators to make Trotsky's former secretary, Andrés Nin, confess to "treason": "Nin was not giving in. He was resisting until he fainted. His inquisitors were getting impatient. They decided to abandon the 'dry' method. Then the blood flowed, the skin peeled off, the muscles torn, physical suffering pushed to the limits of human endurance. Nin resisted the cruel pain of the most refined tortures. In a few days his face was a shapeless mass of flesh."

International involvement

The Nationalists showed much greater cohesion. Without help from Fascist Italy and Nazi Germany, however, the Nationalist counter-revolution would have quickly fizzled out. German aircraft ferried the bulk of Franco's troops from Morocco to Spain, and large-scale supplies of ammunition plus tens of thousands of so-called

ABOVE **The bombing of Guernica on 26 April 1937 by Franco's German allies was one of the most controversial episodes of the Civil War. Picasso's painting,** *Guernica* (RIGHT) **helped to make the destruction of the town a propaganda triumph for the Republic.**

volunteers from Italy and Germany helped to turn the tide. Foreign aid bought time for Franco to organize his own forces.

The Republic enjoyed much sympathy abroad, but most governments were unwilling to aid it officially. Soviet assistance was counterproductive. Stalin was not prepared to put troops on the ground and the secret policemen who arrived in Spain were more concerned with rooting out non-Communists on the Republican side than fighting Franco.

The end of the Republic

The Republic was mortally wounded when the Nationalist army reached the Mediterranean on 15 April 1938 and cut its territory in two. It was only a matter of time before Franco's forces wore down the Republic. Having done so much to undermine the Republic's war-effort, the Communists now clamoured for the war to continue to the bitter end. Others began to argue for a negotiated end to the civil war and to the terrible sufferings it had caused.

On 5 March 1939, anti-Communist Republicans staged a coup in Madrid to prevent the Prime Minister and his comrades prolonging resistance while they in fact planned their own escape. Franco reacted to the news by insisting on an unconditional surrender. By the end of March, a general collapse ensued. Floods of refugees at the Mediterranean coast found few boats to take them. Suicide was a frequent alternative to falling into Franco's hands.

The counter-revolutionary survivor

Franco's regime survived the defeat of its former Fascist allies, despite sending troops to fight on the Russian front during the Second World War. From 1945 onwards, Spain gradually became more technocratic. By the 1960s Franco was presiding over a modernizing policy that produced a consumer-oriented society. Relative affluence did not produce affection for the regime, however. Over the long years after his victory, Franco had suppressed any hint of opposition. As many as 200,000 Spaniards died after the civil war ended as a result of his rule. Unlike Hitler and Mussolini, Franco died – surrounded by a bizarre mixture of religious relics and modern medical technology – in his own bed in 1975. But he had failed to find a successor in his own mould. Instead he reverted to the Bourbon dynasty and selected Juan Carlos, the grandson of the last King, to be his heir. At the end of Franco's long rule, his dictatorship died with him and the transition to democracy was remarkably painless.

LEFT **General Franco speaking at the Nationalist victory parade in Madrid at the end of the Civil War in 1939. Unlike his allies Hitler and Mussolini, Franco was no orator. The army rather than a political party was his power base.**

KEY EVENTS	
1923	**23 September** General Primo de Rivera seizes power
1930	**30 January** Primo de Rivera resigns
1931	**12 April** Municipal elections won by the Left **14 April** Fall of monarchy; Republic proclaimed **28 June** Left wins Parliamentary elections **9 December** New republican constitution
1933	**November** Right wins second parliamentary elections
1936	**16 February** Popular Front wins parliamentary election **13 July** Murder of Calvo Sotelo **18 July** Beginning of Nationalist uprising
1937	**12–17 March** Italian "volunteers" defeated at Guadalajara **26 April** Destruction of Guernica **May** Communist-led purge of rivals in Barcelona **11 August** Republic dissolves local collectives
1938	**21 February** Teruel abandoned by the Republicans **15 April** Franco's troops reach Mediterranean **21 September** Prime Minister Negrín announces withdrawal of International Brigades
1939	**26 January** Franco's troops enter Barcelona **27 February** Britain and France recognize Franco **5 March** Casado's anti-Communist coup in Madrid **31 March** Madrid falls to Franco's troops
1975	**20 November** Death of Franco

For much of the twentieth century China has been convulsed by revolutions. Her ninety-year transformation from a helpless giant to a superpower was achieved at an enormous cost. Ironically, all attempts to break with China's past seem to have reinforced key features of her traditional ways. Mao's revolution in 1949 brought to power a generation whose rivalries dominated Chinese politics for over forty years. Mao himself presided like a remote god-emperor over his red kingdom.

Communist Revolution in China

The background to China's twentieth-century revolutions lies in the sudden change in the country's status during the nineteenth century when, after countless generations as the centre of its own world, the Chinese Empire was challenged by the intrusions of Western merchants keen to buy silk, tea and other goods. The ruling Chinese Manchu dynasty opposed foreign trade and led China into war with several Western countries. But, unable to compete with modern weapons, China was forced to capitulate and open her over-populated territory to Western traders. Under the impact of foreign interference, imperial authority began to decay.

Loss of confidence in the Manchu government and economic difficulties resulted in the mid-nineteenth century in the Taiping (Heavenly Peace) Rebellion which, half peasant revolt and half relgious crusade, swept much of central China. For almost fourteen years (1850–64), a large part of the country was controlled by rebels whose leader expounded an eccentric mix of Confucianism and Christianity, with a powerful dose of social revolution. The Taiping regime abolished land ownership and preached equality, but its leaders quarrelled among themselves and the rebellion was eventually crushed by the Manchus.

The collapse of the empire

Anti-foreigner sentiment in China grew towards the end of the nineteenth century and culminated in the Boxer Uprising of

LEFT **An attack on Shanghai during the Taiping Rebellion of 1850–64. Inspired by a mixture of peasant egalitarianism and Western-influenced Christian ideology, the rebellion was a harbinger of the collapse of imperial China some fifty years later.**

1900, which was tacitly supported by the imperial Manchu regime. The Boxers launched violent attacks on foreigners and missionaries in northern China and laid siege to Peking in June 1900. The siege was lifted only when an international army intervened in August.

Resentment was directed not just against the foreigners, however, but also against the Manchu elite, which had failed to protect China from foreign exploitation. The imperial regime's attempt to channel nationalism by encouraging the unsuccessful Boxer rebellion only discredited the imperial family. Despite last-ditch attempts at reform and huge (if inefficient) military spending, the disintegration of the imperial system climaxed in 1911, when troops began removing the symbol of Chinese subjection to the Manchu – the pig-tail – just as Taiping rebels had in the 1850s. Small-scale army mutinies and uprisings soon developed into national revolution,

causing the dynasty to slide into collapse. The Dowager Empress formally abdicated on behalf of the five-year-old Emperor, Pu Yi, in February 1912.

ABOVE **German cavalry (part of the Western forces of occupation) arrive at the Forbidden City in Beijing following the collapse of the Boxer Rebellion in 1900.**

The new Chinese Republic

On 1 January 1912, a new Republic of China was proclaimed and a provisional government established at Nanking with the nationalist leader Dr Sun Yat-sen as President. Sun Yat-sen had spent much time abroad and was keen to apply certain modern Western ideas of democracy (even Socialism) to traditional Chinese principles, but for the sake of national unity he resigned his presidency in March to general Yuan Shi Kai, who quickly began to adopt dictatorial methods and later tried to make himself Emperor. The Republic inherited massive problems from the old regime that were exacerbated when central authority collapsed after the death of Yuan in June 1916. Corruption and local ambitions soon led to the appearance of warlordism.

Patriotic frustration at China's decline and subservience to foreign interests erupted again on 4 May 1919 in student-led demonstrations in Peking calling for the boycott of foreign goods. However, not all Chinese radicals rejected everything foreign. The success of the Russian revolutionaries in establishing a new social order while denouncing imperialism and defeating foreign intervention impressed some intellectuals, and in July 1921 a Chinese Communist Party was founded in Shanghai.

The early years of the Communist Party

The Communist Party attracted a motley group of intellectuals from elite backgrounds, such as the future Prime Minister Zhou En Lai, as well as people born into peasant families, for example the young librarian, Mao Tse-tung.

At first the Communists enjoyed good relations with Sun Yat-sen's Nationalist (Kuomintang) movement based in Nanking. Both parties opposed warlordism and collaboration with imperialists from abroad. But after Sun Yat-sen's death in 1925, relations soured. The new Kuomintang leader, Chiang Kai-shek, was an army officer with some Soviet training, but his political sympathies lay with the West.

The split with the Kuomintang

According to orthodox Marxist principles, Communism can be established only by a proletarian revolution. Taking no account of the fact that China was populated by hundreds of millions of peasants and only a relatively small urban working class, the Soviet regime encouraged the Chinese Communist Party (CCP) to focus its activities in the big cities like Shanghai. Unfortunately these cities were also centres of Nationalist power.

Fearful of a Communist coup, Chiang launched a preemptive purge of his rivals in 1927 and slaughtered thousands of Communists. This started a long civil war between the Communists and Nationalists.

In 1931 the Communists set up a Chinese Soviet government in Ruijin in Jiangxi province, which became the object

LEFT **Southeast China. Revolutionary upheaval, struggles between warlords and war against Japan marked the period of the first Chinese Republic, 1911–49. Communist guerrillas adopted Mao's strategy of first establishing control over the countryside before eventually storming the cities.**

of Chiang Kai-shek's troops. Pitched battles were extremely costly to the ill-equipped Communists and by the autumn of 1934, the Communists were in a desperate position. However, impending defeat brought to the Party's leadership a group led by Mao Tse-tung, who advocated a radical break with existing methods.

It became clear to Mao early on in the civil war that Soviet advice about how to fight the Nationalists was not working. Mao recognized that the only chance of successful revolution in China was to mobilize the great majority of the Chinese population: the peasants. Thus, rather than concentrating his efforts on the urban centres, he left these completely alone and sought instead to build up power bases in the rural areas of south-central China.

Whereas many Chinese Communists continued to follow the advice from Moscow, Mao and his followers decided to ditch conventional tactics and resort to a mobile form of guerrilla warfare. Chiang was deeply threatened and began to block-ade all the Communist strongholds. This led to Mao's bold decision to break out from Chiang's suffocating encirclement in October 1934 and begin what became known as the Long March: an epic trek to Yenan in the north, where the Communists could establish an alternative government.

Harassed first by the Kuomintang and then by the armies of local warlords, the Chinese Red Army of some 90,000–100,000 people marched nearly 6,000 miles (9,660 km) across inhospitable mountain ranges and rivers. Only a tiny proportion of the original army arrived in Yenan a year later, in December 1936. But the survivors of the Long March were to dominate the Chinese Communist Party into the mid-1990s. It was a badge of hon-our and a passport to high rank to have been one of the few thousand survivors.

ABOVE RIGHT The rush for gold as China's most important financial centre, Shanghai, fell to the Communists amid scenes of chaos in late May 1949.

RIGHT Celebrating the Communist victory in Shanghai, June 1949. The posters of Mao Tse-tung and General Chu De indicate that the cult of personality in China had begun.

ABOVE **Communist soldiers guarding the Great Wall against Japan. In the end, Chinese Nationalists proved to be more dangerous to the Communists than the Japanese.**

Yet the days of triumph still lay far in the future. Although Mao's model of guerrilla warfare was to prove effective in the long term, for many years the Communists were marginalized in their northern hideouts. Their self-proclaimed "liberated areas" were poor and remote.

Japanese invasion

Meanwhile, the Nationalists faced a much more serious challenge: a Japanese invasion of China. Although Japan had seized Manchuria in 1931, Chiang had been more preoccupied with his war on the Communists than with Japanese aggression. This had provoked some of Chiang's own – largely Manchurian – generals to

kidnap him in 1936 and force him to agree to stop persecuting the Communists and instead concentrate Nationalist forces against the growing Japanese threat.

In fact Japan launched a full-scale invasion of China in 1937. Together the Nationalists and Communists fought the Japanese, although Chiang's troops did the bulk of the resistance. The Nationalist army lost its best troops in battle against the Japanese while, behind the fighting line, Nationalist politicians proved incapable of organizing an effective war effort. Corruption and inflation were rampant.

By 1940, Japan occupied much of northern China and regular defeats were disillusioning Chiang's supporters. While Kuomintang officials and the wealthy tended to flee areas occupied by the enemy, the Communist partisan forces were able

LEFT **Mao's People's Liberation Army occupies the ancient city of Nanking on 23 April 1949.**

INSET **Mao proclaims the People's Republic of China on 1 October 1949: "The Chinese People have stood up."**

to operate across large areas of China by exploiting the lack of Japanese troops to properly police their conquered territories.

In 1941, Britain and the United States entered the war on the side of the Chinese. The dropping of the atomic bombs on Japan in August 1945 resulted in the sudden surrender of the large Japanese armies in China and an end to the Sino-Japanese war – but renewed hostilities between the Communists and Nationalists.

Many of the Japanese soldiers handed over their weapons and equipment to Mao's People's Liberation Army (PLA), which helped to transform the PLA from a guerrilla force into a regular army. Another benefit came from the Soviet army's lightning advance into Manchuria to destroy the Japanese army there, which opened the way for Mao's forces to operate in that rich province.

The fall of the Kuomintang

Chiang failed to take advantage of Japan's defeat. Although he recovered nominal control of China, all the worst features of his regime meant that civil war against the Communists was renewed, with popular support for it at a low ebb. Chiang's armies were now well-equipped (fearful of a Communist victory in China the US had supplied Chiang with arms), but morale was low. Desertion and corruption were rife.

Meanwhile, the PLA was growing rapidly and Mao's comrades showed that they possessed the ability to organize large-scale military operations as well as partisan warfare. Backed up by populist propaganda calling for land redistribution, the Communist forces swept across China with astonishing rapidity.

Chiang's dependence on American aid was double-edged. Even though the USA was not in fact prepared to send in its own troops to fight in a Chinese civil war, Mao could portray the Kuomintang as a corrupt regime serving foreign interests. Nationalism was as important as Socialist ideas in attracting people to Communism. After decades of war and then civil war, Mao's promises of a better life were very appealing to a population worn down by corruption, repression and famine.

Mao establishes the People's Republic of China

In 1948, Mao changed his tactics and launched an offensive against the Kuomintang. The Nationalists were easily routed and the Communists swept across China. In December they laid siege to Peking, which fell without a shot in January 1949. Mao's troops went on to take most of China's key cities and by autumn 1949 the Communists clearly had control of the country. Mao celebrated the Communist triumph in Peking on 1 October 1949, when he proclaimed the establishment of a People's Republic. In addition to the Marxist rhetoric there was a strong dose of nationalism: "Today the people of China have stood up," Mao announced. Communism and the restoration of Chinese pride were supposed to go hand-in-hand after a century or more of humiliation. Chiang Kai-shek fled to the island of Taiwan where he continued (under American protection) to claim to rule the "Republic of China." A Nationalist government still exists in Taiwan.

The new Chinese government set about establishing a Socialist society. Land was expropriated from large estates, agriculture was collectivized and factories were nationalized. Nationalists and other class enemies, when they were not shot, were sent to do "reform through labour" in prison camps.

For a while, Mao's regime seemed relatively moderate in its progress towards a fully socialized economy. In 1956, after the death of Stalin, some liberalization seemed in the air. Mao talked in May 1956 about "letting a hundred flowers bloom," allowing intellectuals to voice their opinions. But he soon reacted against the flood of criticism that this policy had unleashed. He identified all critics as enemies and counter-revolutionaries. A period of repression followed liberalization.

Although Mao talked about revolutionary spontaneity, he liked to be its catalyst and to direct popular energies. As he grew older he became anxious to achieve full Communism. He also began to show symptoms of distrusting his comrades.

The "Great Leap Forward"

In February 1958, Mao launched another revolutionary wave. This time it was to be a giant step in the modernization of China.

The so-called "Great Leap Forward" – which aimed to rapidly expand China's industrial base – was supposed to surpass even the forced modernization of the Soviet Union under Stalin twenty years earlier. Instead it produced even worse disasters. It is true that 99 per cent of China's teeming rural population was organized into communes linking agriculture and local industrial production, but the policy was ill thought-out and, based on Mao's cult of willpower over expertise, tens of millions of Chinese peasants starved to death as their whole way of life was swept away. Efforts to boost industrial production failed too. By the early 1960s, China was in an economic crisis and a split in the Party's leadership between Maoists and pragmatists appeared.

The Cultural Revolution

After the failures of the Great Leap Forward, Mao's comrades began to ease him out of day-to-day charge of policy. Their suspicion of his megalomania mixed with his fears about their motives. Mao resigned his position as Chairman of the People's Republic in 1959 to Liu Shao Qi. Publicly Mao was still praised as leader, but he himself complained that his name was invoked like a "dead ancestor."

Rejecting Mao's emphasis on ideological purity, the moderate Deng Xiaoping called for expertise to be the basis of

ABOVE **A Chinese poster of 1949 celebrating the unity of the People's Liberation Army with the Chinese people.**

LEFT **"The Flowers are opening and blooming at the new China," a poster of 1949. Note the portraits of Stalin, Lenin, Sun Yatsen and Mao on the wall in the background.**

appointments: "It does not matter what colour a cat is," he said, "provided it can catch mice." But Mao still possessed effective control over the PLA and the propaganda machine. Suspicious that Liu and Deng wanted to replace him, Mao determined on a counterattack. Open or direct criticism of Party leaders was impossible in China, so intellectuals and politicians had to express their dissatisfaction through other means, particularly essays, editorials and other literary media. The appearance in 1961 of the satirical play, *Hai Jui dismissed from Office*, in

which Mao was implicitly criticized, gave Mao the pretext for a counterattack.

Mao initiated the Cultural Revolution in the mid-1960s to regain ideological control of the Party and to spread more radical revolution to the populace. To implement this new wave of revolution, he enlisted the support of the army commander, Lin Biao, who used his power base to disseminate Maoist propaganda. The famous *Little Red Book* of Mao's thoughts, first printed for the army in 1963, was distributed in tens of millions of copies. Held high by chanting Red Guards wearing Mao lapel buttons it became the bible of the Cultural Revolution after 1965.

Propaganda was used to incite a revolutionary fever across the country. All of China's problems were blamed on a clique of traitors to the Party led by Mao's former close comrades. China had to be purified of them and every kind of

LEFT **Some of the first signs of the Cultural Revolution appear in China in 1965 with the cult of Mao.**

INSET **Rivals for Mao's favour: the army commander Lin Biao and Premier Zhou En Lai wave Mao's *Little Red Book* in May 1967.**

old way of thinking, which was holding up the dawn of a Maoist paradise. Youthful resentment against the older generation was unleashed by the septuagenarian Mao. Orgies of destruction and humiliation took place as young Red Guards insulted and degraded any Party official, teacher or figure of authority considered insufficiently Maoist. Not only symbols of Western civilization but also monuments to China's ancient civilization were randomly vandalized as unworthy of the new era dawning under the leadership of Mao.

Liu Shao Qi was physically beaten by Red Guards and died in sordid conditions. Other leaders of the Party, including Deng, were degraded and imprisoned, or sent to work in the fields. Thousands of ordinary officials lost their lives. So too did Red

ABOVE **Despite the suffering during the Cultural Revolution and the abandonment of Maoist economics under Deng, a cult of Mao survived even into the mid-1990s.**

Guards, as one group clashed with another over who was the most revolutionary.

Self-criticism became obligatory, leading Deng to urge his family to denounce him in order to save themselves. Schools and colleges stopped teaching in the chaos. Endless rounds of denunciations and self-criticism interfered with ordinary work. In the end, the extremism of the Red Guards spiralled out of control and Mao was forced in some instances to send in the PLA to defuse the situation.

Attacking his rivals for "taking the capitalist road," Mao purged his current rivals – but by promoting Lin Biao as his successor, he created another threat to himself. The fall of Liu and Deng did not

> **"When Liu Shao Qi was dragged down we had been very supportive... But the Lin Biao affair provided us with a major lesson. We came to see that the leaders up there could say today that something is round; tomorrow that it's flat. We lost faith in the system."** A CHINESE PEASANT

end the Chinese Revolution's tendency to devour its own children.

The twists and turns of policy and the fallings-out among the leadership began to disillusion even the most fanatical Red Guards. It was possible to believe that one set of Mao's closest associates, Liu Shao Qi and Deng Xiaoping, had turned traitor and followed the "capitalist road," but credulity was stretched when their nemesis, Lin Biao, was exposed (following his death in an air crash in 1971 after allegedly trying to overthrow the government) as an enemy of the people. Why did the Great Helmsman keep choosing the wrong assistants?

An end to revolution?

Mao's wife, Jiang Qing, was the chief beneficiary of the Cultural Revolution. She and three other radical leaders (the Gang of Four) hoped to maintain the cultural revolutionary regime. But this was too much for many senior Communists who had stuck by Mao through so many changes in policy. After his death in 1976, the Gang of Four was arrested and denounced as traitors to the dead Chairman. It was almost the final twist in the tortured development of Chinese politics. Instead of the Maoists, it was Deng Xiaoping who emerged from disgrace to claim the leadership. Rejecting both Maoist fanaticism and liberalism, Deng set about trying to develop a China that was economically efficient but still ruled by the Communists. Yet even Deng's more moderate approach attracted dissent (*see pages 174–75*).

After the Second World War, the colonial empires in Asia and much of Africa waned rapidly, and the struggle in Vietnam against French rule was only the first of many anti-colonial wars to sweep across the globe. The success of Mao's guerrilla armies in winning control of China in 1949 gave an enormous boost to many pro-independence movements, which tried to imitate Mao's example by combining a Socialist vision of the future with partisan warfare in order to win power.

Anti-colonial Conflict

When Indochina (modern-day Cambodia, Laos and Vietnam) was colonized by France in the nineteenth century, many peasants were dispossessed of their land, which made French rule very unpopular. Despite occasional nationalistic outbursts against the French in the 1920s and 1930s, it was not until colonial authority was weakened during the Japanese occupation of Vietnam after 1940 that the nationalist movement truly acquired credibility.

After the Allied defeat of Japan in August 1945, the Vietminh (the League for the Independence of Vietnam) were quick to proclaim a Democratic Republic of Vietnam on 2 September 1945. But the Allies had alternative ideas: according to the postwar settlement, south Vietnam would be restored to France with the support of British troops while the north would be secured for the French by the Chinese. With such different plans for the future of Vietnam, war between the French and the Vietnamese nationalists was the inevitable outcome.

The French faced a formidable rival in Ho Chi Minh, Communist leader of the Vietminh. He had good connections with Moscow, but he had also studied the lessons of the campaigns of Mao's People's Liberation Army against the Kuomintang in China (*see pages 146–51*). Like Mao, Ho and his outstanding commander, General Vo Nguyen Giap,

ABOVE **Ho Chi Minh (1890–1969), who led the struggle for Vietnam's independence from France.**

LEFT **Guerrilla conflicts in Southeast Asia, 1945–75. The attempt of the European colonial powers to take control in Southeast Asia after the defeat of Japan in 1945 and Mao's success in establishing a Communist regime in China, provoked resistance to colonial rule throughout the region.**

BELOW **French troops guarding captured Vietnamese troops in Dien Bien Phu before their own defeat in 1954.**

ABOVE **The war in Vietnam. After expelling the French from North Vietnam in 1954, the Communist regime in Hanoi developed the "Ho Chi Minh" trail through Laos and Cambodia to supply troops and weapons to support the Vietcong in the South. Neither the US army nor the South Vietnamese were willing to sustain more fighting in the jungles to the east to block the trail.**

ABOVE RIGHT **US Marines land by helicopter in August 1967. The US possessed superior technology, but lacked sufficient understanding of the complexity of the situation to effectively fight the Vietcong guerrillas.**

RIGHT **US ground forces in South Vietnam.**

recognized that the key to success was through guerrilla tactics rather than engaging the French in conventional warfare.

Distant France could never afford to deploy sufficiently large forces to control Vietnam, so the French generals tried to defeat the Vietminh by relying on technological superiority. But after 1949 the Vietminh was supported by the Communist regime in China, and received modern weapons across the long Sino-Vietnamese border. The Vietminh also heavily outnumbered the French, and benefited from detailed knowledge of the jungle terrain.

At the end of 1953, having already lost thousands of men and been worn down by continual hit-and-run raids, the French adopted a risky, ultimately suicidal, strategy to try to bring the Vietminh to a decisive battle. They established a base deep behind enemy lines in the jungle at Dien Bien Phu, intending to cut off Vietminh supply routes. The base, which could only be supplied by air, was home to 10,000 French troops. But under the cover of the thick

jungle, General Giap was able to assemble his forces around the base, hauling heavy guns to bombard the French defenders. On 15 March 1954, the French garrison was astonished by a sudden and savage barrage.

Unlike much of the war, the struggle for Dien Bien Phu was a pitched battle. It continued for six weeks. Although the Vietminh suffered much heavier losses than the French, the French garrison was overwhelmed after it became clear that the Americans would not intervene to save it. The French surrender in May 1954, marked the end of war. The truce agreement of 1954 temporarily divided Vietnam in two, establishing a Communist republic under Ho Chi Minh in the north and a French-backed government in the south under Ngo Dinh Diem. The country was supposed to be reunified in 1956 after nationwide elections. These never took place.

The Americans in Vietnam

Diem's government in Saigon (in South Vietnam) was corrupt and authoritarian. Diem refused to countenance free elections, for he worried Ho might win. It was not long before an opposition movement emerged – the National Front for the Liberation of Vietnam (NLF), nicknamed the Vietcong – which began to receive smuggled arms and other supplies from the North along the jungle paths of the so-called Ho Chi Minh trail. Civil war ensued.

As the North Vietnamese steadily eroded the South's position in the early 1960s, the United States became drawn in to the war on Saigon's side: the US had no wish to see Communism spread from China across Southeast Asia. By 1967, half a million US troops had effectively taken over the war. This allowed Ho's regime in Hanoi in the North to portray itself as patriotic and Saigon's leaders as puppets of a foreign power. The Vietnamese in the South often found the Americans – their supposed protectors – more threatening than the Communists in the North. Massive aerial bombardments in the South to soften up Communist guerrilla positions and to protect US forces also caused widespread civilian casualties (far more than the selective bombing of North Vietnam itself).

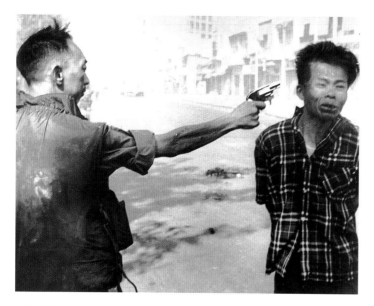

Afraid of provoking China into direct intervention, as had happened in Korea in 1950, the Americans did not invade North Vietnam. Instead the US army set up safe havens for supplying troops operating in the South.

An apparently endless and ill-understood war with a steady flow of casualties demoralized the American public as well as the troops, particularly after the Vietcong launched the Tet Offensive on 31 January 1968: a coordinated attack on the cities of South Vietnam which, though eventually defeated, resulted in thousands of deaths on all sides. Under President Nixon after 1968 the Americans tried, belatedly, to "Vietnamize" the war by training and equipping an effective South Vietnamese army. A ceasefire in 1973 was merely the prelude to a switch in North Vietnamese tactics. With the US army gone and Congress unwilling to authorize air support for the South, the North Vietnamese launched a decisive conventional offensive in spring 1975, capturing Saigon on 30 April. They had demonstrated that they could wage guerrilla warfare effectively even against a superpower. Unfortunately the coming years were to prove that the Communist government was more efficient at waging war than running a country.

Malaya: the exception?
Superficially, the British government after the Second World War faced a similar

ABOVE LEFT **Saigon, 1 February 1968. A propaganda disaster for the South: the head of Saigon's police executes a captured Vietcong guerrilla in front of the cameras during the Tet offensive.**

ABOVE RIGHT **Bodies of Vietcong who had infiltrated Saigon during the Tet Offensive lie in the street on 3 February 1968 after the government's troops recover control.**

threat to its rule in Malaya as the French had faced in Vietnam. Japan had occupied the whole Malay peninsula during the war, and – as in Vietnam – the intentions of the colonial government to return to power after Japan surrendered in 1945 were at odds with the nationalists who sought independence. In June 1948, guerrilla attacks began on British colonial officials and plantations.

The jungle terrain of the Malaysian peninsula was so similar to Indochina in the military problems that it posed that observers might have expected the guerrillas to have enjoyed victories over the British forces similar to those of their counterparts in Vietnam over the French. However, key differences undermined the effectiveness of revolutionary guerrilla warfare in Malaya. Unlike the French, who had been determined to cling to empire to expunge the humiliation of defeat at home in the Second World War, the British were anxious primarily to transfer power in their empire to future independent rulers who would not confiscate valuable investments. By arguing that the Communists' struggle for

KEY EVENTS: VIETNAM
1945 2 September Vietminh proclaims independence of Vietnam
1946 6 March France recognizes Vietnam as "free state" but part of French Union **5 August** Fighting begins between French and Vietminh
1947 22 March Even Communist ministers in France vote funds for war in Vietnam
1948 5 June "Independent Vietnam" adheres to French Union
1953 13 April French lose Chinese border post, Sam Neua
1954 15 March Giap begins onslaught on Dien Bien Phu **7 May** Fall of Dien Bien Phu **21 July** Geneva Agreement: France leaves Indochina
1955 October South Vietnam becomes a republic
1963 2 November Murder of South Vietnamese President, Ngo Dinh Diem
1968 29 January The Vietcong launches the Tet Offensive
1973 27 January Ceasefire between North and South Vietnam
1974 April Open warfare resumes
1975 30 April Fall of Saigon – Communists gain Cambodia as well
1978 25 December Vietnam invades Cambodia
1979 17 February–6 March China attacks Vietnam in reprisal

power was delaying independence, the British had a strong advantage in the propaganda battle. The ethnic balance in Malaya also favoured the British, since the Communists were drawn overwhelmingly from the Chinese population, meaning the British could rally support among the other communities, particularly the Malay and Indian majority, against the Chinese minority. Furthermore, the guerrillas were outnumbered by carefully trained jungle warfare units using modern technology and cooperating with the local people. Malaya became independent in 1957 and the state of emergency ended in 1960, though guerrillas hid deep in the remote jungle for decades to come.

FAR LEFT **The leader of the Algerian nationalist movement, Mohammed Ben Bella (1918–95). Released from a French prison in 1962, he was President of Algeria until he was overthrown in a coup in 1965.**

LEFT **Jacques Massu, the French general whose brutal methods failed to stifle resistance to French rule in Algeria.**

Algeria: French or Algerian?

Unlike France's other colonies, Algeria was legally part of France itself. As well as a large European French-speaking population, the *pieds-noirs*, Algeria also had a very much larger Arab and Muslim population, which enjoyed at best second-class status.

There had been stirrings of nationalism in Algeria even during the Second World War, but these were brutally suppressed. A spontaneous nationalist rebellion on 8 May 1945 saw a hundred or so Europeans murdered, but the French responded by massacring thousands of Algerians. The brutality of the French reprisals converted many people to the nationalist cause.

In 1952, Mohammed Ben Bella, the Algerian nationalist then in exile in Cairo, set up the National Liberation Front (FLN) of Algeria. Bella admired President Nasser's radical Pan-Arab Egypt and looked to the Soviet Union as an ally for a future secular Socialist independent Algeria. But it was the French debacle at Dien Bien Phu in Vietnam in 1954 that was the signal for open revolt in Algeria.

Having been humiliated in Vietnam, the French army was determined to win in what it regarded as France itself. The struggle initially had the character of a rural guerrilla conflict, especially in the east near Tunisia (which supplied military equipment to the FLN). But by late 1956, urban guerrillas had also become active in the capital, Algiers. French paratroopers were brought in to clamp down on the FLN, which they did with the highly publicized use of torture and other brutal methods.

RIGHT **French soldiers with an Algerian prisoner and the bodies of two FLN guerrillas in May 1956. Heavy civilian casualties often accompanied such counter terrorist successes.**

KEY EVENTS: ALGERIA

1945 **8 May**
Rioting in Setif

1948 **4 and 11 April**
Algerian elections

1952 **March**
Ben Bella, in exile in Cairo, establishes the FLN

1954 **1 November**
Beginning of revolt in Algeria

1955 **21 March**
Proclamation of state of emergency in Algeria

1956 **7 March**
Independence for Morocco
October
French seize Ben Bella on Moroccan plane

1958 **13 May**
Coup in Algiers against Fourth Republic in France

1961 **22 April**
General Salan's coup in Algiers

1962 **18 March**
Evian Agreements grant independence to Algeria
20 April
Arrest of Salan
3 July
Independence Day in Algeria

Although the French forces could control the situation in Algeria, the expense of the war and the methods used by the authorities to suppress the nationalists became increasingly controversial inside France. In May 1958, General de Gaulle returned to power with the support of mutinous generals in Algiers who thought he would back them to the hilt. In fact, de Gaulle decided that although the FLN could not defeat the French army in a battle, the war itself was ultimately unwinnable.

By making the war too costly and bloody for the French public to stomach, the FLN provoked de Gaulle into agreeing to Algerian independence in 1962. Ben Bella became President. The last fighting in Algeria was between the military and *pied-noir* extremists who could not accept de Gaulle's volte-face.

Although the FLN was able to unite a large majority of Algerians against French rule, after independence its internal divisions came out into the open. Ben Bella was deposed in 1965 and imprisoned by former comrades until 1979. Despite Algeria's reserves of natural gas, the economy failed to develop rapidly enough to absorb a population explosion. The loss of the *pieds-noirs* and other French loyalists also hit the economy. By the 1990s, a new revolutionary force threatened the FLN's dictatorship: the Islamic Salvation Front (FIS), which challenged the FLN's failed secular Socialist model. Terrorism once more returned to haunt Algiers and the country at large when the FLN tried to suppress the FIS.

WORLD REVOLUTIONARY MOVEMENTS

In addition to Algeria, guerrilla warfare against Western colonizers took place in British-ruled Kenya, Rhodesia (Zimbabwe) and especially the Portuguese colonies of Angola, Mozambique and Guinea-Bissau.

Prolonged rural guerrilla warfare starting in the early 1960s in Portugal's three African colonies encouraged revolution in Portugal itself in 1974 when the authoritarian regime was toppled by disgruntled army officers on 25 April 1974. Portugal

ABOVE **Independence brought civil war to Angola. Here Unita supporters trek through the savannah in 1989.**

granted independence to Mozambique on 25 June 1975, to Angola on 10 November 1975, and gave up its other colonies, Cape Verde and Guinea-Bissau, at the same time.

Divisions among the anti-Portuguese guerrillas complicated the struggle and led to post-independence civil wars in both Angola and Mozambique. The domestic problems of these countries were further confused by international politics. Cuba,

ABOVE **In Mozambique, civil war was the backdrop to Frelimo's rule after 1975.**

RIGHT **An anti-Mau Mau operation by the British security forces in Kenya in April 1954. Thousands of Kikuyu were detained in camps like this one outside Nairobi in the attempt to round up all suspects. Many were severely treated by the British.**

the USSR, the US and South Africa were all major players in the politics of southern Africa in the 1970s and 1980s.

In Angola, both of the main groups jockeying for power were Marxist: the People's Liberation Movement of Angola (MPLA), which had Soviet and Cuban backing, and the Maoist Unita movement, led by Jonas Savimbi, which received South African support. In Mozambique the Soviet-backed Frelimo party took power, but was opposed by the Renamo movement, which also received South African support. South Africa wished to undermine the MPLA and Frelimo parties, both of which opposed the South African regime because of its apartheid policies and resistance to Namibian self-rule.

So long as the Cold War continued, neither Soviet and Cuban involvement nor South African intervention proved decisive. But at the end of the Cold War, the United States and Russia encouraged elections and reconciliation in both Angola and Mozambique. Years of civil war had bred deep distrust, however, especially between the MPLA and Unita in Angola, and a secure peace proved hard to establish.

The Mau Mau rebellion in Kenya

The Mau Mau uprising in Kenya after 20 October 1952 was a mixed revolt against British rule: it was part classic tribal revolt against alien rule and part modern anti-colonial revolution. The Kikuyu tribe resented the loss of traditional lands and rights to white settlers in the Kenyan highlands and formed a secret society, Mau Mau, dedicated to driving away the settlers. Apart from the disparity between the large, well-trained British imperial forces and the ill-equipped rebels, the tribal nature of the revolt – which included much bloodletting among Kenyans of different tribes (more in fact than between the British and the Kikuyu) – meant that Mau Mau could be contained and then crushed. More than 12,000 Kenyans, mainly Mau Mau supporters, lost their lives as against 250 whites. By the end of the emergency in 1960, however, the British government had decided to abandon

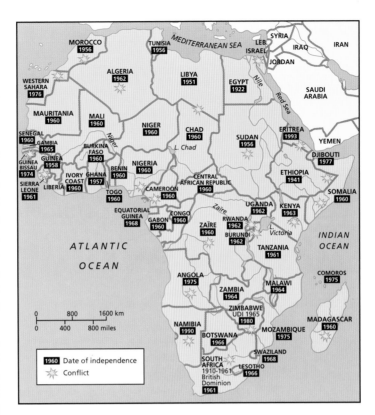

its African colonies so it moved quickly to seek reconciliation with Kikuyu leaders such as Jomo Kenyatta in order to ensure an orderly transfer of power and a guarantee of the rights of the 40,000 settlers.

Rhodesia becomes Zimbabwe

The quarter of a million white settlers in Rhodesia resisted the attempts of the British government to transfer power to independent African states with democratically elected governments. In November 1965, a unilateral declaration of independence (UDI) by the white minority regime led to a break with Britain, which approached the UN for economic sanctions. However, it was the collapse of the Portuguese empire in the mid-1970s that really put pressure on the UDI regime. Exiled black African groups, led by Robert Mugabe in Mozam-

bique and Joshua Nkomo in Angola, began an expensive guerrilla war against Rhodesia in support of a majority-ruled Zimbabwe. In 1979, the white regime agreed to a settlement that permitted a one-person one-vote election while retaining for ten years a limited special representation for the settlers. Robert Mugabe was elected President in January 1980.

Eritrea struggles for independence from Ethiopia

The former Italian colony of Eritrea was reincorporated into Ethiopia after the Second World War, and although after the Ethiopian Revolution of 1974 (*see pages 166–67*) the revolutionary leader Mengistu Haile Mariam briefly flirted with granting autonomy to Eritrea, he soon showed himself more determined to crush the Eritrean rebels than the imperial regime had ever been. The Eritreans used classic Maoist guerrilla warfare tactics against the Marxist Ethiopian regime. Despite famines and heavy fighting, the Eritrean People's Liberation Front (in conjunction with other rebel regions) was able to wear down Ethiopian resistance and gained UN recognized independence in summer 1991.

Unlike many other societies that have experienced revolutions, Cuba in the 1950s was relatively affluent. Both life expectancy and literacy were high. But the stagnating economy and political corruption created a revolutionary situation that brought Fidel Castro to power in 1959. His youthful charisma gave his regime great appeal in its early years; but the collapse of his great ally, the Soviet Union, in 1991 has damaged the economy and left Cuba politically isolated.

The Cuban Revolution

Cuban independence from Spain was achieved in 1898 (with the help of the United States) after a savage war of liberation. The price of Cuban victory, however, was American tutelage, for Cuba had to accept the incorporation into its 1903 constitution the so-called Platt Amendment, which gave the USA the right to intervene in Cuban affairs. This humiliation promoted strong anti-Yankee feeling in Cuba.

Cuba eventually cut its formal links with the USA in 1934 when the Platt Amendment was abrogated, but this did not leave Cuba any more economically independent than it had been. American imports of Cuba's main crop, sugar, remained its chief source of foreign currency (along with earnings from tourism), while US investment in Cuba's economic substructure meant that many of the country's most profitable enterprises were under absentee ownership. What's more, the Cuban government was often forced to look after the financial interests of the American investors at the expense of its own people, which also bred political corruption.

On 10 March 1952, Fulgencio Batista seized power in Cuba in a military coup, just weeks before official presidential elections were due to take place. A former president of Cuba, Batista had once been quite popular. But his coup of 1952 was opposed by many Cubans and the brutality of his second presidential term did nothing to enhance his popularity. A number of groups began to plot his downfall.

A revolutionary movement emerges

Batista's coup had incensed many people in Cuba, but none more so than the young Fidel Castro, who had been planning to run in the presidential elections. Born in 1926, the son of a moderately wealthy Spanish immigrant, Castro was standing as a candidate for the left-wing Ortodoxo party on an anti-corruption ticket.

Fidel came to see armed insurrection as the only way of opposing Batista, and began to plan a raid on the Moncada barracks in Santiago to seize arms. On the night of 26 July 1953, Castro and a handful of other rebels (including his brother) made their way in a convoy of cars across the city towards the barracks. But on their arrival there the attack quickly started to go wrong.

ABOVE **The rebel leader Fidel Castro in Santa Clara on 23 January 1959. The city had been captured by Che Guevara during the only big battle of the revolution.**

LEFT **Jubilant crowds in the centre of Havana in January 1959 hold aloft cartoons of Fidel Castro kicking out the hated former dictator of Cuba, Fulgencio Batista.**

LEFT **Castro's "pick-up militia" search buildings in Havana on 2 January 1959 for supporters of the Batista regime.**

BELOW **Summary show trials of Batista's ex-secret police and other supporters were held in January 1959. Revolutionary justice frequently led to an immediate death sentence.**

It was carnival time and many of the soldiers who should have been asleep were returning from the celebrations. Shooting began (in which three rebels and nineteen soldiers were killed), and Castro and his men were forced to retreat to the country. Castro was caught a few days later and sentenced to fifteen years in prison, but he was lucky to escape with his life: some of his companions were murdered. At his trial, Castro declared, "History will absolve me."

Released after an amnesty in 1955, Castro travelled to Mexico to raise a revolutionary army to topple Batista. It was here that Castro met Ernesto "Che" Guevara, the Argentinian-born revolutionary who was to become Castro's chief lieutenant and great friend. Together they organized a small force of eighty-two men, who on 24 November 1956 clambered into a small boat, the *Granma* (designed to sleep eight

ABOVE **Castro's Revolutionary Party hid in the mountains from December 1956. Many of the guerrillas were women, such as these partisans photographed in 1958. Castro offered women a dramatic alternative to their traditional roles.**

people), that was to take them on the week-long journey to Cuba.

The rebels landed on a beach in the Oriente province of Cuba on 2 December and made for the mountains of the Sierra Maestra, but the group was discovered three days later by government troops and most of Castro's followers were killed or taken prisoner. Castro and Che somehow managed to survive, and they established themselves with fewer than twenty men in the mountains. The mountains provided cover from attack and a good base from which to mount guerrilla raids on military bases to capture weapons. Over the next three years the rebel force grew.

After Batista's forces had failed to capture Castro, his legend in Cuba grew rapidly. Castro cleverly manipulated propaganda (being careful to avoid Communist slogans that might have alienated potential supporters) by using broadcasts over his rebel radio station and agreeing to give an interview to an American journalist, who published Castro's story in *The New York Times* in February 1957. The article lent stature and legitimacy to the rebel cause and won Castro new followers throughout the island – and in America. His anti-Batista rhetoric was even supported by the Catholic Church.

Castro's victory

Batista's venal regime enraged many Cubans: by turning their country's resorts into a playground for the American mafia he had humiliated them. Castro's popularity grew steadily through 1957; even some members of the army began to support him. Any demonstration against Batista was followed by brutal reprisals, which only served to further Castro's cause. But fear of government repression still reigned, and Castro's call in April 1958 for a general strike to topple the Batista regime fell flat. Even the Communist Party ignored it.

In May 1958 Batista launched a major offensive against Castro's supporters in the Sierra Maestra. Rebel victories demoralized the army, however, and Batista was eventually obliged to withdraw his forces. Castro recognized that Batista was losing the long battle and planned his final push.

In the end, Batista's apparent strength proved illusory. His forces began to melt away in late 1958 as Castro's small army began to march across the island towards Havana, taking one town after another. Batista's regime was not worth dying for. The dictator tried to hang on to power as long as he could but finally, in the early hours of 1 January 1959, he left Cuba for the Dominican Republic. Most Cubans had played no part in the struggle but the people of Havana celebrated the fall of Batista in a carnival atmosphere.

Castro establishes Communist Cuba

Fidel Castro's romantic charisma brought him immense popularity, especially because he had managed to lead a successful revolution from an apparently hopeless position. But he was also very ambitious, and had not risked his life to let other people decide what to do. Any hopes that democracy would be reestablished were soon dashed.

Although Castro had not declared himself a Communist during his guerrilla war, he *had* promised extensive land reform and nationalization. On coming to power he began to implement a number of standard Communist measures (such as suspending the American-style constitution and collectivizing agriculture) and soon established control over his own Communist Party. Liberal enemies of Batista who had fought on Castro's side fell from favour when they criticized the new Communist line.

Castro's rapid nationalization of US investments led America to retaliate in October 1960 by imposing a total trade blockade on Cuba. Cuba was pushed into a choice between capitulation to America or turning to the Soviet Union for aid. Castro chose the latter. In the early period of revolutionary enthusiasm, Castro's slogan, "Liberty or Death" was still vibrant and popular anti-Yankee feeling backed a naive policy of economic self-sufficiency. The next few years showed how expensive and futile the policy of relying on Cuba's own resources really was. As old imported equip-ment wore out, the cannibalization of the remaining stock became the only way to maintain industrial machinery.

The Bay of Pigs

Instead of allowing time to wear down support for Castro, the US government became impatient to remove Moscow's new ally in America's backyard. In April 1961, the Americans landed a group of anti-Communist Cuban exiles at the Bay of Pigs in southern Cuba, fully expecting that this small army would be able to topple Castro. Instead, the invasion had the opposite effect and rallied support to Castro's regime. The landing turned into a fiasco when the US airforce failed to back up the exiles on the ground. Worse still for the Americans, the Soviet Union now decided to back Cuba by supplying arms.

In fact, Nikita Khrushchev, the Soviet leader, went further and decided to install nuclear weapons in Cuba, confident that the US would not act after the Bay of Pigs. But US President John F. Kennedy announced in October 1962 that the US

BELOW **Cuba's revolution took place in the USA's backyard. Castro established a Communist regime and helped to provoke the Cuban Missile Crisis.**

INSET **On 17 April 1961, 1,400 Cuban exiles landed on a small beach in the Bay of Pigs to topple Castro's government. The plan failed, largely because the CIA underestimated the support for Castro's regime. Here Cuban tanks head for the "contra" beachhead.**

CHE GUEVARA (1928–67)

Born in Argentina in 1928, Ernesto "Che" Guevara, was radicalized as a young man travelling across Latin America in the early 1950s and became a professional revolutionary. He was in Guatemala in 1954 when a US-backed coup overthrew the progressive President, Jacobo Arbenz Guzmán. Fleeing to Mexico, he met the exiled Castro brothers and joined them in their landing in Cuba in November 1956. He became a Cuban citizen after Castro's victory and played a key role in establishing the Communist system in Cuba; he was especially involved in land reforms. Suddenly, in April 1965, he dropped out of public view and returned to his life as a guerrilla in the Congo and then Bolivia. His campaign was quickly suppressed and he was captured and shot in October 1967. But his romantic image as a tragic rebel lived on, and his portrait was to decorate radical student bedrooms across the West for years to come. His propaganda picture still hangs all over Cuba like an icon of a Marxist Christ.

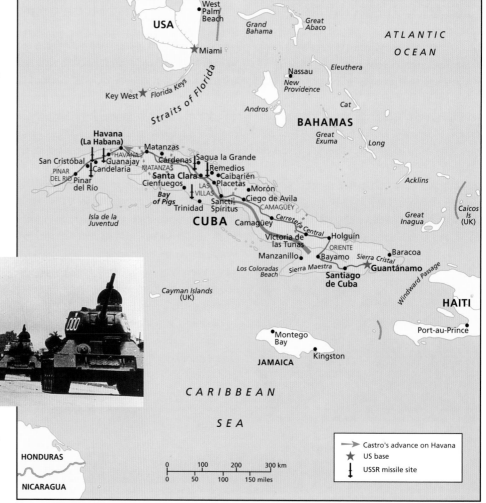

Castro's advance on Havana
US base
USSR missile site

ABOVE **At times the cult of Che Guevara seemed to overshadow Castro himself.**

Navy would quarantine Cuba and force the withdrawal of the missiles. The Kremlin backed down rather than risk nuclear war but it extracted a US promise not to invade Cuba. However, for the next ten years the Central Intelligence Agency engaged in (sometimes farcical) attempts to kill Castro and undermine his regime.

Cuban Communism

Both Castro and Guevara were puritanical in their revulsion against the venality of much Latin American society. They believed public service rather than profit should motivate people. For all their rhetoric about unleashing the people's energies they distrusted individual initiative. In any case, a planned economy left no space for it. Over the decades since 1959, Cuba failed to modernize. Leftovers from the days of Batista such as American gas-guzzling limousines and run-down tourist hotels slowly decayed for lack of investment. The regime could not live up to its promises of an ever better life and instead repeated calls for people to tighten their belts rather than concede to American pressure.

As in some other Communist countries, the Cuban regime became isolated from ordinary people. Worse, it came to be a parody of so many right-wing nepotistic dictatorships across the world, with Castro's brother and son playing central roles in the armed services and the energy programme. Even Cuba's dependence on sugar (which had economically and agriculturally damaged Cuba) was not broken after 1959. Cut off from American markets and aid, Cuba came to rely on the Soviet Union for its energy needs. In return, Castro willingly lent his troops to revolutionary movements in Mozambique, Angola and Ethiopia after 1974.

By 1980, many Cubans were deeply disappointed by the decline in their standard of living and Fidel's endless rhetoric of sacrifice. Thousands of people occupied the Peruvian embassy demanding the right to leave the country. Castro relented and allowed 125,000 Cubans to leave for the United States from the port of Mariel, west of Havana. Perhaps vindictively, he also sent several thousand mentally ill patients and much of Cuba's prison population along with the other émigrés. The regime was stabilized but the Mariel exodus was a symptom of its failure to fulfil its promises.

Castro: A revolutionary survivor

The collapse of Communism in the Soviet Union in 1991 (*see pages 186–91*) left Cuba bereft of Soviet assistance. Castro proclaimed a period of "rectification," which entailed making "more with less." Even the antique American gas-guzzlers gave way to Chinese bicycles as fuel supplies from Russia dried up and Castro struggled to preserve his Socialist system.

By the mid-1990s, Castro tacitly acknowledged that for his regime to survive it had to abandon key features of its revolutionary ideology. Courting the return of foreign tourists, including North Americans, whose dollars were desperately needed to rescue the struggling economy, and ignoring the boom in prostitution at the tourist-only resorts on Cuba's virgin sands, Castro ultimately permitted the revival of the kind of society he had so fervently denounced under Batista.

KEY EVENTS	
1898	**10 December** Declaration of independence from Spain
1902	**20 May** Spain recognizes Cuban independence
1909	**28 January** End of US administration
1940	**10 October** Fulgencio Batista becomes President
1944	**10 October** End of Batista's first term as President
1952	**10 March** Batista returns to power
1957	**13 March** Rebels unsuccessfully attack presi dential palace in Havana
1953	**26 July** Attack on the Moncada barracks in Santiago
1956	**2 December** Castro returns to Cuba with his brother Raül and Che Guevara
1959	**1 January** Fidel Castro assumes power
1959	**7 February** Declaration of Socialist Republic
1959	**16 February** Fidel Castro proclaimed head of government
1960	**May** Soviet Union offers Cuba military aid
1960	**October** Eisenhower imposes blockade of Cuba
1961	**15 April** The Bay of Pigs fiasco
1962	**22 October** Beginning of Cuban Missile Crisis
1962	**28 October** Khrushchev agrees to withdraw missiles
1965	**April** Che Guevara disappears from Cuba
1967	**8 October** Che Guevara captured in Bolivia and killed
1976	**2 December** Fidel Castro unites presidency with head of government

In 1968, a wave of revolution – a combination of student protest, opposition to the Vietnam War and trade union unrest – swept across the United States, France and West Germany. The unrest brought the governments of all three countries very close to collapse. Although the protest movements, which also spread to several other countries, were ultimately suppressed, they were important for being almost the only attempt at revolution in Western, industrialized nations.

Students at the Barricades

The night of 30–31 January 1968 saw the beginning of the Vietnamese New Year: the festival of Tet. It also marked the beginning of a massive offensive by the Communist North Vietnamese and local Vietcong against the South Vietnamese army and its American allies (*see pages 152–54*). Even the US embassy in the southern capital, Saigon, was attacked and several US guards were killed. The Tet offensive shocked the American public, which had been assured that America was winning the war in Vietnam, and it gave a huge boost to anti-war protests in the presidential election year.

Across the Western world the 1960s had seen a rise in radicalism, despite consumer affluence. Opposition to the Vietnam War was a linking thread that ran through the new protest movements not just in America but also in Western Europe (which was not directly involved in the war). The first televized war seemed characterized by overkill and horror. Watched against the backdrop of the economic boom in the West it seemed to illustrate a ruthless hypocrisy on the part of America's leaders.

Vietnam and US student protest

The radical student group, Students for a Democratic Society (SDS), had found little response in the US to its Marxist ideas, but when it started anti-war protests in April 1965 it began to draw in new supporters. In May 1965, a campus teach-in against the war at Berkeley became the first of a growing series of direct actions in US universities.

LEFT **The funeral of Martin Luther King in Atlanta, 9 April 1968. Ironically, the murder of the prophet of non-violence sparked terrible rioting.**

BELOW **A protester is forced into a police car during riots in Los Angeles on 13 August 1965. Violent clashes in America's cities between mainly white police and black rioters in the mid-1960s were impossible for the affluent white suburbs to ignore.**

White middle-class students were the social group least likely to have to go to Vietnam – yet they were the most vocal opponents of the war. The new youth culture, with its emphasis on nonconformity, created a heady atmosphere of rejection of adult authority. But the student radicals and dropouts were only a minority of the US political population, albeit a noisy and frequently effective one. Pictures of the anarchic violence of the Cultural Revolution in China were relayed by television into the homes of affluent Western students. Sympathy for Mao was often less important than the example of youthful nihilism. Waving Mao's *Little Red Book* was an easy way to shock conservative elders.

The other end of the social scale from the radical offspring of the white middle

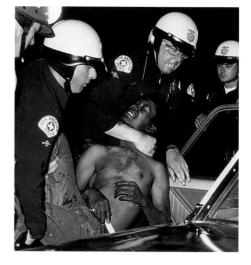

classes was also on the other side of the racial divide. The extension of civil rights and educational opportunities under Presidents Eisenhower (1953–61) and

LEFT **An anti-Vietnam war demonstrator confronts the military police in front of the Pentagon, 21 October 1967.**

BELOW **The price of anti-war protest: National Guardsmen fire tear gas at students on the campus of Kent State University in the US on 4 May 1970.**

Johnson (1963–69) had still left many poor blacks, particularly in the urban ghettos of the north and west, feeling disadvantaged. Symptoms of the breakdown of the black family and the growing crime wave in the ghettos stoked up the flames of discontent. The disproportionate drafting of young black men to fight in Vietnam intensified the bitterness felt by America's black community.

Black ghettos had regularly erupted in violent riots since 1965. But the murder in April 1968 of Martin Luther King, the apostle of non-violent change for blacks in the USA, sparked the worst rioting yet. When it was followed two months later by the assassination of Senator Robert Kennedy – the younger brother of the murdered President, John F. Kennedy – America seemed to be in the grip of a wave of violence and disorder that threatened the social fabric. This climaxed with pitched battles between police and anti-Vietnam radicals outside the Democratic Convention in Chicago in August 1968.

These manifestations of a deep social malaise and the fear of uncontrolled civil disorder promoted the election of the Republican presidential candidate Richard

Nixon, who appealed to conservative sensibilities among whites of all classes. Hard-hatted construction workers famously left their work in New York to attack an anti-Nixon student demonstration. It was a sign that revolutionary sentiment was more likely to be found in America among the children of the middle class than it was among the fathers of the working class.

KEY EVENTS: USA

1965 17 April
First anti-Vietnam War protest in Washington
1968 30–31 January
Beginning of Tet Offensive in Vietnam
4 April
Assassination of Martin Luther King
5 June
Assassination of Robert Kennedy
27 August
Rioting at Democratic Convention in Chicago
1974 9 August
Resignation of President Nixon

May 1968 in France

In 1965, Charles de Gaulle was, by a narrow margin, reelected as President of France's Fifth Republic. The economy was prospering, but social tensions were simmering in the aftermath of the war in Algeria (*see pages 155–56*) and other domestic problems. By the spring of 1968, these tensions came into the open among the French working class, who had not benefited from the economic boom to the same extent as the middle classes, and among the students, who were dissatisfied with the rapidly expanding but very hierarchical education system.

The real disturbances began at the new Nanterre faculty of the University of Paris on 22 March 1968. A student at the faculty had been arrested for planting a bomb at an American Express office in protest against the Vietnam War, and fellow students demonstrated against his "victimization." Heavy-handed actions by the police encouraged further protests at the Sorbonne. The Rector closed the university while the courts worked over the weekend, handing out mostly suspended sentences. But the students and striking junior faculty members reacted with indignation. On 3 May, Nanterre was closed.

Meanwhile, student strikes spread across France. What was more worrying for the government was that the workforce of large factories, such as the Renault car works, also came out in sympathy on 13 May. Despite the economic boom, France still had half a million (mainly young) unemployed, while many workers felt their pay had not risen in step with economic growth. Some 800,000 students and strikers marched through the streets of Paris that day. Workers occupied their factories and students seized university buildings. All kinds of state employees, from doctors to television technicians, joined the stoppages and protests. Famous intellectuals such as Sartre appeared briefly in the occupied Sorbonne to urge ever more radical gestures.

A carnival atmosphere accompanied many of the student protests, despite violent clashes with the police. Although the government rocked on its foundations, the fact that so many of the young protesters seemed more interested in free love and rock-and-roll than genuine revolution gave the regime – and with it much of middle-class France – the chance to recover breath.

But in late May, with about 9 million workers on strike, de Gaulle seemed to lose his nerve. He flew to see the army commander in Germany, General Massu, who reassured him he would deploy his troops to restore order if necessary. On 30 May, de Gaulle appeared on television, making concessions to the workers but not to the students, and ordered fresh elections to the National Assembly. As well as the appeal to the people over the heads of the radicals, de Gaulle's unspoken message from the army was clear: those who refused to take their chance at the ballot box risked civil war.

BELOW **Riot police face student protesters in Paris, May 1968. Heavy-handed police methods helped turn demonstrations into battles.**

LEFT **Students on strike at the Sorbonne. Posters of Marx, Lenin and Mao inspired a new generation of would-be revolutionaries.**

Emboldened by the President's defiance, the Gaullist Party organized the largest demonstrations yet. Huge numbers of the beneficiaries of the economic boom since 1958 marched through Paris, and the electorate voted decisively for the Right in the elections on 23 June.

May 1968 had been a dangerous time for the Fifth Republic, but in the end the alliance of students (mainly children of the boom) and those workers who had done less well out of the 1960s was a fragile one. The students' rhetoric was abstract, and

quite often incomprehensible to themselves as well as the workers on strike. The Communist Party were distrustful of the long-haired students with their heretical tendency to quote Trotsky instead of the current Soviet leader, Leonid Brezhnev. In the end, as so often, the Communists were happier to see the old order survive than the wrong sort of radicals triumph.

After being taken by surprise by the May events, the French Right soon showed itself more cohesive and effective. It also had the advantage of a majority in the polls. Even so, de Gaulle was fatally weakened and resigned in 1969 to make way for the Right's real hero of 1968: the imperturbable Georges Pompidou, the Prime Minister. When everything had calmed down, the government quietly granted the students' original demand for a share in the running of universities – but by then this demand hardly seemed radical.

West Germany

Like France, West Germany was seeing a rapid increase in the student population,

which rose from 384,000 in 1965 to 510,000 by 1970. At the same time, the strict hierarchy of pre-war professorial authority was preserved. Younger teachers as well as radical students were antagonized by the academic elite. Ghosts of Germany's Nazi past haunted the new democracy, as many older teachers and professors had held questionable positions under Hitler.

West Berlin's Free University was the natural focus for unrest because studying there meant that young men could avoid conscription into the West German army. It was a natural haven for all dropouts from West German society who rejected the values of the "economic miracle." However, those students who renounced the bourgeois life of study and went to work in real factories in order to agitate the proletariat found little sympathy among a working class that prized productivity and cleanliness. Arguments in favour of Lenin cut little ice with workers who had fled from East Germany or knew some of the millions that had.

The students, too, had bourgeois scruples. When the radical "Extra-Parliamentary Opposition" called for hundreds of cars to block the entrances to the

premises of the right-wing newspaper publisher, Springer, only twenty came. A student radical, Wolfgang Lefevre, asked bitterly, "Is it because most students fear for their property and do not want their automobiles damaged?"

If this disillusioned question hit the nail of much radical posturing on the head, smaller groups of students and others caught up by the excitement *did* break with bourgeois society. Communes were established, for example, especially in West Berlin. From some of the communes

INSET **During the night of 20–21 August 1968, two Soviet army units moved in on Prague to crush the liberal Czech regime under Alexander Dubček.**

ABOVE **Students block Wenceslas Square in Prague in protest at the Soviet invasion.**

developed the 1970s terrorist group, the Red Army Fraction, which survived so long because it called on the sympathy and help of many student radicals in the 1960s who had since gone straight and taken up successful careers in law, the media, or business, but who would supply money or accommodation to an old comrade in need.

As in France, the authorities astutely recognized that one way to separate the real radicals from students with more basic grievances was to give in on matters such as student representation on university committees and, above all, to permit cohabitation in university dormitories. Revolutionary zeal was often extinguished when elderly professors stopped enforcing traditional morality.

Another factor stabilizing the situation was the Soviet Union's invasion of Czechoslovakia on 21 August 1968. Television pictures of US tanks in distant Vietnam were replaced by scenes of repression in nearby Prague. The festive protests of the student revolutionaries in Germany suddenly seemed rather trivial (and the Marxist rhetoric foolish), given the reality of the suffocation of "socialism with a human face" in Czechoslovakia.

The eclipse of the New Left

Even student revolutionaries grow up. After the heady days of the late 1960s, the radical generation went out into the world of full employment. Capitalism still provided the cash for the expansion of universities and the public sector for those who would not work for profit. But in the long term the hedonism of the 1960s was corrosive to revolutionary commitment. Despite the "long march through the institutions" (as the unrest of 1968 came to be known) of the New Left, whose members came to predominate in many areas of the public services and media across the West, their zeal and influence was ultimately reduced by the realization that capitalism was better able to provide the resources to fund an alternative lifestyle than grey conformist Communism.

KEY EVENTS: WEST GERMANY
1967 2 June
Student demonstrator killed during visit to West Berlin of Shah of Iran
8 June
Beginning of student protests
1968 11 April
Rudi Dutschke badly wounded in West Berlin
April
Easter Week riots and student sit-ins after Dutschke's shooting
21 August
Soviet troops occupy Czechoslovakia

Ethiopia underwent a terrible ordeal after 1974. Impoverished by drought and famine, it was plunged into an ill-conceived economic transformation by revolutionary army officers who tried to create a Communist paradise in a desperately poor society. Soon they were bitterly divided, but while they were supported by Soviet military aid they could maintain their power – despite civil war and terrible famines. The collapse of Soviet support precipitated the collapse of the regime.

The Ethiopian Revolution

Haile Selassie acceded to the Ethiopian throne in 1930. When Italy invaded the country in 1935 he became a popular hero for personally leading his troops against the invading army (he was forced to flee in 1936). But after he was restored in 1941, his efforts to modernize Ethiopia clashed with his determination to hold on to power.

By the 1970s, Selassie was over eighty and showing signs of senility. His rule seemed anachronistic. Soldiers and students returned from their studies abroad full of indignation at Ethiopia's corruption and backwardness. As in many other developing countries, the Soviet model of forced progress appealed to radicals frustrated by slow progress at home and resentful of their Emperor's pro-Western policies.

Catastrophic famine in 1973–74, especially in the Welo region, and discontent about inflation and poverty in the capital Adis Abeba were the backdrop to the collapse of Selassie's power in 1974. When his son, the Crown Prince, suffered a debilitating stroke in January 1973, the fragility of the regime suddenly became apparent.

The revolution begins

Young army officers joined the strikes in February 1974. A wave of mutinies forced the Emperor to dismiss his ministers and appoint a new, reformist Prime Minister. Emboldened by these concessions, the officers demanded more change. Through the spring and summer of 1974, ministers and senior officials were removed at the

LEFT **Ethiopia during Emperor Haile Selassie's reign was a multi-national empire with an ancient Christian tradition. As well as Selassie's fellow Amharic-speakers, there were also the Oromos in the south, Somalis in the Ogaden province and Eritreans in the northeast. Whereas the Oromos, Somalis and Eritreans were mainly Muslim, the dominant Amharic people were Christian. Civil war worsened after 1975 and was complicated by foreign intervention.**

behest of the soldiers, leaving Selassie increasingly isolated. On 11 September, Ethiopian television contrasted the treatment of the Emperor's dogs with the plight of famine victims around the country, undermining what little remained of his authority. Selassie was deposed the next day by a committee of revolutionary army officers known as the Derg. A year later the old man met his end: he was suffocated and his remains disposed of underneath a lavatory in the ex-imperial palace.

Selassie and his ministers were by no means the only victims of change, for in-fighting followed between those who had overthrown the Emperor. First to fall

was the new non-Marxist Prime Minister, Aman Andom, who was killed in November 1974 after he had supported a more liberal line towards Ethiopia's non-Christian regions and Selassie's imprisoned relatives.

While rivalry existed on the Derg between those who advocated the idea of a federation of Ethiopia's many peoples and those who insisted on a unitary revolutionary state, both factions agreed at first on a declaration of Socialism and the nationalization of key industries and the banks. The Derg sent students and other radicals into the countryside in 1975 to redistribute land. But the key group in the Derg led by Mengistu Haile Mariam refused to offer more than an unsatisfactory bogus Soviet-type of autonomy for minorities.

Meanwhile rebels in Eritrea and the Tigray province took advantage of the confusion in Adis Abeba to challenge the central government for control in these two areas. General Tafari, Ethiopia's nominal President, urged compromise with the rebels, but he was suddenly arrested in February 1977 and executed along with his own followers. Mengistu became both head of state and chairman of the Derg. He declared a "Red Terror," a campaign of violence against opponents that engulfed educated radicals and conservatives alike.

ABOVE **Guerrillas of the Eritrean Liberation Front flourish their rifles and make a victory salute in 1977.**

RIGHT **As Ethiopian troops, backed by Soviet and Cuban forces, continued their advance in the Ogaden region, the Somali government announced a general mobilization. This poster in Mogadishu praises the Somali army.**

Civil war and civilian disaster

Mengistu's regime embarked on a programme to suppress regional opposition and to revolutionize Ethiopian society at the same time. But chaotic conditions inside Ethiopia encouraged Somalia to invade the Ogaden province in 1977. Appealing to Ethiopian patriotism and receiving lavish Soviet military aid, Mengistu's forces counterattacked. Victory over Somalia in 1978 only confirmed Mengistu's view of force as the best solu-

tion to his country's problems. He tried to apply the same recipe against domestic rebels, but they were more resilient.

Ironically, each of Mengistu's wars was against another self-proclaimed Marxist–Leninist regime: the Somalian government and the Eritrean and Tigrean Popular Fronts were all loud in their claims to be the true Communist force in the region. The Soviet Union decided to back the Ethiopians as the most strategically valuable ally, but the guerrillas in the northeastern provinces proved tough and their struggle was to survive Mengistu's regime.

War and collectivization would have made life difficult enough for Ethiopia's peasant majority but by 1984 the weather too had turned against them. Drought catastrophically compounded the man-made causes of famine. Mengistu's regime tried to manipulate the flood of international relief aid to bolster its position.

The fall of Mengistu

Changes in Moscow after 1985, when Mikhail Gorbachev became Soviet leader, brought further crisis to Ethiopia. Once Gorbachev withdrew Soviet subsidies, Mengistu's enemies began to crowd in on him. Bitter years of terror and famine had earned his regime few loyal supporters. Mengistu also received security aid from the hardline regime in East Germany, whose agents helped to foil a plot against him in May 1989. Fresh executions of opponents could not stem the demoralization of the regime, however, and in May 1991 Mengistu fled to Zimbabwe. Eritrea became independent in 1991 and a new regime made up of disillusioned followers of Mengistu and former opponents was established in Ethiopia.

Whether Ethiopia will achieve a stable, democratic or even law-abiding government remains to be seen, but the experience of Mengistu's dogmatic and ruthless drive to transform the country ought to be a powerful warning against similar regimes in the near future.

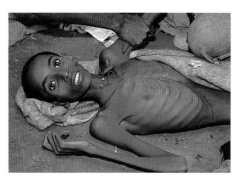

ABOVE **Famine had caused the revolution in 1974; in 1984 it returned with a vengeance.**

KEY EVENTS

1973	**May** Extent of famine in Welo becomes clear
1974	**Mid-January** Mutinies over army pay begin
	18 February Taxi drivers in Adis Abeba begin strike
	1 March Endalkatchew appointed premier
	5 March Haile Selassie promises constitutional monarchy
	18 April Endalkatchew arrests past ministers
	27 June Formation of Derg (army committee)
	22 July Endalkatchew removed from power
	12 September Haile Selassie deposed
	22 November Andom murdered by Derg
	20 December Declaration of Socialism
1975	**February and March** Nationalization of Ethiopian industry
	27 August Murder of Haile Selassie
1977	**3 February** General Tafari and others arrested
	12 February Mengistu declared head of state – beginning of "Red Terror"
	May–June Skirmishing on border with Somalia
	23 July Somalia invades Ogaden province
1979	**18 December** Formation of the Ethiopian Working People's Party
1983	Failure of rains forecasts famine for 1984
1987	**10 September** New Constitution
1990	**9 February** Eritreans begin successful assault on Asmara
	5 March Mengistu announces end of Socialism
1991	**21 May** Mengistu flees to Zimbabwe
	28 May Adis Abeba falls to rebels

During the 1960s and 1970s the Shah (King) of Iran introduced reforms to transform his country into a modern, Westernized nation. But his dictatorial rule and disregard for Islamic values provoked a popular revolution in 1979 that resulted in the establishment of an Islamic Republic. Unlike most secular, modernizing revolutions of the twentieth century, this was a backlash against economic and technical progress, and proved that religion could still be a powerful factor in politics.

The Power of Islam: Iran

Islam was introduced to Iran during the first wave of Arab expansion in the seventh century, and the Shiite branch of Islam later became Iran's state religion. According to most Shiite teachings, religious instruction can come only from an infallible Imam ("guide") descended from Ali, the cousin and son-in-law of the Prophet Mohammed. But because the twelfth Imam disappeared in 878, Shiite clerics or mullahs have had to assume the role of the absent Imam until he returns to redeem the world. The clerics in Iran enjoyed periods of great religious and political authority. Towards the end of the nineteenth century, religious feeling, combined with national pride, intensified as Britain and Russia vied with each other for dominance in the region.

The first Iranian revolution

Western pressure on Iran increased when oil was discovered in Iran in the early 1900s. But foreign interference in domestic affairs caused tremendous dissatisfaction with the government. Protesters organized a series of strikes that almost paralyzed the economy and forced Shah Muzaffar to concede a constitution in 1906.

Muzaffar was succeeded in 1907 by his son, who tried to abolish the constitution,

but he was deposed in 1909 by the army in favour of *his* son, who generally abided by the constitution. All these coups and infighting discredited the regime, however, and it was further destabilized by the outbreak of the First World War in 1914.

Determined to reverse Iran's fortunes, an army officer, Reza Khan, seized power in February 1921 and established a military dictatorship. Becoming Prime Minister in 1923, he went on in October 1925 to depose the Shah and proclaimed himself the first Shah of a new royal dynasty.

The shaky new empire

Reza Shah's support for Germany in the Second World War resulted in an Anglo-Soviet invasion of Iran in 1941. Reza was forced to abdicate, leaving his young son, Mohammed, as the new ruler.

While the occupation of Iran ended in 1946, international disputes over the ownership of oilfields fostered internal political strife and brought the populist politician Mohammed Mossadeq to power. In June 1951, Mossadeq (by then Prime Minister) forced through the nationalization of the foreign oil companies, despite the open opposition of the Shah. The West responded by boycotting Iranian oil exports, which

INSET **Shah Mohammed Reza Pahlavi places a crown on the head of his wife during his coronation ceremony.**

RIGHT **A young Iranian has substituted the head of the unpopular Shah on a bank note with that of the Ayatollah Khomeini.**

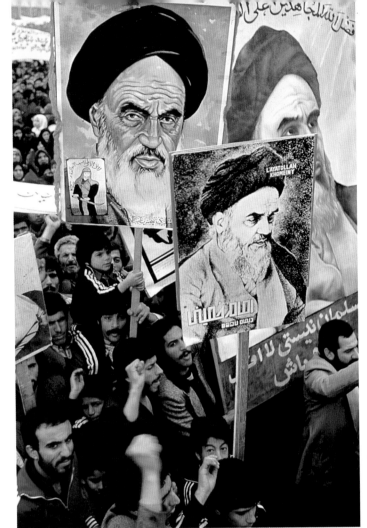

LEFT **An anti-Shah demonstration in the Iranian capital, Tehran. As the protests gathered pace, some of the demonstrators began to wear white shrouds, indicating they would be prepared to die a martyr's death for their cause.**

BELOW LEFT **Riots swept through Iran in 1978. The Shah was indecisive and ill, and his police were not trained for crowd control.**

brought severe economic problems for Iran. The crisis came to a head in 1953 when the Shah briefly fled the country, only to be restored by a CIA-inspired coup.

"The White Revolution"

Back in power in the capital, Tehran, the Shah determined to modernize Iran using its oil revenues. But unlike militant nationalists such as Mossadeq, the Shah believed the way forward was through closer alliance with the West. Thus, in 1954, he invited an international consortium of oil companies to use Iranian oil facilities, the profits to be shared with Iran. In return for support against the Soviet Union, the United States also gave Iran considerable economic and military aid.

It was partly in response to an outburst of popular discontent at the end of the 1950s (caused by a small economic downturn) that the Shah unveiled in January 1963 his plans for a "White Revolution," a massive programme of reforms intended to win the support of Iran's poor with economic and social progress while restoring Iran's international status. It was to be a revolution from above, involving the redistribution of land, compulsory education and other welfare provisions. The Shah may genuinely have hoped to improve the lot of his subjects, but his policies proved impractical – and deeply offensive to many of his devoutly Muslim people.

Critical of the erosion of Islamic values and the increase in royal power, the clergy

began to speak out against the regime. The religious leader Ayatollah Khomeini was arrested in 1963 after publicly attacking the Shah. Within two hours, huge demonstrations were taking place across Iran. These were brutally suppressed by the army, and literally hundreds of protesters were killed. Khomeini was exiled to Iraq in 1964.

The corruption that went with the Shah's breakneck changes alienated even those who did not share Khomeini's dislike of Western "decadence." There was also resentment among many Iranians, particularly the urban unemployed, about the thousands of highly paid foreign technicians and advisers. But rather than coopting

his political opponents, the Shah attempted to buy them off, or, worse still, silence them.

The crisis

Buoyed by oil wealth, the Shah began to pursue absurdly over-ambitious economic plans. These fell apart in 1977, just after the new American President, Jimmy Carter, made clear that he intended to promote human rights in Iran and put pressure on the Shah to liberalize his regime. The US would no longer turn a blind eye to the brutality of the secret police, Savak.

With falling wages and rising unemployment, the Shah united a vast and motley array of people against him. During 1977, strikes gathered pace as workers and the urban poor protested against their living conditions. Soon the religious authorities added their voices to the protest and Khomeini called for the abdication of the Shah. Far from losing influence in exile, Khomeini had extended his power base through pamphlets and cassette recordings that were smuggled into Iran. The opposition groups united behind him.

FAR LEFT **A soldier bends to kiss the feet of the Shah as he leaves Iran on 17 January 1979. The Shah's wife is behind him.**

CENTRE AND LEFT **Potent symbols of revolution: a statue of the Shah being pulled down and revolutionaries burning a picture of the Shah.**

Throughout 1978 strikes and riots swept across the country. The Shah hoped to discourage his opponents on the streets by ordering the police and troops to fire on demonstrators – but the dead were upheld as martyrs, which served merely to fan the flames of revolution. In the crisis the Shah's regime turned out to be woefully short of supporters. While the opposition gathered hundreds of thousands to protest in the autumn of 1978, the Shah's agents could turn out only handfuls of loyalists – even when money was offered.

On 8 September 1978, "Black Friday," the Shah declared martial law and his troops massacred thousands of demonstrators in Tehran. Over the next few weeks strikes at many of the major oil refineries and factories brought the economy to a virtual standstill. As investors panicked, money began to flood out of the country.

The fall of the Shah

The Shah vacillated between repression and concession, but scarcely a day passed towards the end of 1978 without huge demonstrations taking place. Sometimes more than one million people marched through Tehran demanding better wages and political reform. Meanwhile Khomeini had moved to France, where emissaries of the Iranian government were sent to mediate between him and the Shah. But the

Ayatollah refused to be reconciled, and he continued to call for the Shah's abdication.

By the end of the year, the Shah's generals could no longer guarantee control of the capital, let alone the country. Even some of the troops had begun to mutiny. Already sick with the cancer that would kill him two years later, the Shah left Iran on 16 January 1979 – officially for a "temporary vacation" in Egypt. His regime imploded in his absence. On 1 February 1979, just two weeks after the Shah's departure, Khomeini returned to Iran.

The development of the revolution

The fall of the Shah was followed by disputes between the various revolutionary factions about the future. The religious community, which wanted to establish an Islamic republic, proved the most powerful, however, and quickly took over all the key military institutions and state apparatus. Many of the secular radicals thought the aged Ayatollah's influence would be short-lived, but in fact his hold over popular opinion grew. He unleashed his supporters against anyone who opposed his vision

RIGHT **Iran during the Revolution and war against Iraq. Many of Iran's oilfields are concentrated close to the Iran–Iraq border.**

of an Islamic republic. Communist sympathizers and Westernized Iranians were just a few of those who objected to the enforced veiling of women and the reintroduction of Islamic law, but Islamic tribunals passed the death sentence on thousands of opponents (sometimes up to 10,000 a month); thousands of others fled abroad. For almost two years a state of disorder existed as revolutionary guards fought with other radical groups – but the mullahs always had the upper hand.

Khomeini held no formal political office but his word was law. His denunciations of the United States as the "great Satan" of the modern world encouraged frenzied anti-Americanism. In November 1979, radical students seized the US embassy and took its staff hostage. A botched rescue attempt further boosted the Ayatollah's prestige at home. Only when Ronald Reagan became American President in January 1981 did the US unfreeze Iranian assets and secure the release of the hostages. Meanwhile a far more serious crisis for Iran had erupted.

Iraq attacks Iran

In September 1980, Iraq invaded Iran. The Iraqi leader Saddam Hussein clearly believed that the Iranian revolution had reduced the country to chaos and he could seize the oil-rich land in southwest Iran with impunity. Instead the invasion rallied support to the Islamic regime. Iran fought back during a savage war that lasted until shortly before Khomeini's death in 1989.

Prospects for the Islamic Republic

Khomeini's success sent tremors through the Islamic world. Anti-Americanism and fundamentalist ideas motivated the assassination of Egypt's President Sadat in 1980, while militant Islamic groups such as Hamas and Hezbollah (the army of God) have become a greater threat to Israel than the secular Palestine Liberation Organization. Across North Africa, but especially in Algeria in the early 1990s, supporters of an Islamic revival threatened secular regimes that had lost their post-colonial radicalism. Khomeini's legacy has been to make clear that secular revolution has lost its monopoly as the engine of upheaval as the year 2000 approaches.

LEFT **Women in the revolutionary army.**

BELOW **Armed mullahs on parade in 1980. Religious enthusiasm encouraged self-sacrifice among Iranian volunteers confronted with Iraq's modern weapons.**

Peaceful Revolutions

For decades after the Russian Revolution of 1917, Communist rule in many countries across the world had seemed so secure that few people could have foreseen that Communism would be facing a global crisis in 1989. Yet, between 1989 and 1991, the Communist regimes in Eastern Europe and the Soviet Union collapsed with barely a shot fired in their defence. At the opposite end of the spectrum, the negotiated end of apartheid in South Africa confounded prophets of a blood bath between blacks and whites. The peaceful revolutions of the late 1980s and early 1990s did not, however, mark the end of history, as some commentators had predicted. Instead, after the miraculous social and political transformations in these countries had taken place, grubby politics reappeared and bloodshed began again to play its part in the struggle to control the new order.

OPPOSITE **An East German border guard receives flowers from a West Berliner after the opening of the Berlin Wall in November 1989.**

In 1989, the two hundredth anniversary year of the French Revolution, many countries that had been shaped by revolution were in crisis. Both of the Communist superpowers, the Soviet Union and China, were shaken by dissent. The Soviet Union attempted to deal with its problems by implementing limited reforms, but this succeeded only in eroding its power and the Union split apart in 1991. In contrast, the Chinese regime survived by ruthlessly suppressing all opposition.

The Crisis of Communism

During the 1980s, both Marxism, the most influential revolutionary ideology in history, and the Communist states that it had inspired, were in crisis. Marxist doctrine had proclaimed that the fruits of revolution would pass to the working class. In fact, a new class of Communist Party officials emerged to enjoy a privileged position within Communist states. Dissatisfaction with this new elite grew as the dreams of a perfect society faded.

Even sections of the privileged class came to resent the rigid and inefficient system that constrained their lives. Economic and technological progress in the West and Japan only highlighted the faults and limitations of Communist economic policy.

LEFT **In spring 1989, Tiananmen Square in Beijing (so often the scene of mass rallies in praise of the Chinese Communist leaders), became the centre of denunciations against them. Here hundreds of thousands of protesters have gathered in the Square on 4 May 1989.**

"Glasnost" and "perestroika"

After more than twenty years of political stagnation in the Soviet Union, Mikhail Gorbachev took charge in 1985. Younger than his predecessors and his comrades in Eastern Europe, Gorbachev recognized the urgent need to reform the monolithic Soviet political and economic system.

Under the slogans of "glasnost" ("openness") and "perestroika" ("restructuring"), Gorbachev liberalized the Soviet system. He introduced limited democracy to the political system and elements of free market to the economy. However, Gorbachev's reforms only revealed the need for more far-reaching changes. He questioned the need for massive spending on armaments to rival America (although Soviet defence

spending continued to rise as he tried to keep the military on his side), but he could not solve the growing problem of food shortages. Gorbachev released dissidents from the gulag prison system and permitted multi-candidate elections. These actions only brought long-silenced nationalist grievances to the surface and challenged the whole idea of the Soviet Union (*see pages 186–91*).

China after Mao

Mao Tse-tung, founder and leader of the People's Republic of China for over forty years, died in 1976. A period of rapid change followed. Deng Xiaoping, a former Maoist opponent, became China's leader in 1978. He made a decisive break with Mao's radical Communist policies, promoting the idea of "market socialism." He

LEFT **Pro-democracy demonstrators constructed a goddess of democracy (much like the US Statue of Liberty) in Tiananmen Square.**

OPPOSITE **Soldiers attempt to push back the thousands of demonstrators in Tiananmen Square on 3 June 1989.**

also liberated the vast peasant population from Maoist communes and allowed them to grow crops for profit. His declaration that "to get rich is glorious" shocked Maoists. But his policies did help to diminish the problem of China's food shortages.

Although the peasants benefited from economic reform, it was the Communist officials who gained most. They became

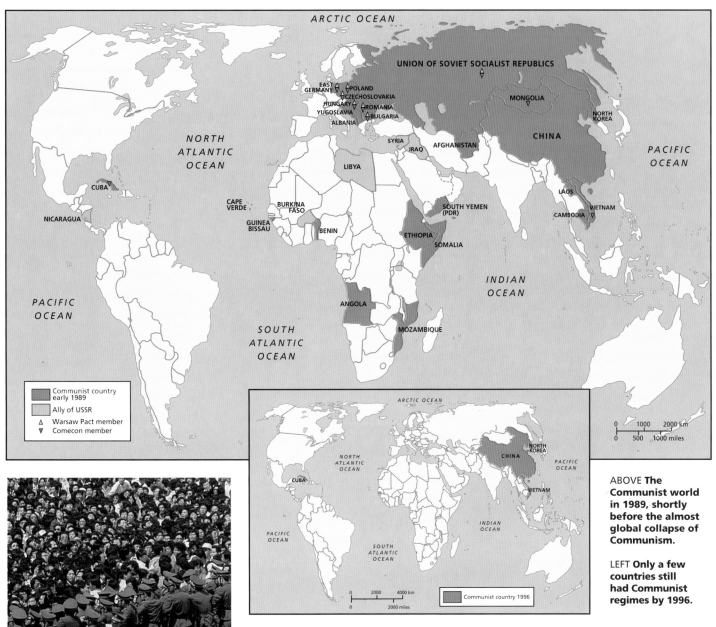

ARCTIC OCEAN

UNION OF SOVIET SOCIALIST REPUBLICS

EAST GERMANY
POLAND
CZECHOSLOVAKIA
HUNGARY
YUGOSLAVIA
ROMANIA
BULGARIA
ALBANIA

MONGOLIA

NORTH KOREA

CHINA

NORTH
ATLANTIC
OCEAN

SYRIA
IRAQ
AFGHANISTAN

PACIFIC
OCEAN

CUBA

LIBYA

LAOS
VIETNAM
CAMBODIA

NICARAGUA

CAPE
VERDE
BURKINA
FASO
GUINEA
BISSAU
BENIN

SOUTH YEMEN
(PDR)

ETHIOPIA
SOMALIA

PACIFIC
OCEAN

INDIAN
OCEAN

ANGOLA

SOUTH
ATLANTIC
OCEAN

MOZAMBIQUE

Communist country
early 1989

Ally of USSR

△ Warsaw Pact member

▽ Comecon member

0   1000   2000 km
0   500   1000 miles

ARCTIC OCEAN

NORTH
ATLANTIC
OCEAN

CHINA
NORTH
KOREA

CUBA

PACIFIC
OCEAN

VIETNAM

PACIFIC
OCEAN

INDIAN
OCEAN

SOUTH
ATLANTIC
OCEAN

0   2000   4000 km
0   2000 miles

Communist country 1996

ABOVE **The Communist world in 1989, shortly before the almost global collapse of Communism.**

LEFT **Only a few countries still had Communist regimes by 1996.**

notorious for corruption and oppression, taking bribes from new businessmen. Officials were especially unpopular in the cities. Students and industrial workers soon began to press for reform and greater democracy. The success of his economic policy did not encourage Deng to initiate political change. Students began to demonstrate for some Soviet-style "glasnost."

Demonstrations accelerated in the late 1980s, culminating in a mass protest in Beijing's Tiananmen Square in April 1989.

Ironically, the protests coincided with the visit to Beijing of the Soviet leader, Gorbachev. This visit signalled the end of twenty-five years of hostility between the countries. While the Chinese government did not act against the protesters during Gorbachev's visit, soon afterwards the army was sent to break-up the demonstration by force. The government controlled the media and were able to prevent further trouble by portraying the protesters as dangerous radicals who wanted to restart the hated Maoist Cultural Revolution.

Repression and revolt

Although Deng Xiaoping had produced a booming economy, which helped to buy the army's loyalty, the government's brutal suppression of opposition left it insecure. Unlike Deng, Gorbachev was either unwilling or unable to use force to stop the slide from Communist authority. Gorbachev's real failure was his inability to revive the Soviet economy. He did not reform the economy as quickly as the Chinese Communists, nor did he fight for power as ruthlessly. In some ways Gorbachev was a Communist idealist who believed that the system would regain popular support once reforms began (*see pages 186–91*).

The Soviet Union effectively controlled Poland, East Germany, Hungary, Romania, Bulgaria and Czechoslovakia in the period after the Second World War. These Eastern bloc countries were one-party Communist states for decades, until anti-Communist revolutions transformed them in 1989. The peaceful, so-called "velvet revolution" in Czechoslovakia set the pattern for the other bloodless revolutions in Eastern Europe.

The "Velvet" Revolutions

Some Eastern bloc countries had tried to break from hardline Communism before the revolutions of 1989. Hungary and Poland, for example, had each experienced turbulent events in 1956. Hungary's Soviet-backed government called in Soviet troops to suppress an anti-Communist revolution in November 1956. The revolutionary leader, Imre Nagy, was subsequently kidnapped and executed on Soviet orders.

In Poland, food shortages prompted demonstrations for change in 1956, which were contained by Polish security forces. Afterwards, the government made some changes to avoid open conflict in the future, such as de-collectivizing agriculture and granting limited freedom of activity to the Catholic Church, but it remained committed to Soviet economic ideals and would tolerate no opposition.

Although many Communist countries found it difficult to manage planned economies, few governments were as recklessly incompetent as Poland's. Efforts to rationalize the economy caused strikes and demonstrations in 1970 and 1976. By 1980, the situation became even worse. Foreign debts escalated and the government could no longer afford to subsidise food. This led to sudden price increases on 26 June 1980 and triggered an unprecedented crisis.

RIGHT **People outside the Lenin shipyard in Gdansk in July 1980 reaching up to catch leaflets being thrown to them by striking workers who have occupied the plant.**

INSET **Lech Walesa campaigning in May 1989.**

The birth and suppression of Solidarity

The Communist nightmare of a workers' revolt in a workers' state became reality in Poland in 1980 when the electrician, Lech Walesa, led his fellow workers at the Lenin shipyard in Gdansk to stop work. Backed by the Catholic Church and intellectuals, the strikers demanded the right to form their own trade union, Solidarity. Strikes spread across the country and the authorities could stop them only by agreeing to the workers' demands. They registered Solidarity as a free trade union and ten million people joined it. Soon, Polish peasants also set up their own union.

The Polish government, backed by the Soviet Union, had no intention of abiding by their agreement with the unions. During the next year and a half, the government waited while splits appeared in Solidarity. Some union hotheads argued that the Communists' power was broken and the union should establish itself as the government. Others, including Walesa, warned of the dangers of pushing the Soviet authorities too far. They realized

that this was not an internal Polish matter. Just as Communism had been established in Poland with Soviet force, a successful revolution needed Soviet consent.

The Communists reasserted their power over the country when General Jaruzelski, the new Polish Communist leader, staged a coup d'état on the night of 13 December 1981. He proclaimed martial law, outlawed Solidarity and arrested the leaders.

The Communist counter-revolution did not last. Jaruzelski could not solve the deep-rooted economic crisis that had produced Solidarity in the first place. During the 1980s, the Polish Communists realized that the only way to reinvigorate a declining economy was to negotiate with former union representatives. Also, Jaruzelski knew that he would have crucial support for reform from the Soviet leader, Gorbachev.

Solidarity's comeback

In 1989, the very men who had stifled Solidarity in 1981 met its leaders in Warsaw to discuss the future. Proposals included the unbanning of Solidarity and elections for some seats in the Polish parliament. The cautious Walesa suspected that the elections would be rigged to guarantee a parliamentary majority for the Communists, but he agreed to the limited electoral concessions in the belief that Solidarity was the key to future reform.

The results of the elections on 4 June staggered both Communists and Solidarity-supporters. So few Communist candidates were elected to the contested seats that Jaruzelski's position was dramatically weakened. No one had foreseen the degree of antipathy towards every candidate supported by the Communist Party. The scale of the defeat made the threat of a hardline Communist backlash a dangerously real possibility. So a compromise was agreed whereby Jaruzelski would remain as head of state, but the day-to-day government would be in the hands of a non- Communist premier, Tadeusz Mazowiecki.

LEFT **The collapse of the Eastern Bloc from 1989.**

BELOW LEFT **The Communist leader General Jaruzelski was Prime Minister from 1981 to 1985 and head of state from 1985 to 1990.**

BELOW RIGHT **The closing ceremony of the Warsaw round-table talks in spring 1989. Change in Poland came through negotiation.**

Emboldened by Soviet non-interference and the gathering wave of revolutions in other Eastern bloc states, the government announced plans for an economic revolution. "Shock therapy" was going to sweep away the planned economy and replace it with a market economy. A rapid start was made by introducing market prices, freeing trade and encouraging entrepreneurs. De-nationalizing huge industrial plants was more difficult. The Polish move from Communism to capitalism reduced the state's power over its citizens. It was one of the few revolutions to do this, and it set a pattern for other Eastern bloc revolutions.

The Czech Revolution

During the so-called Prague Spring in 1968 (*see page 165*), the Czechoslovakian regime had tried to make the Communist totalitarian society more tolerant. The reform process, "socialism with a human face," was crushed by Soviet tanks. A process of "normalization" followed: censorship was strict and pro-reformers were sacked from their jobs.

At the beginning of 1977, a group of dissident intellectuals issued an appeal to the government for greater freedom. This appeal, known as Charter 77, had 243 signatories. The Communist authorities took any public criticism seriously. Despite strenuous efforts, however, they never managed to silence underground literature (*samizdat*) and discussions among dissidents. But the Czech dissidents were unable to gather mass support, unlike their counterparts in Poland.

Public dissatisfaction remained silent while the Soviet Union pursued a policy of crushing any challenge to Communist rule. But when Gorbachev signalled an end to this policy in the late 1980s, change came quickly. Czech dissidents gathered support and led anti-Government demonstrations in 1988 and 1989. The revolution was triggered by a demonstration on 17 November 1989 that was violently dispersed by the police. This brutal action led to demonstrations throughout the country. Within a few days, the Czechoslovakian Communist Party's power had crumbled.

The leader of the Prague Spring, Alexander Dubček, made his first public appearance for twenty years and was greeted by the cheers of 300,000 demonstrators. Dissidents formed an opposition group called Civic Forum, and formulated demands that the demoralized Communists were unable to resist. On 25 November, under pressure from strikes and huge demonstrations in Prague, the Communist Politburo resigned.

By Christmas 1989, the Soviet Union's erstwhile puppet leader, Gustav Husák, had resigned as Czech President. He was replaced by the man he had persecuted, the dissident playwright, Vaclav Havel. The bloodless revolution had occurred within just two months. In the celebratory mood of 1989, few could foresee the major changes that would follow.

Czechoslovakia was composed of two ethnic groups, the Czechs and the Slovaks. The new democratic process revealed differences between them and the Slovaks pressed for independence. In 1993, the country split; Havel's dream of a united democratic Czechoslovakia had failed.

"In Poland it took ten years. In East Germany it took ten weeks. In Czechoslovakia it took ten days. And in Romania it took ten hours." A CENTRAL EUROPEAN COMMENT ON THE COMPARATIVE BREAKDOWN OF THE COMMUNIST REGIMES

Hungary's peaceful transformation

After Hungary's revolution of 1956 was crushed, the Soviets installed a Communist ruler, János Kádár. His collusion in the murder of the revolutionary leader, Imre Nagy, made him unpopular with many Hungarians. But Kádár's regime did permit limited personal freedoms, including some foreign travel, that were denied in other Communist states.

In 1988, the aged Kádár was forced out of leadership by younger officials who looked to Mikhail Gorbachev for support. Hungary's new leaders were disillusioned with hardline Communist policy and were aware of the failure of their economy compared with the affluence of many West European states. Hungary's leaders were

ABOVE LEFT **Soviet tanks crushing anti-Communist dissent in Wenceslas Square in August 1968. The situation had dramatically changed by 1989, however, when the Soviet Union declined to come to the aid of Communist leaders in Czechoslovakia.**

LEFT **A massive rally in Wenceslas Square, 21 November 1989.**

BELOW **A candlelit vigil in Wenceslas Square in 1989.**

confident that a conversion to social democracy and a market economy would be sufficient to stem the growing tide of dissent. To mark this transition to a new democratic political system, a great ceremony to rebury and honour Imre Nagy and his collaborators took place on 16 June 1989. The Soviet ambassador and reformers in the Hungarian Communist Party attended the ceremony. Their presence was testimony to the shift in attitudes. A young radical, Victor Orban, ridiculed the former orthodox Communists as those who "now rush to touch the coffins as if they were good luck charms."

In September 1989, the Communists agreed to de-politicize the army and abolish the Communist Workers' Militia. In the future, political power would be exercised only as a result of the ballot box. The Hungarian Communist Party dropped the word "Workers" from its official title and became the Hungarian Socialist Party in October 1989. A week later, the Hungarian Parliament dropped the word "People's" from the title of the Republic of Hungary.

ABOVE **Alexander Dubček's portrait held aloft in Prague by jubilant crowds, who looked to ex-dissidents for leadership.**

Most importantly, the government agreed to the dissidents' key demand – free multi-party elections. Once these were scheduled for March 1990, the peaceful revolutionary dynamic took on a hectic pace. Within a few months, the Socialists discovered that gratitude for peaceful change was not going to be forthcoming. The various strands of dissident opinion formed political parties and they easily routed the Socialists, who attracted just 8 per cent of the vote.

ABOVE **The reburial in Budapest of Imre Nagy on 16 June 1989. The protégés of his murderers paid their respects alongside the children of 1956.**

The resurgence of Communism

In Hungary, as in other countries of the Eastern bloc, the ex-Communists proved resilient. The survival and comeback of the Communists in the 1990s was partly due to the fact that the new governments did not persecute them. There were no purges to wipe out opposition, such as those that had followed the establishment of Communism after 1945. When they gained power, the Czech reformers chanted contemptuously: "We are not like them" to show their intention not to imitate their humiliated former rulers. With the exception of Romania (*see pages 184– 85*), new Eastern bloc governments did not charge Communist officials with anything worse than corruption. Some were even able to continue their political careers, although their parties had new names.

Democracy was relatively easy to establish in the former Eastern bloc countries: free elections were usually held within a few months of revolution. But the transition to a market economy was more difficult. Unemployment, food shortages and inflation caused discontent in many countries. During the 1990s, many new governments experienced setbacks on the road to establishing capitalist societies. Economic hardships led many electorates to vote in Socialist governments, often run by former Communists. For example, there was certainly a sense of a historic reversal of fortune in Poland in November 1995, when Lech Walesa, the former leader of Solidarity and Poland's President since 1990, was narrowly defeated by an ex-Communist in his bid for re-election.

The dramatic fall of the Berlin Wall in the autumn of 1989 marked the decisive moment in the East European revolutions. Until its collapse, the Wall had divided the city between the democratic West and the Soviet-backed, Communist East. When the East German revolution began, the Soviet Union did not intervene to support the government. This encouraged the people of other Eastern bloc states to start their own revolts.

The Fall of the Berlin Wall

The Berlin Wall surrounding West Berlin was the most bitter symbol of the East–West division of Europe. At the end of the Second World War, Germany was divided between the Soviet Union and other Allies in the West. A split between the Soviet Union and the West developed after the war. Hostility increased, the Cold War developed and East and West Germany polarized politically. The Western Allies loosened control over West Germany in 1949, and it became an independent democracy. In contrast, the Soviets exerted more control over the Communist East. Berlin became the focus of hostility, and, in 1961, the East Germans built a wall around East Berlin. This left the Western section an enclave in Berlin, cut off from the rest of West Germany.

The official reason for the construction of the Berlin Wall was to prevent Western agents infiltrating East Germany. But the real reason was to stop East Germans fleeing to the West. Before 1961, more than two million East Germans had crossed into the West. The Wall helped to halt this flow, but behind it the East German regime failed to solve any of the problems that had led so many of its people to emigrate.

Erich Honecker's regime
The chief political architect of the Berlin Wall was Erich Honecker. He was the second most important person in the East German government (after premier Walter

INSET **An East German soldier jumps to freedom in August 1961, just before the Berlin Wall is erected.**

LEFT **A hole in the Wall is mended after an explosion, 26 May 1962. The East German regime claimed the Wall protected East Berliners from terrorism but at least 184 people were killed trying to flee to the West.**

Ulbright) in the 1960s and became leader of the East German Communist Party in 1971. Honecker was a rigid advocate of the idea that capitalist West Germany and Communist East Germany had almost nothing in common. As late as 1987, he insisted that the Wall would still exist in a hundred years' time. Honecker stated that capitalism and Communism could no more mix than "fire and water."

Honecker had joined the Communist Party during the period when Joseph Stalin ruled the Soviet Union. The spread of hardline Communism during the Stalinist era (1920s–1950s) and after helped to shape Honecker's ideas. He was unsympa-

thetic to reforming measures, such as those introduced by the Soviet leader Mikhail Gorbachev in the 1980s. Honecker wanted to maintain the rigid Communist policies that had governed East Germany for decades – but by the late 1980s, these policies had almost bankrupted the country.

Meanwhile, a whole generation of East Germans had grown up behind the Wall. They had never been allowed to travel to the West, but they could catch a glimpse of the outside world by watching West German television. Unlike their censored media, West German television informed East Germans of the reforms taking place in the Soviet Union, as well as offering entertainment from the capitalist West. Discontent with Honecker's regime grew and was fuelled by economic problems. Food shortages and the limited number of consumer goods in East Germany became more serious. However, there was no organized opposition to the regime until 1989.

Signs of Communist Party fragility

The first challenge to the East German regime came through another Communist country: Hungary. In May 1989, the Hungarian government declared that it would allow its citizens, and those of other Eastern bloc countries, to travel into neighbouring Austria. Until then, all Eastern bloc countries, had operated a "fraternal" policy of preventing their citizens travelling to the West. This had a knock-on effect in East Germany, because many East Germans spent their holidays in Hungary.

In July 1989, the annual exodus began of East German holiday-makers journeying to Hungary. First a trickle and then a flood of people took advantage of the chance to travel to Austria. Despite protests from the East German government, the Hungarians did not change their policy. The anti-Communist reform movement had already begun in Hungary (*see pages 176–79*). Also, Hungary was desperate for investment, and saw a better chance of finding it with

ABOVE **Erich Honecker and Mikhail Gorbachev in East Berlin during the fortieth anniversary celebrations of East Germany.**

the booming economy of West Germany than with its former Communist allies.

Erich Honecker, now 77-years-old, spent much of the summer of 1989 ill in hospital. His government colleagues took no decisive action to try to stem the growing crisis. Although they managed to persuade Communist Czechoslovakia to help them by preventing East Germans from passing through their territory on the way to Hungary, thousands of Hungarians responded by taking refuge in the West German embassy in Prague. This created an embarrassing situation throughout the Eastern bloc.

Within East Germany, open dissent began to appear, really for the first time, as the borders were firmly closed even for travel to other Communist countries. In October 1989, protests escalated, and

there were regular demonstrations each Monday in Leipzig, East Germany's second city. The protesters called for the right to travel freely. Their slogan, "We are the People," was a deadly blow to the claim by the Honecker regime that it represented the people. Soon the demonstrators began to demand free elections as well as free travel. But Honecker knew that concessions to these demands would lead to the collapse of the East German regime, so he could not agree to them.

Honecker loses control

The fortieth anniversary of the creation of the East German state was on 7 October 1989. Grandees from across the Communist world came to celebrate the occasion in East Berlin, which was now in the midst of a growing crisis. Gorbachev was noticeably cool to the East German leader – refusing him the customary embrace – and behind the scenes he may even have encouraged Honecker's rivals to try to replace him with a reformer. Gorbachev took the opportunity to declare: "History punishes those who come late," which was interpreted as an endorsement of the need for rapid reform in East Germany.

Honecker nevertheless clung on to power, and he made plans to suppress the demonstrations in Leipzig – if necessary with violence – much as his Chinese counterparts had already done (*see page 175*). But Honecker was unable to force through his proposals: too many government officials refused to sanction a blood bath. The Soviet Union made it clear that it would not intervene to suppress the protesters. A crackdown was impossible without the backing of the 30,000 Soviet troops stationed in East Germany.

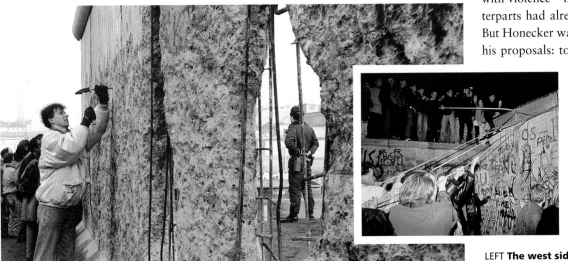

LEFT **The west side of the Berlin Wall: looking through into East Berlin as it is pulled down in November 1989.**

ABOVE **Dismantling the Berlin Wall on the night of 10 November 1989.**

Every day of inaction increased the difficulties of the East German regime. Finally, on 18 October 1989, Honecker was forced out of high office. He was replaced by Egon Krenz, whom Honecker had groomed for leadership, but the change of leader did not result in any immediate action. The new government continued to agonize about what to do. Meanwhile, East German citizens sensed that the regime was in its death-throes and held huge demonstrations to demand change. Next, the Berlin Wall, with its deadly infrastructure, became the main focus for protest by the East Germans.

The Wall crumbles

As people gathered at the Berlin Wall, the government feared that the crowds would try to force their way through to the West and cause a tragic incident. So, the new East German government decided to open the state's borders on 9 November 1989. Farce replaced tragedy when the official responsible for making the announcement

> **"This is a great day for us and a great day for German history. We are and will remain one nation and we belong together."**
> HELMUT KOHL, 10 NOVEMBER 1989

misread his briefing notes. He gave the impression that people could leave East German immediately. Hundreds of thousands of East Berliners promptly swamped to the crossing points with West Berlin. The border guards, who for thirty years had ruthlessly prevented any illegal crossing of the Wall, soon gave up the effort to control the outflow of people.

In a carnival atmosphere, people mounted the previously forbidden Wall and began to demolish it with pickaxes and anything else that came to hand. New entrances were forced through by bulldozers to ease the crush of people wanting to cross into West Germany. In the days after 9 November, more than 2,000,000 East Germans poured through the gaps in the Berlin Wall to visit the West.

Although the Communists remained in power, events meant that their authority had been completely eroded. They agreed to participate in discussions with those representing the demonstrators. These reformers were not an established opposition force: only a few weeks earlier they had been scarcely known. Now they had substantial backing from the East German people and, on 7 December 1989, they were able to make the government agree to free elections. These democratic elections were set for 18 March 1990.

Meanwhile, demonstrators continued to voice their discontent across East Germany. These protests were prompted by revelations of corruption by former officials and abuses of power by the secret police, known as the Stasi. Demonstrators called for investigations into the allegations and they demanded punishment for those guilty of corruption.

The collapse of the Berlin Wall, the inner German border, meant that the chant of the demonstrators changed from "We are the People" to "We are One People." Without the Berlin Wall and with the Communist economic system bankrupt, there was no reason for East Germany to remain separate from the West any longer. Reunification with West Germany had now become a real possibility. The East Germans shared a common nationality with the West. Also, West Germany had the most powerful economy in Western Europe. An alliance offered the chance of a solution to East Germany's bankruptcy. The East German elections held in March 1990 were easily won by parties favouring reunification with West Germany. The West Germans were surprised by the speed of the change. Long-established barriers had fallen and West Germans were left to pay the price of reunification.

1945	**8 May**
	Capitulation of Nazi Germany
1949	**7 October**
	Foundation of German Democratic Republic (GDR)
1953	**17 June**
	Workers' uprising in East Berlin
1961	**13 August**
	Construction of Berlin Wall begins
1971	**3 May**
	Erich Honecker becomes leader of Communist Party
1989	**29 July**
	Start of exodus of East Germans to the West via Hungary
	6–7 October
	GDR celebrates 40th anniversary. Pro-reform demonstrators arrested
	18 October
	Honecker removed as leader of Communist Party
	7 November
	East German government resigns
	9 November
	Berlin Wall opened
	3 December
	Politburo dissolved
	8 December
	Honecker charged with abuse of office
	22 December
	Brandenburg Gate opened and city reunited
1990	**18 March**
	First free elections
	3 October
	German reunification
1994	**29 May**
	Honecker dies in exile in Chile

ABOVE **Jubilant crowds from East and West Berlin help one another to the top of the Wall on 10 November 1989, a few hours after the East German authorities had opened the border.**

LEFT **The German flag is waved during reunification celebrations in October 1990. The first all-German elections since 1933 took place in December 1990.**

One of the most astonishing aspects of the East German revolution was the lack of violence, particularly as the government had exercised such brutal repression. The Communist border guards, who patrolled the East German boundary, had shot hundreds of people who had tried to flee the country over the years. Signs of dissent within the country had been suppressed, often violently, by the Stasi. Yet the East German system collapsed without a single shot being fired. The East German revolution was as bloodless as the other "velvet" revolutions (*see pages 176–79*).

Germany today

Many of the East Germans who helped to pull down the Berlin Wall in 1989 did not foresee the number of problems that reunification would bring. The majority of East Germans did prosper in the new united Germany. However, rationalization and large-scale closure of East Germany's bankrupt industries were unavoidable, this left many people without jobs. Ironically, unemployment pay was of greater value in the new Germany than East German wages ever had been under Communism. Those who did have jobs had to pay higher taxes to fund the change. Social problems of unemployment were more difficult to deal with. Crime and social unrest increased, creating more difficulties for the new state.

Many former East Germans demanded investigations into the past abuses of the Stasi and former government leaders. These calls became more insistent after some of the Stasi's secrets were revealed, such as the names of informers. The new Germany's legal system could not deal with demands to punish those responsible for decades of dictatorship. Even Erich Honecker's trial ended disappointingly, because ill-health prevented him from answering charges. He had been accused of the manslaughter of the people who had attempted to escape over the Berlin Wall during the past decades. As the former East German dissident, Barbara Bohley, commented: "We demanded justice but got the rule of law instead."

The 1989 Christmas Revolution in Romania had more signs of a classic revolution than any other in Eastern Europe. Crowds surged through the streets of Romania, there were violent clashes with authority and a tyrant was toppled from power. Ironically, however, the Romanian Revolution produced much less fundamental change than other Eastern bloc countries had achieved through their more peaceful revolutions.

The Violent Exception

By the end of 1989, Romania was the only East European country that remained under hardline Communist Party control. Romania was the most unreformed of all the East European Communist states. In fact, since Nicolae Ceauşescu became Romania's leader in 1965, the state had adopted progressively more hardline policies year by year. Ceauşescu came from a peasant background and had joined the Communist Party in the years before the Second World War. He was influenced by the Soviet leader, Joseph Stalin, and followed Stalin's example to become a tyrannical ruler.

In addition to keeping the economy rigidly state-controlled, Ceauşescu tried to glorify his position by implementing grandiose projects (*see below*). He also came to bolster his personal power by giving Communist Party and government jobs to members of his family, particularly his wife, Elena. The combination of expensive prestige projects and nepotism led people to joke that if the Soviet Union had achieved "socialism in one country," Romania had managed "socialism in one family."

The emergence of dissent

In 1985, Mikhail Gorbachev became leader of the Soviet Union and soon afterwards began a programme of limited reform. Ceauşescu was not sympathetic with developments in the Soviet Union. He regarded Gorbachev's reforms as a threat to his dictatorship. There was no openness or "glasnost" in Romania. Any sign of dissent was silenced by the powerful Romanian secret police, the Securitate.

The Romanian economy, meanwhile, was declining. The energy industry reached such a state of crisis that electricity was rationed. There were food shortages and delays in paying workers' wages at some factories. Despite the dire economic conditions of the late 1980s, and growing signs of labour unrest, Ceauşescu embarked on an insanely expensive scheme to rebuild Romania's cities. He wanted to reconstruct urban centres in line with his own ideas. Ceauşescu ordered the construction of a massive palace in the centre of the country's capital, Bucharest, at the same time as food and medicine shortages made life a misery for the Romanian people.

Romanian citizens were aware of the reforms in neighbouring countries, but it was the growing disillusionment of key members of the Communist elite that really threatened Ceauşescu. He relied on the security services to stifle opposition, but by the winter of 1989, they too were discontented with the regime.

LEFT **Deceptive enthusiasm. Nicolae Ceauşescu waves to the crowd in Bucharest after the end of the Communist Party Congress on 24 November 1989.**

LEFT **Demonstrators celebrate in front of Ceauşescu's balcony on the Central Committee Building in Bucharest, December 1989.**

The collapse of the Ceauşescu regime

The event that sparked open rebellion in December 1989 was an attempt to deport a clergyman, Laszlo Tökes. He had campaigned for the improved treatment of his fellow Hungarians, who formed a large ethnic community in Romania. Hundreds of people surrounded the priest's home in the Western city of Timisoara, trying to prevent his deportation. The protests grew and resulted in violent clashes with the authorities that left hundreds of demonstrators dead.

A few days later, on 21 December, Ceauşescu staged a massive public rally in Bucharest that was intended to demonstrate support for his regime. Oblivious to his unpopularity, Ceauşescu was unprepared for his reception. For the first time in over twenty years in power, he was hissed by the people he governed.

Demonstrations spread throughout the country and were ruthlessly suppressed by the Securitate. Suddenly, on 22 December, the army changed sides to support the protesters. Later that day, Ceauşescu made a final attempt to quiet the crowd in the capital from the balcony of the Communist Party Central Committee headquarters. He was shouted down by the crowd who shouted "Death! Death!" Ceauşescu and his wife fled: they were airlifted, by helicopter, from the roof of the building as it was stormed by the crowd. They transferred to cars and tried to reach the border, but they were captured by rebel soldiers. On Christmas Day 1989, after a summary trial, Nicolae and Elena Ceauşescu were shot by the same men who had supported them only days earlier. Within the next couple of days the last remnants of opposition to the new regime were wiped out.

The aftermath of revolution

When the dust cleared after four days of jubilation and confusion, the Romanians discovered that they may have killed the hated Ceauşescus, but many of the old regime's apparatchiks (officials) had survived. A few new faces in government did not disguise the basic continuity. When the army sided with the people, army generals staged a coup d'état to install leaders of their choice in the new government. The new president, Ion Iliescu, had been a Politburo member before falling out with Ceauşescu. Much like Gorbachev, Iliescu was in favour of limited reform rather than a complete break with the past.

Many students and intellectuals were unhappy about what they regarded as the hijacking of *their* revolution by ex-Communists. In the run-up to the first multi-party elections in May 1990, demonstrators blocked Bucharest's University Square, where scores of people had been killed in 1989. Iliescu was duly elected President, but only after a campaign marked by the intimidation of his opponents. Once he assumed the Presidency, he summoned thousands of miners from

outside Bucharest as a vigilante militia to disperse the demonstrators. The miners saw the students as privileged urban layabouts and dealt with them with considerable brutality. This episode confirmed Romania's reputation for being less democratic than the other post-Communist states, which in turn discouraged foreign investment. Economic reform and political change has limped along in Romania since 1990 and many qualified people emigrated.

ABOVE LEFT **Crowds surge through Bucharest on 21 December 1989.**

ABOVE CENTRE **Buildings in Bucharest are set alight, 22–23 December 1989.**

ABOVE RIGHT **Celebrating the fall of the Communists, 27 December 1989.**

LEFT **Sheltering from the fighting, 22–23 December 1989.**

KEY EVENTS

1944 23 August
Pro-German dictator, Antonescu, toppled as Soviet troops enter country.
1965 22 March
Nicolae Ceauşescu becomes leader of Communist Party
1974 28 March
Ceauşescu elected President
1989 26 November
Ceauşescu re-elected as leader
16 December
Riots in Timisoara
21 December
Ceauşescu booed in Bucharest
22 December
Ceauşescu flees from Bucharest
25 December
Execution of Nicolae and Elena Ceauşescu

The Russian Revolution of 1917 eventually led to the creation of the first Communist state, the Soviet Union. By the 1950s, the Soviet Union had emerged as one of the world's superpowers. The collapse of the Communist system in its birthplace in 1991 was as dramatic and important as the first Russian Revolution. Both revolutions marked the end of an era and many years passed before new systems emerged.

The Soviet Union Collapses

After the Second World War, an East–West split appeared in international relations and deteriorated into a state of worldwide confrontation known as the Cold War. Hostility was particularly marked between the two most powerful states in the world: the Communist, totalitarian Soviet Union and the capitalist, democratic USA.

The Soviet Union's leader from 1964 until 1982 was the Communist hardliner, Leonid Brezhnev. Under his leadership, the Soviet Union achieved nuclear parity with the USA and pursued an expansionist foreign policy. The Soviet Union backed the triumphant Communist side during the Vietnam War. Communist allies of the Soviet Union gained power in some parts of Africa, Asia and Central America. The only apparent cloud on the horizon was the guerrilla war in Afghanistan where Soviet troops were sent to support the Communist government in 1979. The Soviet troops became embroiled in a war with local Muslim fighters that lasted until the collapse of the Soviet Union in 1992.

In the early 1980s, the Soviet Union seemed to be such a significant superpower that few people suspected that it had peaked and faced a crisis. In November 1980, Ronald Reagan became President of the USA. His election message had been that the Soviet threat to world stability was so real that US defence was a priority. By starting a huge arms build-up, President Reagan helped to expose the problems of the Soviet Union.

Behind the facade of military might and displays of public conformity at May Day parades, the Soviet economy was in decline. Problems were caused by the arms race, which consumed 30 per cent of national resources, and the inefficient production methods. For example, Soviet factories used six times as much electricity to produce the same amount of goods as American or Japanese plants. Such inefficient production and poor distribution meant that fewer and fewer goods reached the shops. A depressing 35 per cent of the agricultural harvest usually rotted before distribution.

Within the Soviet elite, some officials were aware of the seriousness of the stagnation of the economy and society. But a succession of aged and ailing leaders delayed change until 1985, when a reforming leader came to power.

The beginning of the Gorbachev era

Brezhnev died in 1982 and the next two Soviet leaders died in quick succession. Then, in March 1985, the Soviet Communist Party elected a new General-Secretary, Mikhail Gorbachev. He was very different from his recent predecessors. An active and intelligent man in his fifties, Gorbachev was determined to reform the Soviet system and to shake up its stultifying routines. But his actions were ultimately to precipitate a crisis, not avert one.

ABOVE AND LEFT
Military parades in the Soviet capital, Moscow. Such parades were an important means of displaying military force and technology, both to the Soviet peoples and to the outside world (particularly during the years of the Cold War).

"Glasnost" and "perestroika"

Gorbachev could never have become Party leader without the support of powerful elements in the Soviet system who recognized the need for reform. Although there was consensus among officials on the need for change, the form it should take and how it should be implemented were not so clear. One matter that had to be dealt with was the ruinous arms race with the West, so it was important to begin by reducing Cold War tensions. Gorbachev's personal charm helped to improve relations with wary leaders in the West.

Even more crucial than international relations was the need for the Soviet Union to tackle its domestic problems. From early in his period of office, Gorbachev announced the need to end the stifling conformity of Soviet life and to permit more "glasnost" (openness) in discussion. At the same time he wanted to introduce "perestroika" (restructuring) of the economy. It proved difficult to implement these changes, as one of his first reforms was to show. Recognizing that alcoholism was a serious economic as well as social problem, Gorbachev launched a campaign to reduce alcohol consumption. But the plan soon backfired: it was very unpopular, decreased government revenue from vodka sales and also stimulated the black market. These consequences were an early indication that reform could go awry.

The disaster at Chernobyl

On 26 April 1986, there was a major explosion at the Chernobyl nuclear plant in the Ukraine. The effects of radioactive fall-out were disastrous: as well as killing hundreds of people, it contaminated land and animals across Europe. The disaster discredited the Soviet system, which had claimed to be a rational system based on progress in science and technology. Revelations that the Chernobyl plant had been run carelessly, with inadequate attention to safety standards, had shattered assumptions about Soviet

industry. However, Gorbachev's decision, after some hesitation, to publicize details of the Chernobyl disaster was a breakthrough for "glasnost." The Soviet Union had begun to be more open about its past and current events.

The emergence of a rival

As Gorbachev pursued his policies of reform, many Western observers expected him to suffer a hardline backlash. But Gorbachev's political nemesis proved to be Boris Yeltsin, ironically one of the men he brought into the Soviet leadership to speed up change. As head of the Moscow Communist Party, Yeltsin proved to be

FAR LEFT **The last General Secretary of the Soviet Communist Party, Mikhail Gorbachev, at the Party Congress in 1986.**

LEFT **Once Gorbachev's protégé, Boris Yeltsin became his nemesis as the first Soviet politician to break ranks with his comrades.**

radically different from most other officials. He was aware that the system had failed many Soviet citizens and he attacked the privileges of the Communist Party elite.

Tensions between Yeltsin and orthodox officials grew until he decided to take a tremendous gamble with his future. On 27 October 1987, Yeltsin made an astonishing speech to the Soviet Union's ruling Central Committee. He launched an attack on privilege and corruption in the Party elite and argued that "perestroika" had done nothing for ordinary people. Then he announced his intention to resign from his post. Yeltsin's impetuous actions would in the past have marked the end of his career, but now it secured Yeltsin's future as the people's champion against the Communists.

Rumours of Yeltsin's speech spread and made him popular with the silent mass of Party officials. But Yeltsin was aware that he was in a dangerous position. He knew that Party enemies could silence him for good: "They can get rid of me and just leave a damp spot." Gorbachev in fact believed that the popularity of Yeltsin's relatively extreme stance could frighten Party hardliners. Gorbachev hoped that the orthodox officials would see the benefit in implementing his limited reforms now, rather than being forced into extreme reforms later.

Gorbachev promotes democracy

The celebrations in 1987 of the seventieth anniversary of the Russian Revolution took place against a backdrop of rumours about splits inside the Communist Party.

LEFT **A Soviet poster reading "Drunk driver = criminal." Gorbachev's anti-alcohol campaign made him deeply unpopular.**

Mikhail Gorbachev had begun to reverse the repressive policy of his predecessors towards internal critics in December 1986, when he released the famous scientist and dissident Andrei Sakharov and his wife from exile in the city of Gorkiy. Throughout 1988, more revelations about the Soviet Union's grim past under Joseph Stalin (1920s–1950s) were published as part of Gorbachev's glasnost policy to fill in the "blank spots" in Soviet history. At the same time, Gorbachev tried to divest the Communist Party of hardliners by moving the country towards an elected system of government. Gorbachev was convinced that his sincerity as a reformer would rally support to his side, but in practice decades of suppressed disillusionment and cynicism about Communist leaders would be revealed in March 1989 when the Soviet population voted for the new Congress of People's Deputies.

In fact, the beneficiaries of the elections turned out to be the critics of the Soviet system, such as Sakharov and Yeltsin. Gorbachev himself did not risk failure and stand for election in a normal constituency but had himself nominated to one of the 100 seats reserved for the Communist Party. Gorbachev knew that his main weakness was lack of popular support. It was Yeltsin who became the elected representative of the people, while the legitimacy of Gorbachev's power rested on the waning Communist Party.

In the short term, Gorbachev was wise not to stand for election since millions of Soviet citizens voted against high-ranking Communists, even many reformers. The new Congress of People's Deputies opened on 26 May 1989. Soviet citizens watched its sessions on television and saw unprecedented debate and criticism of the system.

During 1989 and 1990, events in other parts of the Communist world influenced the Soviet Union. The Tiananmen Square massacre in China and the "velvet" revolutions in Eastern Europe (*see pages 174–83*) changed Soviet opinion. The collapse of Communism in other countries showed that it was possible to abolish the system, not just reform it.

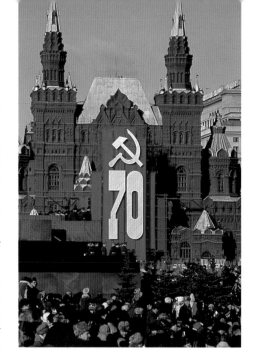

Which way to turn?
Gorbachev could not abandon his lifelong allegiance to the old order and transform himself wholeheartedly into a reformer. Instead, in 1990, he resisted key changes until it was too late. He would not allow private ownership of land and could not decide on a plan to introduce the market economy that he favoured. He did, reluctantly, agree to permit parties other than the

LEFT **Celebrations in Moscow in 1987 of the seventieth anniversary of the Russian Revolution of 1917.**

Communists to participate in politics. But all the time Gorbachev procrastinated, Yeltsin gained influence. In June 1991, Yeltsin was elected executive President of Russia, the largest republic in the Soviet Union. This undermined Gorbachev even further.

Nationalists in the republics around the fringes of the Soviet Union began to demand independence. Economic conditions had worsened, and there seemed to be less reason to remain part of a large, inefficient Soviet Union. Gorbachev sided during the winter of 1990–91 with the hardline Communists who organized crackdowns on the nationalist movements in the republics of Lithuania and Latvia. However, they could not stop the drift to independence. In the spring of 1991, Gorbachev changed tactics and began to negotiate a new constitution for a transformed Soviet Union. This so-called "union treaty" would effectively transfer much of

SOVIET NATIONALITIES

The Soviet Union was one of the world's most diverse states. Westerners often talked about the population of the USSR as the "Russians," but by the late 1980s Russians were only the largest single nation of the USSR (just under 50 per cent of the total) and they shared the territory with a variety of large nations (such as Ukrainians, Uzbeks and Kazakhs) along with small but tenacious nations (Georgians and Armenians, or the Baltic peoples) and numerous small nations ranging from the million-strong Chechens to Siberian tribes with a few thousand members. Russian was the *lingua franca*, but the other languages were increasingly assertive at the local level. "Glasnost" permitted the public expression of an interest in the heritage of individual nations and helped to encourage a revival

of national identity. In December 1986, Kazakhs rioted in protest against Russification. In February 1988, clashes between Armenians and Azeris revealed that tensions existed among non-Russians too. In April 1989, Soviet troops used force to disperse pro-independence Georgians. But by the autumn of that year, millions of Lithuanians, Latvians and Estonians publicly joined hands in a human chain across the Baltic states to protest against their incorporation into the USSR (see *below left*; the flags of the three Baltic states are shown *below right*). Gorbachev seriously underrated the degree of nationalist hostility to the USSR, whether reformed or not: no sooner had the coup of Communist hardliners failed in August 1991 than a number of republics declared their independence from the Soviet Union.

the power of the Soviet central government from the Kremlin to the Union's individual republics. In fact only nine of the republics agreed to sign it (the others considered it too binding), though these included the largest republics of Russia, Ukraine and Kazakhstan. The treaty was due to be signed on 20 August 1991.

ABOVE **During Gorbachev's rule, nationalism and demands for political independence appeared in the Soviet Union's fifteen republics.**

RIGHT **The Caucasus became a hotbed of post-Soviet conflict.**

The failure of Communist hardliners

A group of senior Soviet officials became alarmed by Gorbachev's apparent willingness to concede so many powers to the individual republics. So, on 19 August 1991, they staged a coup in Moscow. The hardliners hoped the coup would halt the slide towards the disintegration of the Soviet Union. Instead their actions accelerated it.

Indecision and poor planning made the coup a failure. Although the plotters kept Gorbachev away from Moscow by preventing him from leaving his holiday *datcha* on the Crimea, they made a major mistake in not cutting telecommunications and not arresting Yeltsin, whose broadcasts and public appearances from his headquarters inside the Russian Parliament building in Moscow, the White House, made him the rallying centre for opposition to the coup.

Key military officers sided with Yeltsin, and the coup collapsed within three days. Only three people were killed, but in effect the Soviet Communist Party had died. The attempted coup had completely discredited the Party. Gorbachev failed to understand this and, on his release from captivity, made a speech calling on the Party to reform itself and to lead reform. This approach proved completely unrealistic. Yeltsin seized the initiative. At a televised session of the Russian Parliament, he humiliated Gorbachev by revealing how Gorbachev's own appointees had betrayed him. Over the next few weeks, the remnants of Gorbachev's authority rapidly drained away. Yeltsin persuaded army generals that an independent Russian state would be a better guarantor of the army's interests than the waning Soviet regime.

The collapse of the coup led directly to the collapse of the Soviet Union. In late August 1991, a group of Soviet republics declared their independence. By December 1991 the Presidents of three of the new independent states – Russia, Ukraine and Belarus declared that the Union of Soviet Socialist Republics no longer existed. They formed a Commonwealth of Independent States (CIS). Most of the former Soviet republics joined the CIS. On 25 December 1991, Gorbachev recognized the absurdity of his position as President of a non-existent country and resigned. The Kremlin's Red Flag was hauled down and the new Russian Federation was created. The great Soviet revolutionary experiment had run its course. But revolutionary events were far from finished in the CIS or the newly independent states around its fringe.

The messy sequel

The end of Communism in Eastern Europe was largely non-violent – apart from in Romania. The break-up of Communist Yugoslavia in 1991, however, triggered savage, protracted warfare. Many feared that this could happen with the collapse of the greatest multi-national Communist state, the Soviet Union. Certainly, democracy did not come easily in many areas. In Central Asia, for example, rigged elections or open dictatorship kept the rulers in power. In the Caucasus, war and coups were used to justify authoritarian presidential rule.

Russia, too, did not have the relatively smooth transition to democratic party politics that most of Central Europe enjoyed. Soon after the collapse of the Soviet Union in 1991, rivalries among Russia's politicians began to surface. For the next two years, Russian politics revolved around the bitter dispute between President Yeltsin and the leaders of the Russian Parliament. Sources of antagonism included economic reform and the hardships that accompanied it; Russia's future role in international politics; and relations with the ex-Soviet republics where 25 million Russian citizens still lived. Personal ambition and fights about who should benefit from the privatization of the state-run economy inherited from the Soviet Union were also causes of growing tension between the President and Parliament. Allegations of corruption and abuse of power were traded back and forth.

Two of Yeltsin's former supporters now turned against him: his vice-President, Aleksandr Rutskoi, and the Speaker of the

ABOVE **Communist icons were toppled by the crowd in August 1991. Here Maxim Gorkiy's statue has been pulled to the ground in Gorkiy Park, Moscow.**

Russian Parliament, Ruslan Khasbulatov. Yeltsin was anxious to enjoy the same level of power as that of the previous Soviet Presidents. He wanted to appoint the heads of regions himself, whereas Khasbulatov and Rutskoi pressed for elections. Both the President and the Speaker had the right to issue decrees. In 1993, each issued hundreds of often contradictory orders to Russian civil servants and the public. The stage was set for conflict.

Yeltsin's second White House siege

In April 1993, popular support for Yeltsin was confirmed in a referendum on his presidential powers. Yet he could not break the resistance of the majority of parliamentarians to his programme of rapid reforms. On 21 September 1993, Yeltsin suddenly decreed the dissolution of the Russian Parliament and elections for a new Parliament. Defiant deputies voted for the deposition of the President and Rutskoi's appointment in his place.

TOP **Tanks block the streets of Moscow during the attempted coup by Communist hard-liners on 19 August 1991.**

ABOVE **Yeltsin celebrates victory with crowds of supporters after the coup has collapsed.**

Rutskoi proved to be a poor strategist in the crisis that followed. Yeltsin had dissolved the Russian Parliament but had not dared to use force to disperse the defiant deputies gathered inside the White House. During the stand-off, supporters of each side gathered around the White House. They were joined by ex-Communists and new Russian Fascists. On 3 October, armed conflict broke out. Yeltsin took the opportunity to call on the army to restore order and preserve civil peace. He appeared to be the person of authority and decisive action while Rutskoi was perceived as the person responsible for provoking the violence. The failure of the protests showed that although many Russians were disillusioned with reform, few were willing to support the extremists against Yeltsin.

RIGHT **Burning barricades in a district of Moscow in October 1993. Yeltsin's opponents staged more of a riot than a coup d'état, and when the Russian Army moved into the city it had little difficulty in restoring order. But the violence marked a break with the largely peaceful evolution of Russian politics since Communism.**

The emergence of Zhirinovsky and the revival of the Communists

Immediately after his triumph, Yeltsin devised a new constitution for Russia that concentrated power in the hands of the President. On 12 December 1993, elections were held for a new parliament, the State Duma, and a referendum to endorse the constitution. The elections produced a shock result: the parties supporting the President did surprisingly badly while the radical nationalist party led by Vladimir Zhirinovsky came first with almost a quarter of the votes cast.

Even before the siege of the White House Yeltsin's foreign policy had already become more assertive towards Russia's neighbours in the so-called "Near Abroad." Now these ex-Soviet republics were more and more pressured to conform to Russia's interests. Russian troops and agents were particularly active in the Caucasus region, which was strategically important and at the crossroad of many economic interests, especially oil and natural gas from the Caspian Sea region.

In December 1994, Yeltsin sent troops into the breakaway Russian republic of Chechnya, which, in 1991, had declared independence. The Russian army bungled the operation and suffered severe losses. The costly and brutal war in Chechnya seemed to contradict Yeltsin's earlier criticisms of Soviet heavy-handedness.

A year later, the Russian Communist Party emerged from the grave to win more than a third of the seats in the elections for the State Duma in December 1995.

> **"Our people knows all too well what revolution is, how great are its temptations, and how tragic its results....We have chosen the path of reforms not revolutionary jolts."** BORIS YELTSIN, SPEAKING IN AUGUST 1992 ON THE FIRST ANNIVERSARY OF THE FAILED COUP

Disillusionment with Yeltsin's failure to stem the fall in most people's standard of living, disgust at the small number of super-rich beneficiaries of the changes since 1991 and opposition to the war in Chechnya all produced a big swing against the Yeltsin camp. Zhirinovsky's party came second. It was an ominous warning that after so much change a reaction was beginning to set in. Few revolutions ever run smoothly, and whether Russia's second great upheaval in the twentieth century will stick to its original course and end peacefully remains an open question.

ABOVE **In December 1994, Yeltsin resorted to violence against the breakaway republic of Chechnya. Here Russian troops patrol Chechnya's devastated capital, Grozny.**

As the rest of Africa underwent decolonization after the Second World War, the survival of white minority rule in southern Africa became an anomaly. In South Africa itself racial segregation was strengthened after 1948 by the introduction of the apartheid system. The next forty-five years saw a bitter struggle for black majority rule. Despite years of violence, the end of apartheid was eventually brought about by compromise.

The End of Apartheid

For the first half of the twentieth century, South African politics were driven by the rivalry between the two parts of the country's white minority: the Boers and the British. While the Afrikaans-speaking Boers (descended from the Dutch colonists) had been living in South Africa since the mid-seventeenth century, the territory was assigned to Great Britain at the end of the Napoleonic Wars in 1815. The British colonial administration riled the Boers by abolishing slavery and attempting to regularize land tenure, which led many Boers to escape British rule by migrating north, where they established their own independent states. Escalating tensions between the British and the Boers resulted ultimately in the Boer War of 1899–1902, in which the Boers were defeated. The independent Boer states were then incorporated into the British Empire and in 1910 a self-governing Union of South Africa was created.

For almost forty years after 1910, an alliance of liberal Afrikaners and British politicians dominated the government. This did not stop it from implementing a number of measures designed to reduce further the limited representation granted the non-whites in the South African Parliament, nor from introducing "pass laws," which restricted the movement and controlled the employment of all blacks by requiring them to carry documents authorized by a white person.

The vast black majority had no say in the government of South Africa. It provided a pool of cheap and unskilled labour for the mines and other industries of the growing South African economy. Ironically, it was the economic development of South Africa that led to increasing demands for segregation and job reservation by whites as, unable to find enough white workers, employers began to recruit and train blacks for skilled work. This threatened the relatively privileged standing of white workers and reinforced racial prejudices. At the same time Boer nationalism found new expression in the National Party led by Daniel Malan.

The liberal Afrikaner–British alliance finally broke down over the question of which side to support in the Second World War (in the event a narrow majority in Parliament voted in favour of bringing

LEFT **Living quarters of the black migrant workers at the Johannesburg gold mine. Although wages in the mines were high by rural standards, the contrast between black and white standards of living was sharper in urban centres.**

South Africa into the war on the side of the Allies) and in May 1948 the National Party won the general election on the back of votes from rural Boers and white skilled workers in the industrial areas. Oblivious to the changes elsewhere in the world following the defeat of Nazism and decol-

LEFT **Apartheid in operation: races are segregated on a footbridge in Capetown. The daily humiliations of petty apartheid were particularly hateful to the black community.**

onization, Malan's new government set about introducing a programme of radical racial segregation – even though, as a founder-member of the United Nations, South Africa had committed itself to a policy of equality for all its citizens.

The introduction of apartheid

The idea of apartheid or "separateness" was intended to secure permanently the position of the white minority in South Africa. In practice, it involved a huge programme to reverse the integrating effects of the modern economy. Strict segregation of the races was decreed. Intermarriage was forbidden. A policy of so-called "influx control" was developed that permitted selected, mainly male workers to come to the industrial areas to work, but without their families. Wives and children were confined to rural homelands where conditions were poor, which was why so many had tried to move to the cities in the first place. The disruption of black family life, the host of petty and demeaning restrictions (such as separate parks, trains and even park-benches), the disenfranchisement of the non-whites and the huge disparity between government expenditure on education for whites and that for blacks gave the lie to claims that apartheid meant separate but equal chances for development.

Resistance to apartheid

The African National Congress (ANC), established in 1912 as a vehicle for black nationalism, was similar to other nationalist movements around the British Empire, and was partly inspired by the Indian Congress movement led by Mahatma Gandhi, who had spent some formative years in South Africa. But there was one major difference between the situation in South Africa and that in India: unlike India, which was ruled by British civil servants, South Africa had its own white government. What's more, the white minority in South Africa was sufficiently large and well-organized to dominate political affairs. Continuing white immigration even encouraged the dream of a white majority, although in reality the demographic bal-

ance began to shift increasingly *against* the minority well before the wave of white emigration in the later years of apartheid.

After the Second World War, new young leaders of the ANC emerged, emboldened by the decolonization taking place elsewhere in the world (*see pages 152–57*). The most impressive of these was Nelson Mandela who, from a Xhosa chieftain's family, had received a good education and was trained as a lawyer. A more enlightened South African government would have tried to coopt blacks like Mandela; instead he was regarded as dangerous.

Throughout the 1950s, Mandela was in trouble with the white authorities as he organized opposition – mainly through strikes, boycotts and civil disobedience – to the growing restrictions of apartheid. At

LEFT **The forecourt of the police station in Sharpeville near Johannesburg is strewn with 70 bodies after police opened fire on a crowd of 12,000 demonstrators protesting against the laws restricting the free movement of black people.**

ABOVE **Residents of the Soweto township drag away the body of a dead man after police opened fire on hundreds of demonstrators on 25 August 1976.**

the same time, the constitutional rights of all South Africans were increasingly limited by new legislation.

In 1959, a new black opposition group to white minority rule was established as an off-shoot of the ANC: the Pan-Africanist Congress (PAC). The PAC advocated a more concerted campaign against apartheid,

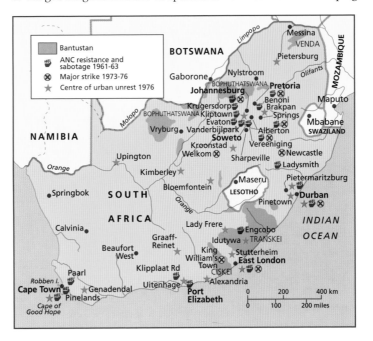

LEFT **Apartheid's attempt to shift the black majority into homelands or bantustans was contradicted by the need of white-owned industries for labour. The black townships around white urban centres became the focus of protest after 1976.**

calling on blacks to refuse to carry pass-books and to present themselves en masse at police stations to demand arrest. It was during one such peaceful demonstration that the so-called Sharpeville massacre occurred in March 1960. Alarmed by the size of the crowd marching to the police station in Sharpeville, near Johannesburg, constables opened fire on the demonstrators, killing about 70 (many of whom were shot in the back) and wounding a further 180. This provoked outrage among the country's black population and led to nationwide strikes and stayaways. The government responded by declaring a State of Emergency and banning the ANC and PAC. Ironically, the massacre encouraged opposition groups to abandon non-violent protest and adopt a more aggressive line. It also stimulated widespread international condemnation. South Africa was expelled from the British Commonwealth in 1961 when the country became a republic.

The National Party government thought all black opposition was inspired by Communism and used the suppression of Marxism to justify a blanket crackdown on all black protests. In fact, the National Party was correct in some of its assumptions. While certain white liberals in the South African Parliament did oppose apartheid, it was the white-led Communist Party that turned out to be the ANC's most dynamic partner. Accustomed to underground activities, the Communists helped to train ANC activists and to provide sympathetic defence counsel during trials.

Mandela and other ANC leaders were at first suspicious of the Communists, but as constitutional ways of protesting were cut off and the authorities used violence against demonstrators, the ANC leadership came to accept that some form of armed struggle would probably be necessary to reverse apartheid. After the outlawing of the ANC in 1960, its leaders set up a guerrilla organization called Umkhonto we Sizwe ("The Spear of the Nation").

Although, starting in the early 1960s, Umkhonto received military training and assistance from other independent African countries such as Algeria, Ethiopia and,

later, South Africa's black-ruled neighbours, guerrilla warfare made little headway. The ANC concentrated on sabotaging government installations but avoided anti-white terrorism, fearing this would be counterproductive. It is striking how few whites died during the anti-apartheid struggle.

In reaction to the attempts at sabotage, the government became harsher. Mandela was caught after a period underground and sentenced to life imprisonment in June 1964. Contrary to the government's expectations, Mandela's authority over the ANC grew with his years in confinement. His long years in the prison on Robben Island turned him into the symbolic figure of the ANC's struggle, and he achieved worldwide fame behind bars.

Although, from the mid-1960s to the mid-1970s, the apartheid regime seemed more secure, its social policies and neglect of the huge black townships for migrant workers on the outskirts of white cities were storing up trouble. Mandela repeatedly voiced his objections to the effect of "influx control" on African family life. Hundreds of thousands of fathers working in the mines or industrial centres were cut off from their wives and children, and even

where families lived together, economic strains and resentment against apartheid's frustrations caused deep tensions.

The Soweto uprising

Low spending on black education as well as the deliberate restriction on job opportunities fuelled black discontent during the years of apartheid. Meanwhile, Afrikaners had always been irritated that the official

In June 1958, Nelson Mandela married the much younger Winnie Madikizela. Their family life was marked from the start by separations for political reasons and then Mandela's imprisonment. During her husband's long years in prison, Winnie Mandela became a political figure in her own right. She faced banning orders and other attempts to gag her. For all her defiant courage, a shadow side of her personality appeared in the 1980s. Her husband had turned to violence as a last resort: Winnie sometimes seemed to glory in the township necklacing – burning to death with rubber tyres – of collaborators with the authorities: "Together hand in hand with our boxes of matches and our necklaces we shall liberate this country." Proud and intolerant of advice, Winnie gathered a group of male supporters around her who became the focus of gossip and allegations of corruption and brutality. The murder by her bodyguards of an alleged boy informer, Stompie Moeketsi, in January 1989 implicated her in a major scandal. It was a key factor in shattering her marriage to Mandela which did not long survive her husband's release from prison. Winnie still enjoyed support among radical youths in townships like Soweto even after the ANC dropped her from its leadership. The divorce did not dent President Mandela's popularity.

TOP **Black students in Soweto in 1976 raise their arms in victory salutes and peace signs as they advance towards the police.**

ABOVE **Vehicles in a Soweto street are set ablaze by students.**

"Your tireless and heroic sacrifices have made it possible for me to be here ...I place the remaining years of my life in your hands" NELSON MANDELA, SPEAKING TO THE CROWDS AFTER HIS RELEASE FROM PRISON

language in black schools was English, an international language, rather than their unique tongue. In an attempt to please the Africaners, the government decided to impose education in Afrikaans on black school children in 1976, but this sparked dramatic events in the vast sprawling township of Soweto outside Johannesburg. On 16 June 1976, large numbers of pupils boycotted classes and 15,000 children marched through the town in protest. Police and then troops arrived and opened fire. Few things are more emotive than the death at the hands of the police of school children, some hardly in their teens, and rioting quickly spread through Soweto and other cities. Hundreds of demonstrators were killed, while the government security forces lost only two men.

Vorster's government determined to act decisively against the new groups demanding majority rule that had begun to emerge in the 1970s. In the ensuing crackdown, the leaders of the "Black Consciousness" movement were arrested. The most famous of them, Steve Biko, died in police custody

in 1977 after terrible maltreatment. Publicity around the world after such deaths aroused widespread hostility to the South African regime and sparked renewed calls for economic sanctions. At the same time, South Africa lost its buffer of white-ruled states to the north: the Portuguese colonies, Angola and Mozambique, became independent under radical Marxist regimes in 1975, then Rhodesia became Zimbabwe in 1980 under black majority rule.

Cracks in apartheid

After Vorster fell from office in 1978 following allegations of corruption, the new South African leader, P.W. Botha, and his Defence Minister, Magnus Malan, recognized that white rule could not survive indefinitely on the basis of alienating the whole non-white population – which amounted to 85 per cent of the total. While continuing to suppress black opposition groups, the Botha regime tried to

RIGHT **The extreme right-wing leader Eugene Terre Blanche threatened war in the event of majority rule. His threats have proved empty.**

entice non-black minorities (Asians and coloureds) into cooperation by improving their status. It also offered limited benefits to the relatively small numbers of blacks who had prospered as businessmen in the townships. At the same time it maintained the policy of creating so-called "independent" homelands or bantustans, hoping to play off the various black tribes and nations against each other.

But with two million black unemployed and an increasing birthrate (while the white birthrate stagnated), Botha's changes had no real impact on the vast majority of the non-white population; indeed, they added

insult to injury because they were so clearly intended to consolidate the basis of apartheid rather than abolish it.

The breakdown of apartheid

By the time illness forced P.W. Botha from office in 1989, "enlightened" Afrikaans politicians like his successor F.W. de Klerk realized that the survival of the whites could not be guaranteed by continuing the old regime. Instead a genuine compromise with the majority had to be sought.

The sudden collapse of the Communist regimes in Eastern Europe in 1989 (*see pages 174–85*) helped de Klerk to push through previously unthinkable change. For decades, fear of Communism had helped justify apartheid's security measures. Now this threat was lifted and the ANC would no longer be supported by the formidable Soviet bloc.

From Mandela's release to majority rule

While P.W. Botha had negotiated with Nelson Mandela shortly before resigning his office, the President had refused to release Mandela from prison unless he gave various guarantees to denounce violence – assurances Mandela declined to offer. De Klerk, on the other hand, took the risk of unbanning the ANC and releasing Mandela in February 1990 without conditions.

The euphoric celebrations of Mandela's release from prison could not disguise the fact that acute tensions still existed. Even though Mandela and the ANC had argued against the black supremacist group, the Pan-Africanist Congress, in favour of a multi-racial South Africa where the whites would have their rights guaranteed along

ABOVE **An ANC mass rally on Freedom Day, 27 June 1992, in Soweto. Demonstrators demand investigation into F.W. de Klerk and others responsible for apartheid crimes.**

ABOVE **Durban celebrations of the Zulu warrior king, Shaka, on 29 September 1992. Zulu consciousness was a great obstacle to black unity in the early 1990s.**

with the rest of the population, nervousness about what majority rule would mean was widespread. Hardline Boers were claiming to prepare for civil war rather than see the end of apartheid, but their leader Eugene Terre Blanche was less of a threat to Mandela and the ANC than Chief Buthelezi and his Zulu-based Inkatha Freedom Party.

The South African government had long pursued a policy of divide and rule. Its homelands were the centrepiece of this strategy, but in fact the only remotely viable black alternative to Mandela was Chief Buthelezi. Unlike other chieftains, Buthelezi was not prepared to accept nominal independence for the bantustan of

Kwazulu by the grace of the white government in Pretoria. To that extent he had kept in the good books of the ANC, but because he was anxious to secure a special status for his fellow Zulus and made no bones about his opposition to the more radical elements in the ANC, he was deeply disliked by many members of the ANC. A savage ANC–Inkatha conflict was waged over the four years after February 1990, even as white ministers negotiated with ANC representatives about a new constitution. Thousands of blacks were killed. Evidence came to light that the security services actively aided Inkatha in the struggle to block the ANC and majority rule.

RIGHT **Black voters in Ventersdorp wait to cast their vote in the elections of 27 April 1994.**

INSET **Voters of various races at the polling station in Ventersdorp.**

RIGHT **An ANC march in Durban, March 1994. The ANC challenged Inkatha's dominance among blacks in Natal.**

FAR RIGHT **Nelson Mandela and Archbishop Desmond Tutu embrace during Mandela's inauguration as the new Head of State on 10 May 1994.**

Despite the in-fighting, on 12 February 1993 the two sides agreed to what the Communist Party leader Joe Slovo called the "sunset clause:" there would be a five-year transition period following the first fully free elections in 1994 to a new Parliament, during which the ANC and the National Party would share power along with other signatories to the agreement.

Although Terre Blanche's Afrikaans extremists made blood-curdling threats to sabotage the elections and set up an Afrikaans-only homeland, it was the inter-black fighting that most threatened the schedule for change. Only at the last minute did Chief Buthelezi agree to participate in the elections. He had feared that the National Party had made a deal with the ANC to preserve a role in the new South Africa at Inkatha's expense.

Election day itself was remarkable. Despite chaotic scenes as unprecedented mixed-race queues formed outside polling stations, which were ill-prepared to deal with the huge numbers, there was no violent disruption of the voting. The results gave each major participant something to cheer about: the ANC received two-thirds of the vote, but the National Party came a respectable second and actually defeated the ANC in the Western Cape, while Inkatha also received representation based on its domination of Kwazulu. Suspicions existed that a degree of benign rigging had occurred to ensure that the major players had a stake in the future workability of the new constitution. The seventy-five-year-old Nelson Mandela was elected President by the new Parliament and took office in a ceremony at which officers of the old white regime presided for the last time. Two years later, the National Party left the government.

Prospects for the future

For whites, the transition to majority rule turned out to be remarkably painless. Fears of a bloodbath or a mass exodus of skilled whites have so far proved unfounded. But life for the great majority in the teeming townships or in the poverty-stricken countryside has not improved as rapidly as was hoped in 1994. Criticism of the ANC's performance in office as well as allegations that its leaders have sold out to a (luxurious) white lifestyle may yet plague it in the future unless economic growth picks up sufficiently to provide jobs and prospects for millions of young black South Africans.

KEY EVENTS

1910	South Africa granted dominion status
1912	**8 January** African National Congress (ANC) founded
1936	Black voters removed from the common electoral roll in Cape Province. Also segregation bills.
1948	**May** Victory of National Party; start of apartheid
1960	**21 March** Sharpeville massacre **8 April** ANC outlawed **5 October** 52 per cent of whites vote to leave Commonwealth
1961	**31 May** South Africa proclaimed a Republic
1962	**7 November** Mandela sentenced to 5 years in prison
1964	**June** Mandela sentenced to life imprisonment
1976	**16 June** Start of school children's strike in Soweto
1977	**12 September** Death of Steve Biko
1979	**4 June** Vorster resigns: P.W. Botha becomes President
1989	**20 September** F.W. de Klerk becomes President
1990	**2 February** Unbanning of the ANC, PAC and Communist Party **11 February** Release of Mandela
1994	**27 April** Election Day **10 May** Mandela sworn in as President of South Africa
1996	**9 May** New Constitution agreed **10 May** National Party leaves government

Further reading

So many books have been published about individual revolutions and the theory of revolution that what follows is just a sample to introduce readers either to other academic interpretations or to guides on particular subjects. Anyone interested in revolutionary manifestoes (such as Karl Marx's *Communist Manifesto*) or memoirs should be able to find them in a library or bookshop by looking up the names of famous revolutionaries.

General

Hannah Arendt, *On Revolution* (Viking: New York, (1965)

Crane Brinton, *The Anatomy of Revolution*, revised and expanded edition (Vintage Books: New York, 1965)

Brian M. Downing, *The Military Revolution and Political Change: Origins of Democracy and Autocracy in Early Modern Europe* (Princeton University Press: Princeton, 1992)

John Dunn, *Modern Revolutions: An Introduction to the Analysis of a Political Phenomenon*, 2nd edition (Cambridge University Press: Cambridge, 1989)

Lewis S. Feuer, *Ideology and the Ideologists* (Basil Blackwell: Oxford, 1975)

Jack A. Goldstone, *Revolution and Rebellion in the Early Modern World* (California University Press: Berkeley, 1991)

Michael S. Kimmel, *Revolution: A Sociological Interpretation* (Polity Press: Oxford, 1990)

Jaroslav Krejcí, *Great Revolutions Compared: The Outline of a Theory*, 2nd edition (Harvester Wheatsheaf: Hemel Hempstead, 1994)

Melvin Lasky, *Utopia and Revolution* (University of Chicago Press: Chicago, 1976)

Theda Skocpol, *States and Social Revolutions: A Comparative Analysis of France, Russia and China* (Cambridge University Press: Cambridge, 1979)

Philip B. Springer and Marcello Truzzi (eds),

Revolutionaries on Revolution: Participants' Perspectives on the Strategies of Seizing Power (Goodyear: Pacific Palisades, California, 1973)

Ellen Kay Trimberger, *Revolutions from Above* (Transaction Books, New Brunswick, New Jersey, 1978)

The Dutch Revolts, 1568–1648

Peter Limm, *The Dutch Revolt, 1559–1648* (Longman: London, 1989)

Geoffrey Parker, *The Dutch Revolt* (Penguin: Harmondsworth, 1977)

Martin Rady, *From Revolt to Independence: The Netherlands, 1550–1650* (Hodder and Stoughton: London, 1990)

Civil War and Revolution in England, 1642–60

Martyn Bennet, *The English Civil War* (Longman: London, 1995)

Christopher Hibbert, *Cavaliers and Roundheads: The English at War, 1642–1649* (Harper Collins: London, 1993)

Christopher Hill, *The Century of Revolution, 1603–1714* (Sphere Books: London, 1969)

J. P Kenyon, *The Stuarts* (Collins: London, 1958)

Lawrence Stone, *The Causes of the English Revolution, 1529–1642* (Harper and Row: New York, 1972)

The Glorious Revolution, England 1688

John Millar, *The Glorious Revolution* (Longman: London, 1983)

J. R. Western, *Monarchy and Revolution: The English State in the 1680s* (Blandford: London, 1972)

The American Revolution, 1755–83

Jeremy Black, *War for America: The Fight for Independence, 1775–1783* (Alan Sutton: Stroud, 1991)

Edward Countryman, *The American Revolution* (Penguin: Harmondsworth, 1985)

Edmund S. Morgan, *The Birth of the Republic, 1763–89*, 3rd edition (University of Chicago Press: Chicago, 1992)

The French Revolution, 1789–1815

Geoffrey Best, *The Permanent Revolution: The French Revolution and Its Legacy, 1789–1989* (Fontana: London, 1988)

J.F. Bosher, *The French Revolution* (Weidenfeld and Nicolson: London, 1989)

William Doyle, *The Oxford History of the French Revolution* (Oxford University Press: Oxford, 1989)

Alan Forrest, *The French Revolution* (Basil Blackwell: Oxford, 1995)

François Furet, *Revolutionary France, 1770–1880* (Basil Blackwell: Oxford, 1989)

Gwynne Lewis, *The French Revolution: Rethinking the Debate* (Routledge: London, 1993)

J.H. Shennan, *Liberty and Order in Early Modern Europe: The Subject and the State, 1650–1800* (Longman: London, 1986)

D.M.G. Sutherland, *France, 1789–1815: Revolution and Counter-Revolution* (Fontana: London, 1985)

J.L. Talmon, *The Origins of Totalitarian Democracy* (Penguin: Harmondsworth, 1986)

Alexis de Tocqueville, *The Old Regime and the French Revolution* (Anchor Books: New York, 1955)

Peter Vansittart, *Voices of the Revolution* (Collins: London, 1989)

The Slave Revolt in Haiti, 1798–1803

C.L.R. James, *The Black Jacobins* (Allison and Busby: London, 1938)

Revolution in Latin America, 1808–20

Jorge I. Domínguez, *Insurrection or Loyalty: The Breakdown of the Spanish American Empire* (Harvard University Press: Cambridge, Massachusetts, 1980)

John Lynch, *The Spanish American Revolutions, 1808–1826* (W. W. Norton: New York, 1973)

The July Revolution in France, 1830

John Merriman, *1830 in France* (New Viewpoints: New York, 1995)

Pamela Pilbeam, *Republicanism in Nineteenth Century France, 1814–1871* (Macmillan: London, 1995)

The Springtime of the Peoples, Europe 1848

T.J. Clark, *The Absolute Bourgeois: Artists and Politics in France, 1848–51* (Thames and Hudson: London, 1973)

Frank Eyck (ed.), *The Revolutions of 1848–49* (Oliver and Boyd: Edinburgh, 1972)

Peter Jones, *The 1848 Revolutions*, 2nd edition (Longman: London, 1991)

Priscilla Robertson, *Revolutions of 1848: A Social History* (Harper and Row: New York, 1965)

Jonathan Sperber, *The European Revolutions, 1848–1851* (Cambridge University Press: Cambridge, 1994)

Peter N. Stearns, *The Revolutions of 1848* (Weidenfeld and Nicolson: London, 1974)

The Paris Commune, 1871

S. Edwards, *The Paris Commune, 1871* (Macmillan: London, 1971)

Robert Tombs, *The War against Paris* (Cambridge University Press: Cambridge, 1981)

The Russian Revolutions, 1905–39

Marc Ferro, *October 1917: A Social History of the Russian Revolution*, translated by Norman Stone (Routledge and Kegan Paul: London, 1980)

Sheila Fitzpatrick, *The Russian Revolution* (Oxford University Press: Oxford, 1982)

Geoffrey Hosking, *A History of the Soviet Union, 1917–1991* (Fontana: London, 1992)

Lionel Kochan, *Russia in Revolution* (Weidenfeld and Nicolson, 1967)

Richard Pipes, *The Russian Revolution, Volume 1: 1899–1919, Volume 2: 1919–1924* (Collins Harvill: London, 1990)

Adam Ulam, *In the Name of the People: Prophets and Conspirators in Pre-Revolutionary Russia* (Viking Press: New York, 1977)

Anthony Wood, *The Russian Revolution*, 2nd edition (Longman: London, 1986)

Mexico, 1910–34

Leslie Bethell (ed.), *Mexico since Independence* (Cambridge University Press: Cambridge, 1991)

Hector Aguilar Camin and Lorenzo Meyer, *In the Shadow of the Mexican Revolution: Contemporary Mexican History, 1910–1989*, translated by Luis Alberto Fierro (University of Texas Press: Austin, 1993)

Fascism as Counter-revolution, 1919–45

Joachim Fest, *Hitler*, translated by Richard and Clara Winston (Penguin: Harmondsworth, 1974)

Ian Kershaw, *The Nazi Dictatorship* (Edward Arnold: London, 1985)

Stein Ugelvik Larsen (ed.), *Who were the Fascists. Social Roots of European Fascism* (University of Bergen Press: Bergen, 1980)

Denis Mack Smith, *Mussolini* (Weidenfeld and Nicolson: London, 1981)

Zeev Sternhell, *The Birth of Fascist Ideology*, translated by David Maisel (Princeton University Press: Princeton, 1994)

The Spanish Civil War, 1936–39

Anthony Beevor, *The Spanish Civil War* (Orbis: London, 1982)

Raymond Carr, *The Spanish Tragedy: The Civil War in Perspective* (Weidenfeld and Nicolson, 1993)

Ronald Fraser, *The Blood of Spain: An Oral History of the Spanish Civil War* (Pantheon: New York, 1986)

Paul Preston, *The Spanish Civil War, 1936–39* (Weidenfeld and Nicolson, 1986)

The Communist Revolution in China, 1949–76

Immanuel Hsü, *The Rise of Modern China* (Oxford University Press, 1990)

Andrew J. Nathan, *Chinese Democracy: The Individual and the State in Twentieth-Century China* (I.B. Tauris: London, 1986)

Harrison Salisbury, *The New Emperors: Mao and Deng* (Harper Collins: London, 1993)

Jonathan Spence, *The Search for Modern China* (Hutchison: London, 1990)

Anti-colonial Conflict, 1945–75

Karl D. Jackson (ed.), *Cambodia, 1975–1978: Rendez-vous with Death* (Princeton University Press: Princeton, 1989)

Elbaki Hermassi, *Third World Revolution Reassessed* (University of California Press: Berkeley, 1980)

Stanley Karnow, *Vietnam: A History* (Pimlico: London, 1991)

James Scott and Benedict Kerkvliet (eds), *Everyday Forms of Peasant Resistance in South-East Asia* (Frank Cass: London, 1986)

Anthony Short, *The Origins of the Vietnam War* (Longman: London, 1989)

Cuba, 1959

Carlos Franqui, *Family Portrait with Fidel*, translated by A. MacAdam (Jonathan Cape: London, 1980)

James Nelson Goodsell (ed.), *Fidel Castro's Personal Revolution in Cuba, 1959–1973* (Alfred Knopf: New York, 1975)

Robert W. Quirk, *Fidel Castro* (W.W. Norton: New York, 1993)

Students at the Barricades, 1968

David Caute, *'68: The Year of the Barricades* (Hamish Hamilton: London, 1988)

Ethiopia, 1974–91

Ryszard Kapuściński, *The Emperor: Downfall of an Autocrat* (Picador: London, 1982)

Harold G. Markus, *A History of Ethiopia* (University of California: Berkeley, 1994)

The Power of Islam: Iran, 1979

Nikki Keddie, *Roots of Revolution: An Interpretative History of Modern Iran* (Yale University Press: New Haven, 1981)

Ryszard Kapuściński, *Shah of Shahs* (Picador: London, 1986)

Barry Rubin, *Paved with Good Intentions: The American Experience and Iran* (Oxford University Press: Oxford, 1980)

Amin Saikal, *The Rise and Fall of the Shah* (Princeton University Press: Princeton, 1980)

The East European Revolutions, 1989

Mark Almond, *Retreat to Moscow: Gorbachev and the East European Revolution* (Institute for European Defence and Strategic Studies: London, 1990)

— *The Rise and Fall of Nicolae and Elena Ceausescu* (Chapmans: London, 1992)

Timothy Garton Ash, *We the People: The Revolutions of '89 Witnessed in Warsaw, Budapest, Berlin and Prague* (Granta: Cambridge, 1990)

W.J.F. Jenner, *The Tyranny of History: the Roots of China's Crisis* (Penguin: Harmondwsorth, 1992)

Thomas W. Simons, *Eastern Europe in the Post-War World*, 2nd edition (Macmillan: London, 1993)

Gale Stokes, *The Walls Come Tumbling Down: The Collapse of Communism in Eastern Europe* (Oxford University Press: Oxford, 1993)

Vladimir Tismaneanu, *Reinventing Politics: Eastern Europe from Stalin to Havel* (The Free Press: New York, 1992)

George Weigel, *The Final Revolution: The Resistance Church and the Collapse of Communism* (Oxford University Press: Oxford, 1992)

The Collapse of the Soviet Union, 1991

Robert V. Daniels (ed.), *Soviet Communism from Reform to Collapse* (D.C. Heath: Lexington, Massachusetts, 1995)

Suzanne Goldenberg, *Pride of Small Nations: The Caucasus and Post-Soviet Disorder* (Zed Books: London, 1994)

John Miller, *Mikhail Gorbachev and the End of Soviet Power* (Macmillan: London, 1993)

John Morrison, *Boris Yeltsin: From Bolshevik to Democrat* (Penguin: Harmondsworth, 1991)

Nicolai N. Petro, *The Rebirth of Russian Democracy: An Interpretation of Political Culture* (Harvard University Press: Cambridge, Massachusetts, 1995)

The End of Apartheid, South Africa 1994

Mary Benson, *Nelson Mandela: The Man and the Movement*, 2nd edition (Penguin: Harmondsworth, 1994)

Merle Lipton, *Capitalism and Apartheid* (Wildwood House: Aldershot, 1986)

Index

Acknowledgments

Abbreviations
b = bottom; BC = back cover; c = centre; FC = front
cover; l = left; r = right; t = top

FCt Réunion des Musées Nationaux/Musée du
Louvre, Paris. *Liberty Guiding the People*, 1830
by Delacroix.
FCb Magnum Photos/Gilles Peress.
FCflap Mary Evans Picture Library.
BC Metropolitan Museum of Art, New York, Gift of
J.S. Kennedy. *Washington Crossing the
Delaware*, 1851 by E.G. Leutze.
2 Magnum Photos/James Nachtwey.
4tl Scottish National Portrait Gallery, by permission
of the Earl of Roseberry. *Execution of Charles I*,
Anon.
4br Metropolitan Museum of Art, New York, Gift
of J.S. Kennedy. *Washington Crossing the
Delaware*, 1851 by E.G. Leutze.
5tl Réunion des Musées Nationaux/Musée du
Louvre, Paris. *Liberty Guiding the People*, 1830
by Delacroix.
5c Magnum Photos/Steve McCurry.
5bl Mary Evans Picture Library.
6 Camera Press.
8tl Magnum Photos/Stuart Franklin.
8br Magnum Photos/A. Abbas.
9tl David King Collection.
9br Rex Features.
10tr National Portrait Gallery, London. *Portrait of
Tom Paine* by A. Milliere. Acc. no 897.
10bl Yale University Art Gallery. *Death of General
Warren*, 1832 by John Trumbull.
11c Lauros-Giraudon/Musée Carnavalet, Paris.
Dead in Paris, 1848 by Andrieu. Musée
Carnavalet, Paris.
11b Roger-Viollet.
12b Bryna/Universal (courtesy Kobal).
13tl Peter Newark's Pictures.
13b Magnum Photos/Steve McCurry.
14t Lauros-Giraudon.
14b Magnum Photos/Gideon Mendel.

15t Rex Features.
15b AKG London.
16cl Corbis-Bettmann.
16cr AKG London.
16bl AKG London.
16br Magnum Photos/Wu Yinxian.
17b Camera Press.
18c David King Collection.
18bl Gosinko (courtesy Kobal).
18br David King Collection.
19tl AKG London.
19tr Popperfoto.
19b David King Collection. *Koslinskii poster*, 1921.
20t AKG London. *Swearing the Oath of the Horatii*,
1784–5 by J.L. David.
20b Rex Features/© Les Films Gaumont.
21cl AKG London.
21cr AKG London.
21bl Camera Press.
21br Magnum Photos/Gideon Mendel.
22t Frank Spooner Pictures/Gamma/M Deville.
22b Hulton Getty.
23t ET Archive/Musée Carnavalet, Paris. *Storming
the Bastille*, 1789.
23b Bridgeman Art Library/British Library.
24t Robert Harding Picture Library/FPG.
24c Magnum Photos/Paul Fusoc.
24b Rex Features/Sipa.
25t Musées de la Ville de Paris/Musée Carnavalet,
Paris. *Women at barricades*, Paris, 1830.
25b Mary Evans Picture Library.
26t Hulton Getty.
26b Popperfoto.
27t Giraudon/Château de Versailles. *The National
Guard*, 1792 by Cogniet.
27b Camera Press/Y. Khaldei.
28t Rex Features/Sipa.
28b Camera Press.
29t Magnum Photos/Stuart Franklin.
29bl AKG London/Château de Versailles. *Louis XVI*
by J.-S. Duplessis.
29br Novosti, London.

30tl David King Collection.
30tc BBC Picture Archives.
30tr Rex Features/Sipa.
31t Hulton Getty.
31b Magnum Photos/A. Abbas.
32t Statens Konstsmeer, Stockholm. *Heads of the
Guillotined* by Géricault.
32b Camera Press/Ray Hamilton.
33t Rex Features/Sipa/Pasche.
33cr Hulton Getty.
33br David King Collection.
34l Giraudon. *Scene of the Revolution of 1830* by
Bouviere.
35t AKG London/Musée d'Orsay, Paris. *A Street in
Paris, May, 1871* by Maximilian Luce.
35b Hulton Getty.
36t Frank Spooner Pictures/Liaison/Anderson.
36b David King Collection/© VG Bild Kunst and
1996 DACS, London. *Beat the Whites with the
Red Wedge* by El Lissitzky.
37t Rex Features/Sipa.
37c Novosti, London.
37b Network/Gideon Mendel.
38b Bridgeman Art Library/Giraudon. *Execution of
Marie-Antoinette*, 16 Oct 1793.
40 Scottish National Portrait Gallery, by permission
of the Earl of Roseberry. *Execution of Charles I*,
Anon.
43t Bridgeman Art Library/Prado. *Philip II of Spain*
by A. Moro.
43c Museum Catharijneconvent, Utrecht.
43b Bridgeman Art Library/Fitzwilliam Museum, Cambridge. *A Village Festival in Honour of St Hubert
and St Anthony*, 1632, Pieter Brueghel the Younger.
44t Mary Evans Picture Library.
45t Bridgeman Art Library/Prado. *Surrender of
Breda*, 1667 by Velázquez.
45b National Gallery, London. *Ratification of the
Treaty of Munster*, 1648 by G. Ter Borch.
46t Bridgeman Art Library/Burghley House. *Charles
I* by Mytens.
47t Peter Newark's Pictures.

48c Bridgeman Art Library/Giraudon/Château de Versailles. *Oliver Cromwell* by Gaspar de Crayor.

49t Ashmolean Museum, Oxford. *England's arke secured* by Sutherland.

49b Scottish National Portrait Gallery, by permission of the Earl of Roseberry. *Execution of Charles I*, Anon.

50t Bridgeman Art Library/British Library.

50c Trustees of the Victoria and Albert Museum.

51b Bridgeman Art Library/Museum of London. *Coronation procession of Charles II*, 1661 by Dirk Stoop.

52tl National Museums and Galleries on Merseyside. *Charles II*, by G. Kneller.

52tr National Portrait Gallery, London. *James II*, 1684 by G. Kneller.

53tc British Museum, London.

53tr British Museum, London.

53b Mansell Collection.

54b British Museum, London.

55t © 1996 Her Majesty The Queen, The Royal Collection. *Landing of William of Orange at Torbay.*

55cl Bridgeman Art Library/Scottish National Portrait Gallery. *William III* by G. Kneller.

55cr Bridgeman Art Library/Guildhall Library. *Queen Mary II* by J. Van der Vaart.

56 Metropolitan Museum of Art, New York, Gift of J.S. Kennedy. *Washington Crossing the Delaware*, 1851 by E.G. Leutze.

58b Peter Newark's Pictures.

59b Bridgeman Art Library/Private Collection.

60t Peter Newark's Pictures.

60c Bridgeman Art Library/Private Collection.

61cl Corbis-Bettmann.

61b Corbis-Bettmann.

62c Peter Newark's Pictures.

62b Yale University Art Gallery. *Death of General Montgomery* by John Trumbull.

63c Yale University Art Gallery. *Declaration of Independence* by John Trumbull.

64t Pennsylvania Historical Society.

64b Peter Newark's Pictures.

65c Corbis-Bettmann.

65b Yale University Art Gallery. *Surrender of General Burgoyne* by John Trumbull.

66t British Museum, London.

66c John Carter Brown Library at Brown University/British Museum.

67c National Portrait Gallery. *General Cornwallis*, 1783 by T. Gainsborough.

68c Bridgeman Art Library/Lauros-Giraudon/ Château de Versailles. *Surrender of Yorktown*, 1781 by L. Blaenberghe.

68b Bridgeman Art Library/Giraudon/Château de Versailles. *Siege of Yorktown*, 1781 by L. Couder.

69c National Portrait Gallery, Smithsonian Institution, Washington DC. *George Washington*, 1795 by R. Peale.

70c Bridgeman Art Library/Giraudon/Musée Carnavalet, Paris. *Pillage of Les Invalides*, 1789 by J.B. Lallemand.

70b Bridgeman Art Library/Musées de Ville de Paris/Musée Carnavalet, Paris.

71tl Bridgeman Art Library/Château de Versailles. *Louis XVI* by J.-S. Duplessis.

71tr Bridgeman Art Library/Giraudon/Château de Versailles. *Marie Antoinette and her children*, 1787 by E. Vignée-Lebrun.

71c Jean-Loup Charmet /Bibliothèque Nationale, Paris.

72t AKG London, *Meeting of the Estates General at Versailles*, 1789 by Helman.

72cr AKG London/Eric Lessing/Institut & Musée Voltaire. *Voltaire* by Nicholas de Largilliere.

72bl Musées de la Ville de Paris/Musée Carnavalet, Paris. *National Guard* by Les Sueur Brothers.

72br AKG London/Scottish National Gallery. *Rousseau in Armenian Dress*, 1766 by Allan Ramsay.

73t ET Archive/Musée Carnavalet, Paris. *Tennis Court Oath* by J.L. David.

74t Bridgeman Art Library/Giraudon/Musée Carnavalet, Paris.

75t Mary Evans Picture Library.

75br Hulton Getty.

76t Bridgeman Art Library/Musées de Ville de Paris/Musée Carnavalet, Paris.

76c Mansell Collection.

77t Bridgeman Art Library/Giraudon/Musée Carnavalet, Paris. *Cry of Liberty*, 1792 by Les Sueur Brothers.

77b Bridgeman Art Library/Giraudon/Musée du Louvre, Paris. *Battle of Valmy*, 1792 by J.B. Mauzaisse.

78tl ET Archive/Musée Carnavalet, Paris.

78tr ET Archive/Musée Carnavalet, Paris.

78b Giraudon.

79bc AKG London/Musée Carnavalet, Paris.

79br Jean-Loup Charmet/Musée Carnavalet, Paris.

80bc ET Archive. *Death of Marat*, 1793 by J.L. David.

80br Bridgeman Art Library/Château de Versailles. *Charlotte Corday*, Anon.

81tl Bridgeman Art Library/Prado. *Saturn Devouring his Children*, 1820–23 by Goya.

81tr Peter Newark's Pictures. *Wounded Robespierre*, 1794 by M. Melingue.

82bl Bridgeman Art Library/Château de Malmaison. *Napoleon Crossing the Alps*, 1800 by J.L. David.

83t Bridgeman Art Library/British Library.

84c Corbis-Bettmann.

85c Hulton Getty.

86 Réunion des Musées Nationaux/Musée du Louvre, Paris. *Liberty Guiding the People*, 1830 by Delacroix.

88b Bridgeman Art Library/Index/Prado. *The Third of May 1808*, 1814 by Goya.

89c ET Archive/Canning House.

90t South American Pictures.

90c South American Pictures.

91t Peter Newark's Pictures.

92t Bridgeman Art Library/Apsley House, The Sir William Wellington Museum. *Battle of Waterloo, 1815*, 1843 by Sir William Alan.

93t Bridgeman Art Library/Giraudon/Bibliothèque Nationale, Paris.

93b Caisse Nationale des Monuments Historiques et Sites/SPADEM/DACS, London 1996.

94c Giraudon/Musée du Petit Palais. *Combat de Hôtel de Ville*, 1833 by V. Schnetz.

95t Lauros-Giraudon. *The Duc d'Orléans leaving the Hôtel de Ville, 1830*, 1833 by H. Vernet.

96t Jean-Loup Charmet/Musée Carnavalet, Paris.

96c AKG London/Gebietsheimatmuseum. *Eisenwerk* by Wologda.

96b © Her Majesty The Queen, The Royal Collection. Great Chartist Meeting, 1848, William Kilburn.

98t Jean-Loup Charmet.

98c Hulton Getty.

98b AKG London/Musée Carnavalet, Paris. *Storming of the Château d'Eau*, 1848 by Hagenauer.

99c Bridgeman Art Library/Giraudon/Musée des Beaux Arts, Lille. *The Republic*, 1848 by Ziegler.

100t Réunion des Musées Nationaux/Musée d'Orsay, Paris. *La Barricade* by Meissonier.

101t Hulton Getty.

102c ET Archive/Museo Correr, Venice.

102bl Mary Evans Picture Library.

102br AKG London/Civiche Raccolte Storiche, Milan. *Porta Tosa*, 1848 by Canello.

103c Mary Evans Picture Library.

104t Hulton Getty.

105t AKG London/Landesarchiv, Berlin.

105c AKG, London/Stadtgeschitcheliche Dokumention, Berlin.

105b AKG London/Neuruppin Heimatmuseum.

106c ET Archive.

107t Mary Evans Picture Library.

107c AKG London. *R. Wagner*, 1871 by Franz Hainfstaeng.

108t AKG London. *Bismarck*, 1890 by Lembach.

109t ET Archive/Museum der Stadt, Vienna.

109c AKG/Heeresgesischichteliches Museum, Vienna.

110t AKG London/Akademie der Bilden Kunste, Vienna. *Franz Joseph I*, 1853 by Schonbrunn.

110b Jean-Loup Charmet.

111t Jean-Loup Charmet/Musée de l'Armée, Budapest.

111b ET Archive/National Historical Museum, Bucharest.

112c AKG London.

113t Jean-Loup Charmet.

113c Musées de la Ville de Paris/SPADEM/DACS, London 1996. *Toppling statue of Louis XIV* by Trocaz.

113b Jean-Loup Charmet.

114c Hulton Getty.

114cr Jean-Loup Charmet/Musée Carnavalet, Paris.

115tl Museum Folkwang, Essen. *The Firing Squad* by Manet.

115cr Hulton Getty.

116 Mary Evans Picture Library.

118c Jean-Loup Charmet.

119t Hulton Getty.

119cl Novosti, London.

119cr Bridgeman Art Library/Novosti.
119b Kobal Collection.
121t David King Collection.
121b Jean-Loup Charmet/Bibliothèque Nationale, Paris.
122t Hulton Getty.
122b David King Collection.
122inset Hulton Getty.
123b Peter Newark's Pictures.
125tl Peter Newark's Pictures.
125tr John Massey Stewart.
126t David King Collection.
127t Bridgeman Art Library/Novosti/Tretyakov Gallery. *Winter Palace* by Savitsky.
127c Mary Evans Picture Library.
127b Mary Evans Picture Library.
128t Peter Newark's Pictures.
129t Peter Newark's Pictures.
129b Hulton Getty.
130t David King Collection.
130bl Hulton Getty.
130bc David King Collection.
131t Peter Newark's Pictures.
133t Jean-Loup Charmet. *Berengy poster*, 1919, Budapest.
133c Hulton Getty.
135t Peter Newark's Pictures.
135bc Peter Newark's Pictures.
135br Peter Newark's Pictures.
136t AKG London.
136c South American Pictures/ Pedro Martinez.
136b Photri.
137t Mexicolore/Sean Sprague. *Mural* (detail) by Diego Rivera.
137b Magnum Photos/A. Abbas.
138t Popperfoto.
138b Hulton Getty.
139t Popperfoto.
139c AKG London.
139b Hulton Getty.
140c AKG London.
141tl AKG London.
141tr Hulton Getty.
141c Hulton Getty
142t Popperfoto.
142c David King Collection.
143t Popperfoto.
143c Hulton Getty.
144t Bridgeman Art Library/E. Arroyo, Paris/ © ADAGP, Paris/DACS, London 1996. *Aidez Espagne* by Miró.
144b David King Collection.
145tl David King Collection.
145tr Bridgeman Art Library/Prado/© Succession Picasso, Paris/DACS 1996. *Guernica* by Picasso.
145b David King Collection.
146t ET Archive.
146b Hulton Getty.
148t Camera Press.
148c Magnum Photos/Henri Cartier-Bresson.
148b Magnum Photos/Henri Cartier-Bresson.
149tl Magnum Photos/Henri Cartier-Bresson.

149tc David King Collection.
150tr ET Archive/W. Sewell.
150c ET Archive/W. Sewell.
150bl Magnum Photos/Marc Riboud.
150bc Hulton Getty.
151c David King Collection.
152bl AKG London.
152br AKG London.
153c Popperfoto.
153b Popperfoto.
154tl Associated Press, London.
154tr Popperfoto.
155tc Hulton Getty.
155tr Hulton Getty.
155b Frank Spooner Pictures.
156t Rex Features/Jan Schneider.
156bl Rex Features/Sipa.
156br Popperfoto.
157c Camera Press/Mike Wells.
158c Magnum Photos/Burt Glinn.
158b Magnum Photos/Burt Glinn.
159t Magnum Photos/Burt Glinn.
159c Magnum Photos/Burt Glinn.
159b Rex Features/Sipa/Durschmied.
160b Frank Spooner Pictures/Gamma.
161tl David King Collection.
161tr Frank Spooner Pictures/Gamma/Antonio Ribero.
162t Corbis-Bettmann.
162b Corbis-Bettmann.
163t Corbis-Bettmann.
163c Corbis-Bettmann.
164t AKG London/Paul Almasay.
164b Hulton Getty.
165t Magnum Photos/Joseph Koudelka.
165c Magnum Photos/Joseph Koudelka.
165b AKG London.
167t Frank Spooner Pictures/Gamma.
167c Camera Press/ B. Gysembergh.
167b Camera Press/ B. Gysemburgh.
168c Associated Press, London.
168b Magnum Photos/A. Abbas.
169t Magnum Photos/A. Abbas.
169c Rex Features/Sipa.
170tl Associated Press, London.
170tc Magnum Photos/A. Abbas.
171tr Magnum Photos/A. Abbas.
171c Rex Features/Sipa/Reza.
171b Magnum Photos/A. Abbas.
172c Magnum Photos/ Steve McCurry.
174t Frank Spooner Pictures/Gamma/Marc Deville.
174c Magnum Photos/Stuart Franklin.
175c Frank Spooner Pictures/Gamma/Marc Deville.
176c Frank Spooner Pictures/Gamma/Chip Hires.
176b Camera Press.
177cl Frank Spooner Pictures/Gamma/Chip Hires.
177cr Frank Spooner Pictures/Gamma/KOK.
178c Magnum Photos/Joseph Koudelka.
178bl Frank Spooner Pictures/Gamma/Chip Hires-Eric Bouvet.
178br Camera Press/B. Gysemburgh.
179t Camera Press.

179c Camera Press/B. Gysemburgh.
180tl Rex Features/Sipa/Jacques Witt.
180c AKG London.
181t Frank Spooner Pictures/Gamma/G. Merillon/P. Piel.
181bl Magnum Photos/E. Hartmann.
181br Frank Spooner Pictures/Liason/Gamma/S. Ferry.
182–3t Rex Features/Sipa
183cMagnum Photos/Bruno Barbey
184t Rex Features/Sipa/Gerard.
184b Magnum Photos/L Freed.
185tl Rex Features/Sipa/Tudor.
185tc Rex Features/Sipa/Luc Delahaye.
185tr Rex Features/Sipa.
185c Rex Features/Sipa/Luc Delahaye.
186c Rex Features/Sipa.
186b Rex Features/Sipa.
187tl Novosti, London.
187tr Rex Features/Sipa.
187b Novosti, London.
188t Rex Features/Sipa/Bocchon.
188bl Rex Features/Letikhuva Oy/Sipa.
188br Rex Features/Sipa/G Stravinski.
190t Novosti, London.
190c Frank Spooner Pictures/Gamma.
190b Network/A. Suau.
191t Network/H.J. Burkhard/Bildberg.
191b Rex Features/Sipa/Joey Abraityte.
192t Popperfoto.
192b Camera Press/Andrew Bailey.
193t Popperfoto.
193c Popperfoto.
194t Popperfoto/Reuter.
194c Camera Press/Sam Knox.
194b Camera Press/Sam Knox.
195t Rex Features/Sipa/Kuus.
195c Popperfoto/Reuter.
195b Magnum Photos/Ian Berry.
196tl Rex Features/Sipa/Kuus.
196tr Rex Features/Sipa.
196bl Magnum Photos/Ian Berry.
196br Magnum Photos/Ian Berry.
197tl Network/Gideon Mendel.
197tr Magnum Photos/Ian Berry.

While every effort has been made to trace the present copyright holders we apologize in advance for any unintentional omission or error and will be pleased to insert the appropriate acknowledgment in any subsequent edition.

Author's acknowledgments
I am very grateful to Frances Gertler of De Agostini for thinking up the concept of this book and to Peter Robinson of Curtis Brown for putting the idea to me. Rachel Aris steered me through much of modern history with great patience and shaped the sometimes unwieldy text with great skill. Manisha Patel, Zoë Goodwin and Diana Morris all helped to make this such a visually striking book. Christine Stone compiled the very thorough index. My thanks to all of them.